THE
SILVER BULLET
OF GOD

XTREME BIG GAME HUNTING
IN THE HEAVENLY
AND EARTHLY REALMS

A FIELD MANUAL FOR SUPERHEROES

AL COLLINS

WayOfTheEagle.org

The Silver Bullet of God

Xtreme Big Game Hunting

A Field Manual for Superheroes

Copyright © 2018 Al Collins

All scripture quotations are in New King James Version, unless otherwise noted.

All rights reserved. No part of this book may be reproduced or transmitted in any form or by any means, electronic or mechanical, including photocopying, recording, or by an information storage and retrieval system - except by a reviewer who may quote brief passages in a review to be printed in a magazine or newspaper - without permission in writing from the author.

TESTIMONIES

"VERY GOOD BOOK!"

Dr. C. Peter Wagner
Theologian, missionary, Professor
Founder/Chancellor-Wagner Leadership Institute
Former Presiding Apostle Emeritus
of International Coalition of Apostles
Author of over 80 books - USA
(August 15, 1930 – October 21, 2016)

"Dear Al… Greetings to you in the Name of Jesus Christ.

We are unceasingly praying for you & about your ministry; we thank you very much for (your) book. (It is) in very much need to Biblical Students, Christians Leaders, Educational Institutions, and Youth Leaders & Sunday Schools. We appreciated you and your love towards encouraging the Lords harvest in India.

Our Emmanuel Bible College Faculty of Theology, unanimously decided to teach this syllabus in our Bible College, Churches and Seminaries. All of our Bible college teaching staff & students, Bible women, Youth Leaders, and Evangelists, are blessed by your syllabus. When I shared about your vision and newsletter, which is impacting the world of many leaders, after meeting many pastors, they came to me in conferences and said we need leaders like you to our nation to visit us and bless our land. I believe that we can train many leaders and send them to all nations to establish the Kingdom of God. You are welcome any time to India. Our doors will be open all the time for you. In my 36 years (of) Ministry experience, I am really Blessed to be a Part of sharing Bishop Al's vision in teaching lessons to our Bible College. These lessons are going to be (a) big impact upon our Youth Leaders & Bible college Students. They are going to be empowered for Almighty God.

Myself and all of our Ministries from India appreciate Al whole heartedly, that he is doing a Great Job for God and winning lost souls for Lord's Kingdom. {Amen}

TESTIMONIES

Th(ese) are) my words from the bottom of my Heart that he is a Great Man of God and (that) he's got Great Call of God upon his Life. He is going to win many souls & his messages will be a blessing to many nations.

Yours in Him, **Dr. Mera Jesudass," India**

Rev. Dr. Jesudass heads over 150 congregations, a Bible College, a Christian school, an orphanage, church planting, a widow's home, and youth ministries across India.

"You are the first person I have ever heard of that deals in the Spiritual realm at the level that you do. You are like a "Green Beret "or "Navy SEAL" in the spiritual and I don't think that there are that many like you in the world."

Rochelle H.-USA

"Man of God, we offer Certificates and Diplomas in Christian ministry in many ministry fields, at 28 training centers across Uganda and Kenya. Part of our curriculum is teaching Xtreme Big Game Hunting. Many students have been empowered, because there (are) some who come from Baptist backgrounds who were taught that Christ fought all their battles so they should not bother themselves to wage spiritual warfare. But after being illuminated, they begin to experience the power of God setting the captives free.

Brother Al, your book is more practical, (and) in case you come across some who oppose it, just know that it is not them, but some evil powers behind them to oppose the revelation which the Lord gave you." Much Blessings

Charles M.-College Director/International Speaker –Uganda

"Dear Al and Rhoda,

Thank you for the teachings on spiritual warfare. I shared your book with a pastor friend and he and a group of children have fasted and prayed using the teachings of your book. There are about 60 people in the group. Majority are children and teens with a few adults, some who are parents of the children. They are now experiencing spiritual encounters such as visiting heaven and hell, travelling to England, USA and Australia praying for sick people. Just last month a group of children travelled with Angels of God down to the Bermuda Triangle and closed the gate of hell there. Initially, only 4 children ages between 8 and 13 got caught up in the spirit during a fasting and prayer meeting. Now the number has increased from 4 to 12 which includes some teens. The impact of your teachings is astounding.

TESTIMONIES

We have never seen spiritual warfare of such nature. The children related instances of how they went into the spirit realm and followed the Archangel Michael into battle against the strongman of the town. Spiritual experiences are still taking place at this time, but are too many to capture in writing. The outstanding of all these is, God the Father's command for holiness, righteousness and truth in the lives of His people. This is the last revival before Christ returns.

Please remember us in your prayers. God bless you.

Martin R, Papua New Guinea

"Dear beloved, Al and Rhoda. Greetings in the name of Jesus Christ our LORD. We wish the whole Christian world would turn to your teachings now. Because we are of Jesus Christ; and the real meaning of the Great Commission. (Matthew 28:29-20)

We do appreciate so much the mobility ministry that you're performing here in Tanzania, while you're physically in USA/Canada.

Muslim families are receiving Christ. Many other religious people, too, are being freed from different bondage. Demonized, sicknesses, and illnesses, including HIV/AIDS victims are instantly healed in JESUS' NAME. We'd like to invite you to visit us this summer, please. We believe that your skill will enable us to advance in the battlefields.

You've been blessings to so many very poor/needy people. We are reaching (preaching) them in the very fields (villages). When we suffer for Christ's sake on invasion and attacking the enemies, in their realms, destroying their strongholds, and kingdoms, you're with us financially and prayerfully. Physically you're in USA but spiritually walking, running into wilderness, jungle, forests, and fields in Tanzania. You're quite different from the modern apostles, prophets, evangelists, pastors and teachers, whose ambitions are earnings, after money, prominence and really corrupted and misinterpreting the true Word to fit to their own interests.

People are being freed from captivity, curses, diseases, illnesses, troubles, etc. From your donations, we've bought a generator, fare for transport, and tents.

The Tents of Meetings are being built in each village we are hunting or planting churches.

We'd say that the missionary role, through your revelation of teachings, has been revived in Tanzania, but, I also believe that it shall spread out all over the world.

TESTIMONIES

Many trainees, from various nations, shall be coming to be trained, learning how to run into the essence of this new program, lively. It's a big challenge to some ministers, gospel preachers, who just concentrate on areas where it's not necessary; health and rich lands, cities, towns, people, rather than reaching out to the poor communities, (DO the HUNT), as well as Jesus and His apostles did it.

May you be blessed exceedingly and continue to listen more and more to the HS, receive new revelation daily.
In His Fields,"

David N.-Pastor/Missionary/Teacher/Speaker-Tanzania

"I've gone in the spirit and seen Jesus, angels and the Apostles and fought many evil entities. I bound a giant evil entity over an area and many drug addicts were brought to salvation. Physical infirmities of people (lung problems, TB, eyesight problems) were healed. I fast and conduct spiritual warfare in the heavenlies and destroy the evil power over an area and am able to conduct many successful evangelistic meetings afterwards. I teach Xtreme Big Game Hunting to Sunday school children and the children are going and worshipping in the spirit, manifesting spiritual gifts… going into heaven and seeing Jesus and angels. My 18-year-old son read your book and told me it has set him on fire to fulfill his destiny as a great world-wide evangelist. I printed 50 copies of your book for all the leaders across the Philippines."

Freddie D.- Pastor, Teacher, Evangelist, Missionary, Church Planter -The Philippines

"I found your website and this completely changed my life. Am from Kenya though have been working in Saudi Arabia and I wanna thank The Holy Trinity for using you to help others. Have been reading the eBook and am so happy for it's what I have been looking for. It covers everything and I pray that God uses me into advancing His kingdom through these principles you've outlined. Thanks a lot, and God bless you."

Patricia E.-Kenya

"This ministry has actually changed my life and enabled my own ministry to go to higher heights doing things that I previously never imagined doing. I now consider Al a friend and spiritual mentor/teacher.

Clinton J.-TV Host/Author/Prophet/International Speaker/Teacher-USA

TESTIMONIES

"Am introducing all to my University students here in Nigeria. We in Kingdom Life Christian University will be using Xtreme Big Game Hunting as part of our study materials to open the eyes of our students to have more knowledge about (the) spirit realm and how to be victorious"

Bishop Dr. Godwin O.-University Director-President/Founder The Africa Project (TAP)/Founder of International Network of Bishops and Archbishops (INBA)/International Evangelist

"Hi, first of all I would like to thank Mr. Al Collins-Man of God, for such a Wonderful & Powerful book. I must admit that this book is a great gift to all the true Christians who want to live like Jesus in their Life. I Pray to God to use each one of us to expand His Kingdom here on Earth as it is in Heaven. In Christ."

Nikhil G.-India

"I read your book last week and it is the most powerful and most knowledgeable book I have read on spiritual warfare. In fact, I taught aspects of it to my Prayer Group of about 20 prayer warriors. I also applied the book at a recent crusade we had last Friday attended by 2500 people in Dubai. After the Crusade, it was announced that the church will be expanding to a new territory outside Dubai called Sharjah. This was announced by the evangelist after we had prayed for the expansion of the kingdom in the UAE. This was a shock, as the evangelist did not know what we prayed. I have shared the book with up to 10 Pastors in Dubai and more than 10 Brothers and Sisters in the UK, my home country. I have also shared it with more people in Dubai, Doha and Lagos Nigeria. TO GOD BE THE GLORY FOR SUCH GREAT REVELATION. My prayer is that God will continue to establish and reward you for your faithfulness."

Leye A.-United Arab Emirates

"I would like to share with you as to what I experienced on Friday. When we started soaking I heard the Lord tell me to go out of my (spiritual) garden... I saw a waterfall, but it was an unusual waterfall. The waterfall had like 7 parts and I could move each waterfall part to the sides like you could to with a curtain. There was a cave behind the waterfall, and I went in. I saw 2 treasure boxes, I opened both. In one of them there was something in there that was like a sword upgrade. I could stick it to my sword, and it would extend it. A few minutes later, all of the sudden I saw a big snake. It had no wings or anything to fly, but I never wondered why it could fly. Suddenly I stood in front of it on my horse (which really surprised me) and I said to

the snake standing about 1 meter in front of it (the snake was maybe 20 meters long) "I don't fear you". I then wanted to use my sword to kill it, but somehow, I couldn't do it, something didn't let me, or wouldn't work, like my sword was somehow incompatible versus this snake. Then I remembered the sword upgrade I just got from the cave. I put it on my sword and then tried to kill the snake. I set my sword at the end of the head where it goes over to the body, because I wanted to cut off the head, and thought this is what I would do now. Now I was expecting to cut off its head any second, but much to my surprise, my sword basically, instead of cutting vertically, it cut horizontally through the whole 20-meter-long body and I heard the snake shouting out in great pain. Finally, after that I was able to cut off its head. After this I did not see anything else. Really appreciate that God introduced you into my life."

David G.-Germany

"I thank you from the bottom of my heart for the insight you have given me... I'm in the heart of Islam, the lies are real and the kids are mostly affected. Can't do much about the grownups, infection too deep... If I lose my life, so be it... this is for me..."

Sharna W.- Saudi Arabia

"While I was reading your book, when Jesus took you to The Final battle on your white horse, I saw it too. My wife is seeing much more too. She was sitting at home soaking with the Lord and was brought to heaven and her body shook a lot in the chair. An angel came and handed her our baby boy. I appreciate how you have encouraged me brother, THANK YOU!"

Chris P.-USA

"I want to be involved in this battle for me and my family, which includes my wife and my children... I just finished reading your book and I sense that I need to thank you for this material. Our region has the reputation to be hard to evangelize. Thank you for your counsel."

Samuel B.-France

"I want to thank you for visiting me in the spirit and revealing to me what was going on there. Honestly, I was shocked to see that you yourself visited and wrote to me. I am reading your book... Since I have been battling, winning and conquering throughout this week and last week, I have been having new spiritual experiences on my bed (my most tense spiritual activities usually happen here whether I am awake/asleep). Thank you once again for your time, attention and assistance."

Donovan R.-Trinidad

TESTIMONIES

"I have never had such an experience ever since I was born, like I was entering the spiritual realm. As we have not been getting paid at the company I work for, for the past three months, I and other two ladies decided to come together and seek God... God showed me what had gone wrong in the company... he showed me there was no holiness in the company... breakthrough... on Friday 1 June 2012, the Chief Executive Officer of the company wrote to the Financial Director, instructing him to pay all employees without fail, the outstanding salaries to maintain good relations and they have since started paying us our March salaries and April salaries, to be paid as soon as we have all got our March salaries. Thank you so much for your book. God bless."

Anna M.-Zimbabwe

"We are a Pentecostal Church, following the footsteps of the apostles and Jesus Christ is the center of our focus, through to God with the help of the Holy Spirit. Our main teachings are based on salvation, deliverance, healing and worship. The eBook has brought so much to our understanding in the ministry as we will continue to give you to the searching of the knowledge of God through the power of the Holy Spirit in Jesus name. Thank you so much."

Pastor Shadrack U.-England

"After reading your book, I have realized there was so much lacking in my life, and my wish and destiny is to have a deep, true and personal relationship with God and dwell in his presence. Reading your book gives me the confidence that your lessons and wisdom will truly help me connect with God."

Thetologo N.-Botswana

"I live in Lahore. I am Evangelist. I appreciate what you have been doing for His glory. You are welcome to Pakistan for the ministry work, i.e. seminars, conferences, Bible study centers, evangelism and other welfare work to help (the) needy and poor in Pakistan."

Emmanuel-Pakistan

"I am a minister of the Gospel and I work in Brazil where there is plenty of darkness. Many churches are ignorant of the spiritual battle. I started reading your book. Very deep, a very great blessing for me and for body of Christ, everyone should know Him. Thank you very much for your encouragement, for your prayers, that the Lord is in full control and bless us through your ministry. God bless."

Aimé-Claude Z.-French Guiana

TESTIMONIES

"I have just discovered your website and I feel so excited to knowing that I will learn so many things as a Christian, my prayers are for Our Mighty to continue to use you to win others to Christ."

Rose M.-Zambia

"Remember the Islam-Muhammad document you sent me? Well, I changed the title to 'For Your Eyes Only' and forwarded it to many of my friends. Do you know that in Malaysia, one is legally bound by law to convert to Muslim if one marries a Muslim? They have jails for those who don't do so. But now you've confirmed for me the demonic elements of the religion. I never wanted to ask this of the religion because I didn't want to have to face the uncomfortable thought of having to be actively opposed to the religion. But I suppose I'm 'stupid'... I've known all this, while that they regard us as 'kaffir' (disbeliever) and can do anything to us, even kill us and they believe they will be in the right. That was a great article... a lot in it struck home."

Roslyn T.-Malaysia

"I also "go in the spirit" on a daily basis, just for intimacy with Father God. This is extra special for me! I personally thank you! You have been instrumental in transforming my life!"

Diane M.- Prophet – Canada

"We really had a blessed time teaching people all about strategic warfare & praying for the World Cup. So far, news reaching me indicates, that my province is the only one free from child trafficking. We have also seen the government clamping down on crime during the World Cup & 54 mobile courts established to deal with crime all because we prayed."

Pastor Leo D.- South Africa

"Since Al's 2007 conference, I have been engaged in Hi- level spiritual warfare directed by our Triune God. I have encountered and defeated many demonic entities including a fallen angel!"

Richard G.-Retired Scientist-USA

"How are you doing dear man of God. The lady who was paralyzed is called Mrs. Boniventure. She had the paralysis for seven years. After applying the deliverance and healing principles (book) which you sent to me, the lady was completely set free."

Pastor Johnstone K.-Tanzania

TESTIMONIES

"I believe that anyone who reads "Xtreme Big Game Hunting" will be blessed immensely as their spiritual eyes will be opened even wider. God is willing to provide us with His knowledge; we just have to be open to receiving it. "For lack of knowledge my people perish." Before this experience I would have thought that someone was making all of this up. I consider myself to be a Spirit-led person grounded in biblical principles, yet I must admit that I was a little skeptical. Now I know better! There are things in the Spirit that call for deeper things as the bible says that the "deep calls unto the deep." I pray that people will be open to the things of God that has been revealed through Al Collins…deep!"

Karen Y.-Minister/Counselor-USA

DEDICATION

TO GOD

"Blessed be the Lord my Rock, Who trains my hands for war, and my fingers for battle—" Psalm 144:1

Thank You Father, Jesus and Holy Spirit, for my life and my destiny!

TO MY PARENTS

I can't imagine being where I am today without the strength and character of my parents, Gord and Lynn.

You set a high bar!

TO MY MENTORS

Thank you, for sharing your wisdom and experience.

It would have been a rockier road without you all!

TO THE SILVER BULLETS
AND XTREME BIG GAME HUNTERS OF GOD

Embrace your destiny advancing God's Kingdom!

"You are My battle-ax and weapons of war: for with You I will break the nation in pieces; with You I will destroy kingdoms."
Jeremiah 51:20

ZONES AND SECTORS

TESTIMONIES iii
DEDICATION xiii
ZONES AND SECTORS xiv
INTRODUCTION xxi
SECTOR ONE: THE KILLING FIELD 1

ZONE ONE: WHY HUNT?

SECTOR TWO: WHY DO XTREME BIG GAME HUNTING? 6
    Why do we do it? Why become a Silver Bullet of God? 8
    Each and every one of us! 9
    What is God's plan? 12
    The Xtreme Superman! The Ultimate Silver Bullet! 13
SECTOR THREE: TRUE CONQUEROR 23
SECTOR FOUR: YOUR DESTINY 28
    Christians are Israel 31
    According to the New Testament there are now two Israel's! 33

ZONE 2: THE PERFECT HUNTING EXPEDITION

SECTOR 5: SAFARI…GOD'S HUNTING AND FISHING CAMP 38
    Failed Fishing 40
    Every Christian group should be a SAFARI Camp! 70

ZONE 3: HUNT PREPARATION

SECTOR SIX: YA GOTTA GET B.A.D. 74
    Baptism 77
SECTOR SEVEN: S.I.T. NO MORE 90
    Sin 90

    Iniquity *95*

    Transgression *99*

SECTOR EIGHT: S.A.C. TIME 101

    Silence *101*

    Alone *102*

    Communication *102*

SECTOR NINE: GIVE HIM YOUR P.A.W. 105

SECTOR TEN: COMPROMISE 108

    The Standard Of God *112*

    Deliver To Satan *116*

    Cave Of Adullam Decision *120*

SECTOR ELEVEN: D.I.G. FOR IT 124

    The "D" Word *125*

    The "I" Word *127*

    The "G" Word *128*

    Superheroes *129*

SECTOR TWELVE: BE F.I.T. 134

    F... Fearless *136*

    I... Incorruptible and T... Tenacious *139*

SECTOR THIRTEEN: FASTING TO GET RESULTS 142

SECTOR FOURTEEN: GOING IN THE SPIRIT, SPIRIT TRAVEL, BILOCATION, TRANSLATION, TRANSLOCATION, TELEPORTING, MULTI-TRANSPORTING 146

    Astral Projection *150*

    Can we Go to Heaven Now? *150*

    Biblical Examples of Going in the Spirit *151*

    Post-biblical Testimonies of Going in the Spirit *152*

    But my "church" Doesn't do That *155*

    Access into Heaven Now! *156*

    What you will Experience *157*

    Dreams *158*

Don't Remember 159

Going in the Spirit While Awake 159

Visions 159

Progression 160

Portals to the Spirit Realm 160

Spiritual Weapons 161

Heavenly Mansion 161

Heavens Scenery 161

Angels and Evil Entities 162

Hunting Evil Entities in the Spirit 162

Transported or Translocation 163

Healed at a Distance in the Spirit 164

Going in the Spirit for a City 165

Is there an age limit to Going in the Spirit? 166

Top Spiritual Secret Revealed 168

I call it Multi-Locating! 171

Conclusion 171

SECTOR FIFTEEN: WEAPONS AND HUNTING GEAR 173

Close Quarter Combat 202

Angels 206

The Secret Of God's Power 208

SECTOR SIXTEEN: SPIRITUAL MAPPING 212

ZONE 4: THE GAME/QUARRY

SECTOR SEVENTEEN: TROPHY OR XTREME BIG GAME 222

Satan 223

Anarchy 248

Endgame 253

Queen(S) Of Heaven 264

Olafing 271

How To Save A Nation 276

Prayer & Fasting Changes Nations 276

SECTOR EIGHTEEN: XTREME SMALL GAME 284
- *Bait* 305
- *The Process Of Deliverance* 308
- *Catch and Release (CAR) Spiritual Warfare* 312
- *Mass Deliverance* 314
- *Self-Deliverance* 316
- *Spiritual Warfare "Techniques"* 317

SECTOR NINETEEN: XTREME RABID GAME, SNAKES, WOLVES AND OTHER CRITTERS 323
- *International Rabid Game* 324
- *Local Rabid Game* 329
- *Rabid Denominations* 331
- *Resurrecting a church* 332
- *Christian Witchcraft* 360
- *Rebuking In Public* 364
- *Can Christians Kill?* 369

ZONE 5: GUIDED HUNTS

SECTOR TWENTY: HUNTING 4 HEALING 376
- *A Hunting Guide's Testimony* 377
- *What can we do?* 379
- *Miracle Crusades* 380
- *Awakenings/Revivals* 380
- *Conferences* 381
- *Healing Rooms* 381
- *Religious "Church"* 381
- *Missionaries* 383
- *One-on-One* 383
- *Pain* 385
- *Stop It!* 389
- *Hunting 4 Healing List* 389
- *Disease from God?* 390

Salvation *391*
Body Abuse *391*
Robbing God *392*
Our Time is Done *393*
Evil Roots *394*
Generational Curses *394*
Curses put against You *394*
Curses against yourself *395*
Soul Ties *395*
Unforgiveness and Bitterness *395*
Corupts *396*
Sin *397*
Sin unto Death *398*
Occultism *399*
Idol Worship *399*
Victimization *399*
Disobedience to God *400*
Fear and Evil Spirits *401*
Self-hatred *404*
Exposure to Chemicals and the Environment *404*
Get Right with God *406*
Unbelief *406*
Prayer *407*
Misguided Prayer *408*
Laying on of Hands *408*
Sanctification *411*
Word of God *412*
Miracles *412*
Divine Intervention *412*
Going in the Spirit *412*
Angels *413*

Coma and Raising the Dead *413*

Doctors and Medication *413*

Disease Prevention *414*

Still Healing doesn't come… Now what? *414*

Final Word from God *415*

SECTOR TWENTY-ONE: RAISING THE DEAD 417

Who raises the Dead? *426*

Permission *426*

Continued Handicap/Injury *426*

What's the Process to Raise the Dead? *426*

SECTOR TWENTY-TWO: POW's 428

Are you a POW? *430*

soul Imprisonment *434*

The Dual Strike Force Escape Plan *437*

Be humble. *443*

Look for Him. *444*

The Saints and Angelic Prison Break Plan *450*

The Commando Prison Break Plan *454*

Going in the Spirit Prison Break Plan *455*

SECTOR TWENTY-THREE: ALTARS, STRUCTURES,
AND STRONGHOLDS 459

Evil Altars *465*

SECTOR TWENTY-FOUR: POAR IT ON -PURSUE, OVERTAKE
AND RECOVER 482

ZONE 6: HUNTING EXPEDITIONS

SECTOR TWENTY-FIVE: XTREME BIG GAME HUNTING STORIES
AND TESTIMONIES 494

SECTOR TWENTY-SIX: AUSTRIAN/HUNGARIAN, NETHERLANDS,
HUNTING EXPEDITION 502

SECTOR TWENTY-SEVEN: CANADIAN HUNTING EXPEDITION 509

Messages From Father And Jesus .... *512 some More Heaven* *513*

The Court Of Heaven *514*

SECTOR TWENTY-EIGHT: THE CARIBBEAN.. 515

SECTOR TWENTY-NINE: GERMAN HUNTING EXPEDITION 519

SECTOR THIRTY: MEXICAN/AMERICAN HUNTING EXPEDITION 524

SECTOR THIRTY-ONE: NORTH CAROLINA USA,
HUNTING EXPEDITION 528

SECTOR THIRTY-TWO: PAPUA NEW GUINEA HUNTING EXPEDITION 532

The Seed, the Plant and the Tree of Holiness *533*

How To Go In The Spirit While Having Dinner *534*

How to practice going in the spirit *541*

SECTOR THIRTY-THREE: SWISS HUNTING EXPEDITION...................... 543

SECTOR THIRTY-FIOUR: DRAGON SLAYING... 546

SECTOR THIRTY-FIVE: THE SPIRIT OF DEATH 554

ZONE 7: HUNT'S END

SECTOR THIRTY-SIX: THE SILVER BULLET OF GOD 558

SECTOR THIRTY-SEVEN: GLORY TO GOD.. 562

THE LAST SHOT.. 564

BIBLIOGRAPHY... 568

INTRODUCTION

> **HUNTING TIP**
>
> The only easy day was yesterday! (US Navy SEAL motto… I love it!)

In the mid-1960's, the Holy Spirit came upon me in my bedroom, with such an in-filling, that I had no idea what was happening. I had to hold onto the side of the bed, as I thought I would fall out. This kind of thing, reminded me of what happened in the Biblical book of Acts.

The Lutheran church, where I was attending at that time, never talked about the Holy Spirit, or such spiritual experiences, so the next Sunday, I decided to ask the pastor if he believed miracles were still happening today. I guess I shouldn't have been too surprised, when he proclaimed that miracles had ended when the last disciple died. Even though this didn't make sense to me at the time, I decided not to mention my experience to anyone.

Church services became dull, giving me a feeling of being drained, rather than renewed. I mistakenly thought that God was dead, not realizing that God was alive in me now. God wasn't dead—it was religion that was dead—to Him and to my spirit!

Attending "church"* since childhood (Sunday school, confirmation classes, worship services, summer Bible school, Bible camp) I was becoming bored and wanted a way out, at the ripe old age of twelve! Unfortunately, my Mom didn't see it my way, so I had to endure this "religious-church" until I was sixteen.

My Dad was not a church-goer, which probably helped in my escape from prison ("church"), on the day that I told my Mom, that I wasn't going anymore.

INTRODUCTION

At that time, my Dad owned a gun shop and was a fur trapper and deputy game warden. In his adventurous past, he'd served as a British commando in WWII and as a police constable. He was a no-nonsense kind of guy.

Before I started school, I would tag along with him as he hunted, while tending his trap line for muskrat, raccoon, mink and fox.

The first time that he let me shoot his gun, I wasn't yet five years old. Holding his 12-gauge shotgun up to my shoulder, he had to pull the trigger for me, because I couldn't reach it!

I remember the recoil of the gun sending me backwards, skidding into a pile of snow!

Painful… but hey… I had shot a gun!

It was at his side that I learned about trapping, hunting, and guns.

To this day, I still enjoy it all—especially big game hunting!

The late '60s and early '70s found me driving motorcycles, becoming a hippie, and immersing myself into the darker counter-culture, that rose up alongside of the Christian "charismatic movement."

My Mom, meanwhile, was introduced to the phrase "being filled with the Holy Spirit", "being slain in the Spirit" and the practice of "laying on of hands" on people, for healing.

She was fifty years old, before finding out that the gifts of the Holy Spirit, and His miracle-working power, were still in force! This is when her ministry of healing and faith began, and she tried hard to point these things out to me. Even though I listened to her, read books, and saw people "falling down in the spirit", I was confused, and still turned off by "church". The world, and all its pleasures, was more of an attraction.

I attended college, moved around often, and had many different jobs—house painter, auto body worker, bar waiter, amusement park ride operator, miner, factory worker, advertising salesman, and mutual funds and insurance salesman. Always drifting, I was never happy or satisfied. During this period, I obtained a pilot's license and enjoyed flying around northern Canada. My plan was to become a bush pilot, but this dream soon bored me, too.

INTRODUCTION

After years of difficult, dirty, low-paying jobs, I decided that it was time to settle into something better… in an office. I applied for an office job as a credit supervisor. Even though I had no experience in this field, mysteriously, I was hired! My boss later told me, that I was the only one who applied, who would accept such a low pay rate! Those were my qualifications… a warm body that would work cheap!

After additional studies at the university level, my experience eventually landed me a management position at another company, with a substantial pay increase. I had a private office with a window, and people who reported directly to me. This time I was chosen from a large pool of qualified applicants—I wasn't just a warm body anymore! Then I bought a dream house on a huge, wooded lot. As they say, "I had arrived"!

Working in an office was a sedentary lifestyle, so I became determined to get myself in shape. Beginning with weight training, I blended that with classes in kickboxing, mixed martial arts, and tai chi; eventually training with the deadliest fighters that I could find.

There was a Russian Spetsnaz soldier/commando; a Delta Force Close Quarter Combat officer/instructor (who later certified me as a Close Quarter Combat Instructor); a grandmaster who had trained U.S. Marine snipers; a Chinese Kung Fu grandmaster; and other master martial artists.

I eventually obtained a Black Belt… one of only three ever handed out, by my combat martial arts instructor! Throughout this training, I never entered into the pagan chanting, worship, etc., that is associated with many martial art disciplines—I just trained my body and learned fighting skills—as I still considered myself a Christian. This extensive training, coupled with my skills with weapons, made me a formidable force... or so I thought.

So, I had arrived—but where?

And was a formidable force—but against what?

My Mom continued to minister to people, praying with them in person and on the phone, using anointed cloths, and they were being healed. Thousands of them! She had even raised people from the dead!

INTRODUCTION

I began to realize that I hadn't actually arrived anywhere. Even with the achievement of my dreams, the world that I had created, now seemed as dead to me, as the Church world had been, so many years ago.

The Holy Spirit was doing His job of convicting me.

I began reading the Bible again, and reread books I'd had since the 1970's, focusing on deliverance and spiritual warfare. I obtained every book that I could find on spiritual warfare, and studied countless others on theology and religion.

Then, I happened upon some gold mines!

It's not every day one finds spiritual gold mines, as most people don't look for them and although some know about them, most don't partake of their wealth.

The first gold mine I'll mention is Smith Wigglesworth.

He was a British, Christian leader in the early 20th Century who travelled the world, even into my home town. Through the many books written about him, he showed me a gold mine!

What did he have that other Christian leaders failed to grasp and still to this day don't grasp?

He showed me that *through personal, uncompromising commitment to God and your destiny,* a person can raise the dead, cast out evil spirits, heal the sick, and even grow missing limbs! I had never heard of anyone commanding missing limbs to grow! Christian leaders couldn't stand in the same room with him when he was communicating with God… only Wigglesworth could withstand God's power!

Actually, many years later, I personally met and learned from Arthur Burt, a Welsh minister who worked with Wigglesworth. Mr. Burt had been preaching for over 80 years! A few of his golden words to me were, "Go… Do!"

If this wasn't enough of a bonanza, I kept digging around and found the mother lode! I found some Christian men and women in the Egyptian desert.

INTRODUCTION

Although I have visited Egypt, I didn't find them literally in the sand. I found them in a set of old books, that were first written around the 4th Century and translated into English in 1904, *The Paradise of the Fathers,* Wallis Budge (2 Volumes).

These books reminded me of Matthew 13:44, "Again, the kingdom of heaven is like treasure hidden in a field, which a man found and hid; and for joy over it he goes and sells all that he has and buys that field".

I read about thousands and thousands of Christian men and women, who gave testament to their holy lives of <u>total commitment to God</u>. They fled into the desert from persecution, from a compromising, corrupt, religious church and from a world full of sin, that they couldn't stand anymore. Some lived in isolation and others in groups. Many lived a harsh existence for over 50 years, just to live closer with God. They are best known as the Desert Fathers and Mothers.

They defeated all kinds of spiritual creatures, such as a hippo-centaur, satyrs, wolves, lions, snakes, scorpions, a half-man-half ass, dragons (one was 70 cubits long, which is about 32 meters or 105 feet- page 1J of Vol. 1), as well as legions of devils and many creatures that took various forms.

People begged one monk to kill a serpent that was killing their sheep and cattle. He agreed to do so and the serpent attacked him three times before it was destroyed, bursting open just by a word from the monk!

Satan also appeared to them numerous times, in many forms, as well as many evil spirits pretending to be ordinary men, women and children, in an attempt to trick them.

They regularly walked on water, destroyed evil entities and could stop the sun as Joshua had done (Joshua 10:12) (See Besarion page 244 Vol. 1 and Petarpemotis page 367 Vol. 1)

Using Petarpemotis as an example, he could stop the sun, walk on water, raise the dead, destroy evil entities, and one time he stood for over half an hour in a blazing fire to expose a false teacher, (page 370-371 Vol. 1)!

INTRODUCTION

<u>A fantastic discovery</u> for me was like many others, he could not only see, hear, and smell the spiritual realm; he could <u>travel in the spirit</u>! He could travel anywhere, anytime, even into locked rooms and appear before people! He could also <u>travel physically into the heavens</u>!

<u>Once Petarpemotis went physically to heaven</u>, as Enoch** had done, and returned with a fig tree that was planted where he lived, that was seen by many people. It was a remarkable fig tree with unusually large figs… the aroma from this heavenly tree healed anyone instantly! (page 367-369 Vol. 1)

I couldn't cover all the miraculous things here, that were done and witnessed, but let me say that after reading all of these testimonies by numerous Christian holy people, recorded from various locations at different times, I can only say I was stunned! What further amazed me was their humility and indifference, to any grandeur attached to these miraculous occurrences.

It was just a way of life to them!

Who was doing this now?

Why weren't Christians being taught about such capabilities and aspiring to this level?

I begged God to give me what these Desert Fathers had or take me home, as I couldn't live in Christian mediocrity anymore!

Since I wasn't hit by lightning, I took it as a sign God had accepted my request.

God showed me that a radical life change or metamorphosis was required!

The path was longer than what I'd hoped.

As I hadn't heard of nor met anyone in the world who was at this level, it seemed I had to move through lower levels, to work my way up the ladder of Divine Ascent, as John Climacus called it in 600 A.D.

As was my usual pattern, when I trained in fighting, I searched out the best to train with them. After a lot of searching and processes of elimination, I found and trained with a deliverance minister in California, spending a lot of time with him and his wife in their home. After 25 years of deliverance ministry, this teacher presented me with the only certificate (Certificate #1) he had ever issued to a person for deliverance ministry.

This was more than most Christians were doing, but still I was not even close to the Desert Father's level.

Along the path, God showed me the richest gold mine I'd ever seen!

God was using all of my background, training, and experience as stepping stones, as He was leading me towards a ministry that few ever talked about or heard about. High-Level Spiritual Warfare, it has been called; dealing with evil principalities, spiritual powers and rulers over entire cities, areas and regions; finance/business, education, religion, government, and groups of people.

This ministry can affect 100's of thousands and millions of people at a time! One could even call it, the <u>Black Belt</u> or <u>Elite Special Forces of Xtreme Spiritual Warfare</u>!

Now this was something a Black Belt, hunter, son of a commando, and faith-healing minister, was born and bred to do!

I had studied some books by the most internationally recognized authority on high level spiritual warfare, Dr. C. Peter Wagner, but such people were "as scarce as hen's teeth" (as my father used to say) to find in order to work with "in the field". Eventually, I tracked down some like-minded individuals and worked along with them in Europe and North America, on different high-level evil spiritual hunting expeditions.

I was soon seeing, hearing and smelling the spiritual realm and travelling in the spirit, like the Desert Fathers had done, to all parts of the earth and into heaven. Some have called this travelling in the spirit, going in the spirit, teleporting or bilocation; being in two places at the same time. In occult circles, it is called astral projection or OOBE (out-of-body experience). The evil realm didn't invent this ability as they are only counterfeiters of the holy aspects of it.

By the way, Dr. C. Peter Wagner, was the President of the Global Harvest Ministries and Chancellor of the <u>Wagner Leadership Institute</u>;

INTRODUCTION

was a professor for 30 years at Fuller Theological Seminary School of World Missions, who taught students from nearly every country in the world; had served on numerous global missions, committees and organizations; had written over 80 books and was also the Presiding Apostle of the International Coalition of Apostles. As I had said, he was the most internationally recognized authority on high level spiritual warfare. He stepped into his eternal destiny in 2016.

We met and talked several times in 2006, at his spiritual warfare conference in Florida. He's the only one that I asked to review this book and I'm pleased that he enjoyed it, saying that this is a very good book!

During these years, Father, Jesus, and the Holy Spirit, were putting me through fiery baptism training, which included wilderness time, stripping away the old nature, giving me spiritual gifts and weapons, and much revelation through the Word, holy dreams and visions, experiences in the spirit realm, and more. I was becoming a new creature; a conquering creature for the glory and Kingdom of God!

I then came into contact with a man in his eighties, Rev. Dr. Rex Shanks, who had a spiritual warfare ministry for over thirty years in the USA, and had also served God in many other parts of the world. God told him it was time to lay down his ministry, and directed him to hand over Crown of Life Ministries, Inc., (COLM) to me, which he did, before he went home to be with the Lord.

At that time, I was appointed and anointed Bishop by Rex and the board of directors.

Around the same time, I was anointed an apostle by a Southern Cheyenne Sioux from Oklahoma named Roaming Buffalo. This man is more commonly known as Apostle Dr. Jay Swallow, and was an apostolic father to many ministers from the Arctic Circle to Central America, years before he was asked to be a member of Dr. C. Peter Wagner's International Coalition of Apostles. He said until that moment, in over 45 years of ministry, he had never been led to anoint anyone as an apostle!

I never asked for, nor was hunting to receive any of these titles or certificates. They don't hold any real weight.

INTRODUCTION

As my Dad used to say, "A bunch of fancy titles and certificates and 10 cents can buy you a cup of coffee at the diner". Inflation puts it at about three dollars at Starbucks now!

One of the things we learn from my Dad, from Jesus, from the disciples, from the Desert Fathers and Mothers is, that titles and certificates aren't needed to get it done.

Many years ago, visitors used to wave their Black Belt certificates from Japan in our faces at the fight club, to try to impress us.

Our smiling response was, "Yeah, but can you fight"!

Unfortunately, they were more concerned with getting a certificate from a recognized, "accepted" martial art, rather than learning to become the best fighter, in a real dangerous world.

Here's another way to say it… a person one time was debating with me about spiritual warfare, when I made a visit to their stated, non-denominational, spirit-filled, Church assembly. She was trying to convince me that spiritual warfare wasn't needed once someone became a Christian, as satan is under our feet and that's where she keeps him.

She was a long-time "church attender", with many bells and whistles, such as star of David and Cross chain around her neck, pretty Sunday clothes, nice shoes, dancing in front of the congregation during worship, "scripture-spouter", and tongues speaker. She certainly looked the part.

She had a small group with her, nodding their heads in agreement. I pointed out several Bible passages to them to prove their position was wrong. Still they fought me.

Then I said, "Have you ever seen an angel or an evil spirit"? A few dropped their heads and walked away. Guess their answer was "No". The leader didn't answer me and tried to change the subject. So, I asked her the same question again. She finally said, "No".

Then I said, "So you're speaking from spiritual blindness and ignorance and I'm speaking from experience and Biblical substantiation."

INTRODUCTION

This person and her group were Christians, perhaps, but spiritual duds! (I say perhaps, as they may all be living secret, deliberate sinful lives. They were following a made-up, religious doctrine on spiritual warfare. When you ignore parts of the Word of God, you are sinning.) These people would have impressed me, if they admitted their shortcomings and asked to be enlightened, when they were shown the truth. They instead, preferred to arrogantly continue living in the spiritually dysfunctional, doctrinal world that they created.

Evil entities won't be impressed with the "church" you attend or the seminary that you graduated from… they will smile and say, "Yeah, but can you fight"?

Through all my interest and studies since a child in fighting, military tactics of the world, and God's military tactics in the Bible, God made it apparent to me how important it is, to get to the leadership or the head, to bring the decisive blow, that can end battles, end wars, and end evil governments.

The removal of one person, such as a Hitler, Stalin, or Mao, can affect the lives of millions of people, and the world. In the Bible, we can use examples such as Kings Zebah and Zalmunna of Midian, King Saul, Ahab and Jezebel; where circumstances changed, when they were ousted. Bringing down the "Big Game" causes things to change! God taught me that changes in the spiritual realm produces changes in the physical realm!

I'm still learning from the best in Person!

One day, during a 40-day fast, I went in the spirit. At this place, Father God started talking to me, as a large white eagle came down carrying two swords. I reached up and took both swords from Him (this eagle and these swords became the logo for Crown of Life Ministries and Way of the Eagle International).

As I took them, lightning went out from the sword in my right hand, across to my left, and lightning from the sword in my left hand went out across to my right.

A great wind came up as I saw that I was standing on top of a huge mountain, having no vegetation, and all the rocks were smooth, rather than jagged. There wasn't much more room on the top, than where I was standing. God our Father spoke to me and said, "These swords are given to you from Me and they will always be with you". I asked Him, "What do I do with them"?

He said, "You will slay the wicked, and destroy the enemy". I was moving the swords around very fast, to get their feel in my hands. Then I placed the swords at my sides. They stuck and hung there.

I asked Father, if I still had the sword that Jesus gave me years ago and He said that I did.

Next, Father sent down a flat piece of stone that had writing on it, with words I couldn't understand. I reached up, took it and threw it off the top of the mountain. I looked over the side and saw it splash into waters that were surrounding the mountain, watching as it floated away.

I asked Father, "What was that and why did I do that"? He said, "That is the book you are writing and My Words will go out across the waters".

As I looked up, I could see the white eagle still flying overhead. Father told me, that this white eagle was from Him and would be with me wherever I went, assisting me. I looked around at where I was standing and asked Father, "Where am I"? He said, "This is our secret place for just you and Me. Although Jesus and the Holy Spirit are always with you… at this place it is just you and Me".

I asked Father, "Whom should I teach about high level spiritual warfare"? He said, "Teach anyone who wants to learn". I asked Him if I should go in the spirit, or go physically to places to do spiritual warfare and He said, "You may do both if you want". I asked Him if it was alright to write about this experience in the book and He said that I could. I asked other questions. He told me other things, until I didn't want to ask any more questions… I just wanted to dance, because I was so happy!

I started dancing in the spirit, on top of this spiritual mountain. The two swords that Father had given me were still at my sides, flapping around as I was turning, spinning and dancing. I have used them as He has directed since that time.

INTRODUCTION

Father was very happy with our entire meeting and I was happy, too!

Father referred to this mountain as "The Rock".

"For in the time of trouble He shall hide me in His pavilion; In the secret place of His tabernacle

He shall hide me; He shall set me high upon a rock." Psalm 27:5

"Be my rock of refuge." Psalm 31:2

"For you are my rock and my fortress!" Psalm 31:3

Like a Silver Bullet of God***, I go in the physical and in the spirit, <u>to hunt and bring down the most dangerous predators and monsters known to exist, and to set free for Him the most precious beings known to exist… people!</u>

Although I'm a guy who like the Desert Fathers and Mothers, prefers the solitude with God as a spiritual recluse, shunning the limelight, God has asked me to write this book and to train and guide others to be successful as Xtreme Christians… as a Silver Bullet for Him!

His will be done!

However, I'm not an entertainer and neither is God. If you're not willing to give everything to God, then pass this book now, over to someone who is serious and will succeed, as it will be too tough for you.

This book has gone into over 190 countries!

Bible teaching centers in many countries, are utilizing this book right now to train leaders and children! (The same Holy Spirit is in children, that are in adults.)

Although many Christians are not led to be Xtreme Big Game Hunters, they do need to learn to be a Silver Bullet of God, operating in the spiritual realm, with their Holy Spirit gifts and with their spiritual senses, if only to worship Him in spirit, as He commands. ("God is Spirit, and those who worship Him must worship in spirit and truth." John 4:24)

If you happen to also become a fighter along the way, that's a bonus that will come in handy when the enemy attacks you. (If you don't think the enemy wants to destroy you, your family and your life, then you live a fairytale life!)

<u>This book will assist any and every person!</u>

<u>Countless have been instantly healed of physical, emotional, mental and spiritual afflictions!</u>

<u>Lives and families have been restored!</u>

<u>Success, has risen out of failures!</u>

This book's guidance, is geared to point the way to an eyes-wide-open, personal, intimate relationship with God <u>in</u> the heavens, and to utilize <u>all</u> your spiritual senses, abilities, gifts, power and authority in the physical and spiritual realms, which is how and why God built you the way He did.

The guts to get there are your guts!

Here's some reality for you. NASA says that there are over 2 trillion galaxies in the Universe. That's trillion with a "T". (There's more). This doesn't account for the size of heaven, the spiritual realm and all the dimensions and realms created by God. A true child of God is a saint, a royal-priest, a joint-heir with Jesus and a ruler in all of this… right now! A true child of God is in dominion of all that God created! God wants you equipped to operate in your position. Sitting around in a "church", using Jesus as a "fire insurance policy" or as a "magic-ticket" to heaven, isn't being equipped. It isn't your destiny. You are robbing yourself, robbing others and robbing God of His glory when this spiritually dead position is adopted and taught to you. Abandon all flesh-driven, religious ways. Anything less, God says, is a sin.

"For those who live according to the flesh set their minds on the things of the flesh, but those who live according to the Spirit, the things of the Spirit. For to be carnally minded is death, but to be spiritually minded is life and peace. Because the carnal mind is enmity against God; for it is not subject to the law of God, nor indeed can be. So then, those who are in the flesh cannot please God." Romans 8:5-8 *religious "church" is a structure/system/organization/government/building designed after the Old Testament temple-system, which became obsolete after the resurrection of Jesus. The Church is a body or assembly (Ekklesia-Greek) of followers of Jesus Christ, who are directed by the Holy Spirit and under the perfect will of Father God.

**1 Enoch, 2 Enoch, 3 Enoch in Pseudepigrapha Vol. 1
***THE SILVER BULLET…
…something that acts as a weapon; especially one that instantly solves a long-standing problem.
The term traditionally originates from ancient days; said to be the only kind of bullet that is effective against monsters.
There's a Silver Bullet of God for each of your monsters!

SECTOR ONE
THE KILLING FIELD

> **HUNTING TIP**
>
> When you lose the fear of death... you will become a force to be reckoned with!

The female-looking creature, was flying around high above me wearing a grayish, tattered dress... the long sickle it carried out in front of it, had its blade set forward. Was it hunting me... waiting for the right moment to attack? I didn't have to wonder long, as it came streaking down at me—and we clashed—its blade just missing me...this hunt was getting serious!

I had a different sword this time, much longer like a broad sword. Although it felt very light and easy to swing, I used two hands to fight with it.

Our combat was fierce and face-to-face... its eyes were black and its face had an emotionless, death-like appearance.

Although my blade cut it a few times, it wouldn't let go of its sickle and we continued to struggle, pushing and battling back and forth with its sickle locked against my sword! It moved back a bit, then swung down at me and missed... its sickle ramming and sticking into the ground.

As it was struggling to get its sickle loose, I slashed and cut its hands. When it let go of the sickle, I wasted no time, immediately driving my sword up through it.

It had a lot of fight left in it, when I asked angels to come. They bound its body and eyes and took it away, still struggling!

There was little time to relax. Another creature, a smaller version of the last one, came down and attacked me. This one, though, was easily defeated and disappeared, when I swiped my sword through it.

Next came two ghosts, or transparent apparitions, of very angry old men… one after the other, they swooped down on me and were also defeated, disappearing, when I sliced through them with my sword.

Then, a giant-headed octopus with many small tentacles appeared and just sat there in front of me… I wasted no time, putting my sword to it.

Now I was at a heightened sense of alert… looking around in all directions.

As I called for angels to come, ten huge creatures with sea horse bodies and human heads materialized, forming a semi-circle in front of me… they were about three times bigger than me!

All of them were just floating there, not making any moves towards me! Perhaps they were deciding on how best to make fish food out of me! I saw no weapons, and didn't intend to wait until they had a plan, so I quickly attacked them from left to right. They vanished in an instant, as I slashed across each of them with my sword.

There wasn't anything else that showed, so I started banging the edge of my sword on the ground with both hands, as I was looking around and up, yelling out, "Anything else want some"? The blade of my sword was making a loud clanging sound as it hit the ground. Phantom creatures dove down on me out of the dark clouds, but I couldn't tell what they were, as I only saw part of them. I swung up with the sword, but they stayed out of range and flew back up out of sight.

I asked the angels to come again and as they came down, surrounding me with their golden chariots and horses, a bright light engulfed us. I was reminded of the angels on the golden chariots, that I had seen around a mountain in Germany once, while I was in the spirit.

I'm not sure if this combat was for part of Canada, where I was physically positioned, or the continuance of a U.S. city's evil spiritual stronghold, that I had just torn down a few weeks before, where prisoners of war were also released from their spiritual prison. This was a possibility, as that mission continued into a second phase; when evil snakes had been trying to break through the membrane barrier that I had set over the gates of hell, in that city. These snakes were desperately trying to squeeze through these barriers, so, I resealed these gates with a mixture of the blood of Jesus and oil from heaven, assisted by an angel, who was working at lightning speed.

Or perhaps, it was just retaliation for some past hunting trip.

As for this mission, my spirit eventually moved back, away from the angels and their chariots, while His Light was still shining down on them… this successful hunt was over!

All Glory to You; God… the victory is Yours!

WARNING

The evil spiritual realm does not want you to read this book!

They especially don't want you to fulfill any of this information in your life.

If you have God and the spiritual realm in a box this book will shake you up!

Ask the Holy Spirit to assist you through this book.

Be prepared to become a mouth-dropping, awe-inspiring,

no-nonsense, destiny-driven, can-do-anything conqueror for God!

One who will enjoy advancing God's Kingdom, one who will be Xtremely successful at defeating the enemies of God; one who will learn and grow from this book and also teach it to others!

Moving in the spiritual realm will be challenging… your destiny won't be easy!

Yet you'll find as I have, The Way of God has no substitute in life!

Be bold… As Smith Wigglesworth would say, "Only Believe!"

ZONE ONE

WHY HUNT?

SECTOR TWO
WHY DO XTREME BIG GAME HUNTING?

> **HUNTING TIP**
>
> All the nations… all the enemies… are in our hands!

So, is all of the fighting, detailed in Sector One, some sort of fantasy game or fictional story meant for entertainment? Neither. What I described actually happened in the spiritual or supernatural realm or lower heaven, while I was in the spirit! For those who think going places in the spirit is not possible or is evil, let's look at where the Apostle John was when he wrote Revelation:

"I was in the Spirit on the Lord's Day, and I heard behind me a loud voice, as of a trumpet." Revelation 1:10

or Elisha

"But Elisha said to him, "Was not my spirit with you when the man got down from his chariot to meet you?" 2 Kings 5:26

or Ezekiel:

"and the Spirit lifted me up between earth and heaven." Ezekiel 8:3

"The spirit lifted me up." Ezekiel 11:1

"The hand of the Lord was upon me and brought me out in the spirit." Ezekiel 37:1

or Paul:

"I know a man in Christ who fourteen years ago-whether in the body I do not know, or whether out of the body I do not know, God knows-such a one was <u>caught up to the third heaven</u>. And I know such a man-whether in the body or out of the body I do not know, God knows- how he was <u>caught up into Paradise</u> and heard inexpressible words, which it is not lawful for a man to utter." 2 Corinthians 12:2-4

"For though I am absent in the flesh, yet I am <u>with you in spirit</u>..." Colossians 2:5

or Jesus seeing Nathaniel under the fig tree before they ever met!

"Before that Philip called you, when you were under the fig tree, I saw you." John 1:43-50

or Philip, taken body and spirit, 25 miles away in an instant,

"The Spirit of the Lord, caught away Philip... but Philip was found at Azotus." Acts 8:39-40

or how about an entire boat full of people being transported about 4 miles!

"<u>immediately</u> the boat was at the land where they were going." John 6:16-21 (They rowed about 3-4 miles and so, were about half way across the sea of Galilee.)

There are those who say that these spiritual occurrences only happened in the Bible and that they don't happen anymore... yet the Bible says, "Jesus Christ the same yesterday, and today and forever". Hebrews 13:8

Is it really conceivable, that God stopped being God and that the spiritual realm stopped, or was suspended, 2,000 years ago? Any leader that stifles your spiritual growth by saying such things, (like the pastor I had when I was a kid), usually do so because their spiritual life is dead or stunted. One day, their actions will be judged. They will be held accountable. Anyone who has such a leader, needs to find a new one, that follows the entire Word of God.

'Nuff said (for now).

Many more of these Silver Bullet and Xtreme Big Game Hunting experiences will be shared... some from me and some that are in the Bible! Teaching <u>YOU</u> how to become a Silver Bullet of God and Xtreme

Big Game Hunter; how to operate in the spiritual realm and fulfill your destiny with God, are the missions of this book.

WHY DO WE DO IT? WHY BECOME A SILVER BULLET OF GOD? WHY DO XTREME BIG GAME HUNTING?

The ultimate end is evangelization… on a huge scale. Also, we do Xtreme Big Game Hunting because God commands us to (not using this <u>exact</u> wording of course) and we do it to teach a lesson to all of creation.

The evil spiritual realm is highly organized, with some of its main goals being to prevent, discourage, and make the evangelism process a failure, to keep Christians ineffective, and to destroy God's plans. Perhaps those in the evil realm still believe, that they have a shot at the title and so continue to make attempts at ultimate victory. Although the war was won by Jesus, we must still battle until the end. If this sounds weird, remember that in WWII, there was a moment when it became obvious that the war was won by the allies and the end was inevitable; however, battles continued on for another year or more.

So, let's examine this kind of hunting, as many would say it is unique, if not dangerous, and many have said Christians are not to do it! Unique, yes… although it shouldn't be… dangerous… it <u>can</u> be Xtremely dangerous… saying Christians are not to do it is un-Biblical.

Strategic-Level Spiritual Warfare; High-Level Spiritual Warfare; Prophetic Spiritual Warfare; Intercessory Prayer and even "redeeming the land", as people have labeled this kind of hunting, has its root in Paul's letter to the Ephesians.

Keep in mind that although Paul was the writer of this epistle, God is the author. God says,

"For we do not wrestle against flesh and blood, but against principalities, against powers, against the rulers of the darkness of this age, against spiritual hosts of wickedness in the heavenly places." Ephesians 6:12.

The Greek word for wrestle is "pale", which refers to warfare, that we Christians have with the main, high-level, or leader evil spiritual entities. The Greek word for "high" here is "epouranois", meaning heavenlies. Therefore, the short version of this scripture verse could say that... "Christians war against leader evil spiritual entities in the heavenlies."

This is a fact.

It doesn't say that Christians shouldn't be warring against these creatures, nor does it say that just some elite, self-professed "generals" are allowed to war against these creatures, nor does it say we only fight against unclean evil spirits in people, physical objects and on earth… it says we Christians war against evil leader spiritual forces <u>IN</u> the heavenlies.

EACH AND EVERY ONE OF US!

The war is on, and they are warring against us, so Christians can decide to either sit and be a target, or be a weapon! When you become a Christian, you volunteer in God's army and evil forces now intensify their attack against you. You can fight back against them or you can sit around in the "church" basement, drinking coffee and eating crumb cake, oblivious to the war against you, all the while getting beaten up and possibly destroyed, as you let others do your work! (The evil realm has no problem with your religious "church"-system attendance. They encourage it. Billions of religious spirits attend "church").

Tough talk—I know, but war is serious and too many Christians are just sitting around doing nothing for God, themselves or others!

We have heard much about small, evil spiritual forces such as demons and human evil forces, such as witches and satanists, but little is known about the "Big Guys." We'll cover them all in this book and what they do to your life, your family, your city and your country. We'll discuss what they do and how you, as a Silver Bullet of God, can stop them.

In physical wars in the Bible, evil rulers controlled their subjects and kept conflicts and wars going until they died or were defeated. The same is said of the modern physical world… so why would it be different in the spiritual realm?

We now know that we are in a war, so let's see what else the Word says about our adversaries:

2 Corinthians 4:4… "whose minds the god of this age has blinded, who do not believe, lest the light of the gospel of the glory of Christ, who is the image of God, should shine on them."

This says that satan (god of this age) and his realm, are blinding the minds of people from accepting the gospel, from being evangelized <u>and</u>, a seldom acknowledged fact—from keeping the gospel (salvation) when they get it.

The evil realm also tries to keep Christians unaware… and most Christians are. Some of the evil spiritual realm's biggest weapons that they deploy, are ignorance, confusion, fear and complacency.

Are any of these adjectives, accurately describing you?

Principalities and powers have little need to war against nominal or notional people, who consider themselves Christian, as they are, for the most part, being controlled by them. They are weak, spiritually blind, and powerless and pose no threat to them. The Word says, that these non-Christians are lost and will be joining all evil entities one day in the lake of fire!

"And I saw the dead, small and great, standing before God, and books were opened. And another book was opened, which is the Book of Life. And the dead were judged according to their works, by the things which were written in the books. The sea gave up the dead who were in it, and Death and Hades delivered up the dead who were in them. And they were judged, each one according to his works. Then Death and Hades were cast into the lake of fire. This is the second death. And anyone not found written in the Book of Life was cast into the lake of fire.." Revelation 20:12-15

If you're reading this book and Jesus is not your personal Lord and Savior, you are full of evil, unclean spirits—attempting to be a Silver Bullet of God or do Xtreme Big Game Hunting will be impossible. You won't be able to go with God in the spirit, nor receive God's guidance to do it; evil entities would destroy you if you came against them. You would get chewed up and stomped on, on a much larger scale than did the sons of a Sceva, who tried casting out evil spirits like Paul.

Acts 19:13-16, "Then some of the itinerant Jewish exorcists took it upon themselves to call the name of the Lord Jesus over those who had evil spirits, saying, "We exorcise you by the Jesus whom Paul preaches." Also, there were seven sons of Sceva, a Jewish chief priest, who did so.

And the evil spirit answered and said, "Jesus I know, and Paul I know; but who are you?" Then the man in whom the evil spirit was leaped on them, overpowered them, and prevailed against them, so that they fled out of that house naked and wounded." Principalities and powers control non-Christians and also many Christians, with the use of evil spirits and with the help of deceived or deliberately evil people. Evil spirits or Xtreme Small Game, use people as hosts, as one can see from the many times Jesus had to cast evil and unclean spirits <u>out</u> of people.

There is also another adversary that I call, Xtreme Rabid Game, such as witches, satanists and their ilk, who astral-project in the spirit, who won't attempt this kind of hunting, as they are already full of evil spirits and willingly living in spiritual darkness... and wouldn't come against their own kind.

Witches, who say they only want to "help" people get rid of evil spirits by using chants, potions, formulas, charms, astrology, and psychic readings, are only inflicting additional evil on people and themselves, as many find out later.

Only obedient, spirit-filled Christians, who sincerely repent of their sins every day and keep their hearts pure, can safely join in on some Xtreme Big Game Hunting!

WARNING

If you are a Christian who is involved in deliberate sin, iniquity, transgressions and disobedience and/or who doesn't spiritually see, hear or go in the spirit or accept direction from God, attempting this type of hunting is not recommended!

Any Christians in these categories can continue through this book and receive guidance to set themselves right with their Lord and prepare themselves as an Xtreme Big Game Hunter!

Evil forces have a plan in place to try and disrupt God, evangelization, the Church and Christians.

WHAT IS GOD'S PLAN?

We know that God has a plan for the future, which we can read in Revelation, but what is the "now plan"?

To see the "now plan", we go to the "beginning plan".

Ephesians 3:9-11, "and to make all see what is the fellowship of the mystery, which from the beginning of the ages has been hidden in God who created all things through Jesus Christ; to the intent that now the manifold wisdom of God might be made known by the church to the principalities and powers in the heavenly places, according to the eternal purpose which He accomplished in Christ Jesus our Lord,"

God knew that Lucifer (satan) would plan a revolt, and that He would kick Lucifer and his followers down to the earth to dwell. The rebellious beings that joined Lucifer are the principalities and powers now operating IN the heavenlies, or spiritual realm, around the earth.

Why, you ask, didn't God just "bump them off" or toss them right away into the lake of fire, and save everyone all this headache, death and destruction? He could have just dumped them and created some replacements. It would seem a wonderful lesson to any future creatures, with an eye on God's throne. They would see what happened to satan and his crew, when they came up against the omnipotent God. You'd think that'd be enough! But God had another plan and God's plans are better than what we think.

He decided to make a different kind of spirit/physical being (mankind) and put us in the same place as all these mean and nasty bad guys, to make us rulers and teach them a lesson!

God knew that mankind would sin and lose command to the bad guys; and that we'd pretty much lose our ability to see them and deal with them… (but they can see us).

Oh, and also, because of the sin of man, we all must now work hard and die!

What'd ya think of God's plan so far?

It gets better!

Rather embarrassing perhaps for God, was that His new creation (us) was such a flop right out of the starting gate, and the bad guys were looking pretty good.

But, God knew before He created us, that we'd sin and get in a jam, so His plan had a continuation.

Dominion over these bad guys would come through man, by the incarnation of the Word… as Jesus Christ.

THE XTREME SUPERMAN!

THE ULTIMATE SILVER BULLET!

Jesus God came, to personally rub satan's and his army's noses, in the futility of their rebellion and plans for rulership; and to give man the pleasure of doing the same thing—when He handed ALL power and ALL authority over to us, after He regained it!

"Beware lest anyone cheat you through philosophy and empty deceit, according to the tradition of men, according to the basic principles of the world, and not according to Christ. <u>For in Him dwells all the fullness of the Godhead bodily; and you are complete in Him, who is the head of all principality and power.</u>" Colossians 2:8-10

"And you (Christians), being dead in your trespasses and the uncircumcision of your flesh, He has made alive together with Him, having forgiven you all trespasses, having wiped out the handwriting of requirements that was against us, which was contrary to us. And He has taken it out of the way, having nailed it to the cross (took away our spiritual death sentence). <u>Having disarmed principalities and powers, He made a public spectacle of them, triumphing over them in it</u>." Colossians 2:13-15

What was that last verse?

Jesus defeated evil principalities and powers <u>and</u> made an open show of them, to all of creation, that they were defeated!

Jesus called these "big bad guys", snakes and scorpions in Luke 10:19, "Behold, I give unto you the authority to trample on serpents (principalities) and scorpions (powers), and over all the power of the enemy (including satan and all evil forces): and nothing shall by any means hurt you".

Not only <u>can</u> we do this, but in Mark 16:17a and 18a, Jesus <u>commands</u> us to stick it to them; "And these signs shall follow them that believe…. They (Christians) shall take up serpents (principalities)".

Every time we stick it to them, we're showing them and all of creation, just how stupid and weak evil principalities and powers are, compared to God. God is giving us, His children, the honor of doing it!

The Lord gave me a spiritual dream in February 2007 and He has asked me to share the teaching.

In this dream, I was deep within "Indian Country", as they called it in the old western movies, which is also a phrase that is used by U.S. soldiers today, when they are behind enemy lines.

This is where we are on earth… behind enemy lines!

I was alone in this land, that was controlled by Apaches and I was hunting them alone. Usually not done by white men during the settler days, due to the extreme danger of being in Indian territory, alone.

I was standing in a hollowed-out tree, looking out over a wide area, through knot holes in the tree. I was hidden… and waiting… specifically for chiefs!

Some wild horses ran by and I could see an Apache's legs dangling under a horse's belly. This Apache was hanging by his arms between the horses, making it difficult for anyone to see or attack him, even from a distance.

I then heard a noise in the distance, that was getting louder. I looked through the knot hole to my right and I could see a wagon train coming. The wagons and all the "pilgrims" were in bright, rainbow colors, dancing and singing and acting like they hadn't a care in the world.

I thought, "These people must be nuts, moving through Indian country like this in broad daylight"! I decided to come out of the tree, to warn them about how dangerous it was in this place, and that what they were doing would bring an attack upon them.

They were moving along slowly; dancing, singing and being happy, as I approached the man in front.

I explained to him the dangers of what they were doing, yet he just kept dancing and smiling with the others all the while trying to convince me to join them. He wasn't listening to me or caring about anything that I was saying!

I kept looking for us to be attacked at any moment!

I shared this dream with a prophetic friend of mine at the time in Germany, who gave this wagon train the title of "Charismatic Woodstock"! This was a commentary about Christians who wander around oblivious to spiritual reality, much like the hippies of the 60's and 70's, who decided to ignore society's realities and "dropped out".

The hippie movement peaked in the summer of 1969, in Woodstock, N.Y., with a frenzied event fueled by sex, drugs and rock and roll.

I was one of these hippies during this time frame and can therefore relate. My warnings to the pilgrims were to no avail, so I decided to get away from these people who wouldn't listen to reason and truth.

I asked the Holy Spirit to explain this dream to me, which is pretty much self-explanatory.

I was doing Xtreme Big Game Hunting… waiting for opportunities to destroy the enemy, especially the leaders.

These people and their wagons were Christians, their religious-churches and organizations moving along oblivious to the evil realm around them, refusing to believe or be concerned about evil spirits or being attacked.

As we know, those 19th century wagon trains that heeded the warnings of scouts, mountain men and other trailblazers, met with better fates, than those who refused to listen to anyone, as they went into Indian country! Native Americans did what was always done, when danger came into their territory.

Evil entities are here—and they also attack to protect their territories.

Acting like they aren't here or can't hurt you, or thinking that we should just leave them alone, is neither Biblical nor wise!

We are given <u>all</u> wisdom, knowledge, power, authority, guidance and the necessary weapons to defeat the enemy!

Myself…I prefer to use <u>all</u> of what God gives to me…I choose to use <u>all</u> the big guns that God gives me!

Are you on a Charismatic Woodstock Wagon Train or are you on a <u>SPIRITUAL BATTLESHIP</u>?

Are you a True Conqueror or wandering around lost and dead?

I apologize to Native Americans for using a negative characterization of them in this dream, yet it was the dream given to me by God, to make His spiritual point. What was done to the Native Americans by so-called Christian whites and a so-called Christian government, (albeit, influenced by evil entities to do so), was a holocaust not unlike that under the Nazi regime that controlled Europe during the Second World War. Innocents were also segregated, murdered, raped, tortured, and robbed because they were different. Had more Christians in the 1700–1800's America and in the 1940's Europe, known about how evil spiritual entities can control people and areas, and then spiritually fought against it, perhaps such brutality and sin would have been avoided.

Rees Howells, a Welshman, was a Silver Bullet of God who understood Xtreme Big Game Hunting. In the 1930's and 1940's, he worked against the Xtreme evil spiritual leaders controlling Hitler, Mussolini, and Stalin.

Quote from Rees Howells' Bible College Website regarding those years:

"One form that this prayer warfare took was intercession on a national and international level concerning anything that effected world evangelism. Every Creature must hear; therefore, the doors must be kept open. <u>Their prayers became strategic. They must face and fight the</u>

enemy wherever he was opposing freedom to evangelize. God was preparing an instrument—a company to fight world battles on their knees. Over the next few years the founder, (Rees Howells) led the college into a path of intercession and prayer warfare on international levels. These prayers included the crisis with the Rhineland, Ethiopia, Dunkirk, the Battle of Britain, Russia, North Africa, Italy, 'D' Day, and the intercession for the establishment of the state of Israel."

See also, *Rees Howells Intercessor*, Norman Grubb. 1952.

Mr. Howells understood what was going on. He knew he was more than a conqueror with God. He knew his destiny and he acted on that knowledge. He and his group came against the Xtreme-level evil spiritual entities <u>IN</u> the heavenlies that were behind Nazism and brought them down, allowing the physical war to succeed.

High level spiritual warfare is needed more so now than ever before in history, as the war is escalating. More people like Reese Howells are needed in every country, to combat the Christian Holocaust for instance.

What is the Christian Holocaust?

In 2002, a study called *The New Persecuted*, was presented at a conference in Italy by Antonio Socci. His study concluded, that approximately 70 MILLION Christians have been martyred since Christ!

The most shocking finding was that 45.5 MILLION were martyred, just in the 20th Century!

The 20th Century saw 65% of all Christian martyrs!

And… I million were killed between 2010 and 2016. 90,000 Christians were martyred in 2016. Roughly 1 Christian every six minutes is being murdered every hour somewhere in the world because of their faith! December 30, 2106 and January 17, 2017 Christianpost.com

Christian martyrdom is growing at a rapid pace!

This doesn't include, the countless millions imprisoned, tortured, attacked, maimed, sold into slavery and victimized… just because they are Christian!

Where's the Fox News and CNN exposé for these atrocities?

Where's the UN sanctions or destruction of regimes that allow and perpetuate these crimes?

Where's the hunting down everywhere and anywhere in the world of these criminals, to bring them to justice, like the Israelis did of the Nazis?

Where's <u>our</u> Holocaust Museum?

A corrupt, New Age world, manipulated by evil spiritual principalities and powers, is in the business of Christian genocide!

Why do we battle principalities and powers? Because they are behind such atrocities as the Christian Holocaust. They are behind a great many things, as you will learn. You will read more testimonies later, of what happens when we attack and conquer them!

Principalities, powers and evil forces continue to battle us and succeed when we do nothing or submit to them. When we fight, we are following God's will and commands; we are adhering to the Word, allowing multitudes to be set free; we rob the lake of fire of more souls; we follow our destiny and we build up our treasures in Heaven!

AND best of all, showing all of creation, that these evil forces are losers and only the one true God deserves all glory and all praise and all worship!

Those of us who are striving and battling for God, are happy to do it <u>just</u> for God and no other reason. Yet, there are some <u>special</u> spiritual eternal rewards… reserved just for Conquerors! Father is Pure Love… it is in His Nature to bless and reward His children. In addition to the usual rewards for Christians, there are special rewards for the Overcomer… the Conqueror!

In Revelation Chapters 2 and 3, Jesus is speaking to us about the different doctrines, of seven different Church groups. We must be careful to heed Jesus' warnings, as not all who call themselves "followers of Christ", are His sheep.

<u>These Chapters in Revelation, also act as a treasure map!</u>

Many people think that when they die, they'll be floating around in heaven somewhere, on a cloud plucking a harp. Oddly, many believe that they will become angels when they die! Many believe, in error, that everyone goes to heaven. This thinking is the dead fruit of the false doctrines of man! I don't know about you, but I love it that God tells me <u>exactly</u> what I'm going to get for being a Conqueror!

Let's examine the condemnations and the rewards spelled out in Revelation:

The Ephesus Christian

<u>Condemnation</u>: Despite looking good on the outside…persevering, working for the Master, "trying spirits," exposing false apostles, against evil, not giving up… the inside of this Christian is sick, as "You have forsaken the love you had at first" (2:4b) Their hearts are no longer on fire for the Lord Jesus Christ. This type of Christian has embraced religion and " These people draw near to Me with their mouth, and honor Me with their lips, but their heart is far from Me. And in vain they worship Me, Teaching as doctrines the commandments of men." (Mt. 15:8-9)

<u>Reward</u>: to those who keep their first love… 'To him who overcomes, I will give to eat from the tree of life, which is in the midst of the Paradise of God." (2:7b)

The Smyrna Christian

<u>Condemnations</u>: None.

<u>Rewards</u>: To the Christian that Conquers worldly wealth, persecution, trials, tribulations, is faithful unto death, will receive… 'Be faithful until death, and I will give you the crown of life." (2:10b) <u>and</u> 'He who overcomes shall not be hurt by the second death (lake of fire)." (2:11b)

The Pergamos Christian

<u>Condemnations</u>: Accepts the doctrine of Baalam (idolatry and sexual immorality) and the doctrine of the Nicolaitanes (impure/immoral/false doctrines, adultery and fornication).

Rewards: "To him who overcomes I will give some of the hidden manna to eat. And I will give him a white stone, and on the stone a new name written which no one knows except him who receives it." (2:17b)

The Thyatira Christian

Condemnations: Despite their good works, faith, patience, and charity, they allow a spirit of Jezebel to teach and seduce them and others to commit fornication and participate in idolatrous practices. Many are seduced by a dynamic personality and a slick presentation, which does not guarantee that they are teaching truth—some leaders and Christians knowingly and deliberately deceive others.

Rewards: "And he who overcomes, and keeps My works until the end, to him I will give power over the nations— 'He shall rule them with a rod of iron; They shall be dashed to pieces like the potter's vessels— as I also have received from My Father; and I will give him the morning star. He who has an ear, let him hear what the Spirit says to the churches." (2:26-29)

The Sardis Christian

Condemnations: Reputation of being a "live" Christian, but actually is spiritually dead, imperfect works and few remaining good qualities.

Rewards: "He who overcomes shall be clothed in white garments, and I will not blot out his name from the Book of Life; but I will confess his name before My Father and before His angels." (3:5)

The Philadelphia Christian

Condemnations: None

Rewards: "He who overcomes, I will make him a pillar in the temple of My God, and he shall go out no more. (And) I will write on him the name of My God and the name of the city of My God, the New Jerusalem, which comes down out of heaven from My God. And I will write on him My new name." (3:12)

The Laodicea Christian

Condemnations: Spiritually lukewarm… do-nothings, lovers of worldly material things and prosperity.

<u>Rewards</u>: "To him who overcomes I will grant to sit with Me on My throne, as I also overcame and sat down with My Father on His throne." (3:21)

OK... sit down, get a firm grip on your chair and read this one again:

As a Conqueror like Jesus... you will sit with God on His throne!

Feel like conquering now?

As we can see by these 7 types of Christians, anyone can <u>say</u> they're a Christian, yet most will be condemned—most will <u>not</u> receive a Conqueror's Rewards. Some Christians will war <u>when the fight comes to them</u>; but as we can see, many warriors will be conquered and will <u>not</u> receive a Conqueror's Rewards. Jesus says that the <u>few</u> who conquer will <u>definitely</u> receive these 18 rewards!

And what are the rewards for being a Silver Bullet of God? For hunting and conquering principalities and powers?

Be Ready!

Don't just sit around.

Don't just defend.

Don't just be a warrior.

Go... Hunt... Conquer!

Why did I start doing it... hunting Xtreme Big Game?

As I explained in the Introduction, I went through many life experiences and training, to arrive where I am today. Getting past Christian mediocrity was a necessity for me, as did the Desert Fathers and Mothers of Egypt in the 4th Century and others since then that we can read about.

Coming against evil principalities and powers, rather than continually contending with the evil pawns for the rest of my life, was a God revelation. I had also learned in my youth that many wars and battles ended, when leadership was destroyed. In addition, I learned in martial arts and military combatives, that you go after the most vulnerable areas and then, finish the job. It all came together for me to move against the most vulnerable areas to cause the most damage possible to the evil kingdom.

I was to <u>hunt</u> them down!

Then it got interesting!

After time, Father pointed out to me, that I can do greater damage to the enemy by multiplying myself… teaching others to hunt them too!

Leaders in many countries that I've never met, have contacted me about what they've learned and applied through this book and… <u>that they are teaching others</u>! Their testimonies are awesome!

How are we able to hunt such large, dangerous monsters? God says we can, "Yet in all these things we are more than conquerors through Him who loved us!" Romans 8:37

A conqueror goes out and conquers!

That's what we do!

And hunting season is always open!

SECTOR THREE

TRUE CONQUEROR

> **HUNTING TIP**
>
> Elisha conquered an entire army... your turn!

The Art of War, written by Sun Tzu, a Chinese General in 500 B.C., is said to be, the oldest military thesis in the world.

Sun Tzu said," <u>All</u> warfare is based on deception. Thus, when able to attack, we must <u>seem</u> unable.

Hold out bait to entice the enemy. Feign disorder, and crush him. If he is in superior strength, evade him. If your opponent is quick to anger, seek to irritate him. Pretend to be weak, that he may grow arrogant".

All of this seems perfectly wise... for one wearing blinders!

The Art of War first came to the west, with a French Jesuit in 1782, and has since been studied by generals from Napoleon to Rommel. It is still required reading, in most military academies of the world, including the U.S. National Defense University and at the U.S. Naval War College, as a text for senior military officers.

Although meant to be a practical guide to warfare on a battlefield with weapons, corporate and government leaders also apply its lessons in a different battlefield—using words, pens, phones and computers.

The majority of the Bible was written long before 500 B.C., and it contains God's directions on <u>conquering in the spiritual</u>.

The Bible is the greatest war manual ever written!

Sun Tzu had this <u>major</u> flaw in his military tactic manual. Why do I say conquering in the spiritual, when the Bible is full of mostly battles and wars in the physical?

God teaches, that warring only in the physical, would be like tearing off a leaf from a tree and believing that you have conquered the whole tree! This is the immense gaping hole in Sun Tzu's writing, that he and other military tacticians have failed to realize. This gap is their non-existent consideration, of the spiritual dimension.

This most important factor is ignored!

Perhaps 95+% of all people in the world have the same limitation and will never be true conquerors or Silver Bullets of God or Xtreme Big Game Hunters.

People blame governments, global warming, crime, poverty, disease, war, terrorism, religious extremism, etc., for the world's problems—never acknowledging the true origin.

They pluck away at these areas with their naive activities, bringing the evil spiritual realm to their knees in laughter, at their feeble efforts!

Any seeming victories are, in reality, shallow, limited, hollow and false.

They are pawns of evil spiritual entities.

Only those who know what's going on, can teach and lead the blind to bring God's Silver Bullet solutions to the table!

"In the kingdom of the blind, the one-eyed man is king."
Desiderius Erasmus (1466? -1536)

How can a person leave this kingdom of the blind?

Only one doorway opens, to allow a person onto the road from blindness, to being a king or a true conqueror.

No true conqueror exists prior to entering this door… the door of death!

The door of death is in front of each person… physical (first death) and spiritual death (second death).

According to the U.S. Census Bureau, the world population as of end of 2017 is approximately 7.7 Billion.

The population is broken down into these main groups of people by faith. Smaller groups not included in detail. *

Christians** 2.2 Billion (28% of world)

Roman Catholics 1.2 Billion

Protestants 430 Million

Independents*** 356 Million

Orthodox 277 Million

Anglicans 89 Million

Islam 1.6 Billion

No religion/agnostic/atheist 1.1 Billion

Hinduism 1 Billion

Buddhism 376 Million

Chinese Universists 494 Million

Sikhism 30 Million

Spiritism 15 Million

Judaism 14 Million

*Wikipedia estimates in 2017.

**Terminology used by many denominations and people, even when not following Christian scripture.

***This term denotes members of Christian Church groups and networks that regard themselves as post denominationalist and neo-apostolic and thus independent of historic, mainstream, organized, institutionalized, confessional, denominationalist Christianity.

Over 41,000 separate Christian groups have been identified in the world. Many consider themselves the only "true" denomination!

From these statistics, it shows that 72% of the population of the earth will never pass through the spiritual door of death and thus will never be true conquerors.

They will die both physically and spiritually.

"And anyone not found written in the Book of Life was cast into the lake of fire." Revelation 20:15

"This is the second (spiritual) death." Revelation 20:14

Even death and hell really have conquered nothing as "death and hell were cast into the lake of fire". Revelation 20:14

68% of the world's population equals approximately 5 Billion people who will die spiritually!

<u>And this figure is constantly growing, as the birth rate exceeds the death rate!</u>

*World Birth Rate:	*World Death Rate:
19 births/1,000 population	8 deaths/1,000 population
131.4 million births per year	55.3 million people die each year
360,000 births per day	151,600 people die each day
15,000 births each hour	6316 people die each hour
250 births each minute	105 people die each minute
4 births each second of every day	almost 2 people die each second

*The World Fact Sheet (CIA) (2016 est.)

These 5.5 billion spiritually lost people, are the Silver Bullet of God and Xtreme Big Game Hunter's ultimate objective, in addition to bringing down Xtreme Big, Small and Rabid Game.

We will find out later that this figure is much, much higher than reports indicate!

There is only one way to be a true conqueror.

One must <u>first</u> conquer the second or spiritual death. Without initially going through this door, all else is a waste of time and amounts to nothing.

Going through this door of death, starts one off on the first level of a conqueror.

A very important level and foundation, upon which all else grows.

<u>There is only one way to go through this door</u>, despite what many religions and purported Christian groups teach.

"That whoever believes in Him (Jesus Christ) should not perish (experience second death), but have everlasting life." John 3:15

Notice… a person must <u>believe</u> in Him… that means, a life in action, that follows His entire Gospel… not just through "lip service".

Many Christians' beliefs and actions, are far from matching up with the title that they give themselves of Christian. Calling oneself a winner or victor or conqueror, when personal spiritual death hasn't been defeated, is sad and foolish.

Forget Sun Tzu and any other military-religious-political-scientific-social "geniuses". The true genius of all time and eternity, is Jesus Christ and through Him, true Christians are "more than conquerors." Romans 8:37

On the way to becoming a Silver Bullet of God, you must first come out of the kingdom of the blind, by conquering spiritual death first, and then discover your destiny with God.

SECTOR FOUR
YOUR DESTINY

> **HUNTING TIP**
> Acquire the target… pull the trigger… next!

Take a moment or more and answer this question… your life may depend on it!

<u>What is my destiny</u>?

Not your destiny with family, or career, or finances or retirement… I mean your destiny with God! You are a creation of His and you were created for a reason. What is that reason? Do you think the reason you are here, is to make a name for yourself at work, or to own property, or to accumulate wealth, or be the best golfer that you can be?

"Do not lay up for yourselves treasures on earth, where moth and rust destroy and where thieves break in and steal; but lay up for yourselves treasures in heaven, where neither moth nor rust destroys and where thieves do not break in and steal. For where your treasure is, there your heart will be also." Matthew 6:19-21

Is the main purpose of life, to live as long as possible? If so, do you exercise, eat right, take vitamin supplements and medications and get regular checkups from the doctor?

Let's say that you are a physical marvel and that you live to be a mere 115 years old. What about the rest of your trillion-to-the-trillionth-power years and more after that?

OK… suppose you're a pretty nice person, who regularly reads the Bible, goes to "church" for a few hours every week and helps people… perhaps you're very busy with "church" activities all the time… and you also give hundreds or thousands of your dollars, to see to it that the "church" meets its budget? Just because <u>you think</u> that you're doing well and <u>you think</u> that God will like all that you do… <u>is that His will for you and your destiny</u>?

<u>Is all that you do Biblical?</u>

Is all that you do, what <u>you</u> want to do, what <u>people</u> want or expect you to do, or what <u>God</u> has for your destiny?

"He who speaks from himself seeks his own glory" John 7:18a

God says what <u>our</u> good works and activities, without His will, are worth.

"But we are all like an unclean thing, and all our righteousnesses re like filthy rags; We all fade as a leaf, and our iniquities, like the wind, have taken us away." Isaiah 64:6

No matter how well-intentioned or nice we are or people think we are… without God's will… it is all worthless! Imagine… everything that you've ever done in your life, being worthless!

Wow… that's hard to believe, isn't it?

Yet God's Word is truth!

What do you do if your mechanic, your financial advisor or your dentist isn't doing a proper job?

You find a person who does what they are supposed to do for you, right?

Makes sense.

People will dispense with spouses, friends and relatives, sometimes for the slightest reasons, yet will continue to attend the same "church", no matter what! If your "church", denomination, pastor, minister, or leadership is not teaching you and equipping you on how to find and accomplish your destiny and spiritually grow in God's will for <u>your</u> life, shouldn't you be questioning why you're still there?

Leaders are "for the equipping of the saints for the work of ministry, for the edifying of the body of Christ, till we all come to the unity of the faith and of the knowledge of the Son of God, to a perfect man, to the measure of the stature of the fullness of Christ; that we should no longer be children, tossed to and fro and carried about with every wind of doctrine, by the trickery of men, in the cunning craftiness of deceitful plotting." Ephesians 4: 12-14

Even worse… if you know God's will for your life, but your "church" won't accept it, or won't allow your ministry or anyone else's to flourish, other than perhaps singing in the choir or doing chores around "their church" … you're letting His destiny for you die!

Shouldn't you be upset, when people are teaching you wrong or not at all, robbing you of your destiny and your eternal rewards?

God says you should beware, and depart from them.

"If anyone teaches otherwise and does not consent to wholesome words, even the words of our Lord Jesus Christ, and to the doctrine which accords with godliness, he is proud, knowing nothing, but is obsessed with disputes and arguments over words, from which come envy, strife, reviling, evil suspicions, useless wranglings of men of corrupt minds and destitute of the truth, who suppose that godliness is a means of gain. From such withdraw yourself." 1 Timothy 6:3-5

"For the time will come when they will not endure sound doctrine, but according to their own desires, because they have itching ears, they will heap up for themselves teachers; and they will turn their ears away from the truth, and be turned aside to fables." 2 Timothy 4:3-4

"These things I have written to you concerning those who try to deceive you. But the anointing which you have received from Him abides in you, and you do not need that anyone teach you; but as the same anointing teaches you concerning all things, and is true, and is not a lie, and just as it has taught you, you will abide in Him." 1 John 2:26-27

How do you find your destiny?

Please <u>examine</u> Romans 8 now, and over and over again.

Just recognizing and accepting that God has more for you, than just making it through life or sitting in a pew, is a great start to finding His will for <u>you</u>!

Each of us must disregard our own and others' expectations, traditions and fabricated doctrines and find God's will for our life.

A key to understanding is the realization, that we are a spirit with a physical body, not the opposite. This is a fact that is ignored by most.

Accept that you are a spirit, and strive to find proper direction, encouragement and spiritual understanding through your Comforter and Teacher, the Holy Spirit.

Then you will know His will for you and <u>fulfill your destiny</u>!

"But the Helper, the Holy Spirit, whom the Father will send in My name, He will teach you all things, and bring to your remembrance all things that I said to you." John 14:26

CHRISTIANS ARE ISRAEL

Most people, including Christians, are unaware of their true identity and thus never grasp a hold of their potential. The Bible's Truth shows us, that God considers Christians to be Israel! Its wrong interpretations and false teaching that has lead everyone to believe that ancient lost tribes of people are still God's Israel today. When Jesus came, the new tribe became those who accept Jesus as their Savior… the Christian! The destiny of the Christian, is every promise to Israel in God's Word!

Let's examine God's Truth.

The first time we see the name Israel in the Bible, it is the new name given to Jacob by God to indicate a change in his character.

"And he said, your name shall be called no more Jacob, but Israel: for as a prince have you power with God and with men, and have prevailed." Genesis 32:28 KJ 2000 Bible

Jacob had a new spiritual character and was given a new spiritual name, as Israel literally means "prince of God"! **Remember this!**

Israel (formerly Jacob) had 12 sons that multiplied and were forced into slavery in Egypt, until Moses went to Pharaoh with a message from God… "Then you shall say to Pharaoh, 'Thus says the Lord: "Israel is My son, My firstborn. So, I say to you, let My son go that he may serve

Me. But if you refuse to let him go, indeed I will kill your son, your firstborn." Exodus 4:22-23

Now we see that God refers to His spiritual people... all the descendants of one man (Israel) as a nation of people called Israel, that He calls out of Egypt.

"When Israel was a child, I loved him, and out of Egypt I called My son." Hosea 11:1

We see someone else was called out of Egypt...

"When he arose, he took the young Child and His mother by night and departed for Egypt, and was there until the death of Herod, that it might be fulfilled which was spoken by the Lord through the prophet, saying, "Out of Egypt I called My Son." Matthew 2:14-15

*Israel was called out of Egypt... Jesus was called out of Egypt.

*Israel was baptized through the Red Sea (1 Corinthians 10:2) ... Jesus was baptized at the Jordan River (Matthew 3:13-17).

*Israel spent 40 years in the wilderness (Joshua 5:6) ... Jesus spent 40 days in the wilderness (Matthew 4:1-2).

*Israel is called a vine (Psalm 80:8) ... Jesus calls Himself the vine (John 15:1).

*God calls Israel His son, His first born (Exodus 4:22) ... Paul calls Jesus "the first born of every creature" (Colossians 1:15).

What do these and other parallels with Jesus to the nation of Israel mean?

It means that Jesus is repeating the history of Israel, overcoming where they had failed!

He is the new spiritual Israel, the Prince of God, who overcomes sin, sickness, disease, death, principalities and powers... to give the same to those who decide, to become children of God!

Isaiah called Israel "the seed of Abraham" (Isaiah 41:8) ... Paul wrote "The promises were spoken to Abraham and to his seed."

Scripture does not say "and to seeds," meaning many people, but "and to your seed, "meaning, one person, who is Christ." (Galatians 3:16)

Here in the Old Testament, God calls all of Israel the seed of Abraham, yet Paul says here, that Abraham's seed is now not many, but one… Christ!

In the Old Testament, the name Israel was one man, Jacob, and then later also to his descendants.

We see the same parallel again in the New Testament.

After Paul tells the new Gentile converts about Jesus being "the seed", he tells them, "And if you are Christ's, then you are Abraham's seed" Galatians 3:29.

In the New Testament, Israel is now not only one man again, but also those who are in Him.

Believers also become the seed of Abraham!

Followers or descendants of Jesus as Christ (true Christians) are now God's spiritual ISRAEL!

*Moses made a covenant with Israel with animal sacrifice and blood (Exodus 24:8) … Jesus made a new covenant with His sacrifice and Blood with those who believe and accept Him as their sacrifice to God… "For this is My blood of the new covenant, which is shed for many for the remission of sins." Matthew 26:28

According to the New Testament there are now two Israel's!

Paul said in Romans 9:6, "It is not as though God's word had failed. For not all who are descended from Israel are Israel". He said in Romans 9:3 there is a flesh Israel, "For I could wish that I myself were cursed and cut off from Christ for the sake of my people, those of my own race" and in Galatians 6:16 that there is a spiritual Israel, "Peace and mercy to all who follow this rule-to the Israel of God". Paul also said in Galatians 3:6-7, "So also Abraham "believed God, and it was credited to him as righteousness." Understand, then, that those who have faith (in Jesus as Christ and His Gospel) are children of Abraham".

Many thinks that Israel, is the land between Egypt, Jordan, Syria and Lebanon and only Jews are Israelites and God's chosen, but the Bible says in John 14:6 and in many other places, that only through Jesus are you saved, "Jesus answered, "I am the way and the truth and the life. No one comes to the Father except through me".

The Bible says that Jews who deny Christ, are flesh Israel… no longer God's spiritual Israel.

Only those who accept Jesus as their Savior are spiritual Israel, and are the only Israel that God considers to be His children… they are also called Christians!

God had the obsolete physical temple in Jerusalem destroyed, because the law and flesh sacrifice was now all fulfilled in Jesus. His temple is now a spiritual temple within each believer… "Don't you know that you are the temple of God's and that the Spirit of God dwells in you?" 1 Corinthians 3:16

The temple that Jews and most Christians pray for today to be rebuilt in Israel, is not of God and never would be if it were built! The same goes for those imitation temples that flesh-driven Christians have invented, they today call "church".

All the promises that God made in the Bible applying to Israel, apply to the spiritual Israel today!

"Now we, brethren, as Isaac was, are children of promise." Galatians 4:28

CHRISTIANS… Search through the Bible and get hold of all of your inheritance and all of God's promises, as we each of us, are the true Israel!

"To him who overcomes I will grant to sit with Me on My throne, as I also overcame and sat down with My Father on His throne." Revelation 3:21

Your throne awaits you Israel… Seize your destiny!

Moving along the way to find your destiny, will be a lot easier once you shed yourself of worldly thinking, wrong people and religious doctrines that cage you in. Once you tap into your spiritual senses and are directly hearing from and walking with God, your destiny will become more focused, if it is obscured right now.

Push aside, go around or go over, any who try to stand in your way!

Find people who will train you, equip you, exhort you and assist you, to fulfill your destiny with God, even if it isn't as an Xtreme Big Game Hunter!

Take it more seriously than your career path or your retirement savings program!

It's never too late to start your destiny… Moses was 80 and Aaron was 83 when they met with Pharaoh!

ZONE 2

THE PERFECT HUNTING EXPEDITION

SECTOR FIVE

SAFARI
GOD'S HUNTING AND FISHING CAMP

> **HUNTING TIP**
> God is not in a box...don't try to figure God out...you'll only get a brain cramp!

One day, God gave me an acronym, for the successful process of evangelism, in order to turn out the type of Christian that He is looking for.

This acronym is SAFARI.

This fits in perfectly with the theme of this book, that God wanted me to write. God does do things perfectly!

These letters, S-A-F-A-R-I, stand for <u>S</u>hoot <u>A</u>nd <u>F</u>ish <u>A</u>nd <u>R</u>eady <u>I</u>nteract.

As I hear this word, I imagine a hunting expedition in Africa or Canada, or some other wildly exotic place, in search of big game. A huge camp would be set up, with a large group of adventurers.

Born and raised in Canada, I have hunted many times alone and other times in 'gang hunts', going after big game.

Even before I went to kindergarten, I joined my Dad when he hunted. I was raised in a hunting environment and I am a big game hunter. As a guide at God's spiritual hunting and fishing safari camp, God wants me to help you learn about effective and successful evangelism.

Our SAFARI is divided into 3 main stages:

1. Pre-evangelism stage

2. Evangelism stage
3. Post-evangelism or the stage after evangelism

Let me ask you… how many people have you <u>successfully</u> brought to salvation or witnessed being <u>truly</u> saved in your lifetime?

Are new "church" members being added through pastors, congregational efforts and "revival" meetings—are new members a rarity or are Christians coming in from other "churches"?

Do you know of any "churches" that are locked into and blinded with tradition and religion and are either stagnant or spiritually dead?

How <u>many</u> missionaries do you know, who are truly <u>successful</u> in bringing the lost to Jesus Christ?

"Churches" and Christians seem to be failing everywhere with evangelism, yet they don't know why. No matter how prepared WE are in being fishers of men, as Jesus called us, the fish aren't coming in! There is such a failure rate, that most Christians don't bother with salvation activity anymore, if they ever did. They find it difficult to do, because people they talk to aren't interested. And when there are successes, these ones eventually seem to go back to where they were or perhaps worse… continuing to live an evil lifestyle, claiming to be Christian!

This is what I want to cover in this Xtreme Sector.

Sometimes the biggest problem, is recognizing that there is a problem and what that problem is. I will teach and share with you, about some problem areas.

A man I knew many years ago, told me of his trip to heaven and his conversation with God. I asked him then, "What is the main thing that God wants us to do?" and he said… "Evangelize".

<u>God said</u> the most important thing that Christians should be doing, is evangelism!

In thinking about this, I have examined evangelism and its failures over the centuries and its successes.

I want to focus on what the keys to success are.

There are principal hunting and fishing evangelism strategies and hunting and fishing guidelines, that have eluded Christians for centuries, including many big-name evangelists today!

Do you want to be an incredibly successful hunter and fisher on SAFARI for God?

God has given us a huge safari range and each Christian has a license to hunt and fish anywhere.

There is no catch limit!

Are you ready to go on God's SAFARI?

FAILED FISHING

In order to get across a valuable lesson, I will be following Jesus' example, by using parables to teach, as God has led me to do it this way.

Now imagine, that we're at a beautiful lodge by a lake… a Canadian lake, although any lake will do. Beautiful calm water, sunny day… and everything looks perfect on the surface. While sitting in your boat, fishing, you examine all your equipment: your pole; all kinds of bait and lures; your net; a fancy fish-locating device… and you also have in the boat, the #1 best-selling book on the market… "How to Catch Fish." You have the equipment, training and license to catch loads of fish.

You cast your line in the water and sit there for hours… nothing. So, you decide to change from bait to lure fishing, starting to cast on all sides of the boat, reeling in the lure… nothing. You decide now to troll, so you start your motor on the boat and drag a lure behind the boat, up and down the lake, praying a fish will come after your lure… nothing. You know there are lots of fish here, as you see them jumping out of the water, but nothing you try seems to work. You grab your fishing book, desperately flip through it, trying every tip and method it recommends… still no fish. You come back day after day, trying different times, different places and different ideas… nothing.

Finally, you get a bite—you're excited now! You struggle and struggle with him, finally pulling him close enough to net him and get him into the boat. You're happy; but soon your concentration turns to getting more fish, so you start focusing on getting your equipment ready for the next catch. The fish you already brought in the boat, flips and flops, but you're not paying attention to him, as you want to go after the next one. Then he flips up and goes back into the water—the one you thought you had, is back where he came from! You look into the water, angrily shaking your head, blaming the fish… stupid fish… why didn't you stay in the boat?

But then…another nibble, you play it just right, and BAM! Another one is hooked—you fight and struggle with him for an hour, when he eventually gives up and comes to you. You put him in the boat, smile at all the work it took to get him in and then turn your back again, to get ready for the next one. And bloop… he flips up and over the edge of the boat, back into the water, like the first one.

You think, what's with these stupid fish? You decide to give up on fishing, because it just doesn't work for you.

So, let's review.

You had all the right equipment; all the right training; you were in the right place and could see the fish. But nothing you did was working, even when you caught something. Hmmm… as you start thinking about selling all your fishing gear and your boat, you look out on the lake and notice a professional fishing boat, that has huge nets dragging behind the boat. They're netting some fish, but the fish are slipping and sliding all around on the deck. Eventually, 95% of them are sliding and jumping back into the water. The professionals aren't much better than you!

What is the problem here?

The first problem is, that all of the fish in the lake, are unaware of anything outside their immediate environment, as the water is too murky and cloudy! The next problem is, that when they are hauled in, singly or in massive numbers, they are ignored or not handled properly, and so, end up back in the water. You are using all the right techniques and have the skill, but the fish couldn't sense, what you were trying to give them!

The few that happened to come across you, came in the boat, but eventually figured, it wasn't right for them and went back to where they came from.

The ones brought on the boat in mass numbers by "professionals", were only swept up in the emotional net of the moment, and eventually most of them went back to the water, when they weren't handled properly and left alone on the boat.

Examining the first problem of not catching the fish, Paul tells the Ephesians in 6:12 that, "we do not wrestle against flesh and blood, but against principalities, against powers, against the rulers of the darkness of this age, against spiritual hosts of wickedness in the heavenly places." or "in heavenly realms" as other versions translate.

Notice our initial problem is not with the fish, or people, but with evil spiritual entities; and we must fight them IN the spiritual heavenlies.

Why do we do this?

Paul tells us why in 2 Corinthians 4:4… because… "whose minds the god of this age has blinded, who do not believe, lest the light of the gospel of the glory of Christ, who is the image of God, should shine on them."

Satan, the god of this world, is blinding the minds of people from accepting the gospel.

He is not omnipresent like God and so, cannot do it all himself, so he sets in place around the world his powers, principalities, rulers of darkness and wickedness in high places, lesser evil spirits and evil people.

Another Biblical example of this position, is a revelation that I received from the Lord, about Samson killing a lion, which is in Judges 14. This scripture tells us, that Samson killed a lion with his bare hands and then bees came and made honey in the lion's carcass.

Although lessons in the Bible bring various meanings, I was shown in this revelation, that this lion symbolized satanic powers, principalities and rulers of darkness.

"You shall tread upon the lion and the cobra, the young lion and the serpent you shall trample underfoot." Psalm 91:13

"But the Lord stood with me and strengthened me, so that the message might be preached fully through me, and that all the Gentiles might hear. Also, I was delivered out of the mouth of the lion." 2 Timothy 4:17

"Be sober, be vigilant; because[c] your adversary the devil walks about like a roaring lion, seeking whom he may devour." 1 Peter 5:8

Samson symbolized a Christian conqueror(s), defeating these powers, as Judges 14:6 says that "the Spirit of the Lord came mightily upon him." The Spirit of the Lord comes mightily upon Christians, to defeat evil spiritual leader entities also. And out of this defeat of the lion, or evil, came forth an opportunity to produce honey (honey representing those who receive salvation), after this evil was destroyed.

The summary of this teaching is this:

The honey, which represents those saved at this location (the lion's carcass), would not have been there or been able to be produced, had Samson, (signifying a Christian), not killed the lion (which is evil powers/principalities), making the carcass (area/city/region/nation) ready.

Spiritual warfare against evil powers and principalities has to be done first, before success in evangelization and/or revival in an area can be achieved!

A very important revelation!

Had the bees (signifying missionaries/ pastors/ evangelists) tried to produce honey on the lion prior to his being killed, what success would there have been? The lion would have fought off the bees, had they tried.

Jesus told us in Matthew 12:29 "Or how can one enter a strong man's house and plunder his goods, unless he first binds the strong man? And then he will plunder his house."

Jesus' parable referring to a strong spirit, can be applied to a spirit in a person or in/over an area. In an area governed by evil, you cannot get the spoils (in this case captive people), until the governing evil is dealt with.

A Biblical example of this would be, when Joshua and the Israelites were given the promised land by God.

God didn't just destroy the strong men for them… the Israelites had to go in, fight for themselves and <u>take</u> the land! Can you imagine what the armies of Canaan and the evil spirits over Jericho and the area would have done to Joshua and the Israelites, if they would have peacefully gone into Jericho and Canaan, started building homes and preached to the inhabitants how great <u>their</u> God is?

Strange idea, yet Christians do exactly that every day, all over the world!

Jesus told us in Mark 16:17 that all Christians "shall cast out devils" KJV … the Life Application Version says, Christians "will drive out demons."

Notice here, that it is neither an option nor a request, it is a command. AND very important to note—it doesn't say cast or drive devils or demons out of people, as it is not specific to what or where.

We will and shall cast them and drive them out of anywhere they are: in people, in physical objects, in towns, in cities, in neighborhoods, over financial institutions, over government, over educational systems, over the earth, the waters and in the heavenlies! Religious spirits infect the real Church.

Before you can bring and establish God's Kingdom with people, you must <u>first conquer</u> the evil territorial spirits, powers, spiritual wickedness and principalities ruling particular areas.

Doing it <u>your way</u> can be a hardship; and trying to spread the gospel and accomplish God's purpose will be negligible or futile and sometimes even destructive!

<u>Is there any testimony that shows that this principal works today</u>?

From the aforementioned parable, we learned that hunting the lion or strong man, powers and principalities must be done first, before fishing can properly commence. This has been typically called in most Christian circles, High-Level, Strategic Level, Prophetic Level, or Territorial Level Spiritual Warfare or my favorite—Xtreme Big Game Hunting (XBGH)!

This type of spiritual warfare, has resulted in huge areas suddenly opening up to evangelism and to the gospel, that had been barren for years, decades and even centuries! Results have also included a spiritual renewal among Christians in these areas!

<u>This kind of spiritual warfare affects hundreds of thousands, even millions of people at a time</u>!

We can expect to see dramatic changes in politics, the economy, society, education, media and in Church assemblies and individuals. Heathen festivals, worship and celebrations of idols, witchcraft, occult, and sexual immorality are disrupted and fail, as people lose interest in evil things. Corruption in governments and finance crumbles and is replaced with truth and honesty (can be only temporary based on SAFARI efforts). People actively seek out and accept Jesus Christ, even without evangelism efforts (can also be only temporary based on SAFARI efforts)! XBGH opens up areas and people's minds to the light, allowing evangelism to flourish.

Let's look at some testimony to substantiate this statement:

"In 1974, Eduardo Lorenzo took over a church in Argentina that had never had more than 100 members in 70 years. Through standard church growth procedure, the church added another 150 members but it took 13 years! (That's about 1 new member/month.) Other churches in the area were planted but they all failed. Their church was the only one that survived and was struggling. They admitted that their church "was being kept on a merry-go-round by satan, blinding the minds of the unsaved to the gospel"

Then they learned how to do high level spiritual warfare. They came against the ruling principality over the area and defeated it! Evangelism exploded in the area resulting in mass numbers being converted with 40% of their congregation now coming from that area, when once there were none!" (From "Lessons in Evangelism and Spiritual Warfare from Argentina", by Peter Wagner)

Here's a short excerpt from Chapter 21 of Charles Finney's autobiography commenting on a revival in 1830, after his associate, Daniel Nash, did warfare prior to Finney doing this revival:

"A convert in Rochester, New York, left a description of Finney's revival ministry in that city in which more than a hundred thousand came to saving knowledge of the Lord Jesus within one year. He wrote: "The whole community was stirred. Religion was the topic of conversation, in the house, in the shop, in the office, and on the street…The only theater in the city was converted into a livery stable; the only circus into a soap and candle factory. Grog [beer] shops were closed; the Sabbath was honored; the sanctuaries were thronged with happy worshippers; a new impulse was given to every philanthropic enterprise; the fountains of benevolence were opened and men lived to do good."

The report continues: "It is worthy of special notice that a large number of leading men of the place were among the converts--the lawyers, the judges, physicians, merchants, bankers and master mechanics. These classes were more moved from the very first than any other. Tall oaks were bowed as by the blast of a hurricane. Skeptics and scoffers were brought in, and a large number of the most promising young men. It is said that no less than forty of them entered the ministry…

"It is not too much to say that the whole character of the city was changed by that revival," wrote this eyewitness. "Most of the leaders of society being converted, and exerting a controlling influence in social life, in business, and in civil affairs, religion was enthroned as it had been in few places…. Even the courts and the prisons bore witness to its blessed effects. There was a wonderful falling off of crime. The courts had little to do, and the jail was nearly empty for years afterward."

Finney admits in his memoirs, that the key was the work Daniel Nash did! (More about him coming up!)

Revised Fishing Method

So, let's get back to safari camp… now that we understand how to overcome the first fishing problem.

You get up very early one morning and while sitting by the lake, waiting for someone to buy your boat and gear… you start to see something you haven't seen before. Many large animals are going into the water to eat, drink, swim and walk around, constantly scaring the fish away.

Moose, deer, bear, elk, and caribou are in the lake, and you realize, that the fish will move away from this activity and hide. Also, the waters have become cloudy with stirred up mud.

Keep in mind that these are evil moose, deer, bear, elk and caribou and not to be confused with the good variety found in Canada!

You understand that the fish are scared and confused and so, when some of them attempt to come back from hiding, the water is too cloudy for them to sense any of your fishing attempts.

Your fishing is not the problem nor is the problem the fish; it's an outside factor that's keeping the fish from being caught! You now determine that you must get rid of the big game, so they will no longer be clouding up the water and scaring off the fish. You must become a hunter!

So, you make plans to clear the area of this evil big game.

Shoot First

You and your friends capture some big game and put them in cages and send them away. Still others are brought down, wounded or scared away. You set traps and put guards in strategic areas to keep away any big game that start to move in toward the lake. This is the Xtreme Big Game Hunting phase of evangelism that is being done first, before starting to the next phase, to fish. You're hunting with your power and authority in Jesus' name; the Holy Spirit; angels the weapons God gives you and other hunters.

And Fish

Soon the lake and its surrounding area is free of evil big game. The waters are clear, and you cannot keep up with all the fish that you are catching now. Many are even jumping into the boat on their own! That makes for great fishing testimonies!

We sit down to write in our hunting and fishing journal now… must hunt or shoot first, to get rid of the evil big game before fishing can be successful.

Also… no need to sell boat and gear now!

Next is the word-for-word March 2010 testimony emailed to me from a College Director in Uganda, that applied what he learned about Xtreme Big Game Hunting in this book:

"Recently we have had a Gospel crusade and while praying for the success of this crusade, I was in the spirit and I saw a spirit in form on a man but was a spirit of witchcraft and I commanded it to be bound in the name of Jesus and abruptly <u>I saw a multitude of angels binding it and took it</u> and the results from the crusade where very positive and we saw many souls coming into the kingdom. <u>3453 souls signed the dedication cards in five days and a lady who was practicing witch craft as a priestess leading other women (prostitutes) in blowing the wind pipe while casting spells and chants got saved</u>…praise God."

Charles M. – College Director/Pastor/Teacher/Evangelist/Int. Speaker – Uganda

Great Hunters

We just had a testimony from the famous evangelist Charles Finney, that understood this shoot first and then fish rule. But did you ever hear of Daniel Nash? Probably not.

Daniel Nash worked with Finney for 7 years.

Most consider Charles Finney, the greatest evangelist that ever lived.

That <u>ever</u> lived!

<u>As we just read, that OVER 100,000 people were soundly converted from a single revival</u>!

Today, 100,000 converts at once would be astonishing… but <u>this took place almost 200 hundred years ago, in 1830</u>!

Practically <u>every person</u> in the towns and cities where Finney preached were converted! Theaters and taverns went out of business for lack of customers!

The most ungodly would, on their own, come into Finney's meetings full of anguish and trembling, seeking salvation. The fish were jumping on their own… into the boat.

Why?

What was his secret?

Finney himself never attributed the success to his theology, messages, preaching style, logic nor any method he had to save souls.

The answer was, and still is, spiritual warfare/intercession that was done in advance of the meetings to destroy the enemy first and prepare the area! (They called it prevailing prayer.)

Daniel Nash would slip quietly into an area to get the area ready before Finney would come! Finney would come when Nash was done… and they did this for years!

Daniel Nash and Charles Finney used the 'shoot first' method.

There are no pictures of Daniel Nash, no books or diaries written by him. His messages are forgotten and there are no known descendants. One of the hunters most dangerous to Satan, has all but disappeared from memory.

The success of doing high level warfare was unprecedented in history, as we can read from this further excerpt from Finney's autobiography:

"The greatness of the work at Rochester, at that time, attracted so much of the attention of ministers and Christians throughout the State of New York, throughout New England, and in many parts of the United States, that the very fame of it was an efficient instrument in the hands of the Spirit of God in promoting the greatest revival of religion throughout the land, that this country had then ever witnessed. Years after this, in conversing with Dr. Beecher about this powerful revival and its results, he remarked: "That was the greatest work of God, and the greatest revival of religion, that the world has ever seen, in so short a time. One hundred thousand," he remarked, "were reported as having connected themselves with churches, as the results of that great revival. This," **he said, "is unparalleled in the history of the church**, and of the progress of religion." He spoke of this having been done in one year; and said that **in no year during the Christian era, had we any account of so great a revival of religion."**

Dwight L. Moody followed this same pattern, but only realized a 50% lasting rate of converts… perhaps Moody was not as good a hunter. Perhaps he should have done more <u>after</u> the fish were netted, to retain the other 50% that went back in the water…which we'll discuss later.

The Storms

Back at camp…

Now that you're aware of this 'shoot first' or 'hunt first' fishing system, satan will bring in obstacles (bad weather and broken fishing poles) and distractions from the physical world to keep you from hunting and fishing, under your new guidelines. He'll try to convince you, that you're fishing in the wrong spot, at the wrong time and really, you're not much of a fisher anyway. You'll get busy with other things, so you won't have time to hunt and fish!

He'll try to convince you that you have no license to hunt or fish. Many things will happen, to try to get you to stop hunting and fishing, with the new successful guidelines, even though you know that they work. Because now you know how to clean the lake of impurities, so the fish can see and understand where they are.

What am I saying here with this parable?

We see that satan realizes evangelism and missionary activities will mostly fail, as long as his powers, principalities, rulers, strong men and territorial spirits are in place, clouding people's minds from wanting or accepting the truth of the gospel. Luke 5:1-11 says,

"So, it was, as the multitude pressed about Him to hear the word of God, that He stood by the Lake of Gennesaret, and saw two boats standing by the lake; but the fishermen had gone from them and were washing their nets. Then He got into one of the boats, which was Simon's, and asked him to put out a little from the land. And He sat down and taught the multitudes from the boat. When He had stopped speaking, He said to Simon, "Launch out into the deep and let down your nets for a catch." But Simon answered and said to Him, "Master, we have toiled all night and caught nothing; nevertheless, at Your word I will let down the net." And when they had done this, they caught a great number of fish, and their net was breaking. So, they signaled to their partners in the other boat to come and help them. And they came and filled both the boats, so that they began to sink. When Simon Peter saw it, he fell down at Jesus' knees, saying, "Depart from me, for I am a sinful man, O Lord! For he and all who were with him were astonished at the catch of fish which they had taken; and so also were James and John, the sons of Zebedee, who were partners with Simon. And Jesus said to Simon, "Do not be afraid. From now on you will catch men." So, when they had brought their boats to land, they forsook all and followed Him."

And this same thing happened again after the resurrection in John 21:2-6:

'Simon Peter, Thomas called the Twin, Nathanael of Cana in Galilee, the sons of Zebedee, and two others of His disciples were together. Simon Peter said to them, "I am going fishing."

They said to him, "We are going with you also." They went out and immediately got into the boat, and that night they caught nothing. But when the morning had now come, Jesus stood on the shore; yet the disciples did not know that it was Jesus. Then Jesus said to them, "Children, have you any food?" They answered Him, "No." And He said to them, "Cast the net on the right side of the boat, and you will find some." So, they cast, and now they were not able to draw it in because of the multitude of fish."

These stories of the failure of professional fishermen to catch fish, is remarkably like the failure that we've discussed, until something more was done.

Is Jesus teaching us to hunt first, so fishing can be successful?

Notice also, that both times the professional fisherman couldn't catch <u>any</u> fish until God told them when and where… and that they weren't fishing for just one fish, but for multitudes of fish at the same time! Operate in the spirit under God's will (not yours) and catch multitudes of fish for God!

Great evangelism lessons!

And Ready

Okay… we have cleared the area of big game at safari camp and now fish are swimming to us and we're catching them and netting them and they're even jumping in the boat, <u>but,</u> we remember we have had a problem keeping them in the boat.

How do we conquer that problem?

As any fisher knows, fish tend to flop around and can jump back in the water, so you must make sure they're secured. You don't just leave them in the boat and do nothing with them… they must now be cleaned and made ready.

This is the same with a new Christian. You can't just have them say a sinner's prayer and send them on their way. They can't be ignored and left alone—they must be cleaned.

You must wash dirt from the spirit as you do the physical body.

They need deliverance!

I read this recently:

"A well-known evangelist, who is well financed and highly organized, recently stated that he would be <u>delighted</u> if <u>20 percent</u> of his <u>converts</u> were genuinely converted."

Did you hear that?

He would be "<u>delighted</u>" if 20% <u>stayed</u> saved…

meaning… 80% became lost again, <u>after</u> being converted!

Jesus says in Luke 15:4-7, ""What man of you, having a hundred sheep, if he loses one of them, does not leave the ninety-nine in the wilderness, and go after the one which is lost until he finds it? And when he has found it, he lays it on his shoulders, rejoicing.

And when he comes home, he calls together his friends and neighbors, saying to them, 'Rejoice with me, for I have found my sheep which was lost!' I say to you that likewise there will be more joy in heaven over one sinner who repents than over ninety-nine just persons who need no repentance."

Jesus says we should be <u>distressed</u> over losing just <u>1 percent</u> and diligently work to regain that one! Can we imagine Jesus being "<u>delighted</u>" with losing <u>80%</u> of a flock that was His?

<u>AND</u>… what about all those who never came forward at this well-known evangelist's crusade? Or those who didn't even show up at the crusade in that area, because XBGH (Xtreme Big Game Hunting) wasn't done first?

<u>That's a 100 percent loss of those fish!</u>

Remember the professional's boat at safari camp caught fish, but 95% of them were slipping and sliding and jumping back into the water?

One startling statistic that I learned at Dr. Peter Wagner's 2006 Spiritual Warfare conference in Florida, was that 95% of those evangelized/saved, drop off within one year.

In other words, only 5% of those who were evangelized, are still a Christian after one year!

Yet another astounding statistic at this conference showed, that 85% <u>remained</u> Christian after one year, <u>IF</u> just one additional step was taken… like the first century Church always did… the one thing that the Church today, won't or don't anymore, despite Jesus' command.

That one step is deliverance—again, spiritual warfare!

In addition to deliverance, the fish must also be prepared with baptism of water, with the Holy Spirit and with fire Matthew 3:11/Mark 16:16/Luke 3:16/John 3:5.

They must repent; and be cleansed of and <u>stop</u> all sin; cleansed from iniquity; remove curses against them; break evil soul ties and associations; taught to read the Bible and pray; to fast; take communion often and learn to operate in their spiritual senses and go in the spirit into Heaven. Some fish take longer to clean than others, and it's the same with new Christians.

Interact

After the fish are cleaned and in the freezer or fridge, again, we don't just leave them there. They must be prepared to interact or be used to feed others, with perhaps special oils, butter, seasoning, salt and pepper before they are ready. For a new convert, this is accomplished with Bible study; spiritual praise and worship of God; Holy Spirit gift nurturing; mentoring; teaching; revelation from God; to name a few.

Finally, the fish or Christian is ready for what they were destined for and must now be kicked out of the nest, like an eagle does with the eaglet, when it is ready to soar on its own! They now <u>must</u> interact with others to advance the kingdom of God.

Right now, I want to warn some Christians. Better sit down if you're standing. If you've been sitting around in the nest (pew) for years with no destiny and no ministry, just waiting for other eagles to constantly feed you; do you consider yourself a fruitful "Christian"? Don't blame your leader for not allowing you to do ministry. <u>You</u> will be judged for your failure or success as a fruit producer… "Every tree that does not bear good fruit is cut down and thrown into the fire." Matthew 7:19

Get out of the nest and fulfill <u>your</u> destiny!

In *Matthew 14:19-21* Jesus "Then He commanded the multitudes to sit down on the grass. And He took the five loaves and the two fish, and looking up to heaven, He blessed and broke and gave the loaves to the disciples; and the disciples gave to the multitudes. So, they all ate and were filled, and they took up twelve baskets full of the fragments that remained. Now those who had eaten were about five thousand men, besides women and children."

Jesus proved that a few fish can feed many thousands, but they must be put to use.

Being a fish always at the ready isn't enough.

The Christian must produce fruit.

Where does your destiny take you with SAFARI?

Shoot/hunt <u>And Fish</u>, <u>And Ready</u>/clean and prepare others to <u>Interact</u> like you.

Go on SAFARI!

<u>Falling or Jumping Out of the Boat</u>

Many times, a fish is improperly cleaned or not properly prepared and can be a danger if they interact. Such people are ones who carry on a sinful life, convinced they are Christians, and feed others with wrong food. Such people according to Hebrews 10:26-32, and many other scriptures, are not still saved.

Many Christians believe that they do not willfully sin, because they don't murder or commit adultery. Therefore, they don't even consider they have lost their salvation or that they can be <u>legally</u> attacked by the devil.

Yet these people may be gossipers, idol worshippers, boasters, liars, deceivers or unforgiving and live by their own set of rules or doctrines, rather than God's; believing they are "good Christians" and <u>never</u> asking for forgiveness for these acts.

"Do you not know that the unrighteous will not inherit the kingdom of God? Do not be deceived. Neither fornicators, nor idolaters, nor adulterers, nor homosexuals, nor sodomites," I Corinthians 6:9-10

"Now the works of the flesh are evident, which are: adultery, fornication, uncleanness, lewdness, idolatry, sorcery, hatred, contentions, jealousies, outbursts of wrath, selfish ambitions, dissensions, heresies, envy, murders, drunkenness, revelries, and the like; of which I tell you beforehand, just as I also told you in time past, that those who practice such things will not inherit the kingdom of God." Galatians 5:19-21

Many Christians don't even think that they can lose their salvation. They believe they are <u>permanently</u> covered by grace, no matter what they do, despite what many scriptures such as Romans 1:28-32, Hebrews 10:26-31 and Matthew 6:15, say!

Not only will these people who sin, suffer from demonic attacks, problems, sicknesses in their life and early death, but worst of all, <u>they are deceived in thinking that they will always have salvation</u>!

Any form of healing and deliverance on these people would be limited in success and perhaps temporary, or worse, unless they cease their willful sinning.

If they attempted to pursue a ministry in deliverance or spiritual warfare, life would be even more hazardous for them.

Any form of iniquity we've inherited, and sin or transgressions that we enter into, creates an alliance with the devil, giving him a legal right to you. That right can be broken by <u>true</u> repentance and through the blood of Jesus Christ.

WARNING…
Don't do spiritual warfare if you are a deliberate sinner!

Some may ask about sinning in ignorance, or even worse, sinning with the <u>expectation</u> or the <u>acceptance</u> of their "church". A few major denominations do accept such sin as idol worship (of the dead and their statues or "relics") as an integral component of their man-made doctrine, which is <u>expected</u> of members.

Some denominations <u>accept</u> many sins, even amongst their own religious-priests and bishops, such as idol worship and illicit sexual activity, in the belief that they are not really sinning or are immune, due to their man-made salvation doctrines. Some believe this, even though the Bible clearly states that idol worship and sexual activity outside of marriage between a man and woman are abhorrent to God and lead to death.

See Romans 1:21-32, 1 Corinthians 6:9-10.

Some self-professed "Christians" believe they can do whatever they want. They think that they will just repent afterwards; or confess and say a few prayers and all is well again to continue in their willful sins.

God is not a fool… such thinking leads to spiritual death. Revelation 20:12-15 says, that <u>every</u> person will be judged according to <u>their</u> works.

It is each one's responsibility to find out what is acceptable to <u>God</u>… <u>not</u> what is acceptable to their denomination, or to a personal philosophy. Just knowing some scripture, attended a "church" and saying you're a Christian, doesn't make it so. We must all make sure we don't fall out of the boat once we're in and also not take any others with us.

Many Christians believe "once saved always saved" and act accordingly. "If a drowning man is saved, can he then never drown?"

The Bible says in Hebrews 10:26-32 that there are seven ways to <u>lose</u> salvation:

1. Willfully sin.

2. Renounce Christ as the only sacrifice.

3. Despise the gospel.

4. Tread the Son of God under our feet.

5. Count Christ's blood as an unholy thing.

6. Despise or blaspheme the Holy Spirit.

7. Become an adversary of Christ.

How many Christians willfully sin?

How many Christians come against the Holy Spirit and His gifts, such as tongues? How many Christians accept only the parts of the gospel that fit "their" doctrine and come against those who follow the entire gospel? How many muslims, buddhists, atheists, etc., who were once Christians, now deny, and even hate Jesus?

How many thinks that they are Christian, yet have other gods that they pray to and worship, including people who have died, who are all <u>creations</u>, not the Creator?

How many Christians accept other religions and philosophies and <u>mix it</u> with the <u>only</u> sacrifice and the <u>only</u> gospel acceptable to God the

Father (i.e. Chrislam)? How many entire denominations, accept and embrace various sins?

The people in these examples that think they are Christians, are living a fairy tale Christianity.

What does Jesus say will happen with these self-professing Christians in Matthew 7:21-23?

"Not everyone who says to Me, 'Lord, Lord,' shall enter the kingdom of heaven, but he who does the will of My Father in heaven. Many will say to Me in that day, 'Lord, Lord, have we not prophesied in Your name, cast out demons in Your name, and done many wonders in Your name?' And then I will declare to them, 'I never knew you; depart from Me, you who practice lawlessness!'"

The World Survey we examined in Sector 3, reports that 28% of the world "claims" that they are Christian, but, is this an accurate accounting of those who will spend eternity in heaven?

Let's go to someone who could, from his own experience, give us a more accurate figure:

On August 3, 1979, Rev. Howard Pittman, a Baptist minister for 35 years, died on the operating table during surgery having a 'near-death' experience. After angels showed him the second and third heavens, he was taken before the very throne of God, where he was given a message to share with the world.

Rev. Pittman was taken to heaven and was told to watch as 50 Christians entered through the gates into heaven.

This is an excerpt from Rev. Pittman's book, Placebo:

"It was explained to me (by the Holy Spirit) that at the same time those fifty saints died on Earth, some 1,950 other humans also died; or only 50 out of 2000 made it into Heaven."

That other 1,950 were not there. Where were they? That was only 2 ½ percent going to Heaven! 97 ½ percent did not make it!

Is that representative of the entire world today?

If so, **97 ½ percent of the population of this world today is not ready to meet God!**

We are now in the time when the great majority of churchgoers are only "mouth–professors" and not "heart–possessors." At the outset, I stated that I would not try to convince anyone of anything.

However, I would like to offer as evidence the Parable of the Sower, as told by Jesus in the <u>13th Chapter of the Book of Matthew</u>.

If you read this chapter closely, you will notice that three out of every four people who <u>heard</u> the gospel preached, turned it down. That is seventy–five percent, anyway you look at it. I am talking about three out of every four people who <u>bothered</u> to <u>hear</u> the gospel, turned it down! The sad thing is, <u>the overwhelming majority of the people that did turn the gospel down, do not know that they have turned it down</u>!

They have bought a lie of satan and have been deceived. <u>They have been led to believe something that is not the truth and they have been fooled by satan into rejecting the gospel</u>!

Place the seventy–five percent who turned down the gospel with those in the world who made no pretense of hearing the truth and you have the overwhelming ninety-seven and one-half percent of the population today!"

While Rev. Pittman was in heaven, God told him to deliver this message to the world.

This is a quote from God:

"A high majority of so-called Christians are, in fact, living a deceived life. They talk Jesus and play church, but do not live it. They claim to be Christians and then live like the devil. They have bought the great lie from satan who tells them that they are alright.

He tells them that it is alright to go to church on Sunday and attend mid-week services but as far as the rest of the time is concerned, they are to get all they can out of life.

As far as their Christian life is concerned, they believe they are comfortable and have need of nothing and as a result, they are only lukewarm Christians if Christians at all. To be a true Christian one must follow the teachings of Christ by living it, not just talk. To honor God with your lips and not your heart is not acceptable.

Those who accept the responsibility of teaching, preaching, or any leadership role have much for which to answer."

End of quote from God.

This pastor's experience is a revelation—and what God has to say to Christians is rather shocking!

Examining the 28% again of those who say they are Christian… if only 2 ½% enter into heaven, that means **25 ½% of those people in the world that think and say they're Christians, aren't considered so by God, and aren't going to make it!**

Don't be one who blindly accepts and does things your own way and believes you're saved. Do not compromise with God as the Israelites did in Jeremiah, Chapters 7 and 44, as they saw nothing wrong or any harm in what they decided to do, in addition to worshipping God. In Jeremiah 7:20, God cursed them, the land, the beasts, trees and fruit for their compromise and God told Jeremiah in Chapter 7:16, to not even bother praying nor interceding for them, as it would be a waste of time…" for I will not hear you."

1 Samuel 15:23 says rebellion "is as the sin of witchcraft." Don't rebel against God… read God's Word for yourself to find out what is acceptable and what is not.

It is the most important issue in your existence and you must be sure that you understand it!

If someone or some organization says anything that is contrary to God's word, run, and run fast from them! Well… run initially. Later you can come back to those who are deceived, as "more than a conqueror," as per Romans 8:37 and assist them!

Perhaps the most difficult assignment for a Christian would be, to convince people that think they are Christians, that they're out of the boat and need correction and salvation!

Back at SAFARI Camp

Returning now to SAFARI Camp, we read and continue adding in our journal. There must be a big game hunt first, before fishing can be highly successful. We must then take care of the fish we've labored for, by cleaning and preparing them <u>properly</u> for their destiny, and we must make sure <u>we</u> don't fall out of the boat along the way.

A few fish properly prepared can feed thousands—how long then should it take to feed the world?

Let's now go to heaven for a peek into the future… One day, billions of condemned people will walk by the judgment throne and perhaps point a finger at those who did little or nothing to help them, saying "You didn't care for my soul!"

Those saved—thanks to evangelistic and SAFARI efforts by others—might feel justified and say, "Am I my brother's keeper?" or "I always gave tithes and offerings to "the church" … look to <u>them</u> if they spent it more on themselves and not towards evangelizing the world, as they should have."

Yes, many pastors and religious church leaders will be accountable, but God will look to each of us, as we are each watchmen. Failing our duty… we fail God, we allow others to die lost and we fail ourselves.

Ezekiel 3:17-19 says "… his blood will I require at your hand."

What will God require of those who fail Him?

Many may say, "But I was not suited for (or too ill, or too old) to do missionary or evangelistic work. I had a job and a family and a house and car to pay for; or, that's the job of "the church"."

Sadly, many are not concerned about lost souls in other countries or even those in their own neighborhood that need salvation.

A long time ago, all of North Africa, as well as most of the Middle East, was evangelized and had embraced Christianity. Except for jewish Israel, these countries are all now muslim.

What happened to the watchmen?

Christians at that time, became more concerned about doctrinal pride and arguing with one another, than they did about evangelism.

They also lost the know-how on operating in the spirit! They should have continued to the next village and the next town, until in a short time, all of Africa and Asia would have been saved! Who knows how many people have been lost due to this disobedience.

So, what's changed today?

Christians in North America and Europe and other places in the world today, are much the same as those African and Middle Eastern Christians of long ago—judgmental of each other; full of man-made rules and doctrines and laws; isolated from other Christians; powerless; attending nothing more than friendly social clubs and entertainment centers, that they call "church".

Yet these people seem happy with that! These people don't realize, that the same evil forces over the area where they live, that are blinding and keeping the unsaved from the gospel, are also blinding, oppressing, and hindering Christians, keeping them immobile, in addition to deceiving them into jumping off the boat!

Think about that—evil powers and principalities are right now working against you, to keep you sitting around in the freezer and trying ways to get you out of the boat, so you'll lose your destiny and your salvation!

Getting mad yet?

Some Christians say, they don't support mission work, as the home field or their local "church" is more important. Do they think Paul was wrong and should have stayed home, concerning himself only with the Church assembly in Jerusalem and let the Europeans and Asians look after themselves?

Where would you and I be today, if he had done that?

The last estimate I read, reported 65% of the world has never even heard about Jesus!

One of the most shocking examples of evangelism failure that comes to my mind, was a Christian TV reporter on the street in Hollywood California, interviewing people <u>in front of a "church"</u> building who had never heard of Jesus!

<u>Jesus gave each of us ONE main task…world evangelization</u>.

It's been <u>2,000 YEARS</u>!

I'll say that again; it's been <u>2,000 YEARS</u>!

Most Christians have been focused on what THEY say is important… not what JESUS says is important. Bible teaching in Sunday schools; helping the poor and fellowship is a good thing, but people need to be taught how to move in the spirit and in God's power, not wallow in flesh-driven, man-made doctrines and traditions. Many of these Bible institutions, organizations, and denominations that we consider Christian, are built on Old Testament laws, structures and/or ancient pagan rituals. Some, having little to do with New Testament teaching.

Most Christians are not following His orders and therefore most of the world is still lost. By withholding the gospel from others and by not correcting those in error, the long-awaited return of Jesus is delayed, the kingdom of satan is perpetuated, billions are lost <u>forever</u> and what is the reward for ignoring this ONE task?

"His blood will I require at your hand."

John Wesley used to say, "You have <u>one</u> business on earth… to save souls."

Our duty is plain.

<u>Let's get it done</u>!

Although I pray there are many more out there that I've not heard of, there is only one well-known person in the world that I'm aware of that does a complete SAFARI campaign on a large scale. That's shoot, and fish and ready, interact. It wasn't Billy Graham… it wasn't even Charles Finney… or D.L. Moody… its Carlos Annacondia, in Argentina.

He goes into an area and does Xtreme Big Game Hunting first to bind the strongman… driving it and other evil spiritual leaders out.

Then he holds a crusade. The numbers of people who attend is staggering. People run to salvation at his crusades and are then taken behind the speaker's platform into tents, where deliverance ministers cast demons out of them, just like Jesus and the early Church members did. Then they are matched with a mentor, whose job it is to prepare them to interact one day, as a mature Christian.

They report that 85% of converts remain Christians after one year, where statistics with other evangelists are said to be about 5% of those few fish that came.

Why?

Because these others didn't go Xtreme Big Game Hunting first, nor prepare them properly afterward.

Also, another **key evangelism procedure** that gets and keeps them in the boat, is what Jesus taught us, what the Bible tells us to do, but is usually ignored today!

If a reporter today was to research Christianity for a documentary, by watching ministries on TV, the internet, radio, through books, CD's, DVD's and by personally attending, the major denominations of the world, there would be a sharp contrast with this reporter comparing it to what the Bible says we should be doing.

Let's see what Jesus did when He was doing ministry.

"Then Jesus went about all the cities and villages, teaching in their synagogues, preaching the gospel (truth) of the kingdom, and healing every sickness and every disease among the people (demonstration of power not just words). But when He saw the multitudes, He was moved with compassion for them, because they were weary and scattered, like sheep having no shepherd. (In other words the false Pharisees, false Sadducees, false leaders were failing them) Then He said to His disciples, "The harvest truly is plentiful, but the laborers are few. Therefore, pray the Lord of the harvest to send out laborers into His harvest." Matthew 9:35-38

Paul said: "And I, brethren, when I came to you, did not come with excellence of speech or of wisdom declaring to you the testimony of God. And my speech and my preaching were not with persuasive words of human wisdom, but in demonstration of the Spirit and of power, that your faith should not be in the wisdom of men but in the power of God." 1 Corinthians 2:1, 4-5

A well-educated man like Paul, did not talk to the people with fancy words, in order to persuade them or to get them to idolize him. Even Jesus didn't do that! He knew that talk without demonstration of God's power, makes Christianity just a religion like all the others.

Jesus, the disciples and Paul didn't walk around entertaining people, to build up a personal following or build up their bank accounts! They also didn't compromise with sin, to appease the will of the people.

Without demonstration of God's power when we gather together or when we show our lives to non-believers, we're contradicting the Word of God!

Paul said to fully preach the Word of God, there needs to be mighty signs and wonders. This teaches us that those who are talking, teaching, preaching, doing "church", without miracles, signs and wonders to follow, are not fully preaching the Gospel.

"in mighty signs and wonders, by the power of the Spirit of God, so that from Jerusalem and round about to Illyricum I have fully preached the gospel of Christ." Romans 15:19

Paul ran into people who were poisoning minds in Iconium. What did he do? They decided to stay a long time to fix the problem. How was the problem fixed? Speaking boldly in the Lord, Who bared witness to what they were saying with signs and wonders.

"Now it happened in Iconium that they went together to the synagogue of the Jews, and so spoke that a great multitude both of the Jews and of the Greeks believed. But the unbelieving Jews stirred up the Gentiles and poisoned their minds against the brethren. Therefore, they stayed there a long time, speaking boldly in the Lord, who was bearing witness to the word of His grace, granting signs and wonders to be done by their hands." Acts 14:1-3

Leaders need to fully preach the Gospel with signs and wonders. It's a requirement, not a request nor a suggestion. Let's hope and pray that any reporter doing a documentary on Christianity today, ignores the "persuasive words of human wisdom" and the entertainers on TV, the internet, the radio and what they would experience in most denominational gatherings.

Let's pray that this reporter, would be like Palladius of the 4th Century, who spent years documenting the lives of true Christians, that didn't compromise their faith, that didn't pretend to be Christian and that backed up their talk with demonstrations of the power of God. Palladius could have written about the corrupt "church" in the world, but he wanted the true Christianity to be documented. Palladius eventually became a bishop.

1600 years later I still read what Palladius wrote about these wonderful Christians… the Desert Fathers and Mothers!

Getting back to SAFARI camp, here's a report on Carlos Annacondia from Dr. Peter Wagner:

"After observing the ministry of Carlos Annacondia for several years, I am prepared to offer a hypothesis: <u>Annacondia may well be the most effective citywide interdenominational crusade evangelist of all time.</u> If this turns out to be only approximately true, his approach to winning the masses of the cities to Christ deserves close scrutiny.

Annacondia was the committed Christian owner of a prosperous nuts and bolts factory in Quilmes on the outskirts of Buenos Aires when he was called into evangelistic ministry. It was probably no mere coincidence that the day he launched his first public crusade was the day the British sunk the Argentine Battleship General Belgrano in the 1982 Falkland Islands war. He was 37 years old at the time.

When I use the term "effective evangelism" I follow the lead of Donald McGavran and the Church Growth Movement in arguing that biblical evangelism involves bringing unbelievers to a simultaneous commitment to Christ and also to the body of Christ. Making disciples involves bringing men and women to faith in Jesus and into responsible membership in a local church. Carlos Annacondia is highly successful in seeing this happen. On a recent visit to Argentina I worked with pastors of four cities. Without any leading questions on my part, in each of the four cities I heard Christian leaders in a matter-of-fact way refer to recent trends in their cities as "before Annacondia" and "after Annacondia". In more than 20 years of studying urban crusade evangelism I have never heard such consistent testimonials of one evangelist across the board. Single instances of effective evangelistic crusades such as Tommy Hicks in Buenos Aires and Stanley Mooneyham in Phnom Penh have been recorded. But Annacondia's ministry seems to be unique.

Several pastors showed me new sanctuaries they had constructed to contain the growth after Annacondia's crusade in their city. One showed me a basketball stadium they had been leasing for six years. Another church now holds 17 services a week in five rented theaters. Another pastor reports "a notable change of attitude among the people of our city as a result of Annacondia's ministry."

What Is Different?

What is Carlos Annacondia doing that other urban evangelists do not usually do? Annacondia has a great deal in common with traditional crusade evangelists. He preaches a simple gospel message, gives an invitation for people to come forward and receive Christ as their Lord and Savior, uses trained counselors to lead them to Christ and give them literature, takes their name and address and invites them to attend a local church.

Like Billy Graham and Luis Palau, Annacondia secures a broad base of interdenominational support from pastors and other Christian leaders in the target area. Like Dwight Moody and Billy Sunday he has had no formal academic theological training. Like Reinhard Bonnke and T. L. Osborne he features miracles, healings and deliverance from evil spirits in his meetings. *(Demonstration of God's power.)* He is not the only one who preaches in the open air, conducts three-hour services, or has on-the-spot intercessors praying for the ministry.

If I am not mistaken, <u>the major difference is Carlos Annacondia's intentional, premeditated, high-energy approach to spiritual warfare.</u>

A permanent fixture of Annacondia's crusades is what has to be one of the most sophisticated and massive deliverance ministries anywhere. Under the direction of Pablo Botari, a wise, mature and gifted servant of God, literally hundreds of individuals are delivered from demons each of the 30 to 50 consecutive nights of a crusade. The 150-foot deliverance tent, erected behind the speaker's platform, is in operation from 8:00 p.m. to 4:00 a.m. each night. Scores of teams whom Botari has trained do the actual hands-on ministry.

I have never observed a crusade evangelist who is as publicly aggressive in confronting evil spirits as Annacondia. With a high-volume, high-energy, prolonged challenge he actually taunts the spirits until they manifest in one way or another. To the uninitiated the scenario might appear to be total confusion. But to the skilled, experienced members of Annacondia's 31 crusade ministry teams, it is just another evening of power encounters in which the power of Jesus Christ over demonic forces is being displayed for all to see. Many miraculous healings occur, souls are saved, and so great is the spiritual power that unsuspecting pedestrians passing by the crusade meeting have been known to fall down under the power of the Holy Spirit." *The Awesome Argentina Revival - Lessons in Evangelism and Spiritual Warfare from Argentina*, by Dr. Peter Wagner

He also does high-level spiritual warfare (Xtreme Big Game Hunting) in advance.

This SAFARI Sector is meant to show the process of dealing with areas and people who are blinded, so they can come, and most importantly, stay with Jesus and advance the Kingdom of God.

The only way to advance a kingdom is by offense… as defense, passive resistance, negotiation with evil, and inertia end in failure!

The acronym of SAFARI is being used to help you remember this evangelism process, which has proven to be highly successful. The ultimate safari is successfully bringing in the biggest of all game… those who are lost, held captive, and dying in satan's kingdom.

How do we do that?

SAFARI

S-Shoot, A-And, F-Fish, A-And, R-Ready, I-Interact.

Your life will be altered based on your answers to these questions!

What is your destiny with God?

If you don't know… how do you intend to find out?

How are <u>you</u> going to advance the Kingdom of God?

How are <u>you</u> going to apply what you learn in this book, to <u>your</u> destiny and the destinies of others?

Are you, or are you led to be a hunter/shooter, a fisher and/or one who helps clean and ready others to interact?

After the end of a good day of hunting and fishing, typically hunters and fishers sit around the camp to tell stories of past successes. I'll share some more testimonies from others and some of my own experiences in later Sectors.

Various levels of spiritual insight and spiritual warfare are available and known by Christians throughout the world.

What is the highest form of knowledge and spiritual warfare?

"For God, who commanded the light to shine out of the darkness, hath shined in our hearts, TO GIVE THE LIGHT OF THE KNOWLEDGE OF THE GLORY OF GOD IN THE FACE OF JESUS CHRIST." 2 Corinthians 4:6

The kingdom of heaven is all light… there is no darkness. 1 John 1:5 says God is light, and in Him there is no darkness at all. Genesis says that we are made in God's image, out of His light, so therefore, we are also light. We should seek to tap into who we are. Isn't this the peak of spiritual excellence that we must seek and obtain?

Christians should be producing the light that God designed in each of us!

So why aren't we producing this light?

As Christians, we have access to the God and heaven, as we have received salvation in Jesus Christ. But this is more than just doctrine or theology. Most Christians stay at one spiritual level of understanding or another, perhaps growing a bit once in a while, but usually abandoning their spiritual destiny.

<u>Knowing Him...this is light. This is our purpose</u>.

It's not knowing <u>about</u> Him… it's not an emotional feeling or an intellectual understanding or a theological principle… but it's experiencing Him, and having a daily, intimate relationship with Him.

<u>Grow in His light!</u>

Christians must remember, that hunting and fishing must take place in the spiritual world, when they wonder why their physical attempts and physical means are not working.

ALWAYS–ALWAYS–ALWAYS remember that you are a spirit in a physical body, not the other way around.

We always must <u>consider</u> the spiritual factors, not ignore them.

You have to deal with the evil spiritual kingdom. Go to God's kingdom hunting and fishing book, the Bible; obtain guidance from the Holy Spirit; go in the spirit… and then you can catch and <u>keep</u> a fish from satan's kingdom.

All of your hunting and fishing trips, camps and SAFARI's are logged and recorded in heaven forever! Your living trophies (people) will join you in heaven for eternity!

How many trophies do you want to be a part of bringing into heaven? Every hunting and fishing trip, camp and SAFARI you take part in, even just in prayer or financially—you join in its successes and you'll have memories that will be with you, for time without end!

Endeavor to become part of and start a successful hunting and fishing SAFARI and fulfill your destiny with God.

EVERY CHRISTIAN GROUP SHOULD BE A SAFARI CAMP!

Looking back at Daniel Nash, Finney's assistant, we find, that despite his huge evangelism successes, at the end of his life, Nash had a revelation and he said, "It seems to me that I have always limited God…" <u>Nash realized he should "rationally ask for the whole influence of the Holy Spirit to come down… on a whole people, region, country, and world!"</u>

When Nash had set himself to do this, he said, "The devil was very angry with me." (NOTE that the devil became very angry, when Nash expanded beyond just cities.)

Finney says that near the end of Nash's life, Nash would "take the map of the world before him and pray, and look over the different countries and pray for them, 'til one day he expired in his room, praying."

Nash made a colossal discovery, but never had a chance to complete his revelation!

Remember what Nash discovered… the whole world is our hunting and fishing SAFARI camp!

There is no catch limit, so don't limit yourself or God! Let's put a least one Daniel Nash or Carlos Annacondia in each country. Are you up for the job? When you head out on a SAFARI expedition, do all that you need to do to have success.

I pray that each of you will enjoy being part of very successful hunting and fishing trips in the future… All for His glory!

Ezekiel 21:15 says," I have set the point of the sword against all their gates!"

I pray that the sign on your gate will now read, "Gone Huntin' and Fishin'!"

Heavenly Father… thank You for giving us Your guiding hand. We give only You all the praise and glory and worship for this teaching and in all things. Thank You Jesus for being with us and for coming to set us free, allowing us to move from death into life through Your blood sacrifice and for allowing us to use Your name to be more than conquerors over evil.

Thank You, Holy Spirit, for Your gifts, guidance, revelation and continued teaching… preparing us to interact in order to always be advancing the Kingdom of God.

I ask in Jesus' name that the reader of this book receive an anointing upon them and that holy angels be dedicated to them, to assist them in achieving their destiny.

Anyone reading this book, who wants to go from death unto life and fulfill their destiny… jump into the boat of salvation, stay there, get ready, go and do… become a Silver Bullet of God, perhaps as an Xtreme Big Game Hunter for God!

Let's examine how in the next Sectors!

ZONE 3

HUNT PREPARATION

SECTOR SIX
YA GOTTA GET B.A.D.

> **HUNTING TIP**
> You have the authority to change everything around you!

Before going hunting, you must eliminate certain bad habits and activities, if you are to have a successful hunt. I've hunted with guys who smoked, talked, made noise and drank alcohol when hunting.

How successful do you imagine they were?

I was on a stand, waiting for deer and I could smell a cigarette from another hunter. Although I couldn't see him, I knew he was there in the next section of woods. There would be no deer coming by me that morning, unless passing by me to avoid the smoker. Others have been late, not showed at all, or cancelled at the last minute; and some who showed up, you wish hadn't, because they ruined the hunt.

While Xtreme Big Game Hunting, there are also spiritual factors that will inhibit your success.

B.A.D.

Ya gotta get B.A.D.!

B.A.D is an acronym God gave me that stands for Baptism, Acceptance and Deliverance.

Acceptance

Before you can even start preparing to be an Xtreme Big Game Hunter, you must accept Jesus Christ as your <u>only</u> Lord and Savior, Healer and Deliverer.

Jesus is the <u>only</u> way to salvation and to the heavenly Father.

"And we have seen and testify that the Father has sent the Son as Savior of the world." 1 John 4:14

"Whoever transgresses and does not abide in the doctrine of Christ does not have God. He who abides in the doctrine of Christ has both the Father and the Son." 2 John 9

"For there is one God and one Mediator between God and men, the Man Christ Jesus." 1 Timothy 2:5

"Who is a liar but he who denies that Jesus is the Christ? He is antichrist who denies the Father and the Son. Whoever denies the Son does not have the Father either; he who acknowledges the Son has the Father also." 1 John 2:22-23

The only way you can get to heaven; talk to the heavenly Father; receive the Holy Spirit and His gifts and guidance, and go in the spirit and more, is through accepting Jesus Christ into your heart as your Savior.

To some, this may be a non-issue, yet have you <u>personally</u> accepted Jesus?

A woman that I know in her sixties, that had been attending "church" since she was a child, <u>just</u> accepted Jesus as her personal Lord and Savior. It seems unusual, but many thinks that because they attend "church", they're Christian. If you're not sure, be sure.

For those who refuse to accept Jesus, there is no sense finishing this book, as you are lost and can never become a Silver Bullet of God nor an Xtreme Big Game Hunter.

God Loves You

"For God so loved the world that He gave His only begotten Son, that whoever believes in Him should not perish but have everlasting life." John 3:16

"But God demonstrates His own love toward us, in that while we were still sinners, Christ died for us." Romans 5:8

All Are Sinners

"for all have sinned and fall short of the glory of God." Romans 3:23

"But as many as received Him, to them He gave the right to become children of God, to those who believe in His name." John 1:12

"For I delivered to you first of all that which I also received: that Christ died for our sins according to the Scriptures, and that He was buried, and that He rose again the third day according to the Scriptures." 1 Corinthians 15:3-4

All May Be Saved Now

"Behold, I stand at the door and knock. If anyone hears My voice and opens the door, I will come in to him and dine with him, and he with Me." Revelation 3:20

"For whoever calls on the name of the Lord shall be saved." Romans 10:13

Assurance as a Believer

"that if you confess with your mouth the Lord Jesus and believe in your heart that God has raised Him from the dead, you will be saved." Romans 10:9

"Most assuredly, I say to you, he who hears My word and believes in Him who sent Me has everlasting life, and shall not come into judgment, but has passed from death into life." John 5:24

"but these are written that you may believe that Jesus is the Christ, the Son of God, and that believing you may have life in His name." John 20:31

To make your decision now to receive Jesus Christ as your Lord and Savior, repeat out loud something like this: "Heavenly Father, I am a sinner and I believe that the Lord Jesus Christ died for my sins on the cross and was raised for my justification; and His blood sacrifice has paid the penalty for all my sins, iniquities and transgressions. I do now receive and confess Jesus Christ as my personal Lord and Savior."

After making this decision to receive Christ into your heart, search for a spiritual Christian or spiritual group that will baptize you in water <u>and</u> in the Holy Spirit <u>and</u> deliver you (cast out evil spirits) <u>and</u> help you to grow as a new Christian by the clear teaching of God's Word, the Bible, allowing you to develop your ministry to interact.

Don't settle for a Jesus fan club! (The Holy Spirit gave me that one!)

"but grow in the grace and knowledge of our Lord and Savior Jesus Christ." 2 Peter 3:18

BAPTISM

After you have accepted Jesus as your Lord and Savior, you must receive baptism in water and in the Holy Spirit and fire.

"Jesus answered and said to him, most assuredly, I say to you, unless one is born again, he cannot see the kingdom of God." John 3:3

"Jesus answered, most assuredly, I say to you, unless one is born of water and the Spirit, he cannot enter the kingdom of God." John 3:5

"John answered, saying to all, "I indeed baptize you with water; but One mightier than I is coming, whose sandal strap I am not worthy to loose. He will baptize you with the Holy Spirit and fire." Luke 3:16

Most doctrines, if not all, argue, disagree and separate over the issue of baptism. Some say, it is alright if an infant is water baptized; others accept sprinkling with water, rather than full immersion. Some say water baptism is purely a symbolic act signifying the death of the old self and rebirth of a new creature in Christ. Also, some will say the repentant thief on the cross next to Jesus wasn't baptized—so why bother?

Others do not give much consideration to the baptism of the Holy Spirit. Some insist that the Holy Spirit comes into everyone when they accept Jesus or when they are water baptized, they say it happens then. Some insist tongues must be spoken to prove that the Holy Spirit is present in them.

Most never mention baptism with fire.

The theories and doctrines are plentiful.

Water Baptism

Looking to the Word of God, we see that Jesus, who did nothing on His own, but what His Father in heaven had Him do, had a full, water-immersion baptism, as an adult.

If you were baptized/sprinkled with water as an infant, as I was, I would recommend that you go somewhere to receive a <u>full immersion</u> water baptism. I did so in the Jordan River in Israel years ago, and it didn't hurt a bit! This water baptism can be done to you by any true follower of Christ, as John the Baptist was not a seminary graduate, neither was Jesus nor any of the disciples.

Biblically, a full-immersion baptism is how our Father led Jesus. I can't speak for God, or what he'll accept as alternatives. Why risk it?

Further detailed information on water baptism is available from "The Didache," in that the disciples of Jesus did full immersion in running water and if that wasn't available, then standing water, down to pouring water on the head.

Some may say this is all rather simplistic for such a birth… yet so is accepting Jesus as your Lord and Savior, translating one from death to eternal life.

Water baptism is a spiritual act, signifying a new spiritual birth or awakening. A baby has life in the womb, but has not been born. People are like babies in the embryonic fluid or water in the womb, waiting to come forth or be born into a new spiritual life in this world. Most are never born again.

An example of a water baptism: A person being totally immersed 3 times under the water while another person says something like, "I baptize you in the name of the Father and the Son and the Holy Spirit", as you come up out of the water and down again 3 times.

Holy Spirit Baptism

The Holy Spirit was with the disciples when they walked with Him, yet, they were to wait until Pentecost to receive the baptism of the Holy Spirit. If the baptism of the Holy Spirit comes automatically at the same time as water baptism, why did the disciples need to 'get Him again' at Pentecost? Acts 1:5

As you read the Bible and the book of Acts, you'll notice the changes in the disciples after they received the baptism of the Holy Spirit. The Holy Spirit gives many gifts that further our spiritual growth process, including prophecy, working of miracles, wisdom, knowledge, tongues, interpretation of tongues, faith, healing, discernment and more. These gifts will manifest. Holy Spirit Baptism <u>can</u> happen at water baptism as it did with Jesus. The Holy Spirit <u>can</u> come upon you <u>with</u> or <u>without</u> the laying on of hands by a believer. Some doctrines will say this is not true, yet it happened to Jesus and to the disciples and others in Acts.

"Then there appeared to them divided tongues, as of fire, and one sat upon each of them. And they were all filled with the Holy Spirit and began to speak with other tongues, as the Spirit gave them utterance." Acts 2:3-4

The Holy Spirit also came upon me, in the mid-1960's, when I was alone in my room. It was such an in-filling, that I held onto the side of my bed, as I thought I was going to fall out! The Holy Spirit is God, and He does what He wills, without the guidance of religion or people. If there is no one to impart or lay hands on you for this baptism, ask the Holy Spirit to baptize you and come upon you as He did those at Pentecost.

He will!

And ask the Holy Spirit <u>every day</u>, to continually fill you and recharge you!

Over my lifetime, I have seen many people receive the baptism of the Holy Spirit, in many different places. It was usually accompanied with joy, tears of happiness and sometimes holy laughter... but I never once ever heard or saw that it was accompanied with what I'm about to teach now!

Spirit Baptism-The Good, The Bad and The Ugly!

I was brought up as a Christian; taken to a religious "church" every week as a baby and attended Sunday school starting at around age 5. I had a very peaceful life and mind, until I received the baptism of the Holy Spirit at the age of 12. This was a pivotal point in my life. I wrote briefly about this in the Introduction of this book. At that time, I had no teaching of what happens... good and bad... or what to do when you receive the baptism of the Spirit!

Some of you might be thinking, "Bad? What is bad about receiving the baptism of the Holy Spirit?"

I didn't say it was bad to receive the Holy Spirit, just that there is bad side that comes as a consequence and if you aren't taught how to deal with what comes... good and bad... then you're going to be wandering into a world of hurt!

Not only is it a leader's or mature Christian's responsibility to teach a newly Spirit-baptised person how to develop their ministry, gifts and fruits of the Holy Spirit... the good side, but also how to expect and

Too many leaders lay hands on people to baptize them in the Spirit and dance around with them in joy, but leave them untaught on how to maneuver in this new spiritual realm that they've entered! We must remember that this person is newly born into the spiritual realm and like a baby must be schooled on how to survive.

Who would take a newborn baby from the womb, slap them on the back, wish them the best and send them on their way into the street? Yet, isn't that how a newborn, spirit-filled Christian is usually handled?

After I received the baptism of the Spirit, the "pastor" of my "church" denied that any miracles, signs, wonders, healings, etc. was possible nor happened, after the death of the last of the 12 disciples... that's ugly teaching! Although this didn't make any common sense to me that God stopped being God, this was the leadership and guidance that I had available to me in the mid-1960's. No internet at the time to help me; few books written about this (even if I knew they existed or how to find them) and, I never heard of any leader that thought different than this "pastor". (Same problem still exists today in many denominations!)

I soon felt like a soldier in a foxhole... confusion, doubts, fears, things were going wrong... my life started to unravel and I became worse off than when I just believed in Jesus as my Savior!

I truly believe that if I had the proper guidance from just one person, on how to walk in the spiritual realm in confidence, power and authority, rather than face down in a foxhole, just trying to survive, I would have been a much more prosperous servant of God and a much more dangerous opponent to satan!

Leaders who pastor, preach, teach and guide in a spiritually immature and/or spiritually ignorant way, are a danger to the Body of Christ... they are the ugly side! Avoid them!

One great leader that taught about the bad side of the baptism of the Spirit, was Derek Prince.

In his book, *The Spirit-Filled Believer's Handbook*, Mr. Prince says, "The baptism in the spirit does not merely lead into a realm of new spiritual blessings, it leads also into a realm of new spiritual conflict. As a logical consequence, increased power from God will always bring with it increased opposition from satan. The Christian who makes sensible, scriptural use of the power received through the baptism in the Spirit will be in position to meet and overcome the increased opposition of satan. On the other hand, the Christian who receives the baptism of the Spirit but neglects the other aspects of Christian duty will find himself in an exceedingly dangerous position. He will discover that the baptism in the Spirit has opened up his spiritual nature to entirely new forms of satanic attack or oppression, but he will be without the God-appointed means to discern the true nature of satan's attack or to defend against it."

He goes on to say, that Christians can end up worse-off with the baptism of the Spirit... "Quite often such a Christian will find his mind invaded by strange moods of doubt or fear or depression, or he will be exposed to moral or spiritual temptation which he never experienced before receiving the baptism in the Spirit. Unless he is forewarned and forearmed to meet these new forms of satanic attack, he may easily succumb to the wiles and onslaughts of the enemy and fall back to a lower spiritual level than he was before he entered this new realm of conflict."

Mr. Prince describes exactly what happened to me… as a teenager and young adult, I ended up in a lower spiritual level, than I was in before the baptism of the Spirit! I was exposed to the good, the bad and the ugly and I didn't know how to handle any of it! I wasted many years of my potential, with my life and with God!

There are Spirit-baptised Christians in foxholes all over the world right now, that don't know how to deal with the good, the bad or the ugly.

They need our help!

Their lives and destinies are being delayed and destroyed by our common enemy!

Maybe some of them are foxhole soldiers that you laid hands on to receive the Holy Spirit, but didn't properly prepare or mentor them, on how to do spiritual warfare against the enemy or didn't teach them how to work with the Holy Spirit, to develop gifts to manifest fruit… "for to one is given the word of wisdom through the Spirit, to another the word of knowledge through the same Spirit, to another faith by the same Spirit, to another gifts of healings by the same Spirit, to another the working of miracles, to another prophecy, to another discerning of spirits, to another different kinds of tongues, to another the interpretation of tongues." 1 Corinthians 12:8-10

We need to teach all Christians, to get Spirit-baptized and to do spiritual warfare at all times, every day, for themselves, their families, their friends, their neighbourhoods, their economies and their nations.

Let's bring every Spirit-baptized Christian to their full potential!

If they're sitting around in a foxhole (or pew), with their heads down being pounded by the enemy, not firing back, not taking ground, or not producing fruit of the Spirit, then each true Christian, needs to be a part of the body of Christ that hunts for these soldiers; reaches down into the foxholes to lift them out and help them maneuver around through the good, the bad and the ugly, even when leaders can't or won't do it!

We need "Rambo Christians", not "Foxhole Christians"!!

<u>Fire Baptism</u>

As Christians mature, assuming they have a desire to get beyond just spiritual existence and birth, God will put them through the fire.

In the physical world, we hear of people being "put through the fire" to toughen them up. Such as a piece of ore that is crushed and put into the fire to be smelted and refined… to be purified. Then, as pure metal, it is poured into a form, cooled and put into the fire again. It is now put under intense heat and pressure of hammering to shape and mold. Finally, it is polished and sharpened into something that is useful, perhaps a sword.

This is what God is doing.

Metal that isn't strong enough or malleable enough, goes back to the fire.

God does a 'fire of baptism' in many ways, beyond smelting you of sins, iniquities, transgressions and lack of praise and worship. It can include time spent in the spiritual wilderness, as He did with Jesus after His water baptism. Or perhaps trials like Job experienced, until they are passed and then to the next, more difficult trial. As you spiritually mature, you obtain more wisdom, knowledge, responsibilities, and can achieve more for God, thus fulfilling your destiny!

To be a Silver Bullet of God, refining in the fire of God is a requirement!

Accept whatever fire baptism our heavenly Father puts you through and be honored to be chosen.

*Ecclesiasticus Chapter 2 says:

2:1. Son, when thou comest to the service of God, stand in justice and in fear, and prepare thy soul for temptation.

2:2. Humble thy heart, and endure: incline thy ear, and receive the words of understanding: and make not haste in the time of clouds.

2:3. Wait on God with patience: join thyself to God, and endure, that thy life may be increased in the latter end.

2:4. Take all that shall be brought upon thee: and in thy sorrow endure, and in thy humiliation keep patience.

2:5. For gold and silver are tried in the fire, but acceptable men in the furnace of humiliation.

2:6. Believe God, and he will recover thee: and direct thy way, and trust in him. Keep his fear, and grow old therein.

*Ecclesiasticus is one of the Old Testament apocryphal books.

<u>Ask God to refine you with His fire, to be an acceptable instrument of heaven.</u>

Deliverance

A person can receive deliverance from evil spirits, both before and after he becomes a Christian. Some will disagree on both points and some say a Christian doesn't need deliverance, as evil spirits are not and cannot be <u>in</u> a Christian.

How do those who say you should never conduct deliverance for a non-Christian, explain that the people Jesus delivered were all <u>non</u>-Christians?

'Nuff said.

Can a Christian have a demon?

A controversial question that I'm sure will always be debated.

Theory vs. Bible vs. experience.

People historically criticize those, whose views differ from their own, which would help explain the thousands of Christian denominations and sects that currently exist.

Let's blend some Biblical fact, with some experience, to hopefully replace some theory. Those that say it is impossible for a Christian to "have" a demon in them, usually have as their main argument, that the Holy Spirit will not coexist with evil in the same body.

Doubtful any of these people ever did a deliverance (cast evil spirits out of a person), as they would soon reject this theory. They don't take their theory outside of the human body, where the Holy Spirit and evil do coexist.

The Holy Spirit doesn't exist in one spirit world and evil spirits in another. They co-exist.

Some folks argue that any anger, fear, lust, hatred, or other problems, come from either the "old man" or carnal nature; or some evil applied against Christians from evil spirits; or curses from <u>outside</u> the body. People do get hung up on the word possession, thinking if an evil entity is in them, it would totally possess them. Wouldn't you still have your own spirit and hopefully, the Holy Spirit <u>within</u> your body, no matter what other spirit(s) came in? Of course!

In 2 Corinthians 11:4, Paul says to the <u>Christians</u> in Corinth, "...or if you receive another spirit, which you have not received." Paul is concerned for these Christians learning false teachings, false gospels and receiving another spirit, other than the Holy Spirit, Who they already had. This biblical reference shows that Christians can have the Holy Spirit and accept or receive another spirit, as well.

In the story of Ananias and Sapphira, starting in Acts 5:1-10, these two Christians allowed their hearts to be filled with an unholy spirit, which was discerned by Peter... "Satan filled your heart" ...and both fell dead for lying.

Early Christian history records indicate, that it was standard practice for every new Christian to receive deliverance, <u>after</u> they were saved.

Evil spirits not only afflict with mental and emotional problems, such as depression, anxiety, schizophrenia, psychosis and PTSD, but they also, cause physical disease (i.e. arthritis, cancer, heart attacks); break up families; hinder finances and success; cause accidents; convince people to accept religion and the world/reject God's full gospel; perpetuate crime (i.e. assault, rape); convince people to murder and conduct terrorism and commit suicide; block spiritual senses and block/cripple/divert and destroy destinies.

They stay very busy with you and just love it when you let them work!

Do evil spirits flee from a body, when one becomes a Christian?

This does happen. I have seen where they have, on their own, come out and gone away from a new Christian— gone away meaning usually into another person. Others must be dealt with. I have seen evil spirits affecting people from <u>within</u> them and <u>on</u> them.

Jesus told the disciples and all Christians to deal with them in Matthew 10:8, Mark 16:17, Acts 8:7, Acts 16:18… to name a few references.

To blend this Bible truth, with some experience, one only has to pick up any of dozens of Christian books on the market or go to the internet or YouTube, to be inundated with deliverance experiences from around the world, where <u>Christians</u> are afflicted with evil spirits that are in them.

Are all these different ministers and Christians in various circumstances and in numerous countries all conspiring to lie about their experiences and testimonies?

<u>Is That Logical?</u>

My personal experience has also been in line with the Word and with the experience of others, in that, Christians can and do have evil spirits <u>in</u> them, that must be cast <u>out</u>. Once cast out—problems, sickness, disease, fears, accidents—have suddenly left.

Here's an extreme example:

A <u>Christian</u> friend of mine was put in a mental ward with padded walls, after being diagnosed with every mental disorder they could make up, and a few physical ones. Her parents were told she would soon die.

She had to be strapped down to the bed, which was the only thing in the room. She was also cursing and swearing at the doctors in a deep voice. One time when the doctor came in the room, she got one arm free from her restraints, grabbed him by his white coat, lifted this full-grown man up off the floor, flung him across the room, where he hit the wall and slid down, dazed! A petite woman (just 5 feet tall) did this, while strapped down to a bed! Remind you of any movie we know? Her Christian mother, who was in the room when this happened, turned to her Christian daughter and said she'd had enough, and in the Name of Jesus, cast out the evil spirits that were doing this to her daughter. Her mother had never done a deliverance before, but just got some righteous anger against this evil and exercised the authority that all Christians have, and are told to take. Her daughter immediately regained her full senses, was healed of everything and released from the psychiatric ward. She is a lovely, healthy Christian (and leader) to this day.

Do you think these evil spirits gave her mental, emotional and physical problems from outside or inside the body?

Despite prayer, reading the Bible, going to "church" and being a "good" Christian, are you or any other Christians you know still sick, in hospitals and/or in some kind of therapy?

Why do you think that is?

Aren't we God's children?

Why is this continuing to happen, no matter what we do?

Do you think God wants us to be sick and diseased and have problems?

Do you think it is HIS WILL, like so many Christians shrug and submit to?

His will is for you to be well, as we read in 3 John 2, 'Beloved, I pray that you may prosper in all things and be in health, just as your soul prospers.

"Your will be done on earth as it is in heaven." Matthew 6: 10

Does anyone really believe that there are evil spirits, sickness and disease in heaven? So, His will is the same for us here.

Let's keep in mind… theories and doctrines are interesting, but don't let them replace Biblical truths and spiritual experiences.

Find someone who will deliver you from evil spirits. You will also need to close the doors that let them in, so they don't come back.

More on this topic can be found in S.I.T., POW's, and Xtreme Small Game Sectors.

I realize it is difficult to find any group or Christian who does deliverance, so you may have to cast them out yourself.

If you don't think you could possibly need deliverance… think again! If you've never had deliverance, I'd be surprised if you didn't have evil spirits in you!

Evil spirits usually stay hidden and manifest in simple ways, that a person thinks is just them, such as being too tired to read the Bible or pray; or hates or fears Christian music; has uncontrollable lust or urges or explosive anger; or habitual lying.

A fear or disbelief that they need deliverance is a big sign of evil spirits, as common sense says deliverance can only help a person. Many people won't show up for a deliverance meeting and also run away when deliverance is about to take place. Evil spirits will always try to convince you that you're OK and don't need deliverance.

After you have gone through the Sectors I've mentioned, you can rebuke and bind any and all evil entities, powers and forces that are in you, afflicting, affecting, depressing, oppressing, regressing, or possessing you and <u>command</u> them to go out of you and away from you to never return, and never afflict anyone else, and go into and remain in spiritual prisons, in Jesus' name. Seek guidance from the Holy Spirit for how to do this for your deliverance and for continuing concerns, if outside help is not available.

Jesus never <u>prayed</u> out an evil spirit, He <u>commanded</u> them to go—so do the same.

Once you have done this, ask the Holy Spirit to come in to fill any empty areas with His presence and light, where once there was darkness. Keep doing this until you feel free of everything that is oppressing you, as evil spirits have been known to be stubborn and disobedient. But they must go, as long as they have no right to be there.

They will afflict you again, if you allow it in some way, or let them back in or haven't imprisoned them or destroyed them.

For instance, you can kick intruders out of your house, but if you leave the doors and windows open or invite them back, they can and will come back in. If you don't imprison or destroy them, they can also go to someone else. (More on that later).

Ask the Holy Spirit to reveal to you any open areas that are allowing continual oppression that won't go—or keeps coming back.

Ya gotta get BAD, if you want to get going for God!

Do not skip any of these steps!

SECTOR SEVEN

S.I.T. NO MORE

> **HUNTING TIP**
> Jesus died for your inheritance... so seize it!

Three main areas that need to be addressed after getting BAD, is another acronym the Lord gave me—S.I.T. Sin, Iniquities and Transgressions.

Your body, soul, spirit, heart and mind must all be clear. Your mind is the greatest battlefield. Satan wants your mind. Many people are only taught about sin and not the other two, which the Bible considers separate.

"...iniquity, transgression and sin..." Exodus 34:7

"But he was wounded for our transgressions; he was bruised for our iniquities" Isaiah 53:5

"an offering for sin." Isaiah 53:10

In order to be a Silver Bullet of God and an Xtreme Big Game Hunter, S.I.T. must be handled.

SIN

Many Christians believe that they do not willfully sin, because they don't do such things as murder or commit adultery and therefore, don't even consider that they've lost their salvation, or that they can be <u>legally</u> attacked by evil spirits. Yet committing adultery can even be done in your mind, by lusting for someone.

"But I say to you that whoever looks at a woman to lust for her has already committed adultery with her in his heart." Matthew 5:28

And these Christians may also be gossipers, idol worshippers, liars, boasters, deceivers or unforgiving and live by their own set of rules or doctrines, rather than God's. They believe they are "good" Christians and so, <u>never</u> ask for forgiveness for these acts, nor forgive others who offend them. They are therefore living in sin. If you don't forgive others, God <u>will not</u> forgive you!

"But if you do not forgive men their trespasses, neither will your Father forgive your trespasses." Matthew 6:15

I've mentioned some of this in a previous Sector, which must be addressed again in the sin section. Many Christians don't think they can lose their salvation, as they believe they are <u>permanently</u> covered by grace, no matter what they do! Not only will these Christians suffer from evil attacks, problems and sicknesses in their life, but worst of all, <u>they have lost their salvation</u>! Romans 1:29-32; Hebrews 10:26-31

Any form of healing and deliverance on these people, would probably be limited in success and be temporary, shifted or become worse, unless they ceased their willful sins. If they attempt to pursue a ministry in deliverance or spiritual hunting, life would be even more hazardous to them. Any form of iniquity we've inherited, and sin or transgressions that we enter into, creates an alliance with the devil. He then has a legal right to you, until you break that right, by repentance through the blood of Jesus Christ.

Some may ask what about sinning in ignorance or even worse, sinning with the <u>expectation</u> or the <u>acceptance</u> of their "church!" A few major denominations have idol worship of the dead and their images (statues or "relics") as an integral component of their man-made doctrine, which is <u>expected</u> of members.

Some other major denominations <u>accept</u> many sins, even amongst their own priests and bishops, such as idol worship or illicit sexual activities, in the belief that they are not really sinning. Even though the Bible clearly states, that idol worship and illicit sexual activities, are abhorrent to God and lead to death.

"You shall not lie with a male as with a woman. It is an abomination." Leviticus 18:22 and also 1 Corinthians 6:9-10

Some Christians believe, they can do whatever they want, thinking that they will just repent afterwards or confess, say a few prayers and all is well again to continue in their willful sins. Romans 1:21-32

God is not a fool… such <u>thinking</u> leads to spiritual death. Matthew 7:21-23

Sins of ignorance are still considered sin.

Does ignorance of God's will let anyone off the hook? It does not.

Each person will be judged according to <u>their</u> works according to Revelation 20:12-15. It is each one's responsibility, to find out what is acceptable to <u>God</u>, <u>not</u> what is acceptable to their "church" denomination, or to a personal philosophy. Sincerely ask your heavenly Father to forgive you of all your sins, which were all paid for by the blood sacrifice of Jesus Christ.

This you should do the moment after you realize, that have committed a sin. At least once a day, go to Father during SAC time, to ask for forgiveness of anything you said or did that was offensive to Him or for things you should have said or done but didn't do.

Soul Ties

Part of bondage that I will bring up under sin (although it may not fall under sin at times) is sexual and occult soul ties.

Many times, people are afflicted with ongoing problems despite confession and forgiveness of sin, iniquities and transgressions and despite deliverance. Although one might renounce the sin and iniquities of soul ties, that one of their ancestors has had with idol worship, the occult, sex outside of marriage, cults, religions, etc., there may still be a sexual or occult soul tie keeping <u>you</u> in bondage.

There is more to deliverance than casting demons out of people or out of yourself through self-deliverance. Although some deliverance ministers say, that this is all that is required, it has become apparent that many times it is not enough, as people can remain in bondage and continue to suffer. Evil spirits refuse to leave. Those without discernment, can utilize some specific pre-deliverance questions, to try and determine what is holding a person in bondage. When deliverance and healing and other efforts fail, it is time to consider sexual, occult and bondage ties. (Also see POW Sector)

There may be several factors together that are a soul tie (i.e. both occult and sexual), so each will have to be dealt with and renounced (see also Sector on Altars which may be a factor).

Jesus said in Mark 10:8, "… And the two will become one flesh." Sexual relationships unite separate people into one flesh. Evil spirits that influence or dominate one person can now affect the other! Experience has shown this to be true.

"Or do you not know that he who is joined to a harlot is one body with her? For "the two," He says, "shall become one flesh." 1 Corinthians 6:16

There is more involved than just sexual relations between a married man and woman. It also includes pedophilia (sexual relations with children), fornication, homosexual acts, bestiality (sex with animals), adultery, masturbation and other sexual acts.

Let's use an example of how far-reaching this bondage can be.

Let's say there's a man, who was sexually molested as a child, grew up and had several pre-marital affairs, one with a harlot or prostitute, before finally marrying a woman who had been raped as a teenager. And they both have had adulterous affairs.

This married couple now has soul ties with each other; and with the child molester from years ago; and all the sexual partners that the child molester has had in his life. This couple also has soul ties with the prostitute, the rapist, each person from the husband's pre-marital days and the adulterous affairs… all tied in with all of those people's sexual partners and so on.

The numbers of people that just one person can be of "one flesh" with, can be staggering… numbering in the hundreds or perhaps <u>more</u>!

Even if divorced, these soul ties exist unless dealt with.

Evil spirits have access and rights to move freely between all these people as all are interconnected!

Thus, even <u>IF</u> a person receives deliverance or healing, an evil spirit may have been cast out <u>or</u> perhaps moved over to another soul tie and is able to, and may come back later.

Deliverance on one person still does not stop evil spirits from being able to move into this person and back out again, through one or more of their soul tie connections.

Just to clarify something—many Christians and Christian leaders consider that once a person has confessed that Jesus Christ is their Lord and Savior, the job is done—<u>BUT</u> to enjoy peace and health in this world, other factors must be considered such as deliverance, dealing with iniquity and breaking bondages.

Each person can very easily break their own sexual and occult soul ties by speaking, (not screaming), in an audible voice something like this: "In the name of Jesus, I right now renounce all sexual and occult bondage and break all spirit, body and soul ties and connections that have been established between me and (the name of each individual and occult act)."

Once each person is dealt with by name, the unity is broken. If you can't remember or don't know the person's name (such as with a rape), then mention the occurrence and as much about the person as possible, when breaking the sexual soul tie.

Sexual and occult soul ties are a major bondage affecting people.

Much relief has been experienced once these ties are broken.

There are other major bondages that may also need to be broken and renounced, such as unforgiveness; vows to satan; occult practices; evil altars and religious affiliations (i.e. Freemasonry; false Christianity). Iniquity should be dealt with also.

You can also personally address these in much the same way, although iniquity is a separate bondage.

Also, there are bondages that may be and probably are in your house, such as prayer wheels; pagan idols; Buddha statues; good luck charms; religious idol paintings and statues.

Clean your house of evil things, anoint it and close all demonic doors.

One deliverance minister I know, never thought of this kind of bondage from personal items. He had a prayer wheel at the back of his closet, that someone had given to him as a gift. He and his wife received great relief from insomnia and nightmares when he destroyed it!

When in doubt, throw it out!

God suggests that these things be destroyed, rather than sold or discarded for others to pick up.

Anointing can be done with olive oil in a container that you pray over and ask the Holy Spirit to use as a Holy healing/purifying agent (prophetic act). Put some on your finger or hand and put on doorways and rooms of where you live, where you work, your car, etc... Anointing oil can also be put on people for healing and deliverance and so on.

My Mom had a small vile of anointing oil, that she used on countless people for decades. God told her she would never have to add more oil in the vial, as it is to be used for healing and it would never run out.

I now have and still use this vial! Still going for about 45 years now!

INIQUITY

Sin deals with the action or lack of action, that is against God's word. Iniquity deals more with the character or nature of the act. Iniquity is also a word attached to a curse, that passes down to us from generation to generation.

The Bible says iniquity is passed to future generations.

Ever hear of families passing along diseases such as the same cancers, diabetes, heart disease, etc.? Doctors say it's hereditary or it's in the genes or the DNA.

They're right... it's iniquity!

Besides prayer for forgiveness of personal sin, Christians need to address iniquity, thanks to the unforgiven sins and iniquities of their forefathers dating back three and four generations in most cases and back ten generations in another case.

"you shall not bow down to them nor serve them. For I, the Lord your God, am a jealous God, visiting <u>the iniquity of the fathers</u> upon the children to the third and fourth generations of those who hate Me"

Exodus 20:5

"keeping mercy for thousands, forgiving iniquity and transgression and sin, by no means clearing the guilty, visiting <u>the iniquity of the fathers</u> upon the children and the children's children to the third and the fourth generation." Exodus 34:7

"The Lord is longsuffering and abundant in mercy, forgiving iniquity and transgression; but He by no means clears the guilty, visiting <u>the iniquity of the fathers</u> on the children to the third and fourth generation." Numbers 14:18

"you shall not bow down to them nor serve them. For I, the Lord your God, am a jealous God, visiting <u>the iniquity of the fathers</u> upon the children to the third and fourth generations of those who hate Me." Deuteronomy 5:9

"One of illegitimate birth shall not enter the assembly of the Lord; even to the tenth generation none of his descendants shall enter the assembly of the Lord." Deuteronomy 23:2

Imagine all the sins that builds up in all these relatives of yours over their lives, that they have passed on to you as iniquity!

What an inheritance!

The Bible says that sin and transgressions are not hereditary, but iniquity is.

Christians suffer from all sorts of things because of iniquity.

Humans have a physical genetic code, or DNA, from ancestors' that is like a recording, passing along physical characteristics. The same occurs in the spiritual, with unforgiven sin/iniquity that is attached to a spiritual DNA code and passed along down the line.

"Have mercy upon me, O God,
According to Your lovingkindness;
According to the multitude of Your tender mercies,
Blot out my transgressions.
² Wash me thoroughly from my iniquity,
And cleanse me from my sin.

³ For I acknowledge my transgressions,
And my sin is always before me.
⁴ Against You, You only, have I sinned,
And done this evil in Your sight—
That You may be found just when You speak,
And blameless when You judge.

⁵ <u>Behold, I was brought forth in iniquity</u>,
And in sin my mother conceived me.
⁶ Behold, You desire truth in the inward parts,
And in the hidden part You will make me to know wisdom." Psalm 51:1-6

Many cities are built on iniquity.

"Woe to him who builds a town with bloodshed, Who establishes a city by iniquity!" Habakkuk 2:12

As a Christian, you must get rid of iniquity, especially if you intend on being an Xtreme Big Game Hunter.

"Nevertheless, the solid foundation of God stands, having this seal: 'The Lord knows those who are His,' and, 'Let everyone who names the name of Christ depart from iniquity." 2 Timothy 2:19

How can leaders and evangelists produce lasting and abundant fruit, when <u>they</u> are full of iniquity and don't deal with the iniquity of the people?

Because iniquity is never dealt with, people who initially accept Jesus at a meeting, typically drift back to their old lifestyles and habits, as iniquity is an open door to evil spirits.

Iniquity also inhibits spiritual hearing.

Most Christians can't hear God and think those that can hear God are nuts!

"My sheep hear My voice, and I know them, and they follow Me." John 10:27

"Behold, the Lord's hand is not shortened,
That it cannot save;
Nor His ear heavy,
That it cannot hear.
² <u>But your iniquities have separated you from your God;</u>
<u>And your sins have hidden His face from you,</u>
<u>So that He will not hear.</u>
³ For your hands are defiled with blood,
And your fingers with iniquity;
Your lips have spoken lies,
Your tongue has muttered perversity.

⁴ No one calls for justice,
Nor does any plead for truth.
They trust in empty words and speak lies;
They conceive evil and bring forth iniquity…

Therefore, justice is far from us,
Nor does righteousness overtake us;
We look for light, but there is darkness!
For brightness, but we walk in blackness!" Isaiah 59:1-4, 9

Is it any wonder why assemblies, leaders and Christians cannot hear God when God tells them, that they are separated from Him because of iniquity?

Iniquity also stops people from wanting to praise and worship properly in the spirit and from following God's will.

"These people draw near to Me with their mouth, and honor Me with their lips, but their heart is far from Me. And in vain they worship Me, teaching as doctrines the commandments of men." Matthew 15:8-9

" But the hour is coming, and now is, when the true worshipers will worship the Father in spirit and truth; for the Father is seeking such to worship Him." John 4:23

How can people worship in spirit and truth, when they are full of iniquity and don't operate in the spirit? No wonder most people resort to popular songs and call it worship, instead of doing what God says is a must for worship to Him!

We may know some and certainly not all of what our ancestors did, although the Lord may reveal to you all your iniquities, as you confess your ancestor's iniquities.

You may do something like this, to break the curse of iniquity:

"Heavenly Father, I come before you now in Jesus' name, to confess and ask for forgiveness of the iniquities of my ancestors that I have inherited. I cancel the curse right now, of all iniquity in me, my children, my grandchildren, my great grandchildren out to the tenth generation and beyond. I command all iniquity to find an exit and go in Jesus name by the blood of Jesus Christ from my body, mind, spirit, heart and bones."

Use for <u>each</u> of the following scripture verses: Leviticus 18:6-25, 27/Leviticus 19:4, 11-18,26-33 Leviticus 20:6, 8-15, 17, 19-21, 27/ Deuteronomy 27:15-25/ Deuteronomy 28: 15-19.

Ask the Lord now to open your spiritual eyes and spiritual ears, so that you may operate in the spiritual realm.

TRANSGRESSION

Merriam Webster dictionary defines transgression as: an act, process, or instance of transgressing: and as: infringement or violation of a law, command, or duty.

Many might say, that this is the same as sin.

According to Finis Dake in his Commentary Bible, there are 1,050 commands in the New Testament for Christians to obey!

I won't dispute his research.

As Dake says, "They cover every aspect of man's life in his relationship to God and his fellowmen, now and hereafter. If obeyed, they bring rewards forever; some, if disobeyed will bring condemnation and eternal punishment. They are not to be confused with the 10 commandments which were abolished with the law of Moses."

So those who have confessed their sins; have dealt with their iniquities; have decided not to do some or all of God's commands, choosing their own will instead of God's, are transgressing.

How do we follow all of these commands?

We must <u>not</u> seek or decide to deliberately go against or refuse these commands, required of a Christian. Analyze your life and <u>every day</u>, bowing down to God to confess and ask for forgiveness of every sin and transgression that comes to your mind, that you did that day.

Ask the Holy Spirit <u>every day</u> to bring to your attention what Father would have you do today!

Live in holiness. Be humble.

Be sorrowful for offending God and for not following His will.

You have no authority in God's kingdom, without true repentance.

Be vigilant in dealing with unforgiveness, pride, bitterness, rejection and rebellion.

Once you've confessed and asked for forgiveness of all sin, iniquity and transgressions and cancelled every pact made with territorial spirits in your life that you've established through <u>any</u> religion, idol worship, club or organization pact, pagan rituals, occult activities, illicit sexual activities and have cleaned you house of evil things, anointed your house and closed all demonic doors and gates to you… you're on The Way to going in the spirit and being a Silver Bullet of God and Xtreme Big Game Hunter!

S.I.T. no more!

SECTOR EIGHT

S.A.C. TIME

HUNTING TIP

It's not how much Bible you know... it's how much Him do you know!

Any hunter knows that you must be silent, because not doing so, will allow game to hear you and you not to hear (or see) them. Hunters usually hunt alone, perhaps sitting in a tree stand or walking along in the woods trying to flush something up. Hunting in gangs or with a friend or two, can be rewarding when you communicate to one another, before and during a hunt.

I brought down a deer one time, yelling over to my friend, that another deer was coming his way. Fortunately, deer don't understand English and my words didn't alert the deer to what he was running into.

<u>Silence</u>, being <u>Alone</u> with and <u>Communication</u> with God produces needed results.

The Lord has given me another acronym to help us remember these three important details in spending time with Him... S.A.C.

SILENCE

"Be still, and know that I am God." Psalm 46:10

This is a very well-known scripture that one can find in Christian bookstores as refrigerator magnets and plaques, yet how many pay attention to the words?

This is a society and world full of noise—from outside sources, to self-inflicted sources, making it difficult to hear God when He speaks. Noise can even be from reading material and thoughts of the world, that constantly flood our minds. The more noise, even Christian music, that our brains are busy with, the harder it is for us to hear His Voice.

Shut off the noise… Be in Silence and wait for Him there.

You'll hear His voice.

ALONE

"And when he (Jesus) had sent the multitudes away, he went up into a mountain apart to pray: and when the evening was come, he was there… ALONE." Matthew 14:23

"He (Jesus) went out, and departed into a solitary place, and there prayed." Mark 1:35

"And he (Jesus) withdrew himself into the wilderness, and prayed." Luke 5:16

Many times, we read of Jesus going away into the hills, mountains, wilderness and solitary places to be alone and pray.

Jesus came here to teach us what to do and He showed us that He spent SAC time with His Father.

He expects us to follow Him and do the same.

Many people only pray or talk <u>at</u> God in "church" with hordes of other people around (usually some kind of memorized prayer) and of course, accompanied by all the noise. Or perhaps during some world crises or when a personal problem arises and other such moments.

God says He wants to talk <u>with</u> you… alone!

Do What Jesus Did!

COMMUNICATION

Communication or prayer is a two-sided conversation, yet Christians only seem to be doing the talking part without the listening part.

Remember that God gave us one mouth that can close and two ears that cannot!

I have communication with my Heavenly Father, Jesus and the Holy Spirit and at times, all at the same time—and I know whose voice is whose!

Not difficult… for instance, if three people you know are behind you and each one talks, you know who is who, don't you?

This relationship is available to every Christian.

I cannot imagine not having such a relationship.

PRAY WITHOUT CEASING

1 Thessalonians 5:17 says, "Pray without ceasing", although many people think this means we should pray a lot.

Many years ago, I read about hermits and monks of old that interpreted this verse meant saying the "Jesus Prayer" ("Lord Jesus Christ, Son of God, have mercy on me, a sinner") over and over, repeatedly day after day, year after year in an effort to fulfill this scripture command.

I have to admit that I tried to copy the hermits teaching myself many years ago to fulfill this scripture… but it didn't work… (I couldn't grasp how to do it while I was sleeping!)

It's not a flesh thing.

We can't expect or force a spiritual concept to fit a physical concept!

A sermon on "Pray Without Ceasing" was delivered on March 10th, 1872, by C. H. Spurgeon. To distil his long-winded, theological, definition as a physical activity into one quoted phrase, he says, ""Pray without ceasing," is, if I read it aright, a most sweet and precious permit to the believer to pour out his heart at all times before the Lord".

Spurgeon never grasped the spiritual reality!

It's not a physical process!

To give an example that we can relate to, just like we breathe without ceasing and without thinking about it, (although we can think about and adjust it) so also is prayer without ceasing, only on a spiritual plane!

Of course, we can pray <u>with</u> thinking, <u>with</u> audible words, at specific times, at specific places (prayer closet), with others, for others or for specific reasons, but all of this kind of prayer is not the definition of 1 Thessalonians 5:17.

I searched on the internet to see if anyone had the spiritual answer… sadly I gave up looking as all I could find was about the same definition that Spurgeon had 140 years ago… that it's a "proper heart attitude" or it's a "mental outlook of joyful thanksgiving" or it's "when the Lord lays a burden on our hearts". Not!!

So how do we accomplish this?

When I asked God for His definition, He told me that we are linked to Him like a cord. He's giving us wisdom, knowledge, dreams, visions, ideas, prophecies, direction, power 24/7 and a portion of our brain <u>through the Holy Spirit</u>, is communicating back to Him, even if we don't consciously know it, even while asleep!

Another way to look at is a portion of our brain (soul) can be permanently switched on to the spiritual realm like a cell phone! That's praying (communicating with God) without ceasing. Ask the Holy Spirit to assist you in overcoming all spiritual handicaps and to allow you to tune into your praying without ceasing!

Let's insure that we daily allow the Holy Spirit to work through us to accomplish Father's will on earth as it is in Heaven!

Jesus covered SAC time when He said:

"But you, when you pray, go into your room, and when you have shut your door, pray to your Father who is in the secret place; and your Father who sees in secret will reward you openly." Matthew 6:6

If you want to go and grow more "in the spirit", and know when, where and what to hunt, you're going to have to have SAC time with God!

The Desert Fathers and Mothers proved how effective and enjoyable this key can be, as they loved to live in SAC time with God!!

SECTOR NINE

GIVE HIM YOUR P.A.W.

> **HUNTING TIP**
>
> Never worship a hunter… idols are for dummies!

Hunters, me included, get very excited before a hunt, and especially during and after a successful hunt. This is true also of an Xtreme Game Hunt. Closer bonds with those you've hunted with are formed and one can hardly wait until the next hunt, when you can be together again.

Although this is jubilation and joy, rather than praise and worship, we must remember before, during and after an Xtreme Game Hunt, that without God, there is no hunt. He should be sending you on every hunt (not of your own will and desire).

Develop a closer relationship with Him by continually giving Him your P.A.W.—Praise and Worship!

We are also commanded to praise and worship Him.

The following is just a few examples in the Bible, written by God, advising us to praise and worship Him, and only Him.

"Every man have praise of God." 1 Corinthians 4:5

"Then a voice came from the throne, saying, "Praise our God, all you His servants and those who fear Him, both small and great!" Revelation 19:5

See 1 Chronicles 16:8-12/Psalm 47 and 48.

"Exalt the Lord our God, and worship at His footstool—He is holy." Psalm 99:5

And God wants you to worship Him in spirit and in truth.

"But the hour is coming, and now is, when the true worshipers will worship the Father in spirit and truth; for the Father is seeking such to worship Him." John 4:23

Praise and worship other than that is not what God is looking for. In other words, popular songs called worship, is not what God is seeking. People like popular songs and dancing and clapping, which can boast our emotions and make us feel good (and make song writers and musicians popular and wealthy), but God is looking for worship in spirit and in truth. I'm sensing the daggers from "worship" leaders being thrown at me now! Popular songs would be more accurately described as praise, which is a good thing also.

"These people draw near to Me with their mouth, and honor Me with their lips, but their heart is far from Me. And in vain they worship Me, teaching as doctrines the commandments of men." Matthew 15:8-9/Isaiah 29:13/Mark 7:6

Satan wanted Jesus (and also wants you) to worship him.

"Then Jesus said to him, "Away with you, Satan! For it is written, 'You shall worship the Lord your God, and Him only you shall serve.'" Deuteronomy 6:13/Matthew 4:10/ Luke 4:8

Your spiritual language in prayer, praise and worship is what God loves to hear from us. Read more about your spiritual tongue under T'NT in the Weapons Sector.

Do not overlook praise and worship of God <u>in spirit and in truth</u>. He is deserving of it and all that we have, as He gave us all, including our existence.

Without Him, we are nothing!

<u>PAW is a major key in going in the spirit!</u>

<u>God gave us this key that a few have found!</u>

"Serve the LORD with gladness: <u>come before his presence with singing.</u>" Psalm 100:2

"Enter into his gates with thanksgiving, and into his courts with praise: be thankful unto him, and bless his name." Psalm 100:4

When you praise and worship and sing in the spirit (tongue speech) your spiritual senses will open and you will travel in the spirit into the heavens, through heaven's gates, through heavens court's and directly into God's presence!

Although going/travelling in the spirit can be a spontaneous happening or happen during prayer, PAW is almost like pushing a button to take you into heaven!

PAW is also another major key, that the Desert Fathers and Mothers learned and practiced often and long. They also sang the Psalms. They were constantly in spiritual PAW, which brought them blessings beyond imagination!

SECTOR TEN

COMPROMISE

> **HUNTING TIP**
>
> Short cuts lead to dead ends!

Many times, a hunter will compromise and hunt without a license; poach; hunt at night; take more than is allowed; or hunt by methods that aren't legal (certain trapping methods, illegal bait, and illegal weapons) to make things easier for him or her. They'll also shoot anything that shows up in the woods or even along the road when they're driving!

I've known people like this!

Sadly, this is done all over the world. In Africa, this is taken so seriously, that poachers are shot when caught in the act!

There is a similar affliction that affects Christians and their assemblies in our land—this is called compromise. What does God say about compromise?

In Jeremiah 7:18 we see that the people were making cakes and drink to offer/sacrifice to the "queen of heaven." God said, "They provoke Me to anger."

Jeremiah warned them about this, but they "saw no evil" (Jeremiah 44:17) in doing this and said, that whenever they stop sacrifices to the "queen of heaven" they were "consumed by the sword and famine." Jeremiah 44:18

When the people of Judah were worshipping and making these sacrifices to the "queen of heaven", what did God do about it?

"I will set my face against you for evil, and to cut off all Judah." Jeremiah 44:11

God cursed man, beast, trees, fruit AND the land for this compromise! (Jeremiah 7:20)

<u>Not only that</u>!

Because of their compromise, which was idolatry, <u>God told Jeremiah to not even pray nor intercede for them… it would be a waste of time;</u> "For I will not hear you." Jeremiah 7:16

They wrongly determined that this small compromise could not cause harm, and was, in fact, <u>necessary</u>!

A 5th Century BC Egyptian papyrus was found, that recorded, that the Jews, while they were in Egypt, also worshipped the "queen of heaven!" LAB-NIV Commentary Jeremiah 7:18

"Among the Roman Catholics, Mary is recognized not only as the Mother of God, (declared in Ephesus in 431 AD), but also, according to modern Popes, as the <u>QUEEN OF HEAVEN</u>, Queen of the Universe, Seat of Wisdom, and even the Spouse of the Holy Spirit." Time Magazine, "Handmaid or Feminist?" December 30, 1991, p. 62-66

A "queen of heaven" is worshipped by Roman Catholics, the Orthodox and <u>even</u> many Protestants, as well as Muslims, non-Christians, Buddhists, Hindus, and native Americans. Other religions, cults and cultures, also worship various queens or goddesses of heaven.

Most, if not all of us, would say, that compromise is a way of life, as it is part of government, finance and relationships—all of society! It is difficult to imagine anyone not compromising in some way in their life.

But compromise against God is what people have decided to do… not God.

<u>Compromise is a very deceptive trap of satan to destroy you!</u>

If you were to ask a Christian if they ever compromise against God, which is a sin, they most probably would say "no", regardless of their denomination or doctrine.

They are deceived!

For instance, how many denominations compromise by accepting known deliberate sin amongst its members?

Let's see if you and your "church", will pass this one example, of God's biblical standards.

In 1 Corinthians 5 it says Christians are not to associate with people who call themselves Christian who are fornicators (sexually immoral), greedy, idolaters, slanderers, drunkards (includes drug use), or swindlers.

It says that you are supposed to expel them from you and the assembly and hand them over to satan! In other words, not pray for them or fellowship with them, in the hopes that satan will afflict them to bring them to repentance before it's too late (before they die in sin and are lost forever).

Just in this one chapter of the Bible, do you compromise with God?

Does the "church" you attend compromise with God?

Are any members of your "church" allowed to stay, even though they fall into one or more of these areas?

Would you take the easy path, look the other way and compromise or would you stand with the truth… God's Truth? Sadly, I rarely meet a person who turns from compromise, even when I show them what God's Word says! People about 99% of the time, choose their own doctrine, calling it mercy or grace or patience, etc., when it comes to dealing with compromisers. Usually they consider me too harsh or judgmental or they become offended when I point out God's Truth to them. Truth is absolute.

Are you a people-pleaser or a God-pleaser?

The Desert Fathers and Mothers kept far away from compromisers. They knew how easily they can become corrupted, as 1 Corinthians 5:6 says. They despised lavish lifestyles and mammon, as they realized how deceptively it controls and destroys and gives rise to swindling and theft.

How many leaders live simple lifestyles who won't charge for their services? I have found it almost impossible to find a "church" or ministry that doesn't charge people for their services, such as weddings, baptisms and funerals. Most partnership clubs offer "special" prayers, "special" prophecies or private meetings with leadership *if* one "donates" (pays) a monthly fee. In other words, those who don't or can't pay, don't get!

How many "churches" or ministries do you know, who don't constantly ask you for tithes/offerings/donations?

God told Mel Tari (*Like a Mighty Wind*) and Reese Howells (*Rees Howells: Intercessor*), to never ask people for or tell people that you need money. God said we are to ask Him for any finances. He leads people to supply needed finances.

A poor Desert Father one time was offered more gold than King Solomon had possessed. He told satan and his gold, to both go to hell!

God isn't a dummy; He knows your circumstances and what you need, long before you do!

Problem is, that most want more than they need, to feed their idol (greed, desire, possessions)!

Imagine how many more people would have been saved from the lake of fire, had "churches" and leaders over the last 2000 years utilized the offerings, gifts and tithes for advancing the kingdom of God, rather than advancing their own lavish kingdoms!

"Be shepherds of God's flock that is under your care, serving as overseers—not because you must, but because you are willing, as God wants you to be; not greedy for money, but eager to serve; not lording it over those entrusted to you, but being examples to the flock." 1 Peter 5:2-3 NIV

Compromise.

Each person who says they are Christian, must examine their words and actions. If you think you don't compromise with your faith, you might also be surprised when you read the Sector on Altars.

Your actions not only affect you, but also others around you and even the land!

"You (God) destroy all who are unfaithful to you." Psalm 73:27 NIV

Ever compromised against God?

Sincerely go to Him in repentance—compromise no more!

Satan and the world are hunting you right now! They offer many temptation traps, especially for compromise. A Christian who desires a close, spiritual relationship with God, especially the Xtreme Big Game Hunter, cannot accept compromises for their lives nor associate with compromising people who call themselves Christian.

The Standard Of God

How can we know for absolutely sure, what STANDARD God wants from each one of us?

Is the Roman Catholic standard the right standard or some Orthodox one or the Pentecostal one or perhaps some "non-denominational" group that shuns these man-made religions and meets in someone's home to do their own "organic church"?

Who's right, who's wrong?

Is there right and wrong, is there black and white, or does God consider "gray areas" or sub-STANDARDS acceptable?

Father God told the disciples (and therefore us) in Matthew 17:5, "This is My Son whom I love; with Him I am well pleased. <u>Listen to Him</u>!"

So… THE STANDARD of God is Jesus… what He says and what He does.

Maybe most of you already knew that answer. It's doubtful that Christians would argue for a different STANDARD of God than Jesus, so let's look at what Jesus says is the STANDARD of God…

Jesus said in John 15:5, "I am the vine; you are the branches. If a man remains in me and I in him, he will bear much fruit; apart from me you can do nothing."

So... Jesus, THE STANDARD of Father God, says that apart from Me "you can do <u>nothing</u>". This is extremely black and white (no gray) ... you're in or you're out. You're connected with Jesus, <u>which includes ALL of His teachings</u>, or you're not. A branch is either in The Vine or a worthless stick on the ground... you can't be both! Maybe the stick thinks they have value, but sticks without Jesus "can do nothing."

Sticks aren't THE STANDARD!

Many statistics tell us, that the majority of people in the world that say they're Christian, are following their own standard or a religious standard, rather than THE STANDARD. They may say they believe in Jesus, but the Bible says in James 2:19, "You believe that there is one God. Good! Even the demons believe that - and shudder." Evil spirits aren't saved. Just to believe in God doesn't meet THE STANDARD.

"Get 'em to say the sinner's prayer and we got another one", is what many leaders and denominations think and teach around the world today. This is a gross, sub-STANDARD, that is arguably one of the worst inventions of man!

I was at a conference, where one of the leaders kept a log of how many people she could get to accept Jesus at a bus station once a week! They received no guidance on repentance and no mentoring. Statistics prove that without spiritual warfare... **95% of these people will be lost again within 1 year**, if they ever were serious and saved to begin with! (See Sector 5 SAFARI) This is just one sub-STANDARD example.

Man's (sticks) standards aren't THE STANDARD!

Jesus was consistently coming against the religious leaders and teachers (sticks) of His day for their twisted interpretation of God's STANDARDS.

I know that you might be saying, but Al, Jesus STANDARD'S are such things as love of others, love of God, don't sin, obedience... these are all STANDARD'S of course, but I believe that today's leaders and people have become like the Pharisees and Sadducees (sticks), twisting and interpreting God's STANDARD'S to meet their own standards and thus taking an active (even in ignorance) role with satan in <u>sending</u>

billions and themselves to the lake of fire! These sticks aren't in The Vine! They're not following THE STANDARD!

Publically exposing false teaching/teachers and sub-STANDARDS is what Jesus did. If we don't follow this same STANDARD, then aren't we no better than a stick?

Hey Al... that's tough talk! Yeah... I've been speaking this STANDARD for years. The wolves (sticks) don't listen to me anymore than they listened to Jesus. The sheep rarely listen either... they seem to prefer what they want or accept or do what wolves are saying is the standard!

Many people and groups say they follow THE STANDARD but let's expose just a few twisted standards or compromising...

God says "Love others".

Twisted by man to mean: Non-Gospel belief systems and deliberate sin accepted. Chrislam is a great example of a satanically inspired standard of "love others".

God says "Love God".

Twisted by man to mean: Religion standards come ahead of God's STANDARDS.

God says "Don't sin".

Twisted by man to mean: Sin subject to individual/religion interpretation.

God says "Obedience".

Twisted by man to mean: Self worship or someone else's sub-standards first.

We can take God's STANDARDS that are easily found in the Bible (look them up... don't take someone's word, some denomination's word or the world's word on it) and compare them to our own standards to discover whether it's a God STANDARD or not.

You'll find that God's STANDARDS are very black and white, right or wrong, sin or holy, you're going to the lake of fire or going to heaven kind of STANDARDS. It's people that make up "gray areas", not God.

It really is a simple process. We're either a branch in The Vine (Jesus) or a stick on the ground.

We must each examine ourselves closely to see if we meet THE STANDARD. If we're sub-STANDARD, either deliberately or in ignorance, then stop, repent and pick up THE STANDARD. If we're compromising, involved with compromising people, or a compromising group, then stop, repent and pick up THE STANDARD! If you're not sure, picture Jesus doing it, then decide or ask the Holy Spirit for direction.

You'd think, "Why would anyone want to be a prisoner to a sub-STANDARD"? It's happening all over the world... people imprisoned by social/religious acceptance; family/friend pressure; indifference; ignorance; false teachings; religious status; "church" position; personal agendas; guilt; pride; money. Rhoda and I experience these prisoners all the time. We point out THE STANDARD to people, friends and family, yet, almost 100% of the time, they decide to keep their own standards or compromise anyway. Funny thing, they also don't want to associate with us anymore! That's OK... we prefer to work with people who don't want to shame Jesus. We work with Silver Bullets of God all over the world, who strive for God's STANDARD... who refuse to compromise.

Be proud to follow THE STANDARD and <u>expose</u> those who spit on Jesus and the rest of us with their sub-STANDARDS and false standards and compromising.

Remember... without THE STANDARD we "can do nothing" ... it's black and white... we're either a branch or a stick!

You can't be both!

"All men will hate you because of Me, but he who stands firm to the end will be saved." Matthew 10:22/Luke 21:17

DELIVER TO SATAN

"It is actually reported that there is immorality among you and of such a kind that does not even happen among the Gentiles, namely, that a man has the wife of his father. ²And you are arrogant! Should you not rather be grieved? Put the man who practiced this deed out of your midst. ³For even though I am absent in the body but present in spirit, I have already judged the man who has so committed this as if I were present. ⁴When you come together and I am with you in spirit with the power of our Lord Jesus, ⁵in the name of our Lord Jesus deliver this man to Satan for destruction of the flesh that his spirit may be saved in the day of our Lord." 1 Corinthians 5:1-5

In this teaching, Paul has been told that someone in the Corinthian assembly is committing incest, but that the members of this group have not properly dealt with him. Paul had earlier warned the Corinthians not to associate with immoral people, but they decided to ignore this command from God, by now accepting incest. Paul instructs them to remove this man from their midst and deliver him to satan. Indeed, both the man, because of incest, and the entire assembly, because of failure to impose discipline, are guilty of sin before God.

Why did they compromise and accept sin?

Without sugar-coating it, Paul bluntly tells them in v. 2 because "you are arrogant" (prideful, stubborn and rebellious)! This was a continuing problem with the Corinthians as we see from chapter 4:6, 18, 19. They think they have the right to do anything they want (1 Corinthians 6:12, 10:23) and that they claim to possess superior knowledge (1 Corinthians 3:18 and 8:1-2).

This is a problem for most still today!

Even Paul, their own apostle, has difficulty trying to convince these haughty, disobedient people to deal with unrepentant sin and that when they don't, they themselves are guilty of sin!

Paul is telling them, that this decision is not his personal opinion or personal doctrine, but is pronounced with authority on behalf of Jesus, with His approval (v. 4-5).

Jesus said, "treat them as you would a pagan or a tax collector." Matthew 18:17

Paul is directing this entire assembly, to turn from their compromising rebellion; be grieved; put this man out of their midst; deliver him to satan and repent for not doing so sooner, in order to receive God's forgiveness.

If the Corinthians refuse to follow God's instructions, the Christian community itself will be placed under divine condemnation as outsiders are (v. 13). Those who claim to be Christian must be characterized by holiness and obedience to God's Word and <u>must</u> remove blatant, unrepentant sinners from their midst and turn them over to satan or find themselves in deliberate, unrepentant sin and under judgment!

Paul tells them that this man is found guilty of unrepentant sin in God's court, (as in the case of Ananias and Sapphira in Acts 5) and the sentence is

1. To be put away from them

    <u>and</u>

2. Delivered to satan for the sentencing process to be carried out.

That sounds ominous... delivered to satan!

I've <u>never</u> in my life heard of anyone or any assembly ever doing that. All I've <u>ever</u> seen or heard any Christian or group do or say is, that they either ignore or accept sin or they pray for <u>un</u>repentant sinners, and/or bless them, and/or intercede for them and/or have the "we don't judge 'em, we just love 'em" philosophy… and hope one of these personal doctrines will change their minds, stop their sin and they'll repent, thinking that unrepentant sinners mingling with "loving, moral" Christians will rub off on them perhaps! Some also say, "I'm not led by God to do that".

"A little leaven leavens the whole lump of dough." Galatians 5:9

All of these man-made doctrines/procedures, although good-intentioned, are stubborn, rebellious opposition of God's will! It is all sin!

"Rebellion is as sinful as witchcraft and stubbornness as bad as worshiping idols." I Samuel 15:23

People declare themselves god, when they ignore or overrule God's Word!

We read where Paul delivered two others to satan in 1 Timothy 1:20, "Among these people are Hymenaeus and Alexander, whom I have handed over to Satan in order to teach them not to dishonor God" God's Word translation.

These men were once faithful leaders, who became false leaders and were leading others astray. They had to be dealt with, according to God's will.

As common sense tells us, this isn't a physical handing over such as handcuffing and taking a person or an entire group to prison… it is a spiritual sentencing… a spiritual action… although there are physical repercussions!

As God removed the hedge of protection around Job to allow satan to attack him (with restrictions), so too, when we deliver an unrepentant sinner to satan, God removes His protection "for destruction of the flesh that his spirit may be saved" 1 Corinthians 5:5. The destruction of the flesh serves the purpose of making possible, the restoring of the sinner's soul before they die (i.e. the prodigal son).

I know many of you are not liking God's discipline commands, but we must remember, that we are God-pleasers, not people-pleasers and we don't want to fall into satan's trap like Eve did, that Paul warns the Corinthians about in 2 Corinthians 11:3 -4, "But I am afraid that just as Eve was deceived by the serpent's cunning, your minds may somehow be led astray from your sincere and pure devotion to Christ. For if someone comes to you and preaches a Jesus other than the Jesus we preached, or if you receive a different spirit from the Spirit you received, or a different gospel from the one you accepted, you put up with it easily enough".

How God allows the sentence of the unrepentant to be carried out is His responsibility, not ours. We don't see Paul praying for, interceding for or pleading/reasoning/compromising with Hymenaeus and

Alexander. Paul is done with them unless they repent. Paul's' position and relationship with Father, Jesus and the Holy Spirit, his destiny and his eternity are taken seriously… so should ours be.

Why would anyone follow some distorted, religious, man-made definition of "love", and risk their position with God and with salvation?

As we aren't given directions on how exactly to deliver the unrepentant to satan… how can it be done? Can anyone do it or can only an apostle or large group, do it?

What if a leader, group or even a denomination of millions, are like the Corinthians, who refuse to listen to one person like you or me, regarding following the Word of God?

God tells us through Paul, in 1 Corinthians 2:15, "But he who is spiritual, judges all things, yet he himself is rightly judged by no one. For "who has known the mind of the Lord that he may instruct Him? "But we have the mind of Christ".

God says that just one led by the Holy Spirit "judges all things". <u>God's Word, with the authority of Jesus Christ</u>, <u>backs up just one Holy Spirit-filled person, to judge others of sin!</u>

All who refuse to repent or who choose to rebel against God's discipline, preferring the Corinthian ways, will be guilty of sin themselves and <u>must</u> be put away from you <u>and</u> delivered to satan. An entire unrepentant, sinful leadership and/or group are highly unlikely to leave the building if you judge them, so you will have to do as God directs…

1. Put yourself away from them (leave)

   and

2. Turn them all over to satan!

I've done this by verbally judging, as Paul did, and saying something like, "I deliver him/her/them to satan in the name of our Lord Jesus for destruction of the flesh that their spirit may be saved in the day of our Lord"! The sentencing process then commences and moves forward and continues until repentance or their death! I'm done!

What happens if you don't or won't follow God's will?

After this teaching, do I really need to answer that question?

Whoever reads this biblical teaching and is involved in unrepentant sin and/or stubbornly refuses to obey God in how to discipline unrepentant sinners and/or is rebelling against God and His Word, I judge you now and deliver you to satan in the name of our Lord Jesus for destruction of the flesh that your spirit may be saved in the day of our Lord!

What classifies as sin and how to deal with it, is what God says, not what people or a religious, man-made doctrine says!

CAVE OF ADULLAM DECISION

In 1 Samuel, we read of Saul being anointed king over Israel and his loss of favor with God due to his self will and disobedience. David, the shepherd boy, is anointed by Samuel to be the new king, yet he waited over 20 years for this to be realized.

During these 20 years, God protected David from 21 attempts made on his life by Saul.

David eventually made his way to the cave of Adullam…

"David therefore departed from there and escaped to the cave of Adullam. So, when his brothers and all his father's house heard it, they went down there to him. And everyone who was in distress, everyone who was in debt, and everyone who was discontented gathered to him. So, he became captain over them. And there were about four hundred men with him." 1 Samuel 22:1-2

David and his 400 men had a cave and God on their side. Saul had national (world) acceptance, lived in luxury, many people with him, but without God on their side.

We can identify David as Jesus and his men as the true Church today, who are obedient to God; who reject and prefer to be separate from religion (compromising, false and a spiritually dead "church"). Saul and his many followers can be identified with today's "worldly church";

having the behemoth business organizations, wealth and crowds, but without the power of the Holy Spirit.

400 men chose to be with the chosen of God... separate from Saul's Israel.

Saul's way ended with Saul, his entire house and army being destroyed at the hands of the Philistines on Mt. Gilboa with the survivors fleeing their cities, which were then occupied by the Philistines (1 Chronicles 10).

<u>God killed Saul</u> for his transgressions; for compromising; for working with a witch/familiar spirit and because "he did not inquire of the Lord". God turned the kingdom over to David (1 Chronicles 10: 13-14).

Only then did Israel (what was left of it) and the elders (leaders) rally around David, to accept him as their true king (1 Chronicles 11).

We notice from history, that David and these mighty men separated themselves from Saul, his followers and kingdom. People couldn't confuse David and his men with those of Saul's Israel, as they didn't collaborate or compromise with them.

One camp was obedient to God, the other were disobedient compromisers. Surely Israel, its leaders and people knew for many years, that David had been anointed by Samuel to be king, but instead decided to choose a different path more to their liking.

Can we see this today in the false "church", run by rebellious organizations, and rebellious leaders with a following of rebellious false Christians... choosing to accept/collaborate/compromise with sin, transgressions, man-made doctrines, and "not inquiring of the Lord", when the truth is easily found (and ignored) in the Bible?

False kingdoms cannot join or be part of Jesus and the true Church!

David's first act, was to immediately defeat the Jebusites, to make Jerusalem the new capital of Israel!

We then see great supernatural acts of valor, recorded by the mighty men who had been with David in the cave of Adullam...

"Josheb-Basshebeth the Tachmonite, chief among the captains. He was called Adino the Eznite, because he had killed eight hundred men at one time. And after him was Eleazar the son of Dodo, the Ahohite, one of the three mighty men with David when they defied the Philistines who were gathered there for battle, and the men of Israel had retreated. He arose and attacked the Philistines until his hand was weary, and his hand stuck to the sword (fought an army alone with God's power). The LORD brought about a great victory that day; and the people returned after him only to plunder. And after him was Shammah the son of Agee the Hararite. The Philistines had gathered together into a troop where there was a piece of ground full of lentils. So, the people fled from the Philistines. But he stationed himself in the middle of the field, defended it, and killed the Philistines (fought them alone with God's power). So, the LORD brought about a great victory.

Then three of the thirty chief men went down at harvest time and came to David at the cave of Adullam. And the troop of Philistines encamped in the Valley of Rephaim. David was then in the stronghold, and the garrison of the Philistines was then in Bethlehem. And David said with longing, "Oh, that someone would give me a drink of the water from the well of Bethlehem, which is by the gate!" So, the three mighty men broke through the camp of the Philistines, drew water from the well of Bethlehem that was by the gate, and took it and brought it to David (3 men against the Philistine camp) … Now Abishai the brother of Joab, the son of Zeruiah, was chief of another three. He lifted his spear against three hundred men, killed them, and won a name among these three. Was he not the most honored of three? Therefore, he became their captain. However, he did not attain to the first three.

Benaiah was the son of Jehoiada, the son of a valiant man from Kabzeel, who had done many deeds. He had killed two lion-like heroes of Moab. He also had gone down and killed a lion in the midst of a pit on a snowy day. And he killed an Egyptian, a spectacular man. The Egyptian had a spear in his hand; so he went down to him with a staff, wrested the spear out of the Egyptian's hand, and killed him with his own spear. These things Benaiah the son of Jehoiada did, and won a name among three mighty men." 2 Samuel 23:8-22

This cave was much more than a hiding place; it was where David and his men became intimate with the Lord. These men went into the cave in distress; in debt; hunted and discontented and came out to become known as "The Mighty Men" with God's power, while Saul, his followers and kingdom were destroyed by God.

People today must abandon false kingdoms and false leaders that are failures and doomed to destruction!

Each of us must reject false leaders and false kingdoms and deliberately walk into the spiritual cave of Adullam to join Jesus and His Mighty Warriors… to not only learn to be intimate with God, but also to be blessed as true children of God; to obtain dunamis or God's power in our daily lives; be able to defeat the enemies of God; receive the same protection from God that David received and also to preserve our place within the true kingdom of God… now and into eternity!

We can't accept/collaborate or compromise with what is an abomination to God!

In life, we have two choices… obedience or disobedience to God…

Let's each of us walk into the cave of Adullam and become mighty in the Lord!

True Christians must set themselves apart for God.

Don't try for shortcuts!

SECTOR ELEVEN

D.I.G. FOR IT

> **HUNTING TIP**
>
> No quarter expected… none given!

Hunting is a chosen activity. If you don't want to go and hunt, you don't go. Maybe it's cold, rainy, snowy or windy. Maybe you're tired and it's still dark outside and you haven't had much success lately. Any of these excuses have kept people in bed and from the hunt.

The most success I think I've ever had, was at the crack of dawn, or at sunset, or in miserable weather. Had I stayed home or went home early, my freezer and stomach would be empty! Many times, you have to dig down and force yourself to go, otherwise hunting isn't your thing, so you should think of another pastime.

In the spiritual realm, God is your hunting Guide. He'll sometimes tap you on the shoulder to go on a spiritual encounter—right then and there if you're willing.

So, how do we get God, to give us the nod to go and do something for His glory? Spiritual experiences can and do happen with people of any faith, not just Christians, as many involved in the occult can attest. And we all know of a man named Saul, who hated Jesus and hunted Christians down, who had a spiritual encounter that radically converted him in Acts 9.

So, if spiritual experiences can happen to <u>anyone</u>, even non-Christians, why are they not happening to <u>everyone</u>?

Examining the Bible, we see that God chooses when, where, how and whom He will deal with.

For instance, God came in person and met with Abraham and Sarah (Genesis 18); as well as with Joshua (Joshua 5) to give him war plans (Joshua called Him Lord), and God physically wrestled with Jacob (Genesis 32:24-30), so Jacob must have been a strong guy! The Bible is full of wonderful experiences like these spiritual revelations, dreams, visions and meetings with God and angels—too many to mention.

But can we do anything to <u>get</u> these experiences to happen?

Usually any treasure that we seek, we have to DIG for it!

So how does one DIG for the treasure of doing things in the Spirit?

D.I.G. is another acronym that the Lord gave me, utilizing three very small, yet powerful words of God. There are only six letters in these three dynamite words from God! Three words that can change your relationship and walk with God.

The first very powerful word we'll discuss from the acronym D.I.G., is DO.

THE "D" WORD

This is perhaps the most powerful of the three words.

IF you're following God's Word and directions and then GOing when He directs you to GO, whether physically or "in the spirit," yet you won't or don't DO what you're supposed to DO when you arrive, what good would going "in the spirit" be to you, God or anyone else?

The Lord just brought to my attention the Israelites and how God heard their cries and brought them out of Egypt, but when they finally reached Canaan, their promised land, they were afraid to fight and would not DO the final step to take the land that was theirs! God was so upset He wanted to kill them all right then, yet Moses convinced God to have mercy, so instead He sent them back into the wilderness for 40 years until everyone over the age of 20 died there, except Caleb and Joshua. None would see their promised land, because they wouldn't DO what God wanted them to do! (Numbers 13 and 14). The men who convinced the congregation not to DO as God directed, died by a plague. (Numbers 14:37)

God takes it very seriously when we won't DO as He directs us to DO, especially IF we GO and then back out when we get there!

Fast forward 40 years later and now Moses is dead and Joshua is in charge of the congregation and we all know that he didn't fail to DO as he was told!

Cowardice doomed the Israelites with Moses. Despite all that they had been through and seen with God, they were still afraid to DO the warfare, even though they knew God was with them.

We look at this story today, sitting comfortably in our armchairs, thinking how silly these people were to disobey God, to end up being punished by wandering in the wilderness for 40 years.

Is this a good place to point out how many "Christians" today are DOing the same thing?

How many "Christians" today, are DOing what Jesus said they should be DOing?

How many "Christians" today, even read the Word, let alone follow it?

How many "Christians" live in deliberate sin and disobedience?

How many "Christians" hold this world dearer to their heart, then they DO God and their eternal future?

"For where your treasure is, there will your heart be also." Luke 12:34

Many Christians mistakenly think, they can DO whatever they want and they get a free ride into heaven one day, because God is "so good to everyone."

What does Jesus say about that?

"Not everyone who says to Me, 'Lord, Lord,' shall enter the kingdom of heaven, but he who does the will of My Father in heaven. Many will say to Me in that day, 'Lord, Lord, have we not prophesied in Your name, cast out demons in Your name, and done many wonders in Your name?' And then I will declare to them, 'I never knew you; depart from Me, you who practice lawlessness!" Matthew 7:21-23

When "Christians" like this, stand at their judgment, they shouldn't be surprised when they are treated without mercy!

This is a tough message that is rarely, if ever, said in a "church", as people DOn't want to hear such truths and leaders DOn't want to tell such truths.

We are warned of this!

"For the time will come when they will not endure sound doctrine; but after their own lusts shall they heap to themselves teachers, having itching ears; And they shall turn away their ears from the truth, and shall be turned unto fables." 2 Timothy 4:3-4

THE "I" WORD

God's second small, yet very powerful word from D.I.G., is the word IF.

This word "IF", is used over1500 times in the Bible!

"IF my people… shall humble themselves, and pray, and seek my face, and turn from their wicked ways; then will I hear from heaven…" 2 Chronicles 7:14

"Bring all the tithes into the storehouse, that there may be food in My house, and try Me now in this," Says the Lord of hosts, "IF I will not open for you the windows of heaven and pour out for you such blessing that there will not be room enough to receive it." Malachi 3:10

"IF you ask anything in my name, I will do it." John 14:14

"IF you love me, keep my commandments." John 14:15

"IF anyone loves Me, he will keep My word; and My Father will love him, and We will come to him and make Our home with him." John 14:23

"IF anyone does not abide in Me, he is cast out as a branch and is withered; and they gather them and throw them into the fire, and they are burned." John 15:6

This is only a sampling of God's powerful Word—and what happens is <u>conditional</u>, IF we choose to follow, ignore, or do the opposite of what this Word declares.

God has many conditions for us, including THE BIG IF! We all know what happens <u>IF</u> one chooses Jesus as their Lord and Savior and what happens IF one does not!

I can't DIG into all of God's IF's for you… each person must do their own digging for this "in the spirit" treasure and as you DIG more into the "IF" word of God and follow His conditions, your spirituality will grow and more fruit will be born!

THE "G" WORD

The "G" word in D.I.G. stands for "GO". When God wants us to GO somewhere <u>or</u> not GO somewhere, any disobedience, adversely affects our relationship with Him; our spiritual life and perhaps even our physical life!

What IF Noah had decided not to GO into the ark with his family? What IF Lot didn't GO from Sodom?

And… what IF Paul decided to GO to Asia and Bithynia and preach the word, when he was told <u>not</u> to GO?

"Now when they had gone through Phrygia and the region of Galatia, they were forbidden by the Holy Spirit to preach the word in Asia. After they had come to Mysia, they tried to go into Bithynia, but the Spirit did not permit them." Acts 16:6-7

But wait… isn't preaching the Word a good thing?

Yes, it is, however, God's instructions to us to GO, or not to GO must be followed, even IF we think what <u>we</u> want to do is a good thing.

This comes down to timing or ban issues of when or IF to GO, as God will have us GO or stop us from GOing for a reason… even if we can't see a reason—<u>we must listen</u>!

<u>Every battle is not ours, even when/if people want and expect you to do something. Check with the Holy Spirit if a hunt or battle is yours to undertake.</u>

Although the Word does tell us to GO and carry out certain things… there can be timing restrictions, as we have seen with Paul.

There are also total bans, such as Jesus <u>commanding</u> us, "Do <u>not</u> give what is holy to the dogs; nor cast your pearls before swine, lest they trample them under their feet, and turn and tear you in pieces." Matthew 7:6

These few teachings also show us, that we should GO to His Word, and learn <u>precisely</u> what it is He expects… not what we interpret, or want or think is holy and good; and as we learn, we can discover the TRUE God (not a made-up version). Then our relationship with God and GOing "in the spirit" can develop!

IF one isn't interested in seeing or listening to what God <u>really</u> says and expects, should a person expect to GO in the spirit much, or at all?

IF you will GO and DIG into His Word, you will find many treasures waiting for you to assist you in GOing in the spirit!

IF a person is not willing to GO and meet with God… how can a person meet with God, unless God decides to materialize in front of you, wave and say, "Hi it's Me, you know, the Guy you've been ignoring?"

IF a person GOes to "church" an hour or so every week, perhaps because they think they should, and that's the extent of their relationship with God… is God really their <u>God</u>?

Should they really expect to GO in the spirit or reach new and deeper levels of intimacy with God or be a successful Silver Bullet of God or Big Game Hunter?

IF a person is not hearing <u>or</u> listening to God and they GO where they want in life, where is their life headed? It's on the path of failure according to God's Standard!

SUPERHEROES

A typical definition of a superhero, is someone possessing "extraordinary or superhuman powers" and dedicated to protecting the public.

When I was a boy there were superheroes such as The Lone Ranger, Zorro and Superman. They didn't sit around and let the bad guys win. They were power in action!

Some had superpowers; all were extraordinary.

Does this sound like you?

It better sound like you if you call yourself a Christian!

If you're not a Silver Bullet of God yet, then it's time you strapped on your superhero shoes and get Going!

Jesus said, "Most assuredly, I say to you, he who believes in Me, the works that I do he will do also; and greater works than these he will do, because I go to My Father. And whatever you ask in My name, that I will do, that the Father may be glorified in the Son. If you ask anything in My name, I will do it." John 14:12-14

So according to the Word of God, people who believe in Jesus, will do the same and better works than Jesus did!

That means, that the 2 billion people in the world that say they're Christian, should each be doing greater works than Jesus did, according to the Word of God, which doesn't lie.

Yet, we all know that isn't happening!

If it were happening, the other 5.5 billion people in the world would be astounded, at all the billions of daily miracles and would quickly realize who the true God of Heaven and earth is!

So, who's dropping the ball... God or those calling themselves Christian?

That was an easy question I know!

But is the answer an easy answer?

I believe the answer is an easy one, that is also in the Word.

There are certain factors that come into play, if doing what Jesus did and even greater works, is to become a reality.

Besides the few covered in this Sector already, a very big key is this next scripture.

"Are you so foolish? Having begun in the Spirit, are you now being made perfect by the flesh?" Galatians 3:3

OK... what does that mean? It means that people initially believe and have faith in a spiritual salvation when they accept Jesus as their Lord and Savior and yet continue on living a flesh-controlled life. Even well-intentioned motives are flesh-controlled, if not coming from Father. They don't have or don't let the Holy Spirit power work through them, as guided by the perfect will of Father in heaven!

Jesus never did anything of His own will! He led a totally Spirit-led, Spirit-powered life! Every miracle; every word He said; every action; came to Him from His (and our) Father! Jesus absolutely surrendered to His Father!

Jesus said, "I have glorified You (Father) on the earth. I have finished the work which You have given Me to do." John 17:4

I know of an American missionary couple that spent 5 years in the Philippines. When they came back to the USA, they admitted that they hadn't brought a single person to Christ! Why? Because they thought it would be a good idea to be missionaries there. They weren't Spirit led or Spirit controlled while there. God never sends you out to fail!

I know of a very successful spiritual warfare minister, who twice tried to start a "church". His efforts failed both times. He thought it would be a great addition, to his already successful spiritual warfare ministry. When he finally went to God to find out what happened, God said to him, "Did I tell you to start a church?"

I know of a successful international Xtreme Big Game Hunter from Mexico, who prepared for 2 years to go on a mission in Asia. On her way to the hunt, to join others from other countries, at a stopover in Paris, God asked her where she was going. This person, who regularly operated in the spiritual realm, had accepted an invitation to go on this hunt from people, yet never asked God for His will, approval or direction. God told her to go back to Mexico! She did! Wise move!

I know of another leader, who thinks God wants them in a certain fellowship, yet the people there contradict and compromise with the Word of God. If you think you hear God, but what you're doing contradicts or compromises with His Word, then you're hearing wrong. God never contradicts or compromises with His written Word!

These people that I mention above, are just 4 leaders that are "flesh-foolish" (Galatians 3:3), willfully deciding on their own to follow themselves, thus making themselves god. This kind of pride, disobedience, self-will, self-glory and self-idolization is typical among Christians. It should be rare among leaders! Is it any wonder that Christians aren't doing as Jesus did… or greater? Where's God's Superheroes? Where's all the Silver Bullets of God?

Stop Making Your Own Decisions!

Waiting for God's direction, doesn't mean doing nothing. Being "busy" to "accomplish" something, is the world's production method. If you're in ministry now, surrender to and go to God immediately, and from now on, to receive moment-by-moment instructions. You may be shocked to find out… you're on a collision course with failure!

To Be a True Conquering Superhero for God, you must always fly according to His flight plan… or you're flying solo!

When you are spending SAC time and communicating with the true God everyday as Jesus did, you will hear His voice and know Him. IF He says GO or don't GO, then obey Him… and your relationship will deepen and you will expand more and more spiritually, having revelations and gaining spiritual wisdom and spiritual knowledge and other Holy gifts. Spiritual fruit of miracles will manifest from you and you'll be receiving spiritual dreams and visions and experiencing bilocation and multi-location (more on that later) and be sensing, moving, growing and GOing in the spirit more and more!

That's what God wants!

Never fear to GO anywhere with God… as He GOes with you!

Jesus personally told me this in the mid-1960's, as I could see in the spirit what He wrote to me on the air! It was as if He was writing on a chalkboard with chalk right on the air! The words were printed out and then each letter dropped away after I read it.

He wrote: "Lo, I am with you always, even unto the end of the world." Matthew 28:20

He also said this 2,000 years ago.

I didn't find out that this was in the Bible, until after this spiritual event.

It's your move… GO!

DO You Want It?

DIG For It.

SECTOR TWELVE

BE F.I.T.

> **HUNTING TIP**
>
> Taunt hosts of evil game to attack you...
>
> it means more can be taken down at one time!

Let's look at three men who were FIT.

"These are the names of David's mighty men: Josheb-Basshebeth, a Tahkemonite, was chief of the Three; he raised his spear against eight hundred men, whom he killed in one encounter.

Next to him was Eleazar son of Dodai the Ahohite. As one of the three mighty men, he was with David when they taunted the Philistines gathered at Pas Dammim for battle. Then the men of Israel retreated, but he stood his ground and struck down the Philistines till his hand grew tired and froze to the sword. The LORD brought about a great victory that day. The troops returned to Eleazar, but only to strip the dead.

Next to him was Shammah son of Agee the Hararite. When the Philistines banded together at a place where there was a field full of lentils, Israel's troops fled from them. But Shammah took his stand in the middle of the field. He defended it and struck the Philistines down, and the LORD brought about a great victory.

During harvest time, three of the thirty chief men came down to David at the cave of Adullam, while a band of Philistines was encamped in the Valley of Rephaim.

At that time David was in the stronghold, and the Philistine garrison was at Bethlehem. David longed for water and said, "Oh, that someone would get me a drink of water from the well near the gate of Bethlehem!"

So, the three mighty men broke through the Philistine lines, drew water from the well near the gate of Bethlehem and carried it back to David. But he refused to drink it; instead, he poured it out before the LORD. "Far be it from me, O LORD, to do this!" he said. "Is it not the blood of men who went at the risk of their lives?" And David would not drink it. Such were the exploits of the three mighty men." 2 Samuel 23:8-17 NIV

Each time that I read about these guys, I get a spiritual shiver!

These guys were not warriors, they were conquerors!

They were FIT!

Josheb killed 800 men in one battle! Men who would have been trained Philistine warriors.

Eleazar taunted the enemy to fight and when the Israeli warriors ran, Eleazar stood his ground alone, defeating so many warriors, that his hand froze to his sword! Notice that the cowardly Israeli warriors only returned after Eleazar was done, to take spoils that they weren't entitled to!

Shammah did the same thing at another battle, when the Israeli warriors were afraid and ran. Shammah stood alone and struck down the Philistine warriors, obtaining the victory. No doubt the Israeli warriors returned again, after the fighting, to claim unearned spoils.

At David's minor appeal, all three of them together fought through the defenses of the Philistine army, just to bring their thirsty leader some water!

And let's not forget Samson, "He found a fresh jawbone of a donkey, reached out his hand and took it, and killed a thousand men with it." Judges 15:15

I love these guys—they teach me that with God, the victory is guaranteed! They teach me that being a warrior is not enough… that there is a place beyond a warrior… a place where one is FIT!

These guys enjoyed battling against evil, especially against overwhelming odds. They taunted the enemy to get them to fight! They fought alone when warriors fled from assisting them!

Ever meet a Christian like any of these guys, when it comes to spiritual warfare?

Ever meet Christians that flee in fear from what God wants them to do, only to return to accept the spoils of victory (glory and thanks) for themselves?

These guys had three things that set them apart from warriors.

They were FIT!

FIT is an acronym that the Holy Spirit gave me in this teaching.

F… FEARLESS

Although there are numerous scriptures that we can look at to justify this point, the Holy Spirit gave me Psalm 27.

"The Lord is my light and my salvation;
Whom shall I fear?
The Lord is the strength of my life;
Of whom shall I be afraid?
^{2} When the wicked came against me
To eat up my flesh,
My enemies and foes,
They stumbled and fell.
^{3} Though an army may encamp against me,
My heart shall not fear;
Though war may rise against me,
In this I will be confident.

^{4} One thing I have desired of the Lord,
That will I seek:
That I may dwell in the house of the Lord
All the days of my life,
To behold the beauty of the Lord,
And to inquire in His temple.
^{5} For in the time of trouble
He shall hide me in His pavilion;
In the secret place of His tabernacle

He shall hide me;
He shall set me high upon a rock.

⁶ And now my head shall be lifted up above my enemies all around me;
Therefore I will offer sacrifices of joy in His tabernacle;
I will sing, yes, I will sing praises to the Lord.

⁷ Hear, O Lord, when I cry with my voice!
Have mercy also upon me, and answer me.
⁸ When You said, "Seek My face,"
My heart said to You, "Your face, Lord, I will seek."
⁹ Do not hide Your face from me;
Do not turn Your servant away in anger;
You have been my help;
Do not leave me nor forsake me,
O God of my salvation.
¹⁰ When my father and my mother forsake me,
Then the Lord will take care of me.

¹¹ Teach me Your way, O Lord,
And lead me in a smooth path, because of my enemies.
¹² Do not deliver me to the will of my adversaries;
For false witnesses have risen against me,
And such as breathe out violence.
¹³ I would have lost heart, unless I had believed
That I would see the goodness of the Lord
In the land of the living.

¹⁴ Wait on the Lord;
Be of good courage,
And He shall strengthen your heart;
Wait, I say, on the Lord!"

God tells us to be Fearless… which is the first word making up the nature of these men. I just know that a smile came upon these guys faces, when they knew what was about to happen to the enemies of God!

Putting this in a Jesus perspective, does anyone believe that Jesus was ever afraid?

Jesus came head-to-head against satan and his entire army and beat them all… alone! Not to mention the corrupt religious leaders of the day!

The few warriors that Jesus had with Him, ran away when the going got tough. When these Jesus warriors became FIT after Pentecost… they became Conquerors for God!

Be Fearless… not fainthearted!

Let's look at three other conquerors who were FIT.

"Then Joshua spoke to the Lord in the day when the Lord delivered up the Amorites before the children of Israel, and he said in the sight of Israel: "Sun, stand still over Gibeon; And Moon, in the Valley of Aijalon." So the sun stood still, And the moon stopped, Till the people had revenge upon their enemies." Joshua 10:12-13a

Joshua commanded the sun and moon to stand still during battle and it did for an entire day!

Elijah didn't even lift a finger, when he called down fire from heaven to destroy a captain and fifty men, not once, but twice!

"Behold, there came fire down from heaven, and burnt up the two captains of the former fifties with their fifties." 2 Kings 1:14a

Elisha never broke into a sweat, against <u>an entire army that came against him</u> at Dothan! 2 Kings 6:13-23

This physical army surrounded Elisha, not knowing that a spiritual army of God was surrounding them! "the mountain was full of horses and chariots of fire round about Elisha." 2 Kings 6:17b

The physical army was defeated and the war ended!

These men were FIT… Fearless, Incorruptible and Tenacious!

Some might say that these are all nice stories, but what do they all have to do with me living in the 21st Century, with no warriors or armies coming against me?

Actually, every Christian has evil forces that are set against them every day! As well as, 100 million+ Christians are caught up in physical wars, terrorism and suffering persecution right now because of their faith (ChristianPost.com).

"For we do not wrestle (war) against flesh and blood, but against principalities, against powers, against the rulers of the darkness of this age, against spiritual hosts of wickedness in the heavenly places." Ephesians 6:12

I have seen what Elisha saw at Dothan myself!

I was in the spirit one time and saw that the hills and valley were full of angels on flaming chariots, that formed to the sides and behind me as I rode a white horse… after completing a great battle that God had brought me to.

As we rode through the valley, Jesus was standing on the path. I pulled my horse to a stop and jumped off to prostrate myself at His feet. Jesus brought me up and hugged me and kissed me on the cheek twice and said "Thank you my brother" (for the battle I had just completed). I got back on my horse… the heavenly host on fiery chariots continued to follow me through the valley. (I tell this entire testimony later on.)

I wasn't physically at Dothan like Elisha, although we were both operating in the spirit to overcome evil forces.

We are aware of the results of Elisha's battle in the physical… I am aware of the results of my battle against a principality in the spiritual realm. Had either of us not acted in the battle set before us… only God can determine the loss.

God gives us grace; He gives us weapons; He gives us gifts; but <u>there are some attributes that we must bring to the table</u> AND we must DO, if we are to be FIT Conquerors for God!

We discussed Fearless… Incorruptible and Tenacious are the other qualities of FIT.

I… INCORRUPTIBLE AND T… TENACIOUS

What if David's three mighty men, Joshua, Elijah and Elisha had been easily corrupted; or decided to be just plain old do-nothing children of God, or 'fair weather' children, who ran like chickens to be safe when rough conditions came?

Chickens scratch in the dirt and run and hide when things get rough… it's their nature. Eagles soar up and fly above the storm… it's their nature!

Eagles are FIT!

Conquerors for God are FIT!

Eagles cannot be convinced to be anything but an eagle… neither can Conquerors!

Conquerors will neither procrastinate nor retreat…they must advance; they cannot be corrupted by fame, money, politics, religion, nor the world's attractions; they're driven to advance the Kingdom of God against any obstacles, as God directs… it's their nature!

How much can athletes accomplish if they aren't fit?

How much can a Christian accomplish for God if they aren't FIT?

When you move into this higher spiritual realm with God and into heaven, you will need a "thick hide" or "thick skin", as evil entities will attack you, your family, your friends and your life… even your pets!

They'll attack you when you're awake and when you're asleep.

You may lose your job; your home; your money… and maybe your life, if you're not careful! I heard of one pastor in our area, that lost his mind attempting high level spiritual warfare on his own over the region, ending up in a hospital. I applaud his bravery, but more is needed! You need to operate in the spirit and <u>wait</u> for God's strategy, weapons and timing. (Deliverance fixes this problem of evil spirits attacking his mind.)

Besides spiritual attack, you'll notice "friends" and relatives either directly attacking you or starting to ignore you. They will be jealous, resentful, and/or not-accepting of the "new you."

"Then Jesus told them, "A prophet is honored everywhere except in his own hometown and among his relatives and his own family." Mark 6:4 NLT

You will find Christian leaders, who don't experience the spiritual realm like you do, will avoid you, not believe you, wave their certificate in your face, asking to see yours, and/or openly attack you. These people have issues with spiritual pride, jealousy, position-protecting, and blindness from evil entities keeping them from truth.

It will be the rare Christian, who will insist that you teach them what you know, so they can better their lives, destroy the evil kingdom, set captives free and advance God's kingdom!

Be wise when it comes to discussing this information, as it can bring turmoil.

Jesus gives good advice, "<u>Never</u> give what is holy to dogs or throw your pearls before pigs. Otherwise, they will trample them with their feet and then turn around and attack you." Matthew 7:6 ISV

During a pause while writing this Sector, Father God let me feel some of the anguish that He feels, when His children do not and will not operate in the spirit doing His will.

I have never felt such a burden, and I thank God for not giving it all to me and for taking it back upon Himself!

The love that He has for us, to withstand such grief on account of us, brings me to a higher FITness level.

God gives you salvation, power, authority, direction, spiritual abilities, weapons and much more.

Find out daily, as Jesus did, what Father wants you to DO…then act! Finding out what God wants you to do today is a key… not what you want or what people or the world wants you to do!

As Eleazar's hand froze to his sword in battle (2 Samuel 23:10), keep a firm grip on the spiritual sword that God gives you for your life and pursue your destiny!

Be Fearless… Be Incorruptible… Be Tenacious… Be FIT!!

SECTOR THIRTEEN

FASTING TO GET RESULTS

> **HUNTING TIP**
> Jesus only followed Father's will. So should you!

Fasting is one of those topics, that many Christians don't like to talk about, mostly because they aren't taught about it and/or don't want to do it. Many don't think it's necessary or that it accomplishes anything. I really can't remember a single teaching growing up in "church" or Sunday school, that taught about fasting, even though, God's Word testifies about how effective it is.

God's word tells us that fasting is a Christian's requirement, in order to obtain a powerful, God-directed, life and ministry.

Many people email me saying, that they want a spiritually powerful ministry; they want Holy Spirit gifts and miracles working through them; they want the power of the Holy Spirit; they want to go in the spirit but can't; that their prayers don't work; evil spirits won't leave; spiritual senses are closed. A problem can be a lack of or total disregard for fasting!

To testify to my own experience, I have regularly fasted every week for many years. I learned over 20 years ago, that the disciples of Jesus and the early Church fasted (no food over a 24-hour period) every Wednesday and Friday. I figured if they did it then it must be God directed. Besides these two days per week, I've fasted at various times over the years for 2, 3, 5, 7 and 40-day periods, as directed by God.

My main mentor, my Mom, also fasted regularly over 1, 3, 7, 30 and 40-day periods, which provided her with a powerful ministry and answers to prayer.

Examine in God's Word, what the great ones of God did and taught on fasting and what was accomplished, especially with deepening their relationship with God… a few examples… Moses (Ex. 34:28-29); Elijah (1 Kgs. 19:8); Ezra (Ezra 10:6); Nehemiah (Neh. 1:4), Esther (Est. 4:16); David (Ps. 34:13); Isaiah (Isa. 58:6); Daniel (Dan. 9:3); Joel (Joel 1:14); Paul (Acts 27:33).

The main fasting teaching that we'll get into now is, "What did Jesus do"?

Jesus came here for many reasons, with one of them to teach us to follow by His example, as He did everything according to what Father showed Him.

"Jesus gave them this answer: "Very truly I tell you, the Son can do nothing by himself; he can do only what he sees his Father doing, because whatever the Father does the Son also does." John 5:19

"So, Jesus said, "When you have lifted up the Son of Man, then you will know that I am he and that I do nothing on my own but speak just what the Father has taught me." John 8:28

So, we are to follow what Jesus said and did and what it says in God's Word, IF we are to succeed in pleasing God; IF we are to accomplish His perfect will through us (as Father did with Jesus) and IF we are to have the Holy Spirit operational through us (gifts, power, miracles, wonders, open spiritual senses).

What are the two steps that Jesus takes, before He starts His ministry?

He goes down to the Jordan River and gets fully immersed baptized in water as an adult "to fulfill all righteousness" Matthew 3: 13-15. If anyone hasn't done a full immersion water baptism as an adult, this can be a stumbling block to spiritual advancement. If anyone thinks that this process step is unnecessary, then why would Jesus, His disciples and Paul do it and teach it? Are evil spirits ministering to people to skip this step and skip fasting? What do you think?

Next, we see Jesus going alone into the wilderness, fasting for 40 days (Mt. 4:1-2; Mk. 1: 9; Lk. 4:2).

After these two processes (adult, full immersion, water baptism and a 40-day fast), He <u>then</u> started the ministry of preaching the kingdom of God (Matthew 4:17), and the Holy Spirit performed miracles, signs and wonders through Him.

Many Christians say, "Yeah, but Jesus was God, so that's why He could do miracles and I can't". The Holy Spirit did these acts through Jesus, which the Holy Spirit also wants and waits to do through each person today. Jesus said, "Most assuredly, I say to you, he who believes in Me, the works that I do he will do also; and greater works than these he will do, because I go to My Father." John 14:12

Let's examine a significant difference in the words used by Luke, to describe Jesus before and after His 40 days fast.

In Luke 4:1, Luke says, "Then Jesus, being <u>filled</u> with the Holy Spirit, returned from the Jordan". After the fast, in Luke 4:14, it says, "Then Jesus returned in the <u>power</u> of the Spirit to Galilee".

When Jesus completed His water baptism, He was "full of the Holy Spirit". When He completed His fast, He "returned in the power of the Spirit". The potential of the Holy Spirit's power, which Jesus received at His baptism, only came forth in full manifestation, after He completed His 40-day fast. Fasting was the final step of preparation before entering into ministry.

Many Christians and especially leaders, are now scrambling to argue against this teaching of Jesus, to say perhaps that, "I've never done these steps and my life and ministry is fine, so I don't need to do these acts".

Fight it all you like, but this is what Jesus taught by example (as taught to Him by Father) and Jesus said in John 13: 16, "Most assuredly, I say to you, a servant is not greater than his master; nor is he who is sent greater than he who sent him". This applies to the preparation for ministry. Father sets the order and route, not man or a seminary.

If a 40-day fast was a necessary part of Christ's own preparation, it should be a necessary part in every Christian's spiritual path, IF they want to Xtremely move forward spiritually, as our Father desires for each of us.

A habit of fasting is also done after this initial 40-day fasting process, as Jesus said regarding an evil spirit that wouldn't listen to His disciples, "So He said to them, "This kind can come out by <u>nothing but</u> prayer and fasting" Mark 9: 29. Jesus was prayed and fasted up always in advance, to be ready for any circumstance.

"Now in the church that was at Antioch there were certain prophets and teachers: Barnabas, Simeon who was called Niger, Lucius of Cyrene, Manaen who had been brought up with Herod the tetrarch, and Saul. As they ministered to the Lord and fasted, the Holy Spirit said, "Now separate to Me Barnabas and Saul for the work to which I have called them." Then, having fasted and prayed, and laid hands on them, they sent them away." Acts 13: 1-3

Here in Antioch, five leaders fasted and prayed together (collective process) to receive direction and anointing from the Holy Spirit. This is another divine order. We minister to the Lord first (prayer, fasting, worship, praise) before we minister to people. When we minister to the Lord, then the Holy Spirit provides direction and power required to have an effective ministry. Few leaders or fellowships follow this spiritual advice from God. Notice that prior to prayer and fasting, Barnabus and Paul, and the other three, were recognized as prophets and teachers. After the Holy Spirit sent them out, Barnabus and Paul were now described as Apostles (Acts 14:4, 14).

IF a person truly wants to have their spiritual senses open; wants to have the Holy Spirit operate through them in full POWER, not just an infilling; to go in the spirit; to improve their prayer results; to do Father's will and not their own will, then…. Get fasting! AND follow all the Gospel teachings of Jesus Christ!

There's some more detail on how prayer and fasting changes nations, in the Trophy or Xtreme Big Game Sector.

SECTOR FOURTEEN

GOING IN THE SPIRIT, SPIRIT TRAVEL, BILOCATION, TRANSLATION, TRANSLOCATION, TELEPORTING, MULTI-TRANSPORTING

> **HUNTING TIP**
>
> **Religion cannot replace God!**

What did Jesus do?

"Then Jesus answered and said to them, "Most assuredly, I say to you, the Son can do nothing of Himself, but what He sees the Father do; for whatever He does, the Son also does in like manner. For the Father loves the Son, and shows Him all things that He Himself does; and He will show Him greater works than these, that you may marvel." John 5:19-20

Jesus did nothing but what He saw the Father do. Jesus knew what to do every day, as He operated "in the spirit" and saw in the spirit what to do and did it.

Jesus said, "It is the Spirit who gives life; the flesh profits nothing." John 6:63

"For those who live according to the flesh set their minds on the things of the flesh, but those who live according to the Spirit, the things of the Spirit. For to be carnally minded is death, but to be spiritually minded is life and peace. Because the carnal mind is enmity against God;

for it is not subject to the law of God, nor indeed can be. So then, those who are in the flesh cannot please God." Romans 8:5-8

So, should we then be operating in the flesh or "in the spirit?"

I realize that it is difficult to explain and convince someone, that "in the spirit" experiences are real, if they have never experienced being "in the spirit." Much like trying to explain to someone who is physically blind, what things look like, and also convincing them what you're seeing is reality.

Or convincing someone that you've seen a unicorn-like mammal (a single horn in the middle of the head), without a trophy or picture to back it up. (I have seen these physical creatures which do exist—and I can and will prove it!)

But right now, let's discuss "going in the spirit" or the other names we hear to describe this activity, such as, spirit travel or bilocation or translation or translocation or teleporting.

Many who have died and were resuscitated or resurrected, have also had these experiences, that are typically called near-death experiences NDE (they should be called "actual death experiences" ADE).

This is an email that I received from a friend in Paris, who joined me in an Xtreme Big Game Hunt while I was in Switzerland (her native tongue is French so you'll have to accept her testimony in English, just as I received it):

"Hello Al,

I am so happy for what God has done this weekend in Switzerland. I was with my friends Jo and Florianne and we were worshiping God and we were in the spirit about 2 hours. We had a wonderful time with the Father and Jesus. We were first bowing down before God the Father who was standing at His throne; there were Angels who were taking clothes in their hands for us. Papa (God) gave me a stick as the one of Moses, and after that we all received many gifts; new clothes, one is a white mantle shining as diamonds, we received also other shining clothes; Jo a green one, Florianne a red one and me a blue one. God said to us that we were as precious stones. After that Jesus appeared standing before us; we walked with Him in a beautiful shining garden; we were small girls. He was kneeling and washed our feet in a brook; we were laughing with him and playing with the water.

Suddenly everything became dark and after Jesus explained to us that even when it is darkness and we don't see Him in difficult times, He is still there with us. During this time with Him, He restored our child's hearts. Jesus said that He was very proud of us; we had a long time with Him. His angels were behind us and they were smiling and Jesus made us understand, that He enjoyed and loved very much His Angels, but He enjoyed and loved much more His children, He enjoys to be with us. Jesus gave me a red rose in my left hand. We were walking in the direction of the throne and we received crowns of dignity, God established us in our child dignity and in our human being dignity. He gave us also golden rings.

After that we came back before the Throne and asked God what to do with the stick I received; how I can use it. God's answer was, that He did directly on me the deliverance I wanted for many months… the snake which was around my body (it was not a python as I thought but the Egyptian cobra).

He took off the cobra from my spine and my head as nothing; its head was the size of my head. Its head was cut and it was lying on the floor as a dried thing.

After that the stick that God gave me blossomed as Aaron's stick. After that God put in my spine a column and it was as He was establishing me as a column in the temple of the living God.

I will never forget the two hours we spent in the heavens. This shows also how the church of Christ, His body, must work on earth.

Thousands of blessings, Nacéra"

As we know, John recorded in the book of Revelation, "the things" (Revelation 1:19) he became part of, while "in the spirit." Revelation 1:10

How to Go in the Spirit Testimony

I asked Nacéra to explain in her words, on how to go in the spirit.

Nacéra said,

"Dear Al,

We were just worshipping God and we went before His Throne asking for His strategy, for His help. To be born again is not only when you receive Jesus as your Lord and Savior. When you receive Jesus' seed of Life in you, this is the first step, only this place of your spirit is awakened, not all of your spirit. You have to grow.

When a woman is pregnant, the first step is a seed and after nine months a baby is born. Before anyone is born in the Kingdom of God and moving in His Kingdom, it takes time. It's the work of the Cross, the death of the flesh, the waters of Life that awake your spirit, the work of the Spirit of the Lord. Deliverance is also very important in the process.

Jesus answered, "I tell you the truth, no one can enter the Kingdom of God unless he is born of water and the Spirit." John 3:5

God created us to see and hear Him and He awakes with the waters of Life our spirit step by step. For example, some people can feel God, but they can't hear well His Voice or see Him, others can hear well His Voice, but they can't see Him, others can smell the perfumes of the Kingdom.

Blessings, Nacéra"

So how do you get from here to there?

How does one go in the spirit or bilocate?

What else does the Bible say about this topic?

What does experience teach?

Why don't they talk about, teach this or do this in Church assemblies?

Isn't this stuff New Age or considered occultist, astral projection?

Does God really want us to be and go and do in the spirit?

Let's get into some of these questions more deeply.

Astral Projection

This is a form of spirit travel that is occultism, not Christian. Astral projection is an evil counterfeit to holy going in the spirit. Satan and his ilk have created nothing. All the evil realm can do is, copy, steal, corrupt and distort what God has created, in order to trick and deceive people.

Practitioners of astral projection admit, that this usually happens when they're asleep. They say that they experience buzzing, loud noises, vibrations, floating over their body, fear, numbness and disorientation. Usually it's drifting over their body, although the more experienced travel distances on earth and go through walls.

Many admit to being attached to a "cord of light" attached to their head, chest or back, which can pull or snap them back into their bodies.

I personally have never experienced any of these sensory manifestations, nor have I heard any Christians mention these feelings nor a cord of light attachment.

Christians travel in the spirit while awake and into heaven, also into the past and future (time travel) and multiple places at the same time. While "in the spirit", actions by Christians in the spirit realm can and does affect the physical realm for others (healing, deliverance, miracles, crime reduction, and so).

Testimonies of spirit travel in and to different countries, is provided in the Hunting Expedition Sectors.

A great testimony of mine, is when some angels and I battled some astral projecting witches. You can find this in the German Hunting Expedition Sector.

Can we Go to Heaven Now?

Heaven is open to us now through Jesus' blood… we aren't limited to earth until we physically die.

"For through Him we both have access by one Spirit to the Father." Ephesians 2:18

"Jesus said to him, "I am the way, and the truth, and the life; no one comes to the Father but through Me." John 14:6

BIBLICAL EXAMPLES OF GOING IN THE SPIRIT

The apostle John says that he received the revelation while…

"I was in the spirit on the Lord's Day, and I heard behind me a great voice, as of a trumpet." Revelation 1:10

"And immediately I was in the spirit." Revelation 4:2

"So, he carried me away in the spirit into the wilderness." Revelation 17:3

"And he carried me away in the spirit to a great and high mountain, and shewed me that great city, the holy Jerusalem, descending out of heaven from God." Revelation 21:10

Ezekiel went many times in the spirit… here are a few:

"And the spirit lifted me up between the earth and the heaven," Ezekiel 8:3

and "the spirit lifted me up." Ezekiel 11:1,

"The hand of the Lord was upon me and carried me out in the spirit." Ezekiel 37:1

Elisha went in the spirit…

"Elisha said to him, "Did not my spirit go with you when the man turned from his chariot to meet you?" 2 Kings 5:26

Paul said…

"I know a man in Christ who fourteen years ago—whether in the body I do not know, or whether out of the body I do not know, God knows—such a one was caught up to the third heaven. And I know such a man—whether in the body or out of the body I do not know, God knows— how he was caught up into Paradise and heard inexpressible words, which it is not lawful for a man to utter."2 Corinthians 12:2-4

"For though I be absent in the flesh, yet am I with you in the spirit…" Colossians 2:5a

Jesus saw Nathaniel under the fig tree before they ever met!

"Before that Philip called you, when you were under the fig tree, I saw you." John 1:43-50

POST-BIBLICAL TESTIMONIES OF GOING IN THE SPIRIT

A book by Patricia Treece called *The Sanctified Body*, documents many people "going in the spirit" or "bilocating". Treece spent 11 years doing research for this book and found many people in history, that had gone in the spirit.

"Anne Catherine Emmerich (1774-1824), bilocated frequently". Anne said she "crosses the sea as quickly as thought travels."

María Jesus de Ágreda - the "Lady in Blue" or "Blue Nun" from Spain (17th Century) never left her convent in Spain, yet was seen <u>hundreds of times</u> by various native tribes in Texas USA. Many attributes her to evangelizing Texas, before any Christians set a physical foot there!

Well known 20th Century healer, international speaker and author, Agnes Sanford, tells of such experiences.

Padre Pio, of the 20th Century, was seen numerous times in two places at the same time, sometimes in different countries.

Dr. Dale A. Fife wrote several books about his going in the spirit into heaven and walking with Jesus, *The Secret Place*, *The Hidden Kingdom*, and *Spirit Wind*.

Mary K. Baxter wrote, *A Divine Revelation of Heaven* and *A Divine Revelation of Hell*, testifying of her going in the spirit to heaven and to hell.

Rick Joyner talks of going in the spirit and doing battle, such as in his books, *The Final Quest*, *The Call* and *The Torch and the Sword*.

Choo Thomas, who wrote *Heaven is so Real*, testified of her many trips in the spirit with Jesus into heaven.

Well known Christian missionary Sadhu Sundar Singh from India, knew a man named "Christian" in the Himalayas, who received the gift of life from Jesus until His Second Coming. This man was over 300 years old then and would be about 420 years old now! Impossible you say!

Actually, this is Biblically sound, as 14 people are mentioned in the Bible as living over 430 years and some over 900 years! Who knows how many more there were! Christian often travelled in the spirit all over the world and into heaven, from his mountain cave! He went in the spirit mostly, he said, to help others! He also taught Sundar Singh to travel in the spirit.

Richard Wurmbrand was imprisoned and tortured for 14 years by Communists in Romania, for being an outspoken Christian leader. He was eventually released and in 1966 in Washington D.C. in front of cameras, he showed the scars of his torture, exposing the world to the horrors of the Communist treatment of Christians. He became the voice for the persecuted Church, founded the international organization, "The Voice of the Martyrs" and wrote 22 books.

He said that while he was in solitary confinement in prison, "I would pass hours praying… praying for the whole world. <u>I travelled in my spirit from one country to another</u>"!

You can hear him say this in his own words on YouTube at http://www.youtube.com/watch?v=7_1j5FXC2Aw

The Desert Fathers of the 4th century also typically travelled in the spirit at will, one even physically travelling into heaven, bringing back and planting a heavenly fig tree that healed people with its aroma!

Here are some testimonies from some students who learned how to go and operate in the spirit from this book:

"I also "go in the spirit" on a daily basis, just for intimacy with Father God. This is extra special for me! I personally thank you! You have been instrumental in transforming my life!"

Diane M. - Retired University Professor/Prophet- Canada

"Hallelujah! I've finished reading the whole book "Xtreme Big Game hunting" Last Sunday (at) dawn in the spirit, I fought against two animal creatures. One like a wild-bore(swine) and the other one has a form of a man but very black color and his skin is like a crab shell. And while praying, the Lord handed me a weapon like a sharp iron rod. I am victorious. We've been busy preparing and studying Xtreme spiritual warfare for tomorrow afternoon's activities for the pastors. I printed 50 copies of your manual and 50 cd's for all the pastors that are attending our ministerial fellowship."

Freddie D. - Pastor/Evangelist/Church Planter – The Philippines

"Brother Al and his ministry has actually changed my life and enabled my own ministry to go to higher heights doing things that I previously never imagined doing. Because of what Al has taught me I have fought one dragon, two "cat humans" demons, seen one heart healed, fought with a sword, a sword and a shield, and even built and restored broken stones in the spirit which brought healing in people's lives. While at his conference in the spirit I was able to go back in the past and have a childhood emotional wound healed. Fun stuff! Who says Christianity is boring?"

Clinton C. – TV Host/Prophet/Author/Minister/Int. Speaker- USA

"I go for big game hunting visiting new areas in the spirit and drawing my sword through wild beasts slaying them in the name of the lord of Hosts."

Charles M. - Pastor/Teacher/Evangelist/Int. Speaker - Uganda

"To be honest, before this experience, I would have thought that someone was making all of this up. I consider myself to be a Spirit-led person grounded in biblical principles, yet I must admit that I was a little skeptical about "killing" in the Spirit. Now I know better! I thank God that he reveals to redeem. I believe that anyone who reads "Xtreme Big Game Hunting" will be blessed immensely as their spiritual eyes will be opened even wider. God is willing to provide us with His knowledge; we just have to be open to receiving it. "For lack of knowledge my people perish." There are things in the Spirit that call for deeper things as the Bible says that the "deep calls unto the deep." I pray that people will be open to the things of God that has been revealed through Al Collins… deep!"

Karen Y. - Minister/Counselor - USA

"How are you doing dear man of God? The lady who was paralyzed is called Mrs. Boniventure. She had paralysis for seven years. After applying the deliverance and healing principles (manual) which you sent to me, the lady was completely set free."

Johnstone K. - Pastor - Tanzania

"In August of 2007 I attended a spiritual warfare conference given by Al Collins. Since that time, I have been engaged in hi level spiritual warfare directed by our triune God. My direction has been to attack the dark empire.

Our Lord has supplied:

1. Weapons.
2. Armor.
3. A spirit horse.
4. Battle plans & timing.
5. The ability to travel anywhere in the universe instantaneously.
6. The ability to see the spiritual world.

I have encountered and defeated:

1. A ruler of darkness of this age.
2. Dragons.
3. A fallen angel.
4. Leviathans.
5. Demonic entities."

Richard G. - Retired Scientist/Teacher/Church Elder - USA

You'll read in the following Sectors, many of my own testimonies.

But my "church" Doesn't do That

If you're in a group, assembly or gathering ("church") of Christians that doesn't operate in the spirit, teach them what God says (i.e. Romans

8:8) and if they refuse, they are rebellious against God and the Gospel. Rebuke them and then get away from them.

Jesus said in John 4:24, "God is spirit: and those who worship him (the Father) <u>must worship in spirit</u> and truth."

"True worshippers <u>shall worship the Father in spirit</u> and in truth: for the Father seeks such to worship him." John 4:23

ACCESS INTO HEAVEN NOW!

"For through Him (Jesus) we both have <u>access</u> by one Spirit (Holy Spirit) to the Father." Ephesians 2:18

"Serve the LORD with gladness: <u>come before his presence</u> with singing." Psalm 100:2

"<u>Enter</u> into His gates with thanksgiving, and <u>into</u> His courts with praise. Be thankful to Him, and bless His name." Psalm 100:4

As true worshippers in the spirit, we have access to the Father!

Access means we can actually <u>go</u> to the Father—not just with words in the air with one-way prayer.

Religions, cults, most "church organizations" and most Christians are not operating in the spirit nor with God's power, nor worshipping as God wants, nor doing anything in the spirit. Therefore, their spiritual activities are limited or usually non-existent.

Paul says in 1 Corinthians 2:4-5: "My speech and my preaching was not with enticing words of man's wisdom, but <u>in demonstration of the Spirit and of power</u>: That your faith should not stand in the wisdom of men, but in the power of God."

The Bible here says intelligent, persuasive speakers and words bring about faith in man or man's doctrines/religion. Christians, especially Christian leaders, must operate "in the spirit" and <u>demonstrate</u> God's power!

The same Holy Spirit that "remained upon" Jesus (John 1:32) ... is the same Holy Spirit that remains upon YOU!

Ask the Holy Spirit to open your spiritual senses. He is your Helper (John 14:26). Ask Him to take you in the spirit to visit heaven. Initially you may need to remove all noises and be alone. Later distractions won't affect your ability.

WHAT YOU WILL EXPERIENCE

Godly/Holy "going in the spirit" or bilocation is unlike the occult, as a Christian, while "in the spirit", always has control, there is no possession. Our spirit is in contact with the Spirit of God within us. It is like an overlapping of two simultaneous experiences… one in the physical and one in the spiritual.

You can go in the spirit during sleep or while awake. You can go in the past, future, and to the other side of the planet, besides into heaven.

You may also find yourself going in the spirit to heaven walking on golden streets, eating wonderful fruits, frolicking in streams, going into one of God's throne rooms or just strolling somewhere talking to Jesus.

I have walked with Jesus in heaven numerous times, as well as visited <u>my</u> cottage next to a lake, by mountains, that had a stream and fruit trees growing enormous fruit. I sat and talked with Jesus at the edge of the lake under a large willow tree. This will one day be one of my homes! Can't wait! You should see my chateau (read *The Way* book)!

I've been to the courts of heaven to present my case against satan! Jesus was my Jewish lawyer! Father was the Judge! Guess who won? Satan was dragged off a loser!

It is truly amazing and near impossible to describe at times!

I agree with Paul with having a greater desire to depart and be with Jesus, which is far better than being on earth. Indeed!

"For to me, to live is Christ, and to die is gain. But if I live on in the flesh, this will mean fruit from my labor; yet what I shall choose I cannot tell. For I am hard-pressed between the two, having a desire to depart and be with Christ, which is far better." Philippians 1: 21-23

You can also visit spiritual prisons (you can release soul captives. See POW's Sector). I've visited the lake of fire and come face-to-face with satan.

Jesus taught disciples and us that there is a level beyond just preaching the Word.

"In the spirit" activities can be in different forms and different levels.

One can receive just revelation, dreams and visions and go no further.

"And it shall come to pass in the last days, says God, That I will pour out of My Spirit on all flesh; Your sons and your daughters shall prophesy, your young men shall see visions, your old men shall dream dreams." Acts 2:17

You can work with angels and battle against principalities and powers in the heavens as it says we do in Ephesians 6:12. Many testimonies on this are coming up in the following Sectors.

You can also go to multiple places in the spirit at the same time.

Dreams

"In the first year of Belshazzar king of Babylon, Daniel had a dream and visions of his head while on his bed. Then he wrote down the dream, telling the main facts." Daniel 7:1

Usually people report they have spiritual dreams before they actually experience spiritual occurrences while awake. You should journal these and ask God to interpret what He's trying to tell you. Also, as reference in the future to reread.

One leader I know, goes in the spirit into other people's dreams to counsel them. They call him up the next day to tell him that they had a dream about him last night!

Many times, people won't remember that they went in the spirit, although they've given God permission to take them in the spirit during sleep, to fulfill His will through them.

Don't Remember

You can go in the spirit and not remember it.

One testimony is from my Mom, who was at a conference years ago, in the USA, when a woman approached her. The woman was so glad to see her again she said. My Mom didn't remember her, so the women told her, "Don't you remember me? You came into my hospital room, sat with me, we talked, you prayed for my healing, I was healed and released". (My Mom had done this with countless people but didn't remember her). She said, "It was last year in England". My Mom told her that she had never been to England. The woman said, "Well, isn't your name Lynn?" It was. My Mom had gone in the spirit to England, which resulted in being seen by someone there, talking to them and produced a healing!

Going in the Spirit While Awake

Many times, the first conscience spiritual experience is just seeing light or flashes, such as a new born baby can only see light and slowly over time, images appear more clearly.

Visions

Often in the spirit, you will just be observing what is going on, like watching TV and probably see strange events and creatures. These creatures know you are there—usually—unless you are camouflaged or hidden from their view.

With me, the time came when I was attacking and conquering evil creatures with spiritual swords, bow and arrows, knives, stomping them, throwing them into fire, etc.

I was also directing angels to assist me in battle and to put evil spiritual creatures into prisons.

I also travel instantly to other sides of the earth and above the earth hunting evil entities.

You will probably find it to be an escalating process, as you rid yourself of sin, worldly thinking and its activities and spend more SAC and PAW time with God.

Progression

For some people, going in the spirit is quick. For some, they don't know they're going in the spirit. Many think a supernatural dream from God, is just a weird dream because they ate too much pizza! I asked God every day for six months to open my spiritual eyesight so I could see angels. Then boom, there they were!

Some who were involved in the occult, found the transition easy, as they were already experiencing the supernatural realm, although the dark side of it.

Your goal is to achieve more than dreams and visions, where your spirit is <u>participating</u> in the spiritual experience, such as Ezekiel and John did.

You will be going in the spirit anywhere on earth, in the heavens and into the past and future!

Going "in the spirit" experiences are similar to that of Ezekiel, in Ezekiel 40, or of Paul talking about going in the spirit in 2 Corinthians 12:1-4, when you won't know whether in or out of body.

As I said, when going in the spirit, you can communicate and experience activities in heaven (spiritually) and earth (physically), as you can be in both places at the same time. Actually, we are always in both places at the same time as the physical realm and spiritual realm coexist. It's just that most people are deaf, dumb and blind to the spiritual realm.

Portals to the Spirit Realm

There are places on earth where there were and still are spiritual doors into heavenly places, such as when Ezekiel went to the River Chebar (Ezekiel 1:1, 3/3:15-16, 23/10:15, 20, 22/43:3) for visions and revelation and Daniel went to the River Ulai and Hiddekel for visions (Daniel 8:2/10:4/12:5).

Some places are chosen by God for prophets to go to like Moses on top of a mountain. Although it is not necessary, as I have gone in the spirit while at a variety of places, even sitting down for dinner in a restaurant!

It may be helpful to hunt for your river, mountain, prayer closet or place where a door seems especially opened for you. Rhoda and I go to a special place next to the lake where I grew up, where my Mom went to be with God. It's a habit for us, although we go in the spirit to other places also. You might come across it accidentally. You may also purposely bring about this opening, by developing an altar of praise, worship, thanksgiving and prayer to God.

Ask the Holy Spirit for guidance in this area.

SPIRITUAL WEAPONS

There are times when Jesus and Father will give you spiritual weapons, such as swords, or bow and arrows. You may receive a spiritual horse (I have many of them). You may receive a scepter, crowns, robes, scrolls, rings, etc. You may be knighted in heaven, as I was. Accept the promotions.

HEAVENLY MANSION

You may be taken to your heavenly mansion. You may have more than one. Many people have described their mansions in great detail. Some said they have huge diamonds embedded in the side of their mansion. When they asked what these were for, angels told them every time a person on earth is saved because of their efforts, another diamond is permanently embedded in their mansion for all eternity!

HEAVENS SCENERY

Many visiting heaven report of mountains, rivers with fish, animals, birds, their pet dogs, other people such as their deceased relatives, gardens, forests, fruit trees, butterflies and flowers and so on. Many find the beauty and colors hard to describe. I have seen all these things and it is all truly magnificent!

ANGELS AND EVIL ENTITIES

You'll see angels of many sizes and colors. Some wear robes and some armor. I don't usually see them with wings. They rarely talk to you, but readily assist you with binding evil spirits and taking them away. You'll see them with swords, bows and arrows, spears and driving chariots.

You'll also see and experience evil entities from demons to principalities to dark angels. They can look like people, animals and strange beasts like dragons.

Some are in the water, some are on land and some are in the air over the earth. Some principalities have crowns and sit on thrones, as they're in charge of certain nations (i.e. Prince of Persia in Daniel 10:20). Initially they'll try to scare you. When you hunt them, and attack them they are usually afraid. They always lose against you in battle, when you are doing spiritual warfare under God's directions.

Much more in other Sectors on evil entities.

HUNTING EVIL ENTITIES IN THE SPIRIT

If you don't hunt in the spirit, how will you deal with every spiritual entity, every evil structure, and every evil stronghold and trap that you must conquer at a particular place, that requires exact timing and certain spiritual weapons?

From an Xtreme Big Game Hunting perspective, imagine attacking and conquering principalities, powers and evil entities without being able to see them…without operating in the spirit…without spiritual timing from God… without spiritual weapons!

Many Christians try… splashing holy oil or wine around their town or city claiming it for God. Not having a clue of what they're up against or where they are.

Don't operate blind! Don't do spiritual warfare without operating in the spirit. More detail in other Sectors on spiritual warfare that doesn't require repeating here.

Transported or Translocation

We must also realize that we can go "in the body" or be "caught away" to a place such as the following three examples from the Bible and Apocrypha. Philip was told by an angel of the Lord to go to Gaza, where he ended up bringing an Ethiopian to Jesus and baptized him there. Philip was then bodily "caught away" and instantly was in Azotus, about 25 miles away from Gaza.

"Now when they came up out of the water, the Spirit of the Lord caught Philip away, so that the eunuch saw him no more; and he went on his way rejoicing. But Philip was found at Azotus. And passing through, he preached in all the cities till he came to Caesarea." Acts 8:39-40

Jesus, some disciples and an entire boat were all physically transported immediately about 3-4 miles in John 6:16-21!

This happened to me and two others while driving across Germany when hours were knocked off our trip, mysteriously!

In the book of Bel and the Dragon, from the end of Daniel, an Apocryphal book, Habbaccuc the prophet (Habakkuk) had made a meal and was taken by an angel to Babylon to feed it to Daniel, who was currently occupied in the lion's den. "Then the angel took him (Habbaccuc) by the crown, and bare him by the hair of his head, and through the vehemency of his spirit set him in Babylon over the den. And Habbaccuc cried, saying, O Daniel, Daniel, take the dinner which God hath sent thee. So, Daniel arose, and did eat: and the angel of the Lord set Habbaccuc in his own place again immediately."

I know of three people who were driving along in their car in the USA, ended up on a road in China (Chinese road signs, different landscape, Chinese cars and people on the road) for a while and then were back in the USA. Another, walked into an airport bathroom in the USA and was instantly transported to an airport bathroom in Israel, his intended destination!

Being "caught away" bodily can be an immediate, unplanned event, as going in the spirit can be and we should look forward to and not fear this experience. Being caught away may be something the Lord will do, if it is necessary for a particular hunting expedition. We should always consider all the possibilities with our Almighty God! Amen!

HEALED AT A DISTANCE IN THE SPIRIT

One of the greatest teachings I learned from Jesus is about A Soldier's Faith...

"Now when Jesus had entered Capernaum, a centurion came to Him, pleading with Him, saying, "Lord, my servant is lying at home paralyzed, dreadfully tormented." And Jesus said to him, "I will come and heal him." The centurion answered and said, "Lord, I am not worthy that You should come under my roof. But only speak a word, and my servant will be healed. For I also am a man under authority, having soldiers under me. And I say to this one, 'Go,' and he goes; and to another, 'Come,' and he comes; and to my servant, 'Do this,' and he does it." When Jesus heard it, He marveled, and said to those who followed, "Assuredly, I say to you, I have not found such great faith, not even in Israel! And I say to you that many will come from east and west, and sit down with Abraham, Isaac, and Jacob in the kingdom of heaven. But the sons of the kingdom will be cast out into outer darkness. There will be weeping and gnashing of teeth." Then Jesus said to the centurion, "Go your way; and as you have believed, so let it be done for you." And his servant was healed that same hour." Matthew 8: 5-13

I've really loved this story since I was a little kid!

The magnitude of this teaching I think escapes most people, as it did for me for many years. What eventually grabbed my attention was, that people were being healed at a distance. Jesus never saw nor spoke to the servant. It was handled in the spiritual realm.

A friend emailed us that she was suffering from extreme pain and illness for weeks requiring immediate trips to the hospital and lengthy time in bed. She requested warfare.

I went in the spirit and was in my armor with a lance riding my horse Whitey over the earth. I rode down to where this person was in a room. I got off Whitey to destroy several entities that were afflicting her, particularly her legs and head. Angels were there to assist me with disposing of them. I then saw the Holy Spirit fill her with light.

She emailed me to say that in a matter of a few hours, she went from needing urgent care, to pain free and had her best sleep in weeks. I found out later that she experienced pain in her legs and head. She asked what time the warfare had finished, which turned out to be the exact moment the pain left!

As with the Centurion's servant... I didn't see her or talk to her... I never even said a word out loud; it was all done in the spirit realm by faith and obedience to God's strategy, while I physically sat in my living room!

All Glory to God for the victory!

GOING IN THE SPIRIT FOR A CITY

This next battle I'd like to share, was an "in the spirit" battle for a city!

A leader friend of ours from Tanzania contacted us to say, that muslims in his city were systematically burning Church buildings and leader's homes. Even government officials were involved. He asked us to join his assembly in spiritual warfare to stop this.

We spoke, decreed and commanded into the spiritual realm all that was to change in this city.

Here's his October 22, 2011 testimony email:

"The LORD is in charge of all. None like Him. I firmly, confident and believe that " Also, I tell you that if two of you on earth agree about something and pray for it, it will be done for you by your Father in heaven."
Very well you know brothers and sisters, ever since we agreed together to pray for Mwanza city to be protected from radical Islam attacks, burning churches, etc.
The LORD God head of our prayer and quickly reacted on them. The city is really calmed, covered with a huge silence of peace and tranquility at present.

Really the Word is true: (Matthew 16:18) "On this Rock I will build My Church, and the power of death won't be able to defeat it."
In fact, FERVENT PRAYER MAKES DIFFERENCE.
Just use this strongest spiritual weapon, Prayer.
God bless everyone.
In Him, David Ntagazwa"

This joint warfare affected an entire city of over 1/2 million people!

All Glory to God for the victory!

Let's move into the place where Jesus will marvel at us… which can be done from an "arm-chair" … let's move in faith in the spiritual realm to accomplish the marvelous!

IS THERE AN AGE LIMIT TO GOING IN THE SPIRIT?

For many people who are physically restricted or are slowed down from old age, this kind of warfare is perfect! My 88-year-old aunt operated this way. Some would call this intercession.

There's a four-year-old in Papua New Guinea who was trained from this book, who regularly goes into the heavens, walks with Jesus, eats heavenly fruit, works with angels, and attacks evil entities! Read his testimony in the Papua New Guinea Expedition Sector.

Back to the Future Testimony

On July 27th 2006, I was caught away or taken in the spirit, into the future, like John was in Revelation.

As I was sitting down in a restaurant, I was suddenly riding a horse alongside of Jesus.

As I looked at myself and Him, we were both wearing all white clothing.

I was in an honored position, riding along on His <u>right</u> side on a white horse.

As we were breaking through the clouds, I could see the planet earth below us, a long way off in the distance.

"And the armies which were in heaven followed Him upon white horses, clothed in fine linen, white and clean." Revelation 19:14

The horses were straining hard, snorting and almost screaming.

They knew the importance of this hunt even before I did… all of my senses were at an explosive peak!

Although the earth was a long way off, I knew we were heading to "the battle of that great day of God Almighty." Revelation 16:14.

"Into a place called Armageddon." Revelation 16:16

A day that God, the heavens and the universe has waited for many thousands of years!

I was on a gang hunt… on the hunt of all hunts!

In the Bible, there were times when people had visions such as Daniel or Paul.

There were times that people had spiritual experiences where they <u>participated</u> in these experiences such as Ezekiel.

And, when John had his experience of <u>going in the spirit to the future,</u> to end up writing the book of Revelation.

There are different spiritual situations, that we, as spirit-beings, can encounter.

For me, riding on the greatest future hunt of all with Jesus, brings so much to me, besides tears and trembling… it brings happiness beyond any bliss I have ever imagined… mostly the realization that I will be part of this gang hunt led by God on that day.

Although I am more than a conqueror through Jesus right now, there is nothing that I've ever done that compares to participating in this epic battle.

<u>I actually rode with Jesus into this battle and now have a memory of something that I have yet to do!</u>

Such a consideration is difficult for many to comprehend.

I share this experience with you, to serve as an understanding, that these visits are available to us.

I have also gone in the spirit into the past to see the Israelites crossing into the promised land and I saw Jesus on the cross. I also went in the past to see when satan had set up his principalities over an area, long before people inhabited the place.

"And it shall come to pass afterward that I will pour out My Spirit on all flesh; Your sons and your daughters shall prophesy, your old men shall dream dreams, your young men shall see visions." Joel 2:28

"And it shall come to pass in the last days, says God, That I will pour out of My Spirit on all flesh; Your sons and your daughters shall prophesy, your young men shall see visions, your old men shall dream dreams." Acts 2:17

I share this with you as I want you to anticipate that you can be part of His hunt!

For me…anticipation is the best part of what I know is coming!

I later asked God why and how I am so honored to ride with Jesus on His right side that day… and He showed me the continuation of this visit into the future.

I and my horse moved back to join the army of hunters behind Jesus, as another person rode forward taking this honored position next to Jesus and so on… it seemed everyone was getting this great honor… to remember for eternity!

TOP SPIRITUAL SECRET REVEALED

Now I'm going to reveal something that I've never read or heard about ever before, except in a passing statement made once by Padre Pio. In Patricia Treece's book *The Sanctified Body* (page 341), she refers to a comment by Pio made in a book by C. Bernard Ruffin, *Padre Pio: The True Story*.

Pio said, "Whether it's true or not that I'm found in various places by bilocation, trilocation, or whatever, you'll have to ask God, not me."

Why would Pio mention "trilocation, or whatever", if he hadn't experienced being in 3 or more places at the same time?

Let me quote something from the Bible: "For where two or three are gathered together in my (Jesus) name, there am I in the midst of them. Matthew 18:20

Considering what Jesus said, <u>while He was a physical human being on earth</u>, how many places could Jesus be at the same time?

Jesus also said, "Most assuredly, I say to you, he who believes in Me, the works that I do he will do also; and greater works than these he will do, because I go to My Father. And whatever you ask in My name, that I will do, that the Father may be glorified in the Son. If you ask anything in My name, I will do it." John 14:12-14

Jesus says we <u>will</u> do greater works than He did and <u>anything</u> we ask Father in Jesus' name will be done!

So… now that you've soaked all that in what do you get?

Guess what I asked for?

Let me tell you my testimony:

"The first time I went to multiple places in the spirit it was to 15 different places at the same time. I was doing so many things, with so many people, my head was spinning."

OK… trial runs can be a little bumpy and mind boggling!

Next time went like this:

"I was in the spirit at the ocean, standing on some rocks overlooking the ocean. Jesus came down some stairs of light from heaven. He said to me that I must stay holy, righteous and sanctified. The sky was dark and cloudy over the ocean, approaching night.

I mounted my spiritual white horse Whitey with my sword and shield and we turned around from the ocean.

I looked into blackness.

Jesus said, "The world is black, don't let it stop you."

As I started riding into the blackness I could see a black dragon ahead on my right side with a black face, black eyes, and its red mouth open showing white teeth. I slashed my sword through its head as I rode by. It dropped out of sight.

I was riding above the earth. Black dragons were flying below me. I could hear Jesus tell me, "They want to destroy you, but just stay on the path. The Holy Spirit will lead you. Angels will assist you" I turned to look up and behind me, to see countless angels all on chariots. One row of them was as far back as I could see.

Jesus said, "Your destiny is now, your time is now. Listen to the Holy Spirit's guidance. Destroy evil to open holes in blackness for people to see the gospel."

I stopped riding when I reached a crossroad over the earth. The angels behind me also stopped. There was still blackness everywhere.

I then split into 4 of me (and Whitey) and rode into 4 directions of North, South, East and West. The angels broke off into 4 groups to follow. I went to the 4 corners of the earth.

Jesus said, "All is available to you. Believe it!"

When I reached the 4 corners of the earth at the same time, I then split off in each place into numerous numbers of me to spread out into many more places.

Jesus said, "Some places you go people will see you, other places they won't see you."

People were being healed in some places, evil entities were being destroyed by me in other places, some people I was just sitting and talking to them and so on.

It was difficult to see all the things that I was doing at the same time all over the world. I didn't try to see all of it, I just did it."

And so forth on other missions around the world!

I CALL IT MULTI-LOCATING!

OK… I know some of you are perhaps shaking your head right now, thinking I'm maybe suffering from the effects of a sugar-overload from one too many donuts. All I can say is, ask God to take you for a test ride!

As Smith Wigglesworth was so famous for saying, "Only Believe!"

Heavenly Father… I thank you for these gifts of visits to earth and heaven that you give me and I thank You for giving the same to each person who reads this, who genuinely desires to worship only You and be part of Your army of hunters, riding with you Lord on that great day!

So be it!

I pray that you will embrace your destiny on earth and in heaven with a fierceness that is unrelenting!

CONCLUSION

Certainly, going in the spirit will become much easier and will happen, when you move toward God by getting B.A.D.; dispense with S.I.T.; refuse to compromise against God; spend S.A.C. time and P.A.W. time with God; continue to D.I.G. for it; fast and be FIT.

As elite conquerors prepare themselves for their destiny in battle, so must we be ready to be a Silver Bullet of God and an Xtreme Big Game Hunter for God!

OK… as I mentioned at the beginning of this Sector, I know you still want me to prove that actual unicorn creatures exist and that I've seen them!

Years ago, when I was a pilot, flying low over Hudson's Bay near the Northwest Territories Canada (now called Nunavut) in a Grumman Tiger, I could see narwhal's moving in the water, each with their single ivory tusks clearly visible. Sorry I don't have any pictures of this event; however, pictures of this creature are available on the internet or at your library.

Webster's Dictionary: Narwhal: an arctic cetacean (Monodon Monoceros) about 20 feet (6 meters) long with the male having a long, twisted ivory tusk.

Teaching us, that just because we personally haven't seen or heard of something, doesn't mean it can't or doesn't exist.

God does exist… the spiritual realm does exist… each of us is a spiritual being… the Bible proves that we can and should go and operate in the spirit… numerous testimonies exist from people throughout history who went "in the spirit".

Summary

Going in the spirit, Spirit Travel, Bilocation, Teleporting, Translocation, Multi-Locating, and Being Caught Away, are all terms that can describe moving or going or travelling in the spirit, across earth, into heaven, into the past and future. You can be taken and you can initiate them.

Go for it!

IT'S TIME FOR YOU TO GO AND OPERATE IN THE SPIRIT!

SECTOR FIFTEEN

WEAPONS AND HUNTING GEAR

> **HUNTING TIP**
>
> Be Prepared! (I know… the Boy Scouts use this one too!)

Once anyone has decided they would like to take up hunting, there is the decision of what you will hunt, where you'll hunt and when you'll be hunting, as this will determine the weapons and gear that you'll need. I hunt in all conditions and for all kinds of game, so I have many different kinds of weapons and gear.

Clothing to keep you protected from the elements and terrain, thorny brush and those nasty bugs and perhaps snakes. Knives, maps, axes, rope, lights, knapsack, compass, water, food, tent, matches, first aid kit, even a cell phone, can all be part of hunting gear needed.

Who's to say which one is more important than the other when it's needed.

And let's not forget your weapon and ammo.

I have gone hunting with guys who forgot their guns and others who forgot their ammo!

Perhaps they were going to fling themselves down out of a tree and wrestle their game down to the ground?

I have a list that I keep in a file, and every time I go hunting I pull it out and go through the list, to ensure I am taking with me all that I need. Taking excess can be a burden, especially if you have to lug it around.

When going on any hunt, whether in the physical or spiritual, weapons and hunting gear must be considered.

Pretty difficult to bring down spiritual game by throwing a physical axe at them, so we must consider the right weapons and gear, for the right game.

When I go on a moose, bear or deer hunt, I don't even consider using weapons that aren't meant to get the job done.

In Xtreme Big Game Hunting, God will advise us what to utilize as weapons to bring down the game we're after, as it can be game of many different sizes, shapes and varieties at the same time, as you have seen in Sector One. In that particular hunt, there was multiple game, when God gave me a spiritual broad sword to deal with them all.

In the North Carolina hunt, the weapons were physical objects and elements such as the Bible, red wine, oil, salt, altars and the shofar.

And in Switzerland, it was a combination of both spiritual and physical weapons.

Therefore, we must be led by God on which weapons to use, even if it turns out to be the same Xtreme Big Game (i.e. you can hunt deer with a bow, shotgun, rifle, handgun and many are quite successful with their cars).

Some hunters I've known take everything but the kitchen sink with them on a hunt, and they recommend everyone must do as they do. Difficult to do, as God can have us use anything as a weapon for a prophetic act; such as using my camera once, and also earth from Herrnhut, Germany.

He may never have me use a camera again…so should I cart it around with me everywhere I go, just in case? A little easier now, since we take pictures with our cell phones.

You'll need a pretty large party of arms carriers with you wherever you go, if that is your hunting philosophy.

I can give you a list of what some items _may_ be, that God will call upon you to use, as He has done on other hunts. Some are physical and some are spiritual.

So, let's get started on looking at weapons and hunting gear.

Christ has overcome evil already… we just execute the judgment of God. How do we do that?

A few starting tips.

"Therefore, it is said in the Book of the Wars of the Lord: "Waheb in Suphah, the brooks of the Arnon, And the slope of the brooks That reaches to the dwelling of Ar, And lies on the border of Moab." Numbers 21:14-15

Once you've accepted Jesus as your Savior, you've entered a war. You can be one of the most, who sit on the sidelines, to let the enemy batter them or you can step up to your responsibility, as a saint, a royal priest and ruler, to be a Silver Bullet of God. Have your name in God's Book of War for eternity. Save lives!

Once you've stepped up, God opens His armory and brings forth His weapons of war for you.

"The Lord has opened His armory, and has brought out the weapons of His indignation; For this is the work of the Lord God of hosts in the land of the Chaldeans." Jeremiah 50:25

""You are My battle-ax and weapons of war: For with you I will break the nation in pieces; With you I will destroy kingdoms." Jeremiah 51:20

"And to have power… to cast out devils…" Mark 3:15

"Behold, I give unto you power to tread on serpents and scorpions, and over all the power of the enemy: and nothing shall by any means hurt you." Luke 10:19

Understand and believe, that you are God's battle axe and weapon of war, that can destroy nations and kingdoms!

The Holy Spirit will direct you on the weapons and gear (spiritual and/or physical) that is needed and give you power.

The Holy Spirit, through faith, activates the elements, as they are symbols of the Holy Spirit's power.

When I was in fight training, I was told the number one weapon is my brain. Most of us seem to never use this weapon.

We must remember that every battle is not ours. God may direct others to a certain battle.

Go and do as God directs you.

The list is in alphabetical order, including defensive and offensive weapons, and certainly not a complete listing.

Very Important Weapons/Gear—Pack For Sure

"Jesus answered him, "The first of all the commandments is: 'Hear, O Israel, the Lord our God, the Lord is one. And you shall love the Lord your God with all your heart, with all your soul, with all your mind, and with all your strength.' This is the first commandment. And the second, like it, is this: 'You shall love your neighbor as yourself.' There is no other commandment greater than these." So, the scribe said to Him, "Well said, Teacher. You have spoken the truth, for there is one God, and there is no other but He. And to love Him with all the heart, with all the understanding, with all the soul, and with all the strength, and to love one's neighbor as oneself, is more than all the whole burnt offerings and sacrifices." Now when Jesus saw that he answered wisely, He said to him, "You are not far from the kingdom of God." But after that no one dared question Him." Mark 12:29-34

Have love of God and humanity.

Altar

This comes in Joshua 4, where 12 stones were placed at Gilgal, to give the territory back to the Lord.

I have put together physical altars and been with other hunters who have set them up or put them at a place, them dedicating the place to God. The altars are of 12 stones, such as river stones, not shaped by man, and they don't have to be as big as the one's used at Gilgal.

I have used very small stones, put them in small plastic bags, mixed them with red wine and salt and a microscopic version of the Bible, sealed it all up so that it's all barely the size of an olive! Comes in handy when you want to place them in areas or buildings, especially evil buildings and sites, where they can be hidden from view.

I hunted with one guy who used a slingshot to fire these "altar projectiles" up, out and into places that can't be reached easily!

Then there are spiritual altars, which we've discussed in the Altar Sector, that can be set up in your heart and at a praise, worship and prayer location.

A very powerful and necessary weapon!

Anger of God

God's anger can flow through you.

"And in the greatness of Your excellence You have overthrown those who rose against You; You sent forth Your wrath; It consumed them like stubble." Exodus 15:7

Angels

Angels of God are a very powerful weapon that are overlooked. Some say angels cannot be used by us nor directed to do anything but by God. Bologna doctrines made up by people, that don't understand that they are right now a child of God with all power and authority! Angels must be called upon to protect you and all that you do and to assist you in the hunt and in life.

They are an important weapon for defense and offense. They are discussed more in depth at the end of this Sector.

Animals

One might not consider animals as a weapon that we can use, but let's see what Elisha did with them.

"So, he turned around and looked at them, and pronounced a curse on them in the name of the Lord. And two female bears came out of the woods and mauled forty-two of the youths." 2 Kings 2:24

A little extreme use of animals, however, they can also be considered as a disruption to pagan celebrations and festivals, etc., if God so directs.

Armor

Paul in Ephesians 6:13-17 tells us to, "take up the whole armor of God, that you may be able to withstand in the evil day, and having done all, to stand."

He speaks of girding your loins with truth, the breastplate of righteousness, feet shod with the preparation of the gospel of peace, the shield of faith, the helmet of salvation and the sword of the Spirit, which is the Word of God and also spiritual swords you will receive. He says having done all or done what God has had you do, you stand ready to go when God sends you again. Stand can also mean you do not retreat, but hold ground already taken.

You don't take off your armor… you always wear your armor and refortify daily for any weaknesses that may be in it.

Battle Cry of the Lord

"The Lord shall go forth like a mighty man; He shall stir up His zeal like a man of war. He shall cry out, yes, shout aloud; He shall prevail against His enemies." Isaiah 42:13

"Therefore, prophesy against them all these words, and say to them: The Lord will roar from on high, and utter His voice from His holy habitation; He will roar mightily against His fold. He will give a shout, as those who tread the grapes, Against all the inhabitants of the earth." Jeremiah 25:30

Prophesy as God leads and roar His voice at the enemy!

Battle Dress of the Lord

"For He put on righteousness as a breastplate, and a helmet of salvation on His head; He put on the garments of vengeance for clothing, and was clad with zeal as a cloak." Isaiah 59:17 also Ephesians 6:13-19

Bible/Word of God

Can be buried in the ground with wine, oil, and salt poured over it. Can also be placed whole or in separate pages in certain areas and places. It places the Word of God in this place.

Also, God can direct you to something in the Word for a particular situation that you are confronting. Also make proclamations.

Bind and Loose

"Assuredly, I say to you, whatever you bind on earth will be bound in heaven, and whatever you loose on earth will be loosed in heaven. "Again, I say to you that if two of you agree on earth concerning anything that they ask, it will be done for them by My Father in heaven. For where two or three are gathered together in My name, I am there in the midst of them." Matthew 18:18-20

You can bind and loose with your words… also your authority to loose angels, as it says whatsoever.

Blindness

"So, when the Syrians came down to him, Elisha prayed to the Lord, and said, "Strike this people, I pray, with blindness." And He struck them with blindness according to the word of Elisha." 2 Kings 6:18

Bow and Arrows

"If he does not turn back, He will sharpen His sword;
He bends His bow and makes it ready. He also prepares for Himself instruments of death;
He makes His arrows into fiery shafts." Psalm 7:12-13

"Flash forth lightning and scatter them; Shoot out Your arrows and destroy them." Psalm 144:6

I have used a spiritual bow and arrows to bring down evil entities.

Breath of God

"And then the lawless one will be revealed, whom the Lord will consume with the breath of His mouth and destroy with the brightness of His coming." 2 Thessalonians 2:8

Your breath can blow away evil entities, pain and sickness.

Camouflage or Stealth Technology

I have used camouflage many times, not only with clothing, but also in blinds to keep my body hidden (so the animals are blind to any danger). This is also available to us and is effective in keeping us hidden spiritually and physically, when we need to get close to the enemy or somewhere unawares.

"When they (Peter and the angel) were past the first and the second guard posts, they came to the iron gate that leads to the city, which opened to them of its own accord; and they went out and went down one street, and immediately the angel departed from him." Acts 12:10

The angel came to Peter in prison, released the chains from his hands, walked Peter invisible right past the guards, opened the prison gate and set Peter free. Have angels surround you and cover you or blind those in the physical and spiritual realms from seeing you, hearing you and sensing you.

This has also worked with me against non-other than satan… he didn't know I was there! (Although other times he did see me!)

Clapping

"I also will beat My fists together, And I will cause My fury to rest; I, the Lord, have spoken." Ezekiel 21:17

Cloth

Cloth from Paul was taken to the sick and those with evil spirits and they were set free.

"so that even handkerchiefs or aprons were brought from his body to the sick, and the diseases left them and the evil spirits went out of them." Acts 19:12

Clothes

God may direct you to wear certain clothes, perhaps all white and/or put writing on them. Although it sounds unusual to us, in the spiritual realm it will be important if that's the weapon needed.

"And these are the garments which they shall make: a breastplate, an ephod, a robe, a skillfully woven tunic, a turban, and a sash. So, they shall make holy garments for Aaron your brother and his sons, that he may minister to Me as priest." Exodus 28:4

"Then they made the plate of the holy crown of pure gold, and wrote on it an inscription like the engraving of a signet." Exodus 39:30

Commands/Proclamations

God has given us dominion. Command for things to be done.

Jesus never <u>prayed</u> for people to receive healing. Jesus never cast out an evil spirit with <u>prayer</u>. All were commands.

"For assuredly, I say to you, whoever says to this mountain, 'Be removed and be cast into the sea,' and does not doubt in his heart, but believes that those things he says will be done, he will have whatever he says." Mark 11:23

Communion

Take communion or Lord's Supper often, preferably every day… especially during a hunt. You can give it to yourself. Despite man-made, religious doctrines, the Bible and history tells us, that the Jews used and still use unleavened bread and red fermented wine at Passover. Bread is bread and wine is wine (not grape juice). You obtain and hang onto the power of the Cross through communion.

The evil realm hates communion and does not want us taking it.

Is it important?

"Then Jesus said to them, "Most assuredly, I say to you, unless you eat the flesh of the Son of Man (bread represents His body sacrificed for us) and drink His blood (wine represents His blood shed for us), you have no life in you." John 6:53

"For as often as you eat this bread and drink this cup, you proclaim the Lord's death till He comes." 1 Corinthians 11:26

CAUTION: Do not take communion if you are unworthy, as God's Word says if you do, this can cause weakness, sickness and even death! I Corinthians 11:29-30.

Faith

"So, Jesus answered and said to them, "Have faith in God. For assuredly, I say to you, whoever says to this mountain, 'Be removed and be cast into the sea,' and does not doubt in his heart, but believes that those things he says will be done, he will have whatever he says. Therefore, I say to you, whatever things you ask when you pray, believe that you receive them, and you will have them." Mark 11:22-24

Fasting

Moses, Joshua, Elijah and Jesus fasted 40 days. I have also fasted for 40 days, as God led me. Although the Bible mentions fasting, there are no set rules given as to how often or how long.

Jesus didn't even start His ministry until He had finished His 40-day fast. To follow what Jesus did is to follow His Standard.

In the Didache, the disciples fasted every Wednesday and Friday. I have also followed this habit for many years. (Always ready!)

Fasting is connected to spiritual warfare, as Daniel was fasting (Daniel 9:3/10:2-3) to produce angelic results.

Jesus advises us that there are various kinds of evil spirits, with some that require prayer and fasting to cast out.

" However, this kind does not go out except by prayer and fasting." Matthew 17:21

Let God direct you on fasting… be ready! See the Fasting Sector for more detail.

Fire

"So, Elijah answered and said to the captain of fifty, "If I am a man of God, then let fire come down from heaven and consume you and your fifty men." And fire came down from heaven and consumed him and his fifty." 2 Kings 1:10;12

God's Fire destroys spiritual enemies as well, which I have done.

Fish Heart and Liver Smoke

I thought this title would get your attention!

In the book of Tobit, one of the Apocryphal books, an angel tells Tobias "if a devil or evil spirit troubles any, we must make a smoke thereof before the man or the woman, and the party shall no more be vexed." Tobit 6

When this fish heart and liver was burned, the smoke affected an evil spirit that had killed seven men and "he fled into the utmost parts of Egypt, and the angel bound him." Tobit 8

Although I have never tried this weapon, I thought it was interesting.

Flags/Banners

Can be put in places as a declaration of the place to Jesus, to declare the victory of the Lord and fall of the evil stronghold/structure in a place.

If God directs these be used, He will give you the color and/or what to write on the flag.

These can also be very small in size, in order to place them where they will not be seen or disturbed.

"We will rejoice in your salvation, and in the name of our God we will set up our banners! May the Lord fulfill all your petitions." Psalm 20:5

"Lift up a banner on the high mountain, raise your voice to them; Wave your hand, that they may enter the gates of the nobles." Isaiah 13:2

Flame of Fire

"And of the angels He says: "Who makes His angels spirits and His ministers a flame of fire." Hebrews 1:7 and Psalm 104:4

Be a flame of fire for God.

Hedge

"So, Satan answered the Lord and said, "Does Job fear God for nothing? Have You not made a hedge around him, around his household, and around all that he has on every side? You have blessed the work of his hands, and his possessions have increased in the land." Job 1: 9-10

Satan couldn't touch Job, his family or possessions, as long as God's hedge was around him. This would be a hedge of power such as angels.

Holy Spirit and His Gifts

The Holy Spirit is God. He will give you power, revelation, guidance, gifts and more!

I can't imagine a hunt without Him with me.

"There are diversities of gifts, but the same Spirit. There are differences of ministries, but the same Lord. And there are diversities of activities, but it is the same God who works all in all. But the manifestation of the Spirit is given to each one for the profit of all: for to one is given the word of wisdom through the Spirit, to another the word of knowledge through the same Spirit, to another faith by the same Spirit, to another gifts of healings by the same Spirit, to another the working of miracles, to another prophecy, to another discerning of spirits, to another different kinds of tongues, to another the interpretation of tongues. But one and the same Spirit works all these things, distributing to each one individually as He wills. "1 Corinthians 12:4-11

Hooks

"I will turn you around, put hooks into your jaws, and lead you out, with all your army, horses, and horsemen, all splendidly clothed, a great company with bucklers and shields, all of them handling swords." Ezekiel 38:4

Imprecatory Psalms

David used the Imprecatory Psalms against the children of Belial! God, through David, gave us hundreds of bombs… that we can drop against our mutual foe.

One part of God's Word that I have never personally seen nor heard a Christian utilize, are the Imprecatory Psalms.

Research has shown that many Christians condemn the use of this segment of the Word, even though it is God's Word.

Satan and the children of Belial definitely do not want these Psalms being used against them and the evil realm… because they work!

I call them the "Psalm Bombs!"

"since it is a righteous thing with God to repay with tribulation those who trouble you." 2 Thessalonians 1:6

Can we ask God to recompense tribulation?

Absolutely!

The Old Testament Levites issued curses, as set forth by God.

"Let their eyes be darkened, so that they do not see;
And make their loins shake continually.
Pour out Your indignation upon them,
And let Your wrathful anger take hold of them.
Let their dwelling place be desolate;
Let no one live in their tents.
For they persecute the ones You have struck,
And talk of the grief of those You have wounded.
Add iniquity to their iniquity,
And let them not come into Your righteousness.
Let them be blotted out of the book of the living,
And not be written with the righteous." Psalm 69:23-28

When a person of authority in Christ on earth speaks certain words, our Heavenly Father's power is released in heaven!

"And I will give you the keys of the kingdom of heaven, and whatever you bind on earth will be bound in heaven, and whatever you loose on earth will be loosed in heaven." Matthew 16:19/18:18

Authorized agents of God, can speak these words of God, to release angels.

"Bless the LORD, ye his angels that excel in strength, that do his commandments, hearkening unto the voice of his word." Psalm 103:20

Imprecatory Psalms - Psalms 5, 6, 11, 12, 35, 37, 40, 52, 54, 56, 58, 59, 69, 79, 109, 137, 139 and 143 - were given to us to pronounce against workers of iniquity.

More on this in the Xtreme Rabid Game Sector.

Insects

An unusual weapon, yet insects such as bees, hornets, flies, locusts, mosquitoes, ants, etc., can be directed to go and disrupt evil activities.

"So, the Lord said to Moses, "Say to Aaron, 'Stretch out your rod, and strike the dust of the land, so that it may become lice throughout all the land of Egypt.'" Exodus 8:16

"And the Lord did so. Thick swarms of flies came into the house of Pharaoh, into his servants' houses, and into all the land of Egypt. The land was corrupted because of the swarms of flies." Exodus 8:24

Intercession

There are times when God may ask you to intercede on behalf of people or pray for blessing or protection. When hunting in groups, it can be typical that God will choose some hunters to go out physically to certain areas and for others to remain in a place to pray for the protection of the hunters.

I was an intercessor with others near Mexico and as we prayed I could see God's protecting fire envelop the hunters.

Map

Any spiritual mapping that has been done is another weapon and part of the hunting gear that will be involved, if God directs.

More on this in the Sector on Spiritual Mapping.

Name of Jesus

"For it is written: "As I live, says the Lord, every knee shall bow to Me, and every tongue shall confess to God." Romans 14:11 and Isaiah 45:23

Use this weapon often, as you have been given authority and power with this name.

"It is like a man going to a far country, who left his house and gave authority to his servants, and to each his work, and commanded the doorkeeper to watch." Mark 13:34

Net of God

"Wherever they go, I will spread My net on them; I will bring them down like birds of the air; I will chastise them according to what their congregation has heard." Hosea 7:12

Evil spirits of the air, like birds, come to take away the seeds of truth and the gospel. (Luke 8:5)

During many of my hunts, holy angels have taken evil spiritual creatures away in big nets and bags.

Noise

"For the Lord had caused the army of the Syrians to hear the noise of chariots and the noise of horses—the noise of a great army; so they said to one another, "Look, the king of Israel has hired against us the kings of the Hittites and the kings of the Egyptians to attack us!" Therefore they arose and fled at twilight, and left the camp intact—their tents, their horses, and their donkeys—and they fled for their lives." 2 Kings 7:6-7

Imagine the possibilities!

Olive Oil

Consecrate the olive oil to the Lord. Oil is used to consecrate apostles, teachers, evangelists, and is used for healing and deliverance.

As Jacob did in Genesis 28:18, "And Jacob rose up early in the morning, and took the stone that he had put for his pillows, and set it up for a pillar, and poured oil upon the top of it," you can pour oil over the altar, territory, and area and use as the Holy Spirit guides. 1 Samuel 16:1/ 1 Samuel 16: 10, 13

Praise

A very successful and required aspect of spiritual and physical warfare! Praise God for His success in the battle before, during and after.

He may even say to just praise Him without being required to do anything else but watch the enemy be defeated.

Read 2 Chronicles 20, of how God had the enemy fight each other, while King Jehoshaphat and the people of Judah watched!

Now that's the way to win a war! (Be sure God leads you to use only this method, as it is not for every battle!)

Prayer

Keep in touch with God (SAC time). Don't traipse off hunting on your own, without spiritual senses in operation, because if you do, you move forward deaf, dumb and blind!

Reptiles/Amphibians

"Then the Lord spoke to Moses, "Say to Aaron, 'Stretch out your hand with your rod over the streams, over the rivers, and over the ponds, and cause frogs to come up on the land of Egypt.'" So, Aaron stretched out his hand over the waters of Egypt, and the frogs came up and covered the land of Egypt." Exodus 8:5-6

Imagine what these guys can do at an evil location or event!

Right Hand of the Lord

"Your right hand, O Lord, has become glorious in power; Your right hand, O Lord, has dashed the enemy in pieces." Exodus 15:6

"Oh, sing to the Lord a new song! For He has done marvelous things; His right hand and His holy arm have gained Him the victory." Psalm 98:1

"The Lord is at Your right hand; He shall execute kings in the day of His wrath." Psalm 110:5

Ask God's Right Hand to assist you.

Righteousness

Righteousness is a spiritual force.

"for the kingdom of God is not eating and drinking, but righteousness and peace and joy in the Holy Spirit." Romans 14:17

Sacrifice

Releases spiritual power. Nothing beats the sacrifice of Jesus.

Be led by God.

Salt

This represents a covenant/pact…

"And every offering of your grain offering you shall season with salt; you shall not allow the salt of the covenant of your God to be lacking from your grain offering. With all your offerings, you shall offer salt." Leviticus 2:13

"Should you not know that the Lord God of Israel gave the dominion over Israel to David forever, to him and his sons, by a covenant of salt?" 2 Chronicles 13:5 and heals the earth.

"Then the men of the city said to Elisha, "Please notice, the situation of this city is pleasant, as my lord sees; but the water is bad, and the ground barren." And he said, "Bring me a new bowl, and put salt in it." So, they brought it to him. Then he went out to the source of the water, and cast in the salt there, and said, "Thus says the Lord: 'I have healed this water; from it there shall be no more death or barrenness.'" So, the water remains healed to this day, according to the word of Elisha which he spoke." 2 Kings 2:19-22

You may be led to sprinkle this around at some place that needs healing and declare restoration.

Seeds/Grain

Seed or grain symbolizes the fruit of the spirit and an awakening of the area or place where you spread it.

"There will be an abundance of grain in the earth, On the top of the mountains; Its fruit shall wave like Lebanon; And those of the city shall flourish like grass of the earth." Psalm 72:16

Declare the gospel to grow and spread over an area.

Shadow

"so that they brought the sick out into the streets and laid them on beds and couches, that at least the shadow of Peter passing by might fall on some of them." Acts 5:15

Shofar

Blow as the Lord directs.

"The sons of Aaron, the priests, shall blow the trumpets; and these shall be to you as an ordinance forever throughout your generations. When you go to war in your land against the enemy who oppresses you, then you shall sound an alarm with the trumpets, and you will be remembered before the Lord your God, and you will be saved from your enemies." Numbers 10:8-9

Evil entities flee when this is sounded. There are many reports of people being instantly healed and delivered, just from the blowing of the shofar!

When the shofar is blown, I have seen innumerable angels show up immediately... angels filled the sky as far as I could see, until in the distance, their numbers blended together and they looked like smoke!

This happens often!

This is a very powerful weapon!

Silence

Shut up!

Keep quiet... don't reveal and blab hunting plans around before you get there.

Evil spirits can see, hear and understand your plans and will do everything they can to stop you and others, if you forget to use camouflage.

Cover any conversations that you have with others in person, with the blood of Jesus, and protection from angels, and declare that your communications can not be heard nor understood by any enemies, in Jesus Name.

Keep hunting plans off of the computer, internet and phone as much as possible.

Sleep

"At Your rebuke, O God of Jacob, both the chariot and horse were cast into a dead." Psalm 76:6

Put your enemies to sleep.

Slingshot

David used one on Goliath and I have seen one used by a hunter to project small altars into hard to reach areas!

If God says you need one on the next trip… don't leave home without it!

Stakes

"Enlarge the place of your tent, and let them stretch out the curtains of your dwellings; Do not spare; Lengthen your cords, and strengthen your stakes." Isaiah 54:2

In some Christian bookstores, they sell metal or wooden stakes with scripture on them, that can be driven deep into the ground out of sight.

Can be used as boundaries of an area or city and declare the area within or around as the Lord's.

Do as the Holy Spirit guides.

Surrender

Total surrender to Father's <u>perfect</u> will and the direction of the Holy Spirit for your life, your ministry and all warfare!

Sword of God

"and say, 'O mountains of Israel, hear the word of the Lord God! Thus, says the Lord God to the mountains, to the hills, to the ravines, and to the valleys: "Indeed I, even I, will bring a sword against you, and I will destroy your high places." Ezekiel 6:3

"I have set the point of the sword against all their gates, That the heart may melt and many may stumble. Ah! It is made bright; It is grasped for slaughter." Ezekiel 21:15

Speak to and against the high places, the waters, and the valleys, the gates of hell and evil strongholds and put God's sword against them.

I have several spiritual swords given to me by our Father and Jesus.

I have used them many times to conquer evil entities.

T'NT

All of us have heard of TNT which is also known as dynamite.

In the spiritual realm we have dynamite called Tongue And Tongues… T'NT!

Although this sounds a bit like a slip of the tongue, these are two distinct spiritual activities; and failure to recognize and apply these two functions can cause confusion and dilution of spiritual power.

Many Christians are aware of tongue speech or "speaking in tongues," as it's usually referred to, with some "doing it" and most not. Many who "do it" say those who don't "do it" are not saved or not filled with the Holy Spirit.

That is doctrinal nonsense that serves only to tear away at the unity amongst Christians. God says, when you're born again and baptized with the Holy Spirit …you got the Holy Spirit!

"Now He who establishes us with you in Christ and has anointed us is God, who also has sealed us and given us the Spirit in our hearts as a guarantee." Corinthians 1:21-22

Also, those who think there's no need to "speak in either or BOTH kinds of tongue or tongues speech" are also missing the mark.

Paul said:

"I thank my God I speak with tongues more than you all." 1 Corinthians 14:18

All born-again and Spirit baptized Christians have the Holy Spirit that abides with them and comes upon them.

The teaching on <u>utilizing</u> this anointing is greatly lacking, not the individual Christian!

The question arises with some, whether we can speak in a spiritual language when <u>we</u> want or must we wait until the Holy Spirit comes upon us?

The answer is yes… we do both!

The two different forms of spiritual tongue speech that is in the Bible, is speaking in a tongue (singular) and diversity of tongues (plural).

As Paul taught, we can speak in a tongue by our own will:

"For if I pray in a tongue (singular), my spirit prays, but my understanding is unfruitful. What is the conclusion then? I will pray with the spirit, and I will also pray with the understanding. I will sing with the spirit, and I will also sing with the understanding." 1 Corinthians 14:14-15

"For he who speaks in a tongue (singular) does not speak to men but to God, for no one understands him; however, in the spirit he speaks mysteries." 1 Corinthians 14:2

And we can speak in diversity of tongues, as the Holy Spirit wills and comes upon us, as this is one of the gifts of the Holy Spirit:

"to another faith by the same Spirit, to another gifts of healings by the same Spirit (Holy Spirit), to another the working of miracles, to another prophecy, to another discerning of spirits, to another different kinds of tongues (plural), to another the interpretation of tongues (plural). But one and the same Spirit works all these things, distributing to each one individually as He (the Holy Spirit) wills." 1 Corinthians 12:9-11

"And God has appointed these in the church: first apostles, second prophets, third teachers, after that miracles, then gifts of healings, helps, administrations, varieties of tongues (plural)." 1 Corinthians 12:28

Why should we want to use tongue and tongues or T'NT?

The Bible says T'NT are activities that are available and that we should be engaged with both:

*tongue (singular) speech in our will to spiritually pray, sing and worship God… John 4:23; 1 Corinthians 14:2; 1 Corinthians14:4; 1 Corinthians 14:14

*diversity of tongues (plural), which is the Holy Spirit using us as intercessors to bring God's will on earth. Acts 2:4; Acts 10:46; 1 Corinthians 12:30; 1 Corinthians 13:1; 1 Corinthians 14:18

In both cases, we must be willing to spiritually speak, which we can do as the Holy Spirit anointing is in us and also to spiritually speak as the Holy Spirit gives us utterance (Acts 2:4). And, when the Holy Spirit's special anointing comes for a time to empower us to serve and do specific works of the Father. Both activities build up our spirit!

So, what's going on when the Holy Spirit anointing comes for a time on us to operate in diversity of tongues?

"Though I speak with the tongues of men and of angels, but have not love, I have become sounding brass or a clanging cymbal." 1 Corinthians 13:1

The Holy Spirit gives us a language that may be necessary to speak to people in their own language to reach/teach them, as He did at Pentecost.

"And when this sound occurred, the multitude came together, and were confused, because everyone heard them speak in his own language." Acts 2:6

There are also many modern-day testimonies of God talking to someone in their native language through a born-again Christian of another language.

This happened to my Mom when the Holy Spirit spoke Italian through her, to a woman in the hospital, which brought this woman to Christ before she died!

My Mom didn't speak anything but English!

Obviously a very powerful tool, to convince the unsaved and unbelieving of the presence of God!

Another aspect of diversity of tongues, is speaking the language of angels.

Why would we need to do that?

Do you think angels act when God tells them to do something through you?

You betcha they do!

What would they be doing?

Just imagine!

And all God needs is for you to be willing!

"And the smoke of the incense, with the prayers of the saints, ascended before God from the angel's hand." Revelation 8:4

Praying in the spirit (tongue speech) by your will comes from earth up to heaven and fills God's throne room.

"Then the angel took the censer, filled it with fire from the altar, and threw it to the earth. And there were noises, thunderings, lightnings, and an earthquake." Revelation 8:5

God's Will comes to you, from heaven to earth, and you speak (hopefully) in diversity of tongues.

Why doesn't God just do all this Himself and just fix everything that's in a mess?

God chose to limit Himself by giving man dominion on earth (Genesis 1:26, 28) and thus we are rulers of earth right now, unless we allow satan to steal our dominion.

The earth's in a mess because we allow it to be that way!

Christians have been shown and told by God what to do throughout His Word… yet what are they doing? Christians, for the most part, are working in the flesh, instead of in the spirit and are being eaten alive by unseen, evil spiritual entities!

They keep praying to God, in the flesh, to do something and God says, "But I put you in charge… why don't you do something!"

One thing we can do is use T'NT!

"for prophecy never came by the will of man, but holy men of God spoke as they were moved by the Holy Spirit." 2 Peter 1:21

Notice and expect God's move upon you, especially when you are willfully praying, singing, praising and worshipping in your spiritual tongue speech.

Diverse kinds of tongues will come outside of your own will from the Holy Spirit.

Tongue speech is a language, and every language sounds different, and is important (1 Corinthians 14:10) so listen for a change in tone and sound from your usual spiritual tongue speech.

You will not only be able to hear a change in language, but also sense a change in your spirit, as the Holy Spirit will be in operation on you.

You should notice how your spirit perceives this when it happens, in order for you to develop your spiritual being and perception of God. This perception may be a number of things like heaviness, laughter, sorrow, joy, and love.

Keep speaking in your willful spiritual tongue, giving God your PAW (praise and worship). Then, as God moves on you, and you speak in diverse kinds of tongues, you will be developing your spirit to recognize and act when the Holy Spirit anoints you at certain times, for certain functions. You can then act upon God's perfect will, by speaking His words that He wants spoken for specific reasons at that specific time… perhaps to a person or a group, perhaps to angels to act, perhaps against evil entities!

"Your kingdom come. Your will be done on earth as it is in Heaven." Matthew 6:10

Translate/Teleporting

"Now when they came up out of the water, the Spirit of the Lord caught Philip away, so that the eunuch saw him no more; and he went on his way rejoicing. But Philip was found at Azotus. And passing through, he preached in all the cities till he came to Caesarea." Acts 8:39-40

Philip was translated in body and spirit from Gaza to Azotus, about 25 miles away.

"Then they willingly received Him into the boat, and immediately the boat was at the land where they were going." John 6:21

Jesus, some disciples and an entire boat was moved several miles instantly!

Many instances of the Desert Fathers physically moving in an instant to somewhere else (cutting down on travel time), into locked rooms and even into Heaven!

Enoch went physically into Heaven! (1, 2 &3 Enoch)

No disputing that this is a great weapon!

Traps

"A noose is hidden for him on the ground, and a trap for him in the road." Job 18:10

"Let their table become a snare before them, and their well-being a trap." Psalm 69:22

"For among My people are found wicked men; They lie in wait as one who sets snares; They set a trap; They catch men." Jeremiah 5:26

"And David says: "Let their table become a snare and a trap, A stumbling block and a recompense to them." Romans 11:9

Trapping with my Dad, I realized how very effective traps and snares can be against creatures that are difficult to capture.

Traps are available to us in the spiritual world and the evil realm uses them against you ALL THE TIME, so be vigilant!

I trapped an evil spirit one time that thought I was defeated. I waited until it was in my trap and then… whap!

Isn't hunting fun?

Of course, now they don't seem to want to get close to me anymore.

Voice

"The Lord will cause His glorious voice to be heard,
And show the descent of His arm,
With the indignation of His anger
And the flame of a devouring fire,
With scattering, tempest, and hailstones.
For through the voice of the Lord
Assyria will be beaten down,
As He strikes with the rod.
And in every place where the staff of punishment passes,
Which the Lord lays on him,
It will be with tambourines and harps;
And in battles of brandishing He will fight with it.
For Tophet was established of old,
Yes, for the king it is prepared.
He has made it deep and large;
Its pyre is fire with much wood;
The breath of the Lord, like a stream of brimstone,
Kindles it." Isaiah 30:30-33

He can use our voice or shout through us.

Weather

"He sent out His arrows and scattered the foe,
Lightnings in abundance, and He vanquished them." Psalm 18:14

"Have you entered the treasury of snow,
Or have you seen the treasury of hail,
Which I have reserved for the time of trouble,
For the day of battle and war?
By what way is light diffused,
Or the east wind scattered over the earth?

"Who has divided a channel for the overflowing water,
Or a path for the thunderbolt,
To cause it to rain on a land where there is no one,
A wilderness in which there is no man;

... From whose womb comes the ice?
And the frost of heaven, who gives it birth?...

Can you send out lightnings, that they may go,
And say to you, 'Here we are!'?" Job 38: 22-26; 29; 35

"And it happened, as they fled before Israel and were on the descent of Beth Horon, that the Lord cast down large hailstones from heaven on them as far as Azekah, and they died. There were more who died from the hailstones than the children of Israel killed with the sword." Joshua 10:11

"And Moses stretched out his rod toward heaven; and the Lord sent thunder and hail, and fire darted to the ground. And the Lord rained hail on the land of Egypt." Exodus 9:23

Snow, wind, rain, hail, ice, lightning, thunder can all be used in battle to stop evil ceremonies and pagan festivals and events, to name a few ways.

"When I put out your light, I will cover the heavens, and make its stars dark; I will cover the sun with a cloud, and the moon shall not give her light. All the bright lights of the heavens I will make dark over you, and bring darkness upon your land," Says the Lord God." Ezekiel 32:7-8

Wine

"in a holy place, you shall pour out the drink to the Lord as an offering." Numbers 28:7

Use red wine as a symbol of the blood of Jesus.

I have also dug a hole, broke bread into it, poured wine over it and declared the place holy to the Lord. This brings healing to the earth that has been defiled by sin, iniquity, wars and bloodshed.

Many times, you will be led to mix the oil and wine together and also salt.

Many consider this a standard weapon to automatically take on a hunt, with oil and salt.

Use as directed by the Holy Spirit.

Words

"Then God said, Let there be light: and there was light." Genesis 1:3

God created with words.

The power of words is enormous.

Let the Holy Spirit guide you on what to say and then say it!

Worship

"Saying with a loud voice, "Fear God and give glory to Him, for the hour of His judgment has come; and worship Him who made Heaven and Earth, the sea and springs of water. Revelation 14:7

True worship brings down the power of God and brings down the Xtreme Big Game… like with Elijah on the mountain with offerings and sacrifices (1Kings 18: 17-40). *

Remember that these elements and physical things have no spiritual power of themselves, as they are created objects.

Faith and God's guidance for this hunt, makes all of these physical elements powerful and destructive weapons against the enemy realm.

Don't get obsessed with methods and procedures, throwing elements around with a "shotgun approach", thinking if enough is applied, it'll work.

Don't get stuck on what others have done in the past or thinking that God had you do it in a certain place, so it must work everywhere.

I know many Christians walk around their city doing such things, in a genuine effort to do good, yet many times the fruit has either been small or non-existent or was counter-productive.

Don't just read a book and try that method because it worked in some other city.

This activity can also rile up the evil realm and bring heavy attacks against you.

God will guide you and will honor your obedience.

There are many spiritual weapons that God will give you when you are "in the spirit". These can vary from swords to blowguns! Yes—blowgun—someone that I know was in the spirit when God gave him a blow gun as a weapon!

You can and will also be given horses, chariots, spears and so on.

And of course, angels also have various weapons at their disposal to assist you, as well as the ability to bind and take evil entities away, seal off gates of hell, etc.…

Using "the Name of Jesus"; applying the blood of Jesus; utilizing discernment; prophecy; wisdom; knowledge and even Biblical cursing, are all weapons.

Additional weapons that you can always be ready with ahead of any hunt are the whole armor of God (Ephesians 6), reading the Bible; fasting; asking for and developing the gifts of the Holy Spirit (1 Corinthians 12), SAC time, PAW time, being FIT, etc.…

When I am in the spirit, the correct spiritual weapons are at my disposal and I use them without hesitation. I hear the same with others and trust the same will be with you on your hunting trips.

God's instruments are mightier than any others.

"You are My battle-ax and weapons of war:
For with you I will break the nation in pieces;
With you I will destroy kingdoms." Jeremiah 51:20

Remember… God says that you are His battle axe and weapon of war and with you He will destroy and break nations in pieces.

David knew that with God, he could destroy multiple nations that came against him. So can we!

"All nations surrounded me, but in the name of the LORD I will destroy them. They surrounded me, yes, they surrounded me; but in the name of the LORD I will destroy them. They surrounded me like bees; they were quenched like a fire of thorns; for in the name of the LORD I will destroy them. You pushed me violently, that I might fall, but the LORD helped me." Psalm 118:10-13

Keep in mind that satan and the evil kingdom, also use many of these same weapons and counterfeits.

Also, do not go to places, attack people or destroy property and such things, and end up getting yourself and others arrested, as that is unnecessary and also against the law.

"Forewarned is forearmed," is a good saying.

Another one I used when I was a Queen Scout in Canada (equivalent to Eagle Scout in the USA) was "Be Prepared."

CLOSE QUARTER COMBAT

We must always remember NOT to carry "excess baggage" with us into spiritual warfare (mental, emotional, spiritual, physical).

In Ephesians 6:12 Paul says that we wrestle (war-Greek: pale) NOT against flesh and blood, but against an evil spiritual enemy.

When Paul wrote this, he was using an analogy to describe Close Quarter Combat between two individuals… hands on battle!

When we consider that often the loser in Greek wrestling had his eyes gouged out, with resulting blindness for the rest of his days, we have a taste of how the Ephesian saints who read Paul's letter would have received this illustration. The believer's wrestling against the powers of darkness is no less serious.

Also, when the ancient Greeks wrestled, they did so naked… they didn't weigh themselves down. How many Christians go into battle carrying "excess baggage" with them (mental, emotional, spiritual, religious man-made doctrines)

History teaches us a good lesson, when the army of Alexander the Great was advancing on Persia. At one critical point, it appeared that his troops might be defeated. The soldiers had taken so much plunder from their previous campaigns that they had become weighted down and were losing their effectiveness in close quarter combat.

Alexander commanded that all the spoils be thrown into a heap and burned. The men complained bitterly but soon saw the wisdom of the order. Someone wrote, "It was as if wings had been given to them—they walked lightly again."

Victory was assured!

The Bible also likens Christians to runners. To win the race, we must "lay aside every weight" that would drag us down and rob us of our strength and endurance (Hebrews 12:1).

This weight may be an excessive desire for possessions; the captivating love of money; an endless pursuit of pleasure; slavery to sinful passions; or a burdensome, religious, legalistic mindset.

As soldiers of Christ and as a Silver Bullet of God, we must rid ourselves of anything that hinders us in Close Quarter Combat with our spiritual enemy.

To fight the battle effectively, we must be clad with the spiritual armor of God (Ephesians 6:11-17).

When I go hunting big game such as deer or moose, I don't carry with me things that will hinder me and even though I have all the gear needed to get the job done, I must go to where they are to be effective. If I hunt at home or go to the mall or wander around my neighbourhood with my rifle shooting wildly into space, I won't accomplish anything other than interest from the police!

If I find my way to the woods where the game lives but wear a blindfold, I won't be successful either!

As Christians, we are in fierce and deadly Close Quarter Combat with spiritual entities, so we must be properly prepared or they will beat us! They may win small battles, some big battles and maybe even win the war against you if they lure and trap you into losing your salvation!

If you get smacked down, find out what happened... did you sin; fail to forgive someone; get sidetracked in the world; operate in the flesh instead of in the spirit... find the root... get rid of the root and then get up and press on!

Paul didn't say we wrestle part time nor did he say we take the armor on and off... it stays on as the war against us is always on... every day... the enemy doesn't sleep!

Some "weekend warriors" (1 hour on Sunday Christians) have a very poor chance of survival in all-out Close Quarter Combat with a determined enemy operating on a 24/7 basis. Statistics on various denominations and their watered-down or anti-Gospel doctrines indicate how efficient the enemy has been in infiltrating the Church and destroying from within. The enemy has been so effective, that most people don't realize they have been conquered!

The main Close Quarter Combat tactic the enemy utilizes against us is in our minds. Many are convinced that they're OK and anyone that comes along to point out to them Biblically that they're losing or totally lost, is shunned, ignored and even attacked! (Has happened to Rhoda and me!) The enemy also bamboozles many into thinking that spiritual warfare isn't necessary!

Even when we're beating the enemy at every turn, we must be careful to remain humble and give all the glory to God, as the enemy will toss the "pride trap" in our path to bring us down.

The gist or essence of this study and what Paul is telling us is, that we are in a deadly Close Quarter Battle with spiritual enemies. They are serious, prepared, cunning, ruthless and merciless. Should we be any less?

So, to be the Close Quarter Combat conqueror that we're destined to be, we must:

1. Recognize that the real enemy is spiritual, not physical!
2. Don't carry any "excess baggage" with you into battle!
3. Put on the whole armor of God!
4. Never take the armor off!
5. Don't operate blind or in the flesh... operate in the spirit, with the Holy Spirit's timing, tactics and weapons!
6. Hunt where the enemy is, not where they ain't!
7. Examine ourselves after any loss to find the root and get rid of it!
8. Realize that we are in combat every day!
9. Keep our lives and thinking in tune with the Gospel... make immediate corrections if needed!
10. Give all the glory to God!

11. Be serious, prepared, cunning, ruthless and merciless!
12. Have fun!

What was that last one... have fun?

Yes, as Christians we are to have joy in life, even in Close Quarter Battle (CQC), as we are defeating an enemy that is against God, that wants to destroy us, that wants to destroy the Church, that wants to bring sickness and death, that wants us to suffer... we should enjoy attacking and conquering such enemies!

Once, every soldier (prior to firearms and missiles) was taught and mastered CQC to ready themselves for physical wars. If they didn't, they didn't last long! Now it is usually only offered to elite military special operation groups such Delta Force or Navy SEALS. Martial artists of old were extremely effective in CQC... now they are mostly taught sport or point entertainment fighting, rather than preparing for real CQC encounters!

Sadly, the same goes for the Church today... once, the early Church Christians were trained and prepared for reality! They were lethal in spiritual battle! Who teaches or practises spiritual CQC today? Only a very small percentage are doing what God wants them to do! Too many Christians are only interested in "choreographed routines" (planned memorized services) ... afraid of CQC or to fight back, even when the enemy has them on the ground in a chokehold.

What are they afraid of... dying?

"Cowards die many times before their deaths; the valiant never taste of death but once. Of all the wonders that I yet have heard, it seems to me most strange that men should fear; Seeing that death, a necessary end, will come when it will come." William Shakespeare

"For to me, living means living for Christ, and dying is even better." Paul in his letter to the Philippians 1:21NLT

"Live for nothing, or die for something. It's your call." Rambo

We're in Close Quarter Combat, whether we want it or not so let's make the enemy hurt!

ANGELS

The business side of a gun is the muzzle.

When it is time to use a gun, you bring it up, aim, and pull the trigger, when you are very sure of taking your game.

A weapon is not a toy, and is to be handled properly.

In the spiritual realm, there are angels that have been used as God's weapons, that we can also use as weapons.

"Behold, I have created the smith that bloweth the coals in the fire, and that bringeth forth an instrument for his work; and I have created the waster to destroy." Isaiah 54:16 KJV

The waster refers to a destroyer angel.

The Bible tells us what just one angel did in the physical realm:

"And it came to pass on a certain night that the angel of the Lord went out, and killed in the camp of the Assyrians one hundred and eighty-five thousand; and when people arose early in the morning, there were the corpses—all dead." 2 Kings 19:35

That's 185,000 men slain in one night!

Angels of God are also very effective in the spiritual realm, that can be directed by man, as he/she is directed by God.

I have set angels in place to protect me, my home, others, and certain locations, as well as to close gates to the underworld/hell and to release POW's.

They can be directed and set in place, whether you see them or not.

I have also hunted with angels many times in the spirit, as you will read in other Sectors.

I have seen angels that are 6' tall and some that are taller than a house! Some who have wings, some without wings, some with different weapons, some on chariots, some with various kinds of armor, and some with just robes. They come in various colors also!

The Holy Spirit reveals to us what to do with them and to set the sword's point against objectives! Ezekiel 21:15

The dispatching of angels into battle is available to every spirit-filled Christian who walks in revelation.

Why doesn't God just do all of this and have His angels do what He wants and leave us out of it?

<u>Because He wants US to do it!</u>

A book in my library called, *The Scroll of the War of the Sons of Light Against the Sons of Darkness,* by Yigael Yadin (1962), is the interpretation of what is commonly called The War Scroll found in Qumran, Israel as one of the Dead Sea Scrolls.

It vividly describes war tactics, formations, and weapons, and how they are used in war.

One of the main weapons mentioned was angels, who were directed to assist in warfare against physical and spiritual enemies.

There are other examples in the Bible of when angels were utilized in battle. Unfortunately, many Christians have never thought of nor believe that we can command angels, in the name of Jesus. I wonder if that is based on the fact that they tried and the angels wouldn't move, or because that is their non-Biblical personal doctrine?

Some Christians say we cannot order spirits around.

Really?

If that is so, how can we cast out evil spirits from a person or a place?

"And I will give you the keys of the kingdom of heaven, and <u>whatever</u> you bind on earth will be bound in Heaven, and <u>whatever</u> you loose on earth will be loosed in heaven." Matthew 16:19; 18:18

We have the authority to speak and dispatch angels into battle; to close gates of hell; take away and imprison evil entities; assist with Xtreme Game Hunting and more… freeing up people to come to the Lord!

If you don't think that this is powerful, see what satan had to say to God about Job, as he had no power or ability to get to him.

"Have You not made a hedge around him, around his household, and around all that he has on every side?" Job 1:10

Does anybody think this was a hedge of bushes?

Satan couldn't get past the angels of God around Job!

I asked God <u>every day</u> for 6 months to see angels before I finally did!

Be persistent!

Same goes with moving in the spirit realm… keep asking until you achieve!

(Keep in mind you will also be seeing the dark side of the spiritual realm!)

Angels are waiting for your orders right now—and during a hunt!

Praise God… thank you Lord for this mighty weapon at our disposal. Amen

THE SECRET OF GOD'S POWER

Many people will say, "Yeah all these weapons and strategies sound cool but I'm not Jesus" or "you need a "special anointing" to do this or "it doesn't work because I know people who tried"!

WHAT IS THE SECRET OF GOD' S POWER?

How do we do greater things than Jesus did?

"What I'm about to tell you is true. Anyone who has faith in me will do what I have been doing. In fact, he will do even greater things. That is because I am going to the Father." John 14:12 NIRV

Do we need a special anointing, special ministry, special Holy Spirit gifting, a special calling or to be special like many say, before miracles, signs and wonders… the power of God will manifest?

The Bible doesn't say that we do. What did Jesus just say in John 14:12? He said anyone who has faith in Jesus (as Son of God) has God's power.

After the miracle of the multiplication of loaves and fish to feed thousands, Jesus was asked a simple question in John 6:28… "Then they said to Him, "What shall we do, that we may work the works of God?" (in other words, how do we get this power?) Jesus gave a simple answer "Jesus answered and said to them, "This is the work of God, that you believe in Him whom He sent." John 6:29

So again, Jesus says, to do God's work (miracles, signs, wonders, have supernatural power, etc.) we must believe in Jesus.

But most of you will say… I believe in Jesus, but nothing happens when I pray for someone to be healed or when I pray for a miracle. Many say, "My faith probably isn't strong enough to do it."

But Jesus said, "I say to you, if you have faith as a mustard seed, you will say to this mountain, 'Move from here to there,' and it will move; and nothing will be impossible for you." Matthew 17:20b

So, our belief system must be askew or off the mark, as what God says can't be wrong.

Let's examine some stumbling blocks… "The Dirty Dozen"

1. Many think they can't manifest the power of God, as "only Jesus could do those things" … we've already shown this thinking to be false doctrine.
2. Many think special people or a special anointing is needed… also just proven with a few scriptures that this is false doctrine.
3. Many think their faith is too small… mustard seeds are extremely small… false doctrine again.
4. When people pray, many expect God to do it… Jesus said speak directly to the issue at hand (i.e. mountain) in faith and nothing is impossible (Mt. 17:20b).
5. Many are doing their will instead of God's will… Jesus said in John 6:38 "For I have come down from heaven, not to do My own will, but the will of Him who sent Me." Jesus never did His own will.
6. Many pray and hope, rather than have faith that what they said will

be done.

7. Many have wrong or sinful motives for the power of God to manifest through them, such as personal agendas, wants and desires or to gain fame and fortune.

It's a noble desire to want God's power for the right reasons, not as Lucifer and Adam went about it, but as Jesus taught us.

8. Many limit their belief in Jesus as just a Savior that forgives sins… we need to believe that He is much more and that we receive much more "And I will give you the keys of the kingdom of heaven, and whatever you bind on earth will be bound in heaven, and whatever you loose on earth will be loosed in heaven." Matthew 16:19

9. Many are afraid to try.

10. Many are in rebellion/compromising with what Jesus did and said.

11. Many think and teach that the faith of the mountain (receiver) is required rather than the faith of the giver… everyone that Jesus dealt with was healed, delivered, raised from the dead… no failures, despite dealing with countless people over 3 ½ years that probably had little or no faith (obviously the dead had no faith, neither did the loaves and fish to multiply themselves). Testimonies from around the world also support, that those with no faith (non-Christians) receive healing, deliverance and miracles through Christians.

12. Many are unaware of or don't accept or believe their position as a saint, a royal priest, a ruler, a joint-heir with Christ and that they are more than a conqueror that can accomplish Father's will without fail (Romans 8:17, 37).

If any or all of these "dirty dozen" are in your way of moving mountains; correct them, as they're all mental corrections… No heavy lifting involved!

If an evil spirit is supporting one of the blocks, get rid of it… command it to go!

To summarize in a word what is needed is, "confidence!"

When my Mom started out in her ministry, which she preferred to call a "Faith Ministry", rather than a healing ministry, she dealt with people that had aches and pains and they would be healed instantly. She was confident. Then came the first of many people to her that had cancer. My Mom blinked! Not so confident with cancer. God said to her at that moment, "Do you think it's harder for Me to heal cancer than it is to heal a headache?" Now the confidence was back and it stayed! Many were healed of cancer.

When people would thank her for their healing, she'd always say, "Thank Jesus, don't thank me. I can't heal a hangnail!"

Here's a confidence builder…

I heard a testimony about Heidi Baker. She gathered up a group of people and took them out to a place where she had come across a dead body. She brought a group to witness and to learn. They estimated that the person had been dead for over a week, lying in the African sun. The body had split open and was covered with insects. Heidi then commanded life back into this body. All the insects formed together in a cloud and left. The splits in the body were joining back together before their eyes! The person came back to life! This group was on fire now… they ran to people that needed healing… that needed a miracle! No hesitation! No doubt!

They didn't need to attend seminary, take a course, fly to a retreat, buy a set of teaching CD's or take a bus to a crusade, hoping to get a "special anointing" or that something would "rub off" on them… their mindset changed… the stumbling blocks were gone… they had 100% confidence in The Secret of God's Power that Jesus gave us in John 6:29!

Demonstrations of God's power changes things!

One of the major keys about the John 6:29 Secret is, to have child-like faith.

Ask Father for His will every day like Jesus did… Jesus went to the mountains to talk to Father in order to know which mountains He needed moved today (Matthew 14:23, Luke 6:12)!

Let's be Mountain Movers!

SECTOR SIXTEEN

SPIRITUAL MAPPING

> **HUNTING TIP**
>
> God is your covering and guide, not man!

Before you go on a big game hunt, you can have a good idea where some game is, if you do your homework.

You can go through various areas, scouting for signs of game prior to and even during the hunt. Trails, tracks, rubbings, scrapes, food remnants and of course, actual sightings assist your hunting decisions.

You become familiar with the area and the game in it.

When hunting in a strange area, local inhabitants can be helpful. Make use of a topographical map or a hand drawn map, depending on where you plan to hunt.

Now when hunting day comes, you know where you want to go, in order to achieve the most positive results.

Although I've gone into both well-known and new areas and was very successful without any preplanning.

For the spiritual hunt, the same can be done.

Notice I said "can."

Many will tell you that it's a must. If God leads you to do preplanning, then it should be done.

You'll notice that battles and campaigns fought in the Bible by God's people when He was with them under His plan, had no spiritual mapping required… <u>God's plan and His presence with you were required.</u>

It's the same today… God's plan and Him with you <u>is</u> a requirement!

When Israel refused in fear to enter the Promised Land with Moses, as God told them to do, God told Moses the plan changed, in that they would never see the Promised Land, except for Caleb and Joshua.

They were so upset with the new plan; they decided to swallow their cowardice and do warfare according to God's first plan.

Let's see what happened:

"When Moses reported this to all the Israelites, they mourned bitterly. Early the next morning they went up toward the high hill country. "We have sinned," they said. "We will go up to the place the LORD promised." But Moses said, "Why are you disobeying the LORD's command? <u>This will not succeed! Do not go up, because the LORD is not with you. You will be defeated by your enemies</u>, for the Amalekites and Canaanites will face you there. Because you have turned away from the LORD, he will not be with you and you will fall by the sword." Nevertheless, <u>in their presumption</u> they went up toward the high hill country, though neither Moses nor the ark of the LORD's covenant moved from the camp. Then the Amalekites and Canaanites who lived in that hill country came down and attacked them and beat them down all the way to Hormah." Numbers 14:39-45(NIV)

If you ever think of taking on the enemy with just your own plan, even if you've been spiritual mapping for years and think you have a battle plan in place, remember this history lesson!

Your own spiritual mapping can <u>assist</u> you in understanding the enemy's strategy and strong points.

"See, I have this day set you over the nations and over the kingdoms, to root out and to pull down,
to destroy and to throw down, to build and to plant." Jeremiah 1:10

"For the weapons of our warfare are not carnal but mighty in God for pulling down strongholds" 2 Corinthians 10:4

A real spiritual mapping scenario is when Ezekiel <u>went in the spirit</u> and saw all the abominations occurring, that were hidden in Jerusalem (Ezekiel 8).

Also, Ezekiel 4:1-3 contains the strategy revealed to Ezekiel by God, who ordered him to draw a plan of the city, build a fortress and raise mounds in a spiritual framework.

<u>Only through spiritual revelation and going in the spirit</u> was Ezekiel able to see and know what was truly going on.

Let God do the spiritual mapping.

Spiritual mapping informs you about the area where you're going to be hunting.

This strategy can help you to: see the truth; help identify plans of the enemy; see spiritual structures over the natural ones; consider the military strength of the enemy; see where the enemy is and why they are there; discover the two parts of a city… who built it and why; the spiritual "doors" or "gates" allowing the Xtreme Big Game in; finding the evil spiritual center; and which Xtreme Big Game or evil territorial spirit is highest—all in order to assist you to a victory. <u>Just assist</u>.

People can go overboard with this, taking years to research and mark down everything that isn't tied down, and never work in the spirit.

Some say you have to get other "churches" and Christian groups involved to do spiritual mapping and warfare, yet most "churches" don't operate in the spirit, and would probably think a spiritual mapping project to come against evil spiritual strongholds to be a mad idea.

Also, many "churches" are in competition with another, and just deciding who would be in charge would be a project in itself!

Many will insist they have been led by God to do spiritual mapping of their city or region, so my recommendation for starting would be, to take a map of the area or city, <u>if led by the Lord to do so,</u> and mark where idols, heathen worship and occult centers are located, as these are probably the roots behind the current strongholds, such as drugs, prostitution, corruption, and crime.

Research the area's founders, and their reasons for settling this place, as it usually has an evil foundation and center.

Of interest will be high places, water systems and area/city entrances or gates, as big game will control and operate from these places.

"Then the servants of the king of Syria said to him, "Their gods are gods of the hills. Therefore, they were stronger than we; but if we fight against them in the plain, surely we will be stronger than they." 1 Kings 20:23

This can be expanded as you are led by the Holy Spirit.

If you have several people willing to assist with this project, the area can then be scouted, noting any physical and spiritual points, researching the internet, newspapers or library for history, and so on.

Spiritual mapping, prayer, power manifestations, and Xtreme Big Game Hunting can bring down enemy strongholds in an area, as it did in Ephesus when Diana, the evil principality over Asia, was confronted.

The killer blow against the Xtreme Big Game, Roman goddess Diana, is said to have been dealt by the Apostle John when he was in Ephesus.

He went in the temple of Artemis (Greek goddess combined with Diana) to come against this Big Game, "the altar split in many pieces and half the temple came down."

(*Christianizing the Roman Empire*, p.26, Ramsay MacMullen)

This temple was a former 'wonder of the world'!

Not much spiritual mapping was done there though… pretty much a 'no-brainer', identifying the central evil that was over that area!

To continue into deeper mapping, look at gates that are corridors for spirits to enter and exit, as evil spiritual guardians will guard gates to prevent evangelism from entering… bus stations; train stations; airports; and main roads are transportation gates.

Also, you can look at seven main gates… government that controls the area (mayor); commerce/business; hospitals; absolute powers from courts; casinos (gambling, prostitution); schools (educational systems, universities); and occult/false religions (structures of the freemasons, islam, buddhism, hinduism, satanic/witchcraft/pagan centers, christian science, new age cults, etc.).

The strongman is usually over the center of the city, but not always, as they like <u>high</u> points also.

It is said in both military and spiritual strategy, that those who take the center area or high place, take the city.

Where there are no hills, mountains or high places, occult people build towers or go to high structures like buildings, to do their work. Altars in these high places, with spirits, control the city. Occult ceremonies and sacrifices take place on high places, invoking evil spirits with influence, to fall on people.

In addition, huge gates stand between nations, such as Canada/US; US/Mexico and also between continents, Europe/Asia, etc. Countries of various cultures and beliefs that border each other are large and dangerous spiritual gates such as Islamic countries bordering Jewish, Hindu or Christian countries.

Don't forget that God is your leader and He will guide you concerning how to deal with game in the area you'll be hunting.

Ask God when looking over a map of the city… "What do you want me to see?"

Government places, bars, prostitution, universities, old religious sites, areas of violence… historical information on wars, battles, idol worship and areas of death and bloodshed, should all be considered.

Mountains and bodies of waters are important as territorial spirits can reside there.

You can also examine what the nation/province/state/city's flag, banners, shields, crests, motto and what the name of the city means or stands for, as many times they are evil based.

You can look at occult calendars, which have high days such as full moons; equinox; solstice and halloween. An increase in evil activity can be monitored on those days where the children of Belial operate.

Worship and sacrifices by people and their festivals etc., help keep territorial spirits in place.

Also, a consideration is the "gates of hell" to the underworld. Places where idols are worshipped and evil sacrifices are made are usually "gates of hell."

Command the gates of the underworld/hell prisons to be closed. I have used angels in this activity.

Strongholds are usually of a religious nature or tied to local customs. Centuries of festivals; ceremonies; idol rituals; processions and pilgrimages have built the strongholds.

Destroying these altars, that principalities and powers have maintained, can take time.

Ideology strongholds (atheism, humanism, evolutionism) can destroy entire societies. Territorial strongholds are established through a nation's ideology.

Occult strongholds (multi-religious; new age; satanism; witchcraft) grow stronger every day with rituals, pacts and sacrifices.

Also, sexual strongholds in areas can be mapped (pornography; prostitution; homosexuality; incest and pedophilia).

Before a culture is established, it was first a cult and before it was a cult, it was a god.

First god, then cult, then culture.

All ancient societies had a cult with a god. Culture is everything man does and establishes and originates, and there can be diverse cultures in a nation.

Find out, where did this culture(s) originate in this place?

When images of wood, stone, metal and ceramic are made and worshiped, these idols invite a spirit there. Through that idol, now comes false signs and wonders from the evil spirit (see more in the Sector on Altars).

A hunt can go to different places, cities, mountains, valleys and waters. All the preparation for a hunt at each location can be different.

Let God guide you.

You can find the pillars of iniquity through guidance from the Holy Spirit, where all the evil forces are, as these pillars hold up the city…. key places where all curses are over a city such as pagan religion altars of worship and sacrifice.

Satan controls people through religiosity… idol worship, man-made, false doctrine worship.

People are in bondage when they revere shrines and places, calling it "historical importance" and "part of our culture" and "part of our religious doctrine". Especially when altars, memorials or shrines are put up to commemorate death and war.

Search for any monuments shaped like obelisks, a design which originated in Babylon, as these are usually full of evil spirits and are portals to the underworld! Obelisks are in Washington D.C. (largest in the world built by masons) and at the Vatican (put up by an occultist pope).

When you have more people involved on a hunt, have intercessors at the base camp to protect the hunters, as they go out to various locations.

Some will say 'no intercessors, no hunting'.

Intercessors and extra hunters are a definite bonus, but does it stop God when He has <u>one</u> willing hunter?

The Bible is full of single individuals, willing to be the Silver Bullet of God.

I say, 'no God, no hunting'.

Satan has a plan to destroy humanity and as part of this plan, he utilizes a pattern on the earth called lea lines, which is a spider web-like structure, with a vortex at the end of each line like a circle.

These are usually found in open avenues or roads of satanic power where Xtreme Big Game move.

You can map out lea lines, as led by God, to find an evil vortex or spiritual doors/gates, and close them. Vortexes are usually where lots of sacrifices have been done.

A leading indicator is this: everything on lea lines, and around them, usually fails, such as businesses, marriages, lives, etc.

Usually witches and occultists find lea lines to call up the worst evil spirits.

Schools, cemeteries, hospitals and spiritually dead "churches", can be found on lea lines, where there is spiritual and physical death.

Close doors/gates/vortexes <u>when</u> God shows them to you. Destroy or imprison evil entities and establish the territory for God.

God always took Israel to victory when they relied on Him and they always failed when they didn't.

Keep hunting until God says it's done.

Establish the legal authority that you have through Jesus Christ, over the area and give it to God.

Let the Holy Spirit be your Xtreme Spiritual GPS Mapper!

ZONE 4

THE GAME/QUARRY

SECTOR SEVENTEEN
TROPHY OR XTREME BIG GAME

> **HUNTING TIP**
>
> The Bigger They Are...The Harder They Fall!

So, we finally made it to the Sector about Xtreme Big Game or Trophy Game!

This is a trophy-sized Sector for a trophy hunter, so grab some grub, put the dog out, find a comfortable spot and let's take a look at these Big, Bad Guys!

Trophy Game is that really big one... that one whose head you want hanging on your wall!

"And David took the head of the Philistine (Goliath), and brought it to Jerusalem; but he put his armor in his tent." 1 Samuel 17:54

I've been on many big game hunts in the physical and in the spirit. It is difficult to describe the enjoyment, as there are so many levels that can be discussed.

Hunting in the spirit is 'quantum' leap years beyond big game hunting in the natural. Globe-trotting big game hunters and Safari Club International, can only dream about some of the Xtreme Big Game that I've taken!

New York's legendary Explorer's Club flag has never been taken on expedition, to where I've been in the spirit!

Maybe someday!

You know that you are more than a conqueror through Jesus; you understand that you have a destiny with God and the importance of SAFARI and you're aware of hunt preparations.

You've discovered where these Big Guys can hang out; the many weapons that can be used on them and that God will guide you, take you to them and show them to you in the spirit.

Congratulations… you're on your way to being one of God's lean, mean hunting machines!

But, don't get too cocky… we have more work to do!

Who or what is this Xtreme Big Game we plan to hunt?

They are the evilest levels of hierarchy under satan.

You could call them his chiefs, or generals.

Let's start with "the" big evil guy first and then on to the rest.

Satan

Some say he doesn't exist.

Some say, that he isn't a threat to those who have Jesus and His power and authority.

Some insist, that satan is already chained in the pit, along with all his fallen angels since the crucifixion and therefore, none of them can harm us. The last time I saw him, he wasn't chained!

All this thinking of course is un-Biblical, as the New Testament tells us, that satan and his pals are a threat.

All the books from Acts to Revelation, were written after the Cross and warn Christians of satan; principalities; powers; evil rulers; spiritual wickedness in high places and evil spirits.

Also, if he and his pals are chained down now, who fights Michael and the holy angels in the future that John witnessed in Revelation 12:7-9?

The Bible says, that Satan isn't chained up until a future time after Armageddon (Revelation 20:1-3), and then only for a thousand years, when he is released for a short time, and then cast into the lake of fire (Revelation 20:10).

God's Word says, that he exists and that he is a threat to everyone, including Christians.

Let's take God's Word for it!

Many names are attached to this supreme evil ruler; however, the Bible tells us that he was originally created a holy creature.

We see him called "Lucifer, son of the morning" in Isaiah 14:12 and "the anointed cherub" in Ezekiel 28:14.

Although the Bible discusses the king of Babylon and the king of Tyre in these scriptures, the words have a double meaning, as God uses so often.

Simple examination of these scriptures points out, that God is talking about more than these men, as these human kings were not cherubs nor were they in the garden of Eden nor upon the holy mountain of God, etc.

The Hebrew word for Lucifer is "Heylel", meaning brightness or morning star, from the Hebrew word halal (to shine).

We can learn a great deal about Lucifer and creation in Genesis, Jeremiah, Isaiah and Ezekiel.

"Son of man, take up a lamentation for the king of Tyre, and say to him, 'Thus says the Lord God:

"You were the seal of perfection, full of wisdom and perfect in beauty (he was created wise and beautiful). You were in Eden, the garden of God; Every precious stone was your covering: The sardius, topaz, and diamond, beryl, onyx, and jasper, sapphire, turquoise, and emerald with gold. The workmanship of your timbrels and pipes was prepared for you on the day you were created.

"You were the anointed cherub who covers; I established you; You were on the holy mountain of God; You walked back and forth in the midst of fiery stones. You <u>were perfect</u> in your ways from the day you were created, till iniquity was found in you. "By the abundance of your trading you became filled with violence within, And you sinned; Therefore, I cast you as a profane thing Out of the mountain of God (was cast away from God); And I destroyed you, O covering cherub, from the midst of the fiery stones.

"Your heart was lifted up because of your beauty; You corrupted your wisdom for the sake of your splendor; I cast you to the ground (cast to Earth), I laid you before kings, that they might gaze at you. "You defiled your sanctuaries by the multitude of your iniquities, by the iniquity of your trading; Therefore, I brought fire from your midst; It devoured you, and I turned you to ashes upon the earth In the sight of all who saw you. All who knew you among the peoples are astonished at you; You have become a horror, and shall be no more forever." Ezekiel 28:12-19

Lucifer's beauty, wisdom and position in God's government produced pride and ambition in him, leading him to rebel against God's authority and an attempted coup d'état.

This coup continues up to Armageddon in Revelation 16:16 and then again for "a little season" after his release from imprisonment of a thousand years. (Revelation 20:1-3)

"How you are fallen from Heaven,
O Lucifer, son of the morning!
How you are cut down to the ground,
You who weakened the nations!
For you have said in your heart:
'I will ascend into Heaven,
I will exalt my throne above the stars of God;
I will also sit on the mount of the congregation
On the farthest sides of the north;
I will ascend above the heights of the clouds,
I will be like the Most High." Isaiah 14:12-14

Lucifer, the creature, desired to be over God and become ultimate ruler. He was instead cast down to the ground or earth. Meaning, he was now on some kind of a leash, where before, he had free access to go anywhere.

We can get onto a rabbit trail here about nations and people that existed before Adam, that were destroyed, and try to determine all that happened, but we won't do that.

<u>Let's stay on target.</u>

It appears that these revised names for Lucifer, who used to be the son of the morning and the anointed cherub, came into effect after he was put on his leash.

He has such names now as satan, adversary, accuser, dragon, the devil, a roaring lion, prince of the power of the air, deceiver and even angel of light.

Adam and Eve were created and given dominion over all the earth. They promptly lost their dominion to satan.

In review, we have this former holy creature of God, unsuccessfully attempting to take over God's throne, being put on a leash, and obtaining/stealing dominion (until Jesus) over mankind and the earth.

This is a big job, so how does this one measly being, that is not omnipresent like God, maintain his rebel kingdom?

<u>He needs help.</u>

You can find out about some of those who help him, in the Sectors on Xtreme Small Game and Xtreme Rabid Game.

The "helpers" we want to discuss now, are the rebels that joined him in the rebellion against God.

It is not possible to imagine that Lucifer by himself could overcome God and all his spiritual beings. Lucifer convinced others to join him, no doubt infecting their pride and will with flattery, deceit and promises of higher ranking, kingdoms, and other inducements.

He pulled the same "con job" on Eve.

He tried it on Jesus!

He pulls it on people every day!

Who else could these helpers be at <u>that</u> time?

Does he have a bride, a mistress or… a queen?

I'll tease you with that right now and discuss her/it at the end of the Sector.

"His tail drew a third of the stars of Heaven and threw them to the earth…" Revelation 12:4

Angels and other spiritual creatures of heaven are referred to in the Bible sometimes as stars. Thus, a third of spiritual creatures were drawn to him!

Some argue that this 'third' mentioned in Revelation, is a future figure, rather than a past number of those with satan.

If so, then where did satan's army come from if not from angels rebelling against God? (God gave angels free will also.)

Although God created all things, is it possible God created personal adversaries <u>or</u> that <u>they</u> decided to become adversaries with their free will?

"For we do not wrestle against flesh and blood, but against principalities, against powers, against the rulers of the darkness of this age, against spiritual hosts of wickedness in the heavenly places. "Ephesians 6:12

Let's examine this powerful scripture.

Paul is addressing these words to believers in Ephesus, which encompasses all believers of Jesus Christ as their Savior. Wrestle (and in some versions the word is struggle) is the English translation of the Greek word "pale".

This word only occurs once in the New Testament Greek, which more correctly translates, that we are in an intense fight or combat.

We do not fight against flesh and blood; (Gr: pros haima kai sarka) meaning our main opponents are not physical beings. 2 Corinthians 10:3 confirms this also, "For though we walk in the flesh, we do not war after the flesh."

The next word "but" (Gr: alla), also meaning "rather," gets into what believers are combating, if not flesh and blood.

We are told here, there are four specific entities that we come up against.

3. **Principalities** (Gr: Archas) means chief rulers or first in order or rank and in ancient times this word was used to signify angelic or demonic powers, rather than human powers. These would be directly under or reporting to satan, who would sit on thrones (Gr: thronos) or high positions of authority over dominions (Gr: kuriotes) or jurisdictions.

4. **Powers** (Gr: Exousias) meaning authorities or those who derive their power from and execute the will of the chief rulers.

5. **Rulers of the darkness of this world** (Gr: Kosmokratopas tou skotous) carry out directives of those above them and it is said by some that these are the ones that are behind satanic miracles and power demonstrations. Also considered the ones that produce the spiritual darkness that blinds the world mentioned in 2 Corinthians 4:4.

6. **Spiritual wickedness** (Gr: Pneumatika ponerias) meaning the wicked spirits of satan who would be in direct combat with people to carry out the dictates of the principalities, authorities, powers and rulers. Many say that these are the demons, unclean spirits, familiar spirits, etc., (Xtreme Small Game) mentioned in the Bible. However, this kind are not said to operate in the heavens (plural), but are confined to earth or at best, just one heaven or first heaven and do not function in the upper heavens or heavenlies.

I've read various reports putting these creatures in different ranks, having other functions and some even consider thrones and dominions to be entities.

Some say they are all angels or a mishmash of angels and other evil entities.

They are all evil adversaries that we combat.

"In high places" also translated as "in the heavenly places" or "in the heavenlies" (Gr: en tois epouranios), tells us where these entities manage or rule from or reside.

This scripture also tells us that not all entities are the same, having different titles, functions and ranking.

Although satan is a rebel, he recognizes the importance of discipline and order and so he counterfeits God's divine pattern of ranking, much like the world's military ranking from privates to generals.

Satan divides the world up into sections or territories, giving leadership to his subordinates, which we can substantiate from reading Daniel 10 referencing evil princes of Persia and Greece.

The devil is the "prince or god of this world" according to John 12:31 and 2 Corinthians 4:4, however, the depth of this rule is limited. His ability to hold onto certain areas and peoples depends on a number of factors. Successes and failures are governed by strategies and tactics employed by the evil forces and the holy forces. Corruption, jealousies, miscalculations, imperfections, fears, disunity or weakness, are just some of the factors creating disorganization and failure on both sides.

The imperfect wills of all creatures are involved in this warfare. All of which comes under certain allowances of the perfect will of God.

It is interesting to note that God has his spiritual forces organized and so does satan, yet Christians often feel little need to organize.

Satan works to keep Christians thinking that they don't need others! He doesn't want Christians knowing that they are in union with Christ and thus higher and more powerful than him and his hosts.

Meaning… Christians have the power to defeat him!

More on that later.

Another way of looking at the entities of Ephesians 6:12, is that we can somewhat equate <u>principalities</u> and <u>rulers</u> to being like a king, judge or government dictating laws or orders and <u>powers</u> and <u>spiritual wickedness</u> like a military or police force carrying out those orders.

There is no scriptural evidence indicating that all evil spiritual entities are the same or operate the same. The Bible actually shows us that there are major differences, between higher and lower level evil entities. Lower-level evil spirits or Xtreme Small Game are creatures, evidence shows, that are <u>confined</u> to the first heaven or earth area and are usually seeking the inhabitation of people or an object. This can also be a house or small area, as many people have witnessed and experienced manifestations in houses and graveyards.

Note that I said, that evidence shows Xtreme Small Game to be confined to the earth.

Principalities, powers and rulers are a different set of higher level creatures, that are <u>not</u> bound by earth, as they operate in the heavenlies. This doesn't mean that high level entities can't or don't operate at ground level. Actually, they can and do; and also, they operate in waters.

"to the intent that now the manifold wisdom of God might be made known by the church to the principalities and powers <u>in the heavenly places</u>." Ephesians 3:10

Heavenly places are spiritual places, and the earth and the sky above, are all <u>within</u> the spiritual realm. Their restriction would be certain heaven(s) or areas of heaven, where they are banned by God, due to their rebellion with satan. It is unknown where these restrictions end, since satan has access to God as is evident in Job 1:6: "Now there was a day when the sons of God (angels) came to present themselves before the LORD, and satan came also among them."

Scripture talks of these evil rulers as being on the same level as angels.

"Who (Jesus) has gone into Heaven, and is at the right hand of God; angels and authorities and powers having been made subject unto him." 1 Peter 3:22

"For I am persuaded, that neither death, nor life, nor angels, nor principalities, nor powers, nor things present, nor things to come." Romans 8:38

Note in these scriptures, that angels are separate from principalities, authorities and powers.

Are principalities and powers <u>all</u> angels?

Notice also above in 1 Peter, that these spiritual creatures, are <u>all</u> subject to Jesus and we know that Jesus has given <u>us</u> all authority and all power over them!

Many people consider principalities and powers to be angels that fell with satan, although as we have just seen, they are mentioned as separate beings from angels.

Some say they are fallen angels, some say they are higher than angels and some say they are lower than angels.

There are those that say principalities are lower than powers and that there are also other rulers, princes, dominions, thrones, virtues, and archangels to consider, of those who joined the rebellion against God.

Some suggest that just high-ranking entities in the evil realm are fallen angels.

I've had fallen angels battle me and size me up like a meatloaf sandwich… they are definitely not your regular breed of evil spirit.

Since Michael the archangel is called a chief prince in Daniel, one could say that these evil spiritual princes of Persia and Greece may also be fallen archangels.

"But the prince of the kingdom of Persia withstood me twenty-one days; and behold, Michael, one of the chief princes, came to help me, for I had been left alone there with the kings of Persia." Daniel 10:13.

"Then he said, "Do you know why I have come to you? And now I must return to fight with the prince of Persia; and when I have gone forth, indeed the prince of Greece will come. But I will tell you what is noted in the Scripture of Truth. (No one upholds me against these, except Michael your prince." Daniel 10: 20-21.

Ephesians 1:21 and Colossians 1:16 mentions thrones and dominions: "For by him were all things created, that are in Heaven, and that are in Earth, visible and invisible, whether they be thrones, or dominions, or principalities, or powers: all things were created by him, and for him."

In 1 Peter 3:22 we find the mention of authorities: "Who (Jesus) is gone into Heaven, and is on the right hand of God; angels and authorities and powers being made subject to him."

There are multiple scriptures, writings, experiences, testimonies and doctrines that can be examined, debated and argued concerning their level of authority, power and range.

What's truth… what's fiction?

I've studied this exact question, discussed it with others, debated it and prayed about it.

It really was becoming quite a dilemma… how does one hunt something, when not sure exactly what it is?

How does anyone know if they are dealing with an evil spirit, a foul spirit, an unclean spirit, a familiar spirit, a power, a fallen angel, a principality, an evil ruler, an animal creature spirit, a dominion, or a prince?

Some I've fought were human sized and others were immense that looked like Leviathans or Behemoths or dragons. Some were very odd-looking creatures of various sizes. Some could fly, some did not.

And what are the differences between these evil things?

One night, God gave me the answer.

He told me to look at it just like war in the physical world. In a war we fight the enemy, whether the enemy comes against us in a plane, a tank, a ship or on foot. It doesn't matter if the enemy calls him/herself a pilot, a soldier, a sailor, spy, commando, resistance fighter, general or private, Lucy or Larry.

They're all the same… the enemy!

God said, "You destroy the enemy (spiritual), whatever they call themselves, whatever they look like or whatever form they come in."

In war, Generals don't discuss or care about the enemy's names and where they came from… it doesn't matter.

Then I thought, "What about all the debate about what entity is higher and what they control?"

God took me then instantly in the spirit, placing me on a battlefield with a tank, a plane, and a man with a rifle coming towards me.

God said, "Which one is more dangerous to you right now?"

I said, "They're all dangerous!"

Each one was an immediate threat at that moment.

It didn't matter at that moment that a tank and a plane are more powerful than a man with a rifle.

Each can destroy.

Once I grasped the concept, that everything we come up against is "the enemy," and quit analyzing it all, the confusion was gone.

We can still understand that some are powerful rulers and some are not, but we don't need to argue about their position or ranking or form. God leads us in battle.

Although there is debate about where these evil rulers came from, many point to Revelation 12:7-9 that reveals them as fallen or rebellious entities:

"And war broke out in Heaven: Michael and his angels fought with the dragon; and the dragon and his angels fought, but they did not prevail, nor was a place found for them in Heaven any longer. So, the great dragon was cast out, that serpent of old, called the Devil and Satan, who deceives the whole world; he was cast to the Earth, and his angels were cast out with him."

Revelation tells us that satan has "his" angels with him already in heaven (restricted areas).

Some say this fight or one like it, has already taken place and some say, that it's a future tribulation battle, yet from this scripture we can see that these evil entities exist and operate now in the heavenlies.

Keep in mind that Paul refers to the first and third heaven. Enoch says there are seven heavens and the Bible mentions there is a heaven of heavens (Deuteronomy 10:14).

Again, many disagree about what each evil entity would control.

Regardless of their specific functions, these four areas of spiritual infrastructure mentioned in Ephesians 6:12, has as their ultimate work, to blind the minds of people (2 Corinthians 4:4) from the gospel and destroy the Church, under the direction of satan. Obviously, their mission includes bringing down spiritual Israel (Christianity), and to disrupt prophecy.

There are Christians and denominations that have <u>doctrinal belief</u> that satan and evil entities were destroyed or imprisoned after the Cross. Therefore, spiritual warfare isn't necessary.

Then there are those who believe that <u>all</u> levels of evil spirits exist, but are not a threat to Christians; some also believe we should not do warfare on certain levels, as only God is allowed to deal with higher levels!

Ephesians, 1 Peter, Revelation and other Biblical books written after the Cross, clearly prove these doctrines to be false.

Christians who teach and preach otherwise, will have a great deal to answer for one day, as countless numbers of people are being lost to the lake of fire, due to such dogma, which breeds ignorance and impotency.

<u>Acts 19 alone proves these doctrines to be false</u>, as it covers all areas of hunting after the Cross, of great miracles, which produced the most unprecedented evangelistic results ever recorded in the Bible, backing up the SAFARI principal!

<u>All in just one chapter!</u>

There were "special miracles" God wrought by Paul's hands (v.11). Imagine what <u>special</u> miracles could be!

Handkerchiefs from Paul cast evil spirits out of people (Xtreme Small Game was defeated) (v.12).

Those who practiced divination and magic… "curious arts" … were released from evil spirit influence and occult practices and burned all their occult books. Meaning, Xtreme Rabid Game was defeated (v.19).

Diana, the named principality over Ephesus and all of Asia, lost power and influence due to Paul.

People were no longer buying idols of Diana… as they no longer contained power… which was power from evil entities (Xtreme Big Game was disrupted) (v.24-27). Verse 26 says people "almost throughout all Asia" were "persuaded and turned" to Jesus… evangelism exploded!

Envision the world if just one Christian in every country, would follow Acts 19! Just one Silver Bullet of God!

As I've said, these various levels, ranks and names of Xtreme Big Game can be difficult and impossible to sort out, as to their pecking order and responsibilities.

In the wild, animals will fool you as to their ferocity and what they'll do, even against animals much larger than themselves.

I've seen a wolverine take on a pack of wolves!

I've been attacked and bitten by a mouse that I cornered and grabbed (I had gloves on)! Tough little dude impressed me, so I let him go!

So, keep in mind that an evil entity of any size, name and function is dangerous!

As with animals, evil entities can move alone, in pairs and in herds, although there will be a head/leader, second in command and so on down the line, such as with wolf packs having alphas, betas and omegas.

In the Bible, and in various Egyptian, Greek, German, Incan, Indian, Mayan, Norse, Roman and Oriental mythologies and cultures, there are hundreds of millions of named higher evil entities considered gods and goddesses and worshipped rather than fought against… even today!

An evangelist from India once told me, that his mostly Hindu country, has over 330 MILLION gods and goddesses that are worshipped!

Now that is happy hunting grounds for us as Xtreme Big Game Hunters!

This is not to say that others are less dangerous or will never be encountered, as many of them have changed names over the centuries.

One hunter told me, their group ran into an evil entity calling itself a queen of heaven named Hitler!

The Bible and other writings do give names of certain high level evil creatures, such as satan, Abaddon or Apollyon (Rev. 9:11), Molech, Baal and various gods and goddesses.

Although, the ones that I've come across, never showed me their identification. So, don't get hung up on needing to name what you meet in battle.

One big name we have no doubt of his position and ranking, is in 2 Corinthians 4:4, which tells us that satan is "the god of this world."

Satan is the Biggest of all Xtreme Trophies, but before you get that gleam in your eye (thought of it myself), Revelation says that he will not be "finished off" by any other hunter but God!

Although there are numerous high level evil entities, whether this one or that one is a fallen angel or something else is of little relevance... they are all the enemy!

However, we'll use the names the Bible uses where applicable, to maintain comprehension.

Evidence shows that these ruler entities are not known to seek habitation in people nor objects, as due to their high level, they manage satan's realm, since satan, as I said, is <u>not</u> omnipresent and therefore needs governors.

We see evidence of this in Daniel 10. Daniel had been in mourning, prayer and fasting for 21 days when a holy messenger came and told Daniel that an evil high-level entity over Persia had delayed him from reaching Daniel and that Michael, a chief prince, had to come and help.

"But the prince of the kingdom of Persia withstood me twenty-one days; and behold, Michael, one of the chief princes, came to help me." v.13 a

The word prince or princes is from the Hebrew word "sar" which means a chief ruler.

1 Thessalonians 4:16 and Jude 9 also mentions the word "archangel," another meaning of chief ruler.

An archangel of God, therefore, appears to be equal to or superior to an evil prince, principality or high ruler.

It's interesting that it took Michael three weeks to come onto the battlefield, rather than immediately. Perhaps Daniel wasn't saying the right words for three weeks, as surely his words were being heard.

This scripture also teaches us that princes or principalities rule over large geographical areas or governmental structures.

"No one upholds me against these, except Michael your prince." Daniel 10:21 b

This messenger angel informs Daniel, that Michael came to his assistance. If an archangel or ruler comes to assist an angel or power, then we know the same happens in satan's realm, with a principality personally coming to assist when evil forces are having trouble. This messenger also says that once he leaves Daniel, he will go back and fight this evil prince of Persia until another evil prince of Greece shows v.20, which would have been the evil entity ruler that oversaw and directed Alexander the Great and the Greek empire to destroy the Medo-Persian empire.

This teaching points out, there are different rulers and that holy and evil forces battle one another with some being stronger or more powerful than others.

Also, that evil empires are replaced by other evil empires, presumably as directed by satan, to continually have wars, death, bloodshed and destruction upon God's creation, especially the Church.

Physical wars on earth are won or lost, depending on invisible wars in the spiritual realm or heavens!

Daniel also shows us that dealing with these creatures can be done with prayer and fasting, as his continued prayer brought more angelic warfare to produce results.

It does _not_ say Daniel's prayers _defeated_ any princes... just that Michael's intervention allowed a messenger to get through enemy lines.

Some believe that prayer and fasting is _the_ one and only answer to high level spiritual warfare.

Daniel teaches us that holy spiritual forces (angels) _and_ man's efforts can effect change, countering any thinking that only God can produce changes.

Also, that Daniel prayed until he got results.

Through this study we can determine that principalities, powers and evil princes are high ranking evil officers in satan's realm, controlling, directing and influencing activities in and over regions, cities and large areas.

Their ranking would depend on their responsibility, much like a major under a colonel, under a general in the military, each having areas they are in charge of and reporting up to higher levels.

Perhaps some are promoted or demoted, depending on their successes and failures, the same as in earthly, military forces.

Their high rank would obviously have them in charge of influence directed at world institutions of finance, education, media, politics, government, cities, nations, world organizations (such as the UN), non-Christian religions and especially Christian organizations.

Educational systems are a major target, as this steers especially the youth away from God, and into sin. This includes all school levels and universities (especially seminaries). They want to teach the doctrine of devils as it says in 1 Timothy 4:1, "in latter times some will depart from the faith, giving heed to deceiving spirits and doctrines of demons."

They also pursue the youth through television, radio, movies, books, magazines, music, video games and the internet.

Principalities and powers will also put heavy pressure on people that millions listen to, admire and follow, such as actors, musicians and sports figures... and on world religious and political figures to change laws and government to meet satan's agenda.

They will promote pliable, influential people to higher prominence, to achieve greater results… for them!

We know that satan is "the prince of the power of the air" in Ephesians 2:2 b. This is where he and his leadership operate… in the air or atmosphere or IN the heavens. They prepare and influence our environment and people and the "course of this world" Ephesians 2:2 a, so that people will be subject to allowing demons into them.

Until people are born again to Jesus, they are spiritually dead and easily influenced in mind and flesh by evil forces.

These spiritual forces influence people with words that they speak to them, that are heard in their thoughts, by their spirit. Much like people speak words into the air, are heard and then processed in their minds. The deception here is, people believe evil spiritual thoughts, to be their own thinking.

Christians who operate in the flesh, instead of the spirit, hearing from the Holy Spirit, are also deceived by these evil words, either indirectly by evil spirits talking through others or directly from evil spirits to their own thoughts.

Principalities work from the top and evil spirits work from the bottom or inside, to produce satan's results.

People and areas accept and manifest these evil plans, by sins of idol worship, murder, lying, stealing, fear and addictions, etc. These plans spread through people to their families, friends and into systems of education, commerce, government, religion and also the Church. It keeps spreading and infecting like a plague throughout cities, areas and regions.

Satan will personally influence a major world figure if needed, as he did with Judas, and also with the king of Tyre in Ezekiel 28.

It would make sense that satan or some of his top principalities would have had as their personal project, men such as Nebuchadnezzar, the King of Babylon, Alexander the Great, the Caesars of Rome, Joseph Stalin, Hitler, Mao and the top leaders of the countries of the world.

Another vital plan of the evil realm, is to have entire peoples and nations corrupted and move against Israel (Christianity and nation). Prophecy fulfilled in Israel, equals bad news for satan and his ilk!

They also can direct elements such as the wind and the waters (Mark 4:39).

Satan's hierarchy is managed to corrupt and destroy on a world-wide scale.

God <u>can</u> destroy all these evil entities, but He has decided to allow us the pleasure and honor of doing it, as His children. He has told us that we are more than conquerors (Romans 8:37) and there are heavenly armies of angels awaiting orders from us, to defeat principalities, powers and evil spirits! As with any army, troops wait until they receive their fighting orders.

We must wait; the angels must wait.

God and His angels keep these evil things on some sort of leash, otherwise humans would have been their breakfast long ago. If one is foolish enough to disobey God and walk within their leash zone, then I guess God considers you to be on your own!

Ever walk within a mad dog's leash zone?

How many people on earth are doing it right now?

Satan was on a leash away from Job and couldn't get to him unless God allowed it (Job 1:10-12). This is probably still the case in many degrees upon the earth, that is protecting people from total annihilation. We don't know the full extent of the restrictions. We can only move as we are directed to do and leave the mysteries beyond our understanding to God.

"The secret things belong to the LORD our God" Deuteronomy 29:29.

How we conduct our lives, determines our position with the leash zone and those on the leash.

God allows the leash to come off sometimes, as He did with Job in order to develop us and to further humiliate the evil rulers, like satan's eventual loss to Job.

With the help of God, angels, revelation and action, we can put a pounding on these beasts!

Two of our initial orders from God, were to subdue and have dominion.

"Then God blessed them, and God said to them, "Be fruitful and multiply; fill the earth and <u>subdue</u> it; have <u>dominion</u> over the fish of the sea, over the birds of the air, and over every living thing that moves on the earth." Genesis 1:28

We already know it didn't work out too well, as we lost the power to subdue. As we see in God's orders to Noah in Genesis 9:1, subdue is omitted.

"So, God blessed Noah and his sons, and said to them: "Be fruitful and multiply, and fill the Earth."

Man wasn't able to subdue the earth, because of Adam and Eve, until Jesus came to take dominion and give it back to us. Once we had legal dominion again and the Holy Spirit with us, we could successfully take on the evil spiritual realm, with authority and power, for the last 2000 years.

"Behold, I (Jesus) give you the authority to trample on serpents (principalities) and scorpions (powers), and over all the power of the enemy, and nothing shall by any means hurt you." Luke 10:19

"And these signs will follow those who believe (Christians); In my (Jesus) name they will cast out demons… They will take up serpents (principalities) …" Mark 16:17a-18a

Jesus uses derogatory names for these evil rulers to debase them; to show us that we have all authority and power over these evil entities; and also, how to deal with them.

Notice it says we <u>cast out demons</u>, but we <u>tread on and take up serpents or principalities and scorpions or powers</u>.

Demons that inhabit people and things on earth, are to be cast out of them.

The Greek word for "cast out" in the Bible is "ekballo" and it translates "to throw out." The Greek word "daimonion" is mentioned 52 times in the New Testament Greek text, and 75% of these are cast out.

Principalities and powers are mentioned 8 times in the Bible and none of them are cast out. They are taken or lifted up or displaced, which means to take control over them.

Yet another difference between lower and higher evil entities.

We have determined, that there are high ranking evil entities under satan, the god of this world, operating in the heavens, at war with holy angels and earth's inhabitants, specifically Christians.

<u>Also, that God has put Christians in charge of the war against them. When I say in charge, I mean, that we are the tip of the spear!</u>

<u>This is a concept that you must grasp!</u>

Now that we have this information, we must exercise our authority, by using one of the keys of heaven Jesus gave us— which is to speak words of binding and loosing.

"And I will give you the keys of the kingdom of heaven, and whatever you bind on earth will be bound in heaven, and whatever you loose on earth will be loosed in heaven." Matthew 16:19

While on earth, Jesus used the word "Church" only twice and both times it was regarding binding and loosing principalities and powers!

How many leaders preach that?

Hard to imagine, but this fact is mostly ignored by the Church body!

<u>We are God's principal agents, who have the authority to instruct heavenly angelic powers, to combat evil principalities and powers!</u>

Wrap your head around that one a few times!

Remember when Jesus was asleep on the ship with the disciples,

"And a great windstorm arose, and the waves beat into the boat, so that it was already filling." Mark 4:37 "Then He arose and rebuked the wind, and said to the sea, "Peace, be still!" Mark 4:39

Who do you think was controlling the wind and sea here? Certainly, it wasn't God coming against them. How did the wind and the seas stop, other than angels battling and stopping evil forces, after Jesus spoke? Also notice Jesus spoke a command, not a prayer nor a request.

And Jesus also said,

"Most assuredly, I say to you, he who believes in Me, the works that I do he will do also; and greater works than these he will do, because I go to My Father." John 14:12

Plant that one with the other one and let them swim around in your head for a while! Let it take root… have faith in it… let it grow.

Before you get overly excited about all this authority and power you have, always remember that Jesus said to be excited about something more important:

"Nevertheless, do not rejoice in this, that the spirits are subject to you, but rather rejoice because your names are written in heaven." Luke 10:20

After Jesus made this statement He said:

"In that hour Jesus rejoiced in the Spirit and said, "I thank You, Father, Lord of heaven and earth, that You have hidden these things from the wise and prudent and revealed them to babes. Even so, Father, for so it seemed good in Your sight. All things have been delivered to Me by My Father, and no one knows who the Son is except the Father, and who the Father is except the Son, and the one to whom the Son wills to reveal Him." Luke 10:21-22

He tells you, that not everyone knows what you know and we should rejoice that Jesus has chosen you to now know these hidden truths!

Cool, eh! (Eh is a Canadian word—like hockey and moose—I think donut is also a Canadian word!)

"Then He turned to His disciples and said privately, "Blessed are the eyes which see the things you see; for I tell you that many prophets and kings have desired to see what you see, and have not seen it, and to hear what you hear, and have not heard it." Luke 10:23-24

Now that you know, ask the Great Counselor, the Holy Spirit, to reveal to you how, when and where to fight and set captives free, so that they can have their names written in heaven.

<u>Reveal the truth to other Christians</u>, that they are more than conquerors through Jesus Christ like you!

Christians must remember that they can't just fire this mighty weapon (words from their mouth) into the air and imagine that they are taking back command.

<u>As with any engagement, there needs to be a spiritual plan.</u>

<u>Working in the flesh is not a plan to defeat spiritual forces!</u>

The Bible is the greatest war manual ever written despite what is said about Sun Tzu's, *The Art of War*.

The Bible says, that we can bind and loose as a strategy of war that Jesus taught us because, "<u>Every</u> kingdom divided against itself is brought to desolation" Matthew 12:25-26, Mark 3:24 and Luke 11:18.

When something is recorded in the Bible three times, we know it is a powerful statement!

Jesus is telling us if a kingdom is divided—it is conquered.

"Lest satan should take advantage of us: for we are not ignorant of his devices". 2 Corinthians 2:11

What does all of this say for a non-unified Church, that is ignorant of satan's devices?

The Church has decided <u>not</u> to go to war with principalities and powers, even though God has said they war with us and we are commanded to war with them!

So much for Christians saying, that they only want to do the will of God!

Only small pockets of Christians and individual groups are obeying God in this area and even smaller pockets yet, are those who are doing it properly!

When Jesus belittled principalities and powers, calling them serpents and scorpions, He was pointing out to us their character and their low position, IF we accept our position!

This command of God is so important, that He made a constellation of stars called Ophiuchus, a Greek word meaning "serpent bearer," that is within the constellation of Scorpio.

It shows a warrior taking up a serpent or principality and wrestling it (Ephesians 6:12), while at the same time crushing a scorpion or evil power under his foot (Ephesians 1:22).

This heavenly display has been in place since creation, as a prophecy and message to Christians of what to do… take them up and crush them under your feet!

"And the God of peace shall bruise satan under your feet shortly." Romans 16:20

When Jesus told us to "take up serpents", He was pointing to the Word of God written in the stars in this constellation of Ophiuchus, which couldn't be misinterpreted!

God has told us in the stars; in His written Word and through Jesus Himself, that we are to take on principalities and powers.

Jesus gave us the authority over them.

The Holy Spirit gives us the revelation and power.

Angels are at our disposal.

Now we just have to go and do!

Wrestling problems in the flesh is futile, as the battle is IN the heavens.

You can't wrestle spiritual beings with fleshly solutions.

We are not only conquering them, but we also must replace where they were ruling, with the kingdom of God. If you kick out one force, it must be replaced with another force.

<u>We can't leave the area empty.</u>

Warfare strategy dictates, that we find the weakness and exploit it to our advantage. Attacking and defeating leadership causes confusion, disunity and weakness in the ranks. Divide the forces and conquer. This is what they do, especially to the Church… so this is what we must do to them.

Spiritual Christians understand, that they need the whole armor of God to defend themselves from many-sided attacks. And use the sword of the Spirit, by speaking into the air the Word of God, warring against the evil forces.

Utilize the weapons God gives you!

Go in the spirit and take them out.

Acts 19 shows, that an evil power, most likely an evil religious spirit, was influencing Sceva, a high priest, which wasn't enough to sidetrack Paul. Paul's ministry was so successful, that the principality over Asia, called Diana of Ephesus, personally intervened to have Paul killed.

In Acts 19, we learned of levels of spiritual warfare and how it can change things.

Angels called "ministering spirits" in God's kingdom work to strengthen you, while powers in satan's kingdom work to weaken you. Ministering spirits will bring you comfort and messages. Evil powers will bring you confusion and false messages.

Nice to have so many kingdoms interested in you, isn't it?

Wait until you become a major threat to satan's kingdom and see how much additional interest will be generated!

<u>Be prepared for it!</u>

Jesus warns the seven types of Church groups, in the prophetic book of Revelation, that evil spiritual powers are directly involved in five of them and the other two are showing signs of evil power working against them.

Ephesus lost their first love; people from the synagogue of satan had infiltrated those of Sardis; Pergamos was overcome by false doctrines of the spirits of Balaam and Nicolaitanes; the prophets and teachers of Thyatira were seduced by the spirit of Jezebel; Sardis was influenced by a spirit making them spiritually dead; Philadelphia had the influence and temptation of the synagogue of satan upon them; Laodicea was controlled by the spirit of mammon or wealth and was therefore lukewarm.

This shows us that the evil realm is successful or working on all Christian gatherings.

Evil rulers are also producing pride, fear, hatred, prejudice, control, ignorance, disunity, lust, false doctrine, false gifts and more, in their campaign against ministers, their families and members in the flock.

This knowledge can assist us when we are called to assist with warfare for a person and in an assembly.

Other examples in the Bible of leaders being attacked by evil powers are:

- Satan against Eve, to get to Adam and all of mankind (Genesis 3).
- Spirit of fear against Job (Job 3:25).
- Satan influencing Peter (Matthew 16:23).
- Satan influencing Judas (John 13:27).
- The messenger of satan against Paul (2 Corinthians 12:7).
- The arrogant and spiritually dead Sadducees and Pharisees influenced by religious spirits (John 8:37-47).
- Spirits of disunity and jealousy upon James and Peter to come against Paul's ministry (Galatians 2:11-14).

Expect it to come, as Jesus warned Peter:

"And the Lord said, "Simon, Simon! Indeed, Satan has asked for you, that he may sift you as wheat." Luke 22:31

God warned me with these same words!

I don't imagine being sifted like wheat would be a fun experience!

If you think you are immune and its only others that are deceived or attacked, you better take another hard look at yourself!

What other enemies does satan have but God, spiritually-active Christian leaders, the real Church and Israel?

Don't shy away from it… get prepared and then go get them!

AND, I would ask any "armchair Christians" … not to kick a Christian warrior when they're downed by these evil forces, like so many tend to do. They are casualties, not enemies. The Christian army seems to be the only army that attacks, wounds and tries to bring down their own leaders and troops, and getting pleasure from it, rather than aiding the wounded and restoring them to fighting condition!

ANARCHY

Many years ago I attended Dr. Peter Wagner's Spiritual Warfare Conference in Florida, that had numerous internationally known speakers/apostles in attendance including Peter & Doris Wagner, Dr. Alistair Petrie, Jay Swallow, Chuck Pierce, Dutch Sheets and Cindy Jacobs.

An excellent teaching about "anarchy", by my fellow Canadian Xtreme Big Game Hunter Dr. Petrie, was taught as a major tool for success in high level spiritual warfare for cities and the land (regions/nations).

A definition of anarchy: "Rebellion; chaos; disorder; mayhem; absence of government; a state of lawlessness due to the absence or inefficiency of the supreme power; political disorder."

The order (peace/truth/revival) or disorder (anarchy) in cities/regions/nations involves doorways of law, education, politics/government, education, ecology (land/vegetation/water/air), business, media and spirituality that all pivot around one main doorway... the Church.

If Christians remain in anarchy, so does the city/region/country and the pillars of society and the earth! It's a cycle of anarchy, each affecting the other.

Satan is the god of this world (2 Corinthians 4:4), who builds spiritual strongholds and structures over physical cities/ regions/ nations. These structures, governed by his evil principalities and powers, gain more strength and power through centuries of idolatry, bloodshed, superstition, sexual sins, unforgiveness, addictions, legalism, occult activity and lust (built up iniquity).

All of this spiritual filth builds up and infects the land and people.

The land falls deeper into anarchy (earthquakes, barrenness, terrorism, crime, war, etc.) and so do the people (cycle of sin, blindness to the gospel... 2 Corinthians 4:4).

Satan's evil spiritual structure pushes people and the land to greater anarchy, thus feeding his world.

Only Christians have been given the power to stop it!

Yet when Christians (the Church) are in anarchy, how can they stop satan's plans or be proper stewards of God's plans and His land? (Leviticus 25:23-24/ Exodus 19:5-6, 9:29/ Deuteronomy 10:12-14/ Psalm 24:1)

Examining individual Christians and the Church (body of Christians) we find mostly anarchy on the planet!

Christians fail to understand their responsibilities, the root spiritual problems and how to implement their power and authority to overcome anarchy. They are poorly taught by leaders, who are inadequately taught at seminaries and colleges.

"Whatever is going on in your "church" is indicative of what's going on "out there"", says Alistair.

He says the assembly of Christians is like a litmus test (or gauge) bearing fruit of the roots in the area, city or nation.

He says, "if your church has 3 or more of these following items, then they are picking up what's going on in the spiritual realm in their area":

- History of church/fellowship splits.
- Leadership problems or indiscretions.
- Lack of focused vision.
- Worship problems.
- Financial worries or frustrations.
- Problems with Sunday school and/or Youth Ministry.
- Inability to maintain spiritual growth.
- Poor involvement with other churches in "intra-church" events.
- Little success at community outreach.
- Lack of or poor conversion growth.
- Pastoral or leadership marriage splits.
  *Sickness or illness, especially within families of pastor and leadership.
- Back-biting.
- Gossip.
- Sexual immorality.
- Occult practises.
- General discontent.

Dr. Petrie had these same problems years ago at the "church" he headed and was lost at how to fix it. He pled with God for the answer and this is what God told him!

God reminded Alistair, that he had grown up on a farm in Scotland, asking him, "How did you and your family farm the land"? Alistair said, "Well, we went out after winter and removed any debris and the rocks pushed up by the earth, then we ploughed and fertilized the soil, planted the seed, watered, weeded and nurtured the land and the growing plants and then harvested",

God asked Alistair, if he would consider just throwing seed around and doing nothing else. Alistair said that wasn't a proper way to farm. God told him that it wasn't a proper way to accomplish results in the spiritual realm either.

God then told him to look at Jeremiah 1:10, "See, I have this day set you over the nations and over the kingdoms, to root out, and to pull down, to destroy, and to throw down, to build, and to plant".

God told him (and us) that we must root out, pull down, destroy and throw down evil first... then build and plant over nations!

Not many Christians follow this spiritual, Biblical principle and simple farming principle, for their lives, their assembly, their governments, their businesses, their cities and their nations?

Alistair goes on to say, that spiritual warfare for the area, city and nation is directed through the eyes of God, not our eyes. ("Teach me what I cannot see" Job 34:32a and "Open my eyes that I may see wonderful things in your law" Psalm 119:18). God can point out to us the rocks and debris that need to be cleared out first and so on, in order.

Another XTREME teaching from God of conquering spiritual and physical anarchy, ending the defilement of the land and stopping God's judgment for a city and nation is in 2 Kings 18. Hezekiah became king of Judah... "There was no one like him among all the kings of Judah, either before him or after him" (v. 5b).

Hezekiah was an Xtreme Big Game Hunter!

- *"He did what was right in the eyes of the Lord" v. 3a. "He trusted the Lord... did not cease to follow Him, kept His commands" v. 5-6 (no compromise).
- "He removed the (evil) high places" v. 4a (in life, family, business, Church assembly, society, city, nation). "Smashed the sacred stones" v. 4b (places of evil spiritual leverage).

- "He cut down the Asherah poles" v. 4c (pagan worship places).

- "He broke into pieces the bronze snake" v. 4c (worship of "work of the Lord" rather than the "Lord of the work").

- "He rebelled" against and "did not serve" an evil king. v. 7b (come against and do not submit to evil/corrupt leaders).

- He "defeated" enemy "watchtowers" and their "fortified cities" and "territories." v. 8 (conquer all that is unholy).

- When the mighty Assyrian King Sennacherib and his army came against King Hezekiah and Jerusalem, Hezekiah went to God for an answer to this threat. (2 Kings 18:17-37, 19:1-34).

What was God's answer to the enemy of His faithful steward?

"That night the angel of the LORD went out to the Assyrian camp and killed 185,000 Assyrian soldiers. When the surviving Assyrians woke up the next morning, they found corpses everywhere." (2 Kings 19:35) Assyrian King Sennacherib was killed by his own sons. (2 Kings 19:36-37)

Hezekiah applied a similar plan as in Jeremiah 1:10, to bring himself and his nation into its proper place and in order with God to receive blessings and protection from God.

We each must conquer anarchy in our lives first... <u>then</u>... seek God's direction (Job 34:32a and Psalm 119:18) on how to specifically root out, pull down, destroy and throw down evil structures/ principalities/ powers (Xtreme Big Game Hunting) in an area, city and nation... <u>then</u>... it is prepared to be built upon and planted for it to produce fruits of Church success, ending blindness towards the gospel (2 Cor. 4:4), overall peace, crime reduction, truth, success, prosperity, health, termination of physical/ecological disasters, receiving blessings... a reversal of anarchy!

Rev. Dr. Petrie and his family. have taught high level spiritual warfare in numerous countries for years, resulting in unproductive cities and areas to be restored, even after centuries of anarchy!

ROOT OUT, PULL OUT, DESTROY AND THROW DOWN FIRST, THEN FARM!

THE SAFARI PRINCIPLE!

ENDGAME

Although we go into battle to divide and conquer principalities, powers and demons over people, regions and the Church. to replace with the kingdom of God, we must be watchful for the endgame.

<u>What is the endgame?</u>

Ever watch a sports game where one team believes they have the game "in the bag", only to see the opposing team suddenly rise up for the win? I've seen this many times. Remember Adolf Hitler's overwhelming early victories, and the Japanese victory at Pearl Harbor and how each of them were decisively beaten years later.

This has also happened in the Bible, such as the evil forces coming heavily against Samson after his victories against the Philistines (Judges 16); Paul at Ephesus (Acts 19), after his victories; and Elijah after his showdown at Mt. Carmel (1 Kings 18 and 19).

Principalities and powers will retaliate after a victory against them. They don't have pity parties and a good cry after a defeat. They come back hard… so surprise them, and be ready for them at the gate!

When their guns are turned against you and victory is seemingly theirs, give <u>them</u> an endgame they'll never forget!

You may even anticipate their counter-attack against you for a victory and set traps for them! (My Dad would get a smile with that play!)

Wherever you are, you are more than a conqueror through Jesus Christ.

We have the supreme authority and power in <u>any</u> place.

One very instructive Biblical example of a battle against principalities and powers can be discerned in Nehemiah.

This good teaching in Nehemiah points out to us how high level evil forces operate and what to expect.

The king (representative of Jesus) gave Nehemiah (representing Christians) the authority over Jerusalem (or anyplace) to rebuild the gates and walls (representing cities and areas). Nehemiah prayed to God and was given the "go ahead" (timing) in Nehemiah 1.

Sanballat (representing a principality over an area) was the governor of the area and Tobiah (representing a power in an area) was his servant, who had power over the people as a false, corrupt priest (Nehemiah 7:61-62, 13:4-8).

Religious spirits will get into a Church assembly through deceptive leaders (enemy in the camp), as they did with Tobiah, acting in secrecy, like a scorpion, to bring false doctrine and steal Church funds. Scorpions prefer to work undetected and when found, will act innocent and passive. They will not purposely manifest, so as to not expose themselves, are typically very protective of their position, even killing to keep it and will battle other scorpions or powers that threaten them. (Ran into Xtreme Rabid Game myself like this!)

Despite Nehemiah's letter of authority and the king's men that were with him, these two men in charge of this area were grieved that he had come to help the people and they opposed him (Nehemiah 2).

Principalities and powers will act the same and unite to stop you from helping people or rebuild what is destroyed.

They will despise you, mock you and laugh at your efforts as did Sanballat, Tobiah, and Geshem against Nehemiah (Nehemiah 2:19). These initial attempts will be to question your authority and make you go away humiliated.

As you start having success, they will become very angry; conspire against you; hinder you and fight against you, to stop you, as happened in Nehemiah 4:7-8:

"Now it happened, when Sanballat, Tobiah, the Arabs, the Ammonites, and the Ashdodites heard that the walls of Jerusalem were being restored and the gaps were beginning to be closed, that they became very angry, and all of them conspired together to come and attack Jerusalem and create confusion."

They will try and trick and trap you:

"that Sanballat and Geshem sent to me, saying, "Come, let us meet together among the villages in the plain of Ono." But they thought to do me harm." Nehemiah 6:2

They will distract you with false information and give you fear:

"Then I perceived that God had not sent him at all, but that he pronounced this prophecy against me because Tobiah and Sanballat had hired him. For this reason, he was hired, that I should be afraid and act that way and sin, so that they might have cause for an evil report, that they might reproach me." Nehemiah 6:12-13

Nehemiah's obedience; prayer; going and doing; proper position with God; persistence; discernment; working with God; being FIT and help from others, brought success.

Another key to Nehemiah's success was unity.

Any leaders or Christian groups that are not looking for unity to overcome evil rulers, are not in tune with God.

Loyalty to themselves, is not loyalty to the King of Kings!

Another aspect of fighting these principalities and powers, is utilizing the power at our disposal against their power.

Whoever controls the skies controls the battlefield. This is a warfare strategy that began with flinging rocks, slingshots, catapults, arrows and spears, right up to the aircraft and missiles of today. This is the same in the spiritual realm.

If we control the air (heavenlies) over territories, we can control the territories.

We have the authority, with angelic forces and the Holy Spirit as the power with us.

"Bless the Lord, you His angels, who excel in strength, who do His word, heeding the voice of His word." Psalm 103:20

God commanded us to command— and He commanded His angelic forces to heed the commands. They move when those authorized tell them to!

"The angel of the Lord encamps all around those who fear Him, and delivers them. Psalm 34:7

We must <u>voice</u> the binding and the loosing!

There is another major battle key found in the following scripture. that most people misinterpret:

" And I also say to you that you are Peter, and on this rock, I will build My church, and the gates of Hades shall not prevail against it." Matthew 16:18

Many doctrines wrongly state, that Peter is the rock that Jesus speaks of here and that the Church is built on him, yet Paul is more deserving of that honor. if the rock signified a person.

Would God build the Church upon a man who is now dead?

We have to back up one verse to see what happened for Jesus to make this statement about the rock to Peter.

Peter had just publicly admitted that Jesus was "the Christ, the son of the living God" in verse 16. "Jesus answered and said to him, "Blessed are you, Simon Bar-Jonah, for flesh and blood has not revealed this to you, but My Father who is in heaven" Matthew 16:17.

Jesus is saying the rock that the Church is built on, is revelation from the heavenly Father, not Peter himself!

And then people have also misinterpreted verse 19:

"And I will give you the keys of the kingdom of heaven, and whatever you bind on earth will be bound in heaven, and whatever you loose on earth will be loosed in heaven."

Peter wasn't given the keys… they were given to the Church.

We must work together to utilize these keys against the evil kingdom.

Look for and expect God's revelation!

"For where two or three are gathered together in My name, I am there in the midst of them." Matthew 18:20

Agree, speak and achieve! Then heaven and earth moves against a defeated foe!

"Having disarmed principalities and powers, He made a public spectacle of them, triumphing over them in it." Colossians 2:15

"Beware lest anyone cheat you through philosophy and empty deceit, according to the tradition of men, according to the basic principles of the world, and not according to Christ. For in Him dwells all the fullness of the Godhead bodily; <u>and you are complete in Him, who is the head of all principality and power.</u>" Colossians 2:8-10

Principalities and powers know how effective unified Christians are against them, for this reason they work to disrupt, divide and conquer. Local Christian groups can come against the forces against them and the unity of Church groups can come against forces over the city or area. Once principalities and powers are displaced and replaced with the Holy Spirit and angelic forces from God, we must keep them there with our continued warfare, prayer altars, and spiritual guidance from God.

Some think the war is over with the air campaign, but then must come the ground campaign. Ground troops are required to take and subdue an area. Evangelism; casting out demons; healings; miracles; teaching; preaching and readying/equipping the troops for counter attacks and continued conflicts, are the ground campaign.

God will give us His strategy in every situation on how to deal with the battle at hand.

As with any battle plan, the commander (God) will supply the weapons, the strategy, the battlefield, the timing… all we have to do is show up and follow orders <u>and stay on target</u>!

The book of Joshua gives us another great battle plan that was used for taking an area and evil rulers.

God had Joshua and the Israelites take seven nations stronger than themselves, before they could possess the Promised Land; "seven nations greater and mightier than you." Deuteronomy 7:1

God did not destroy these nations for them, they had to go, in God's timing and do it with God <u>when</u> He delivered these nations to them. They were to utterly destroy them all, make no covenant or compromises and show no mercy.

"and <u>when</u> the Lord your God <u>delivers them</u> over to you, you shall conquer them and utterly destroy them. You shall make no covenant with them nor show mercy to them." Deuteronomy 7:2

They had to ruthlessly take on seven principalities and many cities and towns (powers) within these nations. They moved against these nations as God led them, one at a time, not all at once— and they were successful.

The first battle was against Jericho, the biggest target.

<u>Don't move without God. (Read Numbers 14:39-45)</u>

Stay focused as God focuses you on a single target until it falls. As success comes, principalities and powers will panic and join forces to come against you (They try their "endgame"). This is when God and you smile, as this is what we want!

"And it came to pass when all the kings who were on this side of the Jordan, in the hills and in the lowland and in all the coasts of the Great Sea toward Lebanon—the Hittite, the Amorite, the Canaanite, the Perizzite, the Hivite, and the Jebusite—heard about it, that they gathered together to fight with Joshua and Israel with one accord." Joshua 9:1-2

When the principalities and powers gather together against you, a great victory can be expected, as it was for the Israelites!

"And it happened, as they fled before Israel and were on the descent of Beth Horon, that the Lord cast down large hailstones from heaven on them as far as Azekah, and they died. There were more who died from the hailstones than the children of Israel killed with the sword." Joshua 10:11

Let Him guide you into battle to melt the hearts and the spirits of our enemies for His glory!

"So, it was, when all the kings of the Amorites who were on the west side of the Jordan, and all the kings of the Canaanites who were by the sea, heard that the Lord had dried up the waters of the Jordan from before the children of Israel until we had crossed over, that their heart melted; and there was no spirit in them any longer because of the children of Israel." Joshua 5:1

As the Holy Spirit leads, move with the authority you've been given; loose angels into battle; bind evil rulers and utilize all the weapons that God advises you to use.

In the Going in the Spirit, SAC Time, Give Him Your PAW Sectors, you'll discover how to position yourself to go in the spirit.

Sometimes you'll go in the spirit to visit heaven, other times it's to get a word from Jesus perhaps and other times it will be to go into battle!

You can ask God to take you into battle for something specific or let Him decide where He wants you to go.

You're doing this warfare against Xtreme Big Game in the spirit!

You may find that you'll go in the spirit in the air over the earth or you may be on the earth or you may be over water or you may be in another country, where nothing is familiar! The principality may come to you, although I usually end up going to it! Sometimes I physically go to the area where an evil principality is, other times I don't have to physically leave home. The principality may be in the air coming at you and you're on the ground. You may both be in the air. There may be one or more. Initially you may go in the spirit and just watch and nothing more. Usually God has given me the weapon(s) that I'll use against it or them. (I can't answer your obvious questions on why for all of this!)

God will lead you into what you will come against and how to take them.

He will not take you or put you where you cannot be victorious!

Some say you must use many intercessors, join with other warriors or hunters and go in the spirit to the throne room of God first to receive weapons, angels and orders before you can commence the hunt. I have not found this to be the case and for those who must, perhaps it is a must for them, for some reason.

This "requirement" of some is also not Biblically sound, as God personally came down to earth (Joshua 5:13-6:5) and gave Joshua war plans on how to spiritually take Jericho.

"Yet in all these things we are more than conquerors through Him who loved us. For I am persuaded that neither death nor life, nor angels nor principalities nor powers, nor things present nor things to come, nor height nor depth, nor any other created thing, shall be able to separate us from the love of God which is in Christ Jesus our Lord." Romans 8:37-39

When I have gone hunting Trophy Game in the spirit, I have cut them with various spiritual swords. Sometimes they disappear, sometimes they appear to die with blood coming out, and angels have taken some away bound.

Do they die?

Do they go to some other dimension?

I don't have that answer.

At times, I have instructed angels to put them in a spiritual prison… like some I have seen.

I have also attacked Trophy Game and wounded them and they have fled the area. I would say that these were displaced. Wounded animals in the natural will do the same.

Do they end up coming back or get replaced with other Trophy Game?

These are tough questions and I could venture a guess, but I won't.

Sometimes I have no idea what area I'm in, and sometimes I do.

I have found it best not to concern myself wondering about these things. I just go and do and then wait for the next time.

If the Holy Spirit tells me what happened, then I know; and if He doesn't tell me, then it's not for me to know.

Just be ready and do your job when the hunt is on!

Remember that Jesus defeated them and gave us the authority and power over them. We are to exercise this authority and power against them, remove them, replace them, embarrass them, show no mercy, set captives free and make disciples of all nations.

Hunting season is always open and XTREME BIG GAME are waiting to be taken! The hunting range is huge!

ARE YOU GAME?

THE JOSHUA STRATEGY

I love studying Joshua! He was one of the greatest examples of an Xtreme Big Game Hunter in history! We can also learn from his mistakes such as at Ai and with the Gibeonites.

Let's examine more closely what Joshua does to better assist us in battles for cities, regions and nations?

Joshua defeated 33 kings, however, let's study 5 now.

In Joshua 10, five Amorite kings formed an alliance to come against Gibeon, an ally of Israel. Joshua and his army were sent by God to destroy the Amorites.

This was a 7-part war strategy… let's highlight them:

1. Battle approved by God (v. 8).
2. God threw Amorites into confusion (v.10).
3. God sent giant hailstones to destroy (v. 11).
4. God through Joshua stopped the sun and the moon until the battle ended (v. 12-14).
5. Joshua's army killed many with the sword.
6. God gave strength to Joshua's army to fight for 3 whole days and one night (v. 6-, 9-14).
7. Joshua's captains put their feet on the necks of the 5 kings before Joshua killed them, hung them up and threw them in a cave (v. 15-27).

The miraculous combination of God and man, spiritual and physical tactics to overcome the enemy is important for us to understand. God's approval and tactics are a necessity in every battle! We don't battle in the spiritual or physical realm without God. (Battles in the physical also meaning life's battles, not just war.)

So let's sharpen our swords a bit more by examining the names, meanings and goals of the 5 kings, which are highly significant in Hunting Xtreme Big Game today!

These 5 kings were controlled by evil principalities. Together they were in control of people, cities and regions and planned to further control God's people.

Adoni-zedek, king of Jerusalem – his name means "my lord is righteous". A Lord rules or is master over, so he wants to rule over our position of righteousness. He is king of **Jerusalem** which means "possession of peace" or "teaching of peace". If we lose our peace, we are not trusting in the Lord, and we can't operate in faith. This king is after our peace and will try to instill worry and fear. Do not allow your circumstances (places of testing) steal your peace. Trust in the Lord.

Hoham, king of Hebron – his name means "whom Jehovah impels". As a god over his people, Hoham impels (drives by exertion of strong moral pressure). In other words, he will drive people into religious performance to perfect themselves. The result will be legalism. This driving force will pressure people to try to make themselves better by behavior modification, rather than resting in and leaning on God's Spirit, by which they can overcome the works of the flesh. This will result in a person having a spirit of religion rather than walking in the Spirit of God. **Hebron** means "association". This spirit will try to bring you into relationships with religious people who are legalistic.

Piram, king of Jarmuth – his name means "like a wild ass", which represents stubbornness that refuses to be associated with any, body of believers. This spirit wants to make you wild or unbridled and keep you from the place God would have you to be. **Jarmuth** means "heights", which represents pride to keep you from your destiny, because you don't want to submit to anyone else. Don't allow this spirit to keep you isolated.

Japhia, king of Lachish – his name means shining or show thyself. This spirit will try to get you to shine the light on yourself, call attention to yourself, demand your rights. This spirit will cause you to take God's glory for yourself. You will want to be the light rather than leading others into the light of Jesus Christ. This spirit will influence you to take the credit for yourself.

Lachish means "invincible". This spirit will cause you to think that God can't do anything without you. You will view yourself as irreplaceable. This attitude will come because you have become the light instead of letting Jesus be the Light. You will view yourself as invincible against satan's force, but you will fall. "Humble yourself to show yourself approved". Let Jesus be the Lord; lift Him up so that men will be drawn to Him and not yourself.

Debir, king of Eglon – his name means speaker and sanctuary. This spirit will try to get you to speak against those in the sanctuary… against the household of God. His desire is to cause you to become the voice of the accuser of the brethren. **Eglon** means a bullock or bull-like and represents one who attacks others through the use of words of criticism, accusation, and lies. This spirit will try to get you to trample others under foot and destroy their reputation. Don't be bull-headed! Listen to what the Spirit says.

When Joshua attacked and defeated the power (army) of these 5 kings, they hid themselves in a cave at Makkedah. (v.16)

Makkedah means "place of shepherds". The king's desire was to establish a place of rule over God's people. Evil principalities' desire is to be "shepherds" over people, especially the Lord's flock (Church) through their spiritual influence over God's people. They desire to replace the spiritual influence of our Shepherd, Jesus Christ!

Makkedah is used in the sense of herding, meaning to drive by force to a designated place. So, these 5 kings (and evil principalities) intent is to control and move people, especially God's people, by force and spiritual pressure to a place away from the true Shepherd where they can be slaughtered.

These are the principalities and powers that will try to rule you and over the house of God! It isn't hard to see that all of them are in operation today, in people's lives in various degrees! Perhaps even yours right now!

Do not fear these evil principalities and powers. You're now aware of them and their tactics. Be spiritually guided by God on how to specifically defeat them and their armies for <u>your</u> life, <u>your</u> city, <u>your</u> nation and the people in your region!

God's strategy for final victory with Joshua was…

"And Joshua said, roll large stones against the mouth of the cave, and set men by it to guard them." v.18

To bind them and seal them up (imprison in spiritual prisons), so they will not influence yours or other people's attitudes and actions. Set a guard so they don't break out against you and take you and others captive.

"So it was, when they brought out those kings to Joshua, that Joshua called for all the men of Israel, and said to the captains of the men of war who went with him, "Come near, put your feet on the necks of these kings." And they drew near and put their feet on their necks." v. 24

Put your feet on the necks of these kings (principalities and powers). Take authority over them and put them under your feet.

"And the God of peace will crush Satan under your feet shortly." Romans 16:20

"Then Joshua said to them, do not be afraid, nor be dismayed; be strong and of good courage, <u>for thus the LORD will do to all your enemies against whom you fight</u>. And afterward Joshua struck them and killed them, and hanged them on five trees; and they were hanging on the trees until evening." Joshua 10:25-26

Notice the underlined promise in the Word of God!

Now that your sword is a little sharper, ask God how you can advance His Kingdom and set captives free with this information!

QUEEN(S) OF HEAVEN

<u>Widely circulated</u> and taught in some circles, is that queen(s) of heaven have absolute power and govern over evil forces in every country, given to them by satan.

<u>Some say</u>, satan set up the religion of idol worship and these entities are said to maintain it through three main areas… sensuality/eroticism, war, and the occult.

<u>Said to</u> operate under, the religiosity of the people, to lead them to the adoration of these female idols. They work on the created behaviors and attitudes of people, raising a cult into a culture.

<u>Said to</u> be responsible for, taking the largest numbers of people to hell.

<u>Said to</u> be in charge of, keeping people blinded under religiosity, so they see nothing wrong with what they're doing. People's sins and their consciences send them to religious idols; thus, sin not only stays with them, but gets worse, yet the person thinks they are free.

People worship a variation of this evil entity all over the world, consequently, you don't need to be a satanist or occultist to be an idol worshipper and be lost (see Sector on Altars).

This evil entity, perceived as good and kind, demands offerings, worship, sacrifice, rituals, parades and festivals for the idol, thus trapping souls.

Any mention of a 'queen of heaven' in the Word?

"The children gather wood, the fathers kindle the fire, and the women knead dough, to make cakes for <u>the queen of heaven</u>; and they pour out drink offerings to other gods, that they may provoke Me to anger." Jeremiah 7:18

"Then all the men who knew that their wives had burned incense to other gods, with all the women who stood by, a great multitude, and all the people who dwelt in the land of Egypt, in Pathros, answered Jeremiah, saying: [16] "As for the word that you have spoken to us in the name of the Lord, we will not listen to you! [17] But we will certainly do whatever has gone out of our own mouth, to burn incense to <u>the queen of heaven</u> and pour out drink offerings to her, as we have done, we and our fathers, our kings and our princes, in the cities of Judah and in the streets of Jerusalem. For then we had plenty of food, were well-off, and saw no trouble. [18] But since we stopped burning incense to <u>the queen of</u>

<u>heaven</u> and pouring out drink offerings to her, we have lacked everything and have been consumed by the sword and by famine."

[19] The women also said, "And when we burned incense to <u>the queen of heaven</u> and poured out drink offerings to her, did we make cakes for her, to worship her, and pour out drink offerings to her without our husbands' permission?"

[20] Then Jeremiah spoke to all the people—the men, the women, and all the people who had given him that answer—saying: [21] "The incense that you burned in the cities of Judah and in the streets of Jerusalem, you and your fathers, your kings and your princes, and the people of the land, did not the Lord remember them, and did it not come into His mind? [22] So the Lord could no longer bear it, because of the evil of your doings and because of the abominations which you committed. Therefore, your land is a desolation, an astonishment, a curse, and without an inhabitant, as it is this day. [23] Because you have burned incense and because you have sinned against the Lord, and have not obeyed the voice of the Lord or walked in His law, in His statutes or in His testimonies, therefore this calamity has happened to you, as at this day."

[24] Moreover Jeremiah said to all the people and to all the women, "Hear the word of the Lord, all Judah who are in the land of Egypt! [25] Thus says the Lord of hosts, the God of Israel, saying: 'You and your wives have spoken with your mouths and fulfilled with your hands, saying, "We will surely keep our vows that we have made, to burn incense to <u>the queen of heaven</u> and pour out drink offerings to her." You will surely keep your vows and perform your vows!"' Jeremiah 44:15-25

The Bible is clear that God does not like the worship of idols and punished the Israelites <u>and</u> the land many times because of it.

Who is this queen of heaven?

Is it a goddess, a female god, a bride or perhaps a mistress of satan?

I've heard just about everything imaginable from people.

I've heard it said that the queen of heaven is a half male/half female entity. Saying that the male part wounds the land with bloodshed and war as sacrifices for evil altars and then the female part of this entity takes over, promoting evil idol, virgin, evil god and goddess worship.

I've heard it said that there are <u>numerous</u> queens of heaven all over the world, each with different women's names.

Some evil queens, some say, have names from the Bible, such as:

- Eve (Genesis).
- Hagar (Genesis 16:1-6).
- Delilah (Judges 16).
- Michal (1 Samuel 18:27/2 Sam. 6:20-23).
- Jezebel (1 Kings).
- Vashti (Esther 1:9-12).
- Herodias (Matthew 14:3).
- Mary (mother of Jesus).
- Salome (Matthew 14:6-11).
- Queen of Babylon (Revelation 18).
- The goddess of Babylon had so many names she became known as the "Goddess with 10,000 faces".

These queen(s) or goddess(es) of religions, also seem to move around from one empire to another and can be in many places at the same time, such as:

- Semiramis, Ishtar, Astarte, Beltis (Babylon).
- Isis (Egypt).
- Mother Kali (India).
- Venus, Cybele, Flora, Mary (Rome).
- Ashteroth, Tammuz, Asherah, Baal, Dagon (Canaan).

- Aphrodite, Demeter (Greece).
- Abnoba, Sirona (Gaul).
- Arinna, Astarte, Diana or Artemis (Asia Minor).
- Sophia (early Gnostics).
- Andrasta and Britannia (Britain).
- Kuan Yin (China).

As I've said before, one person told me there's a queen of heaven called Hitler!

One spiritual warfare team spent hundreds of thousands of dollars to climb Mt. Everest to confront the supposed, supreme, queen of heaven… although I prefer going on hunts in the spirit, as it is much cheaper!

Today in the 21st century, many of these ancient names have been adopted by people reviving old religions and cults, including new names like "mother earth", "mother goddess" and "mother god".

Please don't ask me to explain what all these goddesses and queens are supposedly in charge of!

So, let's make sense of all this goop! Goop's a word, right?

Historically in various religions and empires, we've got all these so-called feminine spiritual entities, queens or goddesses that have tens of thousands of names (millions if you go to India).

If it's only one evil entity racing around to all these places, she is one busy goddess!

We know that only the one true God is omnipresent, so it can't possibly be <u>one</u> evil entity present in all these areas in the world.

Unless there <u>is</u> just one in charge and all the others are pretenders and liars.

If satan has a pile of spiritual queens or mistresses all over the place, would he want people worshipping them?

God doesn't permit worship to anyone or anything other than to Himself.

Does anyone really believe that an extremely prideful satan is different… that he would allow people to worship millions of other things or even one other thing (a queen) rather than him?

Saying this, is satan perpetuating a myth, a lie, deceiving people into worshipping <u>really</u> him, <u>thinking</u> they are a worshipping a queen(s)?

<u>If</u> satan was to copy God, and he does, his "bride" would be a religion made up of people, to mimic the "bride" of the true God, which is the Church, made up of true Christians. (God doesn't have a queen so why would satan?)

And… God became man as Christ… Jesus. Satan will mimic this and incarnate a man one day… the antichrist.

The best satan can come up with to mimic the Holy Spirit is his network of Xtreme Big, Xtreme Small and Xtreme Rabid Game.

We are told that we wrestle "against principalities, against powers, against the rulers of the darkness of this world, against spiritual wickedness in high places". No mention of queen(s) of heaven in this scripture. Would God forget to mention this in His Word to us? (Although some will argue queens(s) of heaven is/are a principality.)

<u>Whether one or millions or no actual queens of heaven, it/they all are the enemy!</u>

Don't get bogged down in the analysis, especially if it is satan, or one of his soldiers masquerading under various names and appearances.

"And no wonder; for satan himself transforms himself into an angel of light". 2 Corinthians 11:14

I have seen and battled numerous female-looking evil spiritual creatures and could care less if they were a queen, a princess or Hitler in a dress!

Don't get spooked if some evil entity is sitting on a throne or wearing a crown or is telling you that they are unconquerable because they are so mighty!

If you are a little spooked thinking about this right now, I want you to think of Moses. He was a shepherd who just walked in from Midian uninvited to Egypt, the mightiest empire on the planet, to tell the Egyptian god-king pharaoh to free the people! Sounds impossible doesn't it!

Yet Moses was a god to pharaoh!

"So, the LORD said to Moses, See, I have made you as God to Pharaoh." Exodus 7:1

Pharaoh didn't have a chance, but obviously he needed some convincing, as human logic dictated, that Moses didn't have a chance!

Remember from the Weapons Sector… God says that you are His battle axe and weapon of war and with you He will destroy and break nations in pieces.

David knew that with God, he could destroy multiple nations that came against him. So can we!

"All nations surrounded me, but in the name of the LORD I will destroy them. They surrounded me, yes, they surrounded me; but in the name of the LORD I will destroy them. They surrounded me like bees; they were quenched like a fire of thorns; for in the name of the LORD I will destroy them. You pushed me violently, that I might fall, but the LORD helped me." Psalm 118:10-13

You're in the same position when God sends you against anything or anyone, including evil principalities ruling nations!

Even satan backs away from a true child of God, who is led by God!

"Submit yourselves therefore to God. Resist (defy/oppose) the devil, and he will flee from you." James 4:7

They don't have a chance!

When in this position, jump for joy because you know you're about to knock this loser off their throne and will be setting many people free! Just sort of smile at them and then show them what a child of God can do! If you ever doubt, remember Exodus 7:1!

Any snappy comebacks that come to mind that you want to say back at the enemy, in response to what they say to you, before you zap them, are optional! It is a perk!

Whether real or imagined evil queen(s), many people have not worshipped the one true God and have tied themselves to the evil realm, either deliberately or in ignorance.

Ask the Holy Spirit to show you any alliance with any "queens of heaven". Cancel the covenants of any saints, virgins, gods or goddesses to which you were dedicated. Destroy altars and images and statues in your house, where you have been asking it/them to take care of you and your house. Ask God to forgive you for doing this and cancel this bondage over your life, in Jesus' name.

OLAFING

We've read in this Xtreme Big Game Sector about hunting leader spiritual beings, to produce the greatest results. Also, I had said that satan will focus on one person that is a national leader (such as a Hitler) or a sports, music or entertainment leader and "assist" their position to perpetuate evil, persecution and/or sin over millions of people.

So, let's examine a little strategic Big Game focusing ourselves!

"Wars can be prevented just as surely as they can be provoked, and we who fail to prevent them, must share the guilt for the dead."

Omar N. Bradley - 5 Star US Army General

I know you're probably saying, "But Al, this doesn't apply to us; this applies to politicians and world leaders. How can you or I stop wars or be guilty for the war dead"?

Besides teaching leaders to utilize spiritual warfare and operating in the spirit tactics in their ministries, to have positive physical manifestations occur in their regions, what else can be done?

Jesus teaches us that a few fish can feed multitudes in Matthew 14:13–21, Matthew 15:32-39, Mark 6:31-44, Mark 8:1-9, Luke 9:10-17 and John 6:5-15. Obviously a very important strategy for it to be taught to us so many times by God!

This strategy is targeting specific Xtreme Big Game and the Xtreme Rabid Game that they control, who holds the fate of millions of people.

It's a two-pronged strategy of warfare... spiritual and physical.

I point out in the Xtreme Rabid Game Sector, that there are currently 92 known countries that persecute Christians. (List at persecution.com and persecution.org) Not surprisingly, the countries that are generating all the wars, terrorism and global tension in the world are also in this list, such as Afghanistan, Iraq, Iran, Pakistan, Syria and North Korea. Most of the 92 are Islamic majority nations.

So how can <u>we</u> prevent war and spiritual and physical deaths on a massive scale?

In the Bible, nations of people received relief when national leaders such as Kings Zebah and Zalmunna of Midian, King Saul, Ahab and Jezebel were ousted.

However, now-a-days, actually killing leaders of nations is frowned upon, unless a sudden "accident" or coup d'état by the people brings about this result, ushering in a Christian or a future Christian leadership.

It's amazing that the people of North Korea haven't brought about a change for themselves yet. North Korea once had so many Christians, Pyongyang was known as the Jerusalem of the East. The people should have practiced operating in the supernatural, instead of operating in religion. Having the most "churches" in a region doesn't make it a jewel of heaven and doesn't thwart satan. Perhaps one day, someone will successfully Olaf their "supreme leader".

Let's examine a nation that was once feared and known for war against neighboring nations, to get a sense of what this strategy is all about.

A thousand years ago, Norway was a brutal nation of Vikings that attacked, raped, and plundered without mercy across many lands.

Yet for the last 1000 years, this country and its neighboring Scandinavian countries, are all world renowned and respected as being peaceful.

In fact, every year, the Norwegian parliament chooses a committee to issue Nobel Peace Prizes to those people in the world who they judge "...shall have done the most or the best work for fraternity between nations, for the abolition or reduction of standing armies and for the holding and promotion of peace congresses".

So, what happened?

Olaf of Norway was a pagan Viking known to be a raider and plunderer of many lands.

A prophet foretold to him several things that would happen which came true. This converted Olaf to Christianity.

One prophecy saved his life and changed the lives of millions since then!

God's power brought about a change in his belief system and his conversion to Christianity.

"And my speech and my preaching were not with persuasive words of human wisdom, but in demonstration of the Spirit and of power, that your faith should not be in the wisdom of men, but in the power of God." 1 Corinthians 2:4-5

As the prophet also foretold, Olaf one day became King Olaf 1 of Norway.

He built the first Church building in Norway in 995, promoted Christianity throughout his rule and personally converted and baptized the explorer, Leif Erickson.

Leif Erickson brought and spread Christianity across Greenland and was the first European to discover and settle North America, in what is now Newfoundland Canada, nearly 500 years before Christopher Columbus was born! Thus, North America was first discovered and settled by a Christian! Leif Erickson Day is recognized in the USA on October 9.

King Olaf also converted the people and Earl of <u>Orkney Islands</u> to Christianity.

Prior to his becoming King, Olaf had a Viking friend named Prince Vladimir.

Olaf mocked him for being a pagan idolater. One-day, Prince Vladimir became the King of Russia and realized that his friend Olaf was right; his pagan beliefs were a lie. After Prince Vladimir conducted a "testing of the faiths" (Christianity, Judaism, and Islam) by meeting with these faith's leaders, he realized that Olaf was right in that Christianity was the true path to God.

He decreed that all idols must be destroyed and that all opponents of Christianity would face his royal displeasure. This began what Russians recall as their "Golden Age".

During Vladimir's lifetime, Christianity was adopted in Russia, Norway, Denmark, Sweden, Iceland, Greenland, the Faeroes, the Shetlands, the Orkneys and in fledgling Canada.

Very productive result, stemming from one prophet's demonstration of God's power to the right person!

I call it... OLAFING!

(Olaf Hunting)

Imagine what would happen to the Islamic world, if ISIS, al-Qaeda, Taliban or Saudi, Palestinian or Iranian leadership became Christian! Or if Supreme Leader Kim Jong Un of North Korea converted! Or if the pope of the roman catholic religion renounced and rejected all the false doctrines of man, that they made up over the last 2000 years and embraced God's Truth, as He exactly spelled out in His Word!

The impact of reaching such powerful people can be enormous, affecting the entire world!

Some might say, "But Al, I don't have access to ISIS, al-Qaeda, the Saudi King, Iranians, Taliban leadership or the pope or Kim Jong Un", yet when we move in the spiritual realm, God gives us spiritual access, to conquer for His Kingdom!

God can put us and current or future leaders together.... physically <u>or go to them in the spirit</u>!

Don't forget, you can go in the spirit even into their secret hiding places!

Let's look at another powerful example of Olafing!

In 1937, Christian Wolfkes, an old carpenter in a village in the mountains of Romania prayed like this, "My God, I have served you on earth and I wish to have my reward on earth as well in heaven and my reward should be that I should not die before I bring a Jew to Christ, because Jesus was from the Jewish people. But I am poor, old and sick. I cannot go around seeking a Jew. In my village, there are none. Bring a Jew into my village and I will do my best to bring him to Christ."

God brought a Jew named Richard Wurmbrand to him. Wolfkes introduced him to Jesus and he was converted.

Wurmbrand was later ordained, spent 14 years in prisons being tortured for Christ by the Nazis and communists, wrote 22 books that still reach and comfort people today, became an international speaker and founded the international organization, The Voice of the Martyrs.

I would say millions have been reached by this ministry. My wife Rhoda even heard Wurmbrand speak in Romania, many years ago before he died! Just one old carpenter started it, by Olafing someone who became a Silver Bullet of God, in the spiritual and physical world!

World leaders and even future world leaders, such as Olaf and Richard, come into our vicinity at times or when God brings us to them or them to us <u>or to those who affect them (i.e. their spiritual advisor, a friend or relative)</u>.

Leaders in government, entertainment, sports, and religions, can be a focus of your ministry, to bring about a great harvest with those that look to them for leadership.

Olafing Strategy

One could start with a list of these 92 countries and their leaders and see how you are led!

Or pray over a world map or TV world news, to find out whom God would like you to "Olaf"!

Perhaps God will lead you to one specific country and one person… perhaps more.

History teaches us what one prophet with one future leader accomplished in Norway, that's affected millions of people in numerous countries for 1000 years!!

What we can learn here is, that a highly strategic plan is to go after Big Game that have an effect over multitudes of others. As Jesus said, a few fish can feed many.

Let's not just set our sights on a little prayer group or a neighborhood assembly group.

Eagles don't hang out in chicken yards!

We fly where The Wind takes us!

Don't forget to hunt the Xtreme spiritual game ruling the leader!

Go Olafing!

The only limitation is you!

How To Save A Nation

In Altars, Structures and Strongholds, I discuss that they are both holy and evil.

I've been led to expand on this topic in this Sector with some more insight to assist those who are doing or want to do Xtreme Big Game Hunting (XBGH) for their nation.

Let's examine prayer and fasting.

Prayer & Fasting Changes Nations

Being an Xtreme Christian to change nations like Jehoshaphat, the king of Nineveh, Esther and Daniel did, requires an offensive strategy of "prayer and fasting".

Let's examine 4 quick examples from the Bible and then let's examine 4 20th Century examples, of how nations were changed by these 2-fold spiritual weapons.

Jehoshaphat: In 2 Chronicles 20:1-30, an army from Moab, Ammon and Mount Seir was marching to destroy Judah. Jehoshaphat, king of Judah, turned to God... "Jehoshaphat... proclaims a fast throughout all Judah (v. 3)". Corporate prayer and fasting for God to change the outcome of a war that affected a nation! "So, Judah gathered together to ask help from the Lord; and from all the cities of Judah they came to seek the Lord (v. 4)". They received an immediate prophetic answer from God through Jahaziel, of encouragement and strategy. The people responded with praise and worship, which continued with singing, when facing the invaders. No physical weapons were brought to the battle (v. 22-30). The invading army destroyed itself, with no survivors. It took the people of Judah three days to gather up all the spoils, as they praised God in thanksgiving! Surrounding nations heard of this event and feared ever coming against Judah, leaving the nation in peace for a time.

God says, "if My people who are called by My name will humble themselves, and pray and seek My face, and turn from their wicked ways, then I will hear from heaven, and will forgive their sin and heal their land." 2 Chronicles 7:14

Esther: The entire jewish race was on the verge of destruction by decree of the Persian emperor. This would have been a major victory for satan to destroy the race that Jesus needed to come from. Esther, her cousin Mordecai and all the jews in the capital (Shushan) gathered together for three days of prayer and fasting. The decree was totally reversed, Esther and Mordecai were elevated and the jews across the empire were saved.

King of Nineveh: Jonah (reluctantly) went to Nineveh (Gentile capital of Assyria) to advise them that God had judged them and would destroy them. "Yet forty days, and Nineveh shall be overthrown" Jonah 3:4. This city was idolatrous and cruel. The king ordered everyone including all the livestock to fast, be covered in sackcloth, turn from evil and violence (Jonah 3:5-9). "Then God saw their works, that they turned from their evil way; and God relented from the disaster that He had said He would bring upon them, and He did not do it" (v.10). The city remained safe and prosperous for about 150 years.

Daniel: "in the first year of his (Darius) reign I, Daniel, understood by the books the number of the years specified by the word of the Lord through Jeremiah the prophet (Jeremiah 29:10), that He would accomplish seventy years in the desolations of Jerusalem. Then I set my face toward the Lord God to make request by prayer and supplications, with fasting, sackcloth, and ashes." Daniel 9:2-3

Daniel humbled himself, prayed, sought God's face, interceded on behalf of his people sins and renounced and turned from those sins. Fulfilling Jeremiah's prophecy, Israel was restored to their lands, through one man's warfare!

These weapons worked then and they still work today! I've already discussed earlier in this book about Carlos Annacondia changing Argentina and Rees Howells' spiritual war on Nazism .so let's now look at some testimonies from the world-renowned leader Derek Prince. from his book, *Shaping History through Prayer and Fasting*. (Recommended study to obtain greater insight into these spiritual weapons).

WW II: After the greatest retreat in British history, Derek Prince (in military service in North Africa), guided by the Holy Spirit, prayed, "Lord, give us leaders such that it will be for your glory to give us victory through them". The course of the war immediately changed at El Alamein in North Africa for the Allies, preventing the Nazis from invading and occupying the jews in Palestine, setting in motion a turning point in history against this evil threat from the whole world!

Nation of Israel: Just prior to the re-establishment of the State of Israel, after almost 2000 years, on May 14, 1948, the surrounding Islamic countries declared war on it "their intention to annihilate the newborn Jewish state and to sweep the Jews into the sea" (pg. 77). 150,000 jews with minimal arms and equipment and no military force, were suddenly surrounded by nations of 50 million with well-equipped trained armies! Derek and Lydia Prince were living in Jerusalem at the time and after praying to stand with God's Word, Lydia spoke, "Lord, paralyze the Arabs!" The Israeli defense force had a command post in the Prince's back yard and commented to the Prince's that during battles, when they were vastly outgunned and outnumbered 10 to 1, the Arabs "seem powerless... it's as if they are paralyzed" (pg. 79). Israel went on to defeat Lebanon, Syria, Jordan, Egypt and their backers in many wars and battles.

Russia: In 1953, Stalin, dictator of Russia, planned "a systematic purge against Russian Jews" (pg. 80). Derek Prince and a group in London, England were led by God to pray and fast on behalf of the Russian Jews for 1 day! Within 2 weeks Stalin died. 16 doctors had tried to save him, but in vain. Similar to the death of Herod by an angel in Acts 12, the course of history was changed in Russia. The new leader, Khrushchev, "denounced Stalin as a cruel and unjust persecutor of the Russian people" (pg. 82) and the purge of Russian Jews didn't happen!

Kenya: Derek and Lydia Prince were living in Kenya at the time of its independence from Britain in 1963. Political experts expected bloody internal wars, similar to the Congo's independence in 1960. God led them at a conference to pray for Kenya. The entire group prayed together out loud in unison and finished together. A vision was shared of red, fierce horses led by a "very black man" heading to Kenya being turned away to the north (pg. 86). A bloody revolution broke out in Zanzibar and a revolutionary movement spread from the army of Tanzania to the Kenyan army. The new president of Kenya put down the revolution and the communist attempt to take over the country. The coup failed in Kenya, but was successful in the nation to the north, Somalia. The prophetic vision was fulfilled! Kenya today is a peaceful, democratic nation. Somalia today is an islamic state that breeds and exports terrorism.

There are many examples that can be brought to bear, like the Presidents of the United States proclaiming a national day of solemn humiliation, prayer and fasting in 1798 against war with France; again in 1815 for the war with Britain and again by Lincoln 3 times for the Civil War. We all know the outcomes of these wars!

If people are disobedient (aka rebellious) to Him (His Word), then their house, cities, lands and nations suffer under hardships and cruelty. Examine the Biblical history of Israel and look around the world today at non-Christian majority nations to testify to this fact. When people turn to Him in humility, prayer and fasting, things change, as we see in our few examples… rulers and governments can be replaced or their hearts changed. The efforts of multitudes in unity or just the one righteous going to God, shapes nations! As with Rees Howells (he was in Wales doing warfare against Nazism in Continental Europe/Africa) and Derek Prince (he was in England doing warfare against Russia's leader), you don't need to be standing in the nation that needs change! Let God be your guide in prayer and fasting… follow His direction and strategy.

A good Nation Hunting guide is the "IF/THEN" strategy of God's own Words in 2 Chronicles 7:14… 1. IF My people who are called 2. Humble themselves 3. Pray 4. Seek My Face 5. Turn from wickedness THEN 1. I will hear from heaven 2. Forgive their sin 3. Heal their land.

A nation can be dealt with as easily as with a person! I'm not kidding!

God seeks someone, a Silver Bullet, to do XBGH for their nation!

"So I (God) sought (hunted) for a man among them who would make a wall, and stand in the gap before Me on behalf of the land (do XBGH for a nation), that I should not destroy it; but I found no one. Therefore, I have poured out My indignation on them; I have consumed them with the fire of My wrath; and I have recompensed their deeds on their own heads," says the Lord GOD." Ezekiel 22:30-31

A nation can be destroyed slowly or quickly by God, because of satan's strategies and/or lack of a Silver Bullet of God to save it. Some would say, that people destroy nations through war, yet spiritual forces (holy and evil) are behind physical "war machines" to produce physical results.

Many nations of the world today are suffering from civil war, crime, terrorism, plagues, and economic meltdown. A XBGH must go to God and find out which edge of the sword to use (perhaps both edges) … the edge against satan and/or the edge to stay (stop) God's Hand against the nation (read how Moses stopped God from destroying Israel in Exodus 32:7-14).

Satan's forces work to turn a nation away from God, to bring about its destruction. They infect leaders, families, music, entertainment, education, media, government, and the Church body (compromise/religion).

When a human body is infected, let's say a small tumor, we attack it with some cure to end the spread. Ignoring the tumor can lead to cancer throughout the body and to death of the entire body, even the majority healthy portions. If a nation, like a human body, has a tumor, let's say one corrupt leader (Hitler) that is tolerated, the tumor grows worse, cancer spreads and the entire body (land/economy/education/cities/nation of people) can be destroyed, even the healthy portions.

When a person has a "false-Christianity" (deliberate or in ignorance) or an anti-Christian mind-set (nation = false religions/corrupt government), the evil kingdom has the right and ability to infect it, as the immune system (spiritual power, authority) is down (God's blessings removed or His Hand set against the body/nation). Traumas/accidents (wars), cancer (plagues), job loss (economic woes) come to the body to break it down. The body (nation) will be crippled, experience very poor health and die prematurely… XBGH is needed!

With a person, each (at age of reason) governs their own mind and body… they need to alter their mindset to accept salvation through Jesus.

XBGH is used, under God's guidance, weapons, timing, to combat the evil entity(ies) that are set against their minds, as people's minds are blinded from the gospel (2 Corinthians 4:4). Once the mind is clear, the person must accept Christ (God) to put into motion the cure process. This process differs with everyone, depending on the spread and kinds of infections (i.e. iniquity, unforgiveness, occult, religious and sexual activity, traumas, etc.) XBGH again to do deliverance on a person, to eradicate evil spirits, mental upsets and physical diseases, to bring the body to physical, mental, emotional and spiritual health and strength. The body is brought under God's protection, mercies, blessings, peace, prosperity and life.

A nation is a body made up of many people. Like a body, a nation has many organs (government, police, economy, education, the Church, media, arts). Similar XBGH concepts apply for a nation as for one person. Although we see one physical person or government at the head of a nation (mind-set), a spiritual Silver Bullet of God or XBGH like a Moses, Elijah, Daniel, Isaiah, Jeremiah, or Ezekiel, has affected the spiritual realm to change nations.

A person has a right to govern their own mind/body (even in a dictatorship they can decide).

One Christian has a right, has the power, has the authority and is still hunted by God to "stand in the gap" (Ezekiel 22:31-32) (do XBGH) to save a nation!

As I taught in Olafing, Norway was once a pagan, warring nation that was turned to Christianity by one prophecy from a hermit given to King Olaf. Norway has been a peaceful, Christian nation in prosperity for 1000 years!

Cantons within Switzerland warred with each other until an agreement brokered by hermit Nicolas von Flue, was accepted (no doubt through God's direction) that has kept this country in peace within itself and with and from others for about 600 years, even when it was surrounded by Nazi Germany in WWII!

Once a principality(ies), powers and evil entities are removed from blinding a nation (its leaders/people) from the gospel, infections in organs can be reversed. Think like you're God's doctor for a nation!

If you feel like your faith is too small, try it out yourself on a person (deliverance), then in the spirit for a person, then your neighborhood, then city, then nation. If you have grandiose faith, go hunting in the spirit with God to do XBGH for other cities and nations.

You must be willing. Get and keep yourself right with God. Ask God to show you what to do. You may have to battle certain evil entities in order (as Joshua fought certain battles in order). You may be led to plead with God to hold His Hand of wrath back (like Moses did). You may be led to lead a XBGH team to prevent or stop a war (like Rees Howells from Wales did against Nazi Germany). You may be led to go Olafing (connect with a world leader leader(s) with a word from God like the hermits of Norway and Switzerland). You may be led to back up (be a Daniel Nash) a modern-day Charles Finney.

Be patient and persistent with XBGH, but always wait and work with God, whether for a person or a nation or anything in-between!

If you aren't given weapons or a target, then you don't hunt! Just stay right with God with worshipping, praising and thanking God, until He has something for you to do! Be that one that God's hunting for!

God needs ND's… "Nation Doctors"!

Good Hunting!

Next… let's see what the Xtreme Small Game are up to.

SECTOR EIGHTEEN

XTREME SMALL GAME

HUNTING TIP

They're like shootin' fish in a barrel… here fishy fishy!

Hunting small game is relaxing and enjoyable. Fresh air, exercise, nature and peace and quiet.

Well, at least in the natural!

Rabbits and partridge are my favorites. It brings a smile just remembering those hunting moments.

Most will hunt small game when they are younger, before moving up to big game or trophy hunting, but I have known people who have never hunted small game and enjoy just big game hunting. And the reverse is true… many never go beyond small game hunting.

When hunting trophy or big game, you will run into small game or they will run into you! This goes the same for wolf hunting… a separate breed of game!

I was hunting coyote one day standing by a tree, when I could see a rabbit casually moving along through the woods. He didn't see me. He moved along heading right to me, coming within a few feet of me, before I startled him and he took off.

I've had a squirrel climb my leg (maybe he thought I was a tree); a mouse walk across my body and birds sitting next to me looking at me wondering what I was doing up in a tree, all while hunting big game.

In the woods, there is usually more small game than big game and the same within the evil spiritual realm, where the big game usually control what the small game do and where they go.

Evil spiritual small game are usually called unclean spirits; foul spirits; evil spirits; devils; ghosts; apparitions; imps; poltergeists; phantoms; familiar spirits; animal creature spirits and demons.

These are usually associated with being in, around or on people, in physical objects, in animals, in buildings and smaller areas.

They can be alone; however, they usually are in packs or great numbers, with a leader.

Right now, let's lump them all together and call them Xtreme Small Game or small game for short, through the rest of this study.

My extensive library of books on small game, started in the mid-1970's, has almost as wide a variety of names for these evil things, what they are, and what they look like, as there are books.

Many of those who believe evil spirits exist, seem to think that small game are fallen angels.

Some say they are spirits from a pre-Adamic race of beings.

And there are other beliefs, such as they are interplanetary beings or inter-dimensional beings or the spirits of the unsaved.

Then there are those that insist, that xtreme small game are just some sort of psychological thing or figments of our imagination, that can be dealt with by drugs, counseling, and therapy and/or by reading the Bible and just being a Christian.

These differing beliefs have caused many Christians to segregate!

Many also say, that a Christian can never have a demon in them.

Theories, doctrines and personal opinions of others <u>can</u> be a help to us, although it does cause much confusion and disunity, especially when some "experts" have never personally hunted any small game.

What does the Bible and ancient writings tell us about evil spirits/small game?

We see a glimpse of what they are in Genesis 6:2, 4-5, 11-13.

"that the sons of God saw the daughters of men, that they were beautiful; and they took wives for themselves of all whom they chose." v. 2

"There were giants on the earth in those days, and also afterward, when the sons of God came in to the daughters of men and they bore children to them. Those were the mighty men who were of old, men of renown. Then the Lord saw that the wickedness of man was great in the earth, and that every intent of the thoughts of his heart was only evil continually." v.4-5

"The earth also was corrupt before God, and the earth was filled with violence. So, God looked upon the earth, and indeed it was corrupt; for all flesh had corrupted their way on the earth. And God said to Noah, "The end of all flesh has come before Me, for the earth is filled with violence through them; and behold, I will destroy them with the earth." v. 11-13

The Bible tells us of that sons of God mated with daughters of men, producing hybrid creatures or giants, who were always corrupt and evil. They provoked God to destroy all living creatures on the earth, except Noah, his family and the animals he took on the ark.

These giants are often referred to as Nephilim, a Hebrew word meaning "those causing others to fall."

So, who were these sons of God and what happened to them and their giant offspring?

We must research into other areas, to obtain more detail of this historic story in Genesis, such as in the Book of Enoch, the Book of Jubilees and from certain Dead Sea Scrolls.

Some might say, that these books are not from the Bible and thus discredit anything that they say. But does anyone honestly think, that God has nothing further to say or do, other than what is in the 66 books of the Bible?

Enoch was quoted from by Jesus over 20 times and quoted also by Jude and Peter, so if the Book of Enoch is not worthy, you can take it up with these guys one day for quoting from it!

The Book of Jubilees, included in the jewish canon, and fragments from the Dead Sea Scrolls, support Genesis and what God told Enoch about evil spirits.

We find out from these following passages that these sons of God are angels, that are called Watchers.

"And the angels, <u>the children of heaven</u>, (sons of God) saw them and desired them; and they said to one another, "Come let us choose wives for ourselves from among the daughters of men and beget us children." 1 Enoch 6:2

"they (angels) were altogether two hundred." 1 Enoch 6:6

"and they began to go unto them… and the women became pregnant and gave birth to great giants." 1 Enoch 7:1-2

And also,

"they bore them and these are the giants." The Book of Jubilees Frag. 7

"And they (the Watchers) begot sons, the Naphidim, and all of them were dissimilar. And each one ate his fellow. The giants killed the Naphil, and the Naphil killed the Elyo, and the Elyo mankind and man his neighbor." Jubilees 7:22

In many chapters of 1 Enoch, these angels are referred to as Watchers.

1 Enoch 8 says, that these Watchers also taught people how to make weapons, about incantation, astrology and other practices, that led people and the earth to wickedness. God was very displeased with what these Watchers did. God told Enoch, that these angels "abandoned the high, holy and eternal heaven; and slept with women and defiled yourselves with the daughters of the people, taking wives, acting like the children of the earth, and begetting giant sons." 1 Enoch 15:2-4

The Bible tells us how God still punishes these angels for their sin:

"For if God did not spare the angels who sinned, but cast them down to hell and delivered them into chains of darkness, to be reserved for judgment." 2 Peter 2:4

"And the angels who did not keep their proper domain, but left their own abode, He has reserved in everlasting chains under darkness for the judgment of the great day." Jude 6

Enoch was frightened when he was taken by a heavenly angel to where these angels were being punished. This heavenly angel told Enoch," This place is the prison house of angels; they are detained here forever." 1 Enoch 21:10

Enoch told the imprisoned angels, that what they had done banned them from heaven for eternity and that they "shall remain inside the earth, <u>imprisoned</u>, for all eternity." 1 Enoch 14:4-6

God told Enoch in 1 Enoch 16:3, that these Watchers "will have no peace" for what they'd done.

So, the sinning Watcher angels or sons of God were put into everlasting chains, but what happened to their children?

A Dead Sea Scroll found says, that the Watcher angels begot giants <u>and monsters</u> and they corrupted <u>all</u> the earth.

The Book of Giants is one of the Dead Sea scrolls found at Qumran and it says "they (Watchers) defiled… they begot giants and monsters… all the earth was corrupted by the hand of the giants." 4Q531

Jubilees 7:24 says, "And afterward they sinned against beasts, and birds and everything which moves or walks upon the earth. And they poured out much blood upon the earth. And all the thoughts and desires of men were always contemplating vanity and evil." Sounds here like these giants were involved in bestiality (sex with animals).

Jubilees 5:2-3 sums up Genesis 6 and 1 Enoch 15 for us so far, "And they (the women) bore children for them (the Watchers) and they were giants (Nephilim). And injustice increased upon the earth, and all flesh corrupted its way; man and cattle and beasts and birds and everything which walks on the earth. And they all corrupted their way and their ordinances, and they began to eat one another (cannibalism). And injustice grew upon earth and every imagination of the thoughts of all mankind was thus continually evil."

"Then the Lord saw that the wickedness of man was great in the earth, and that every intent of the thoughts of his heart was only evil continually." Genesis 6:5

God made an interesting statement in Genesis 6:3, that is placed between when the Watchers took daughters of men and their giant children are first mentioned.

"And the Lord said, "My Spirit shall not strive with man forever, for he is indeed flesh; yet his days shall be one hundred and twenty years." Genesis 6:3

What did God mean by this?

Going to "Commentaries on Genesis" found in the Dead Sea Scrolls, we can see a little more detail in 4Q252 Frag. 1 Col. 1:1-4, "In the four hundred eightieth year of Noah's life, he came to the end of them and God said, My Spirit shall not dwell with man forever, and their days shall be determined to be one hundred and twenty years <u>until the waters of the flood come.</u> And the waters of the flood came upon the earth in the six hundredth year of Noah's life."

God was announcing that the flood was coming in 120 years to destroy a corrupt and evil earth! God was even sorry that He had made the beasts and birds and was destroying them also! God gave instructions to Noah to build the ark, right after this statement. God decided to destroy all the earth, due to what these Watcher angels and their brood had done.

But this action just destroys the <u>flesh and blood</u> giants, not their spirits. This is where 'the rubber hits the road' on evil spirits!

"But now the giants who were born from the (union of) the spirits and the flesh called evil spirits upon the earth, because their dwelling shall be upon the earth and inside the earth. Evil spirits have come out of their bodies. <u>They will become evil upon the earth and shall be called evil spirits.</u>" 1 Enoch 15:8-9

This says that when these giants died in the flood, God condemned their half angel/half human spirits to dwell <u>upon and in the earth</u> and God says they are to be called evil spirits!

No speculation or theory here, no ifs, ands, or buts… that's what God says!

Evil spirits are the spirits of corrupted beings, that were created in disobedience and sin outside of the will of God!

So at least now we know where evil spirits come from and that they dwell upon and inside the earth, not in the heavenlies (above the earth), as principalities and powers do.

At least that's what documented ancient evidence tells us, which is more acceptable than baseless theories and conjecture.

More evidence that supports where evil spirits (called demons here), started, is in the Book of Jubilees.

In Jubilees 10:1-14, Noah pleads with God after the flood, to remove the evil spirits that were now plaguing his family.

"The polluted demons began to lead astray the children of Noah's sons and to lead them to folly and destroy them. And the sons of Noah came to Noah their father, and they told him about the demons who were leading astray and binding and killing his grandchildren."

Noah prayed to God for relief from these evil spirits and Noah reminded God that His "Watchers" were the "fathers of these spirits." And Noah points out in Jubilees 10:5-6, that "they were created to destroy".

These demons were leading astray, binding and killing Noah's grandchildren, as they were created to destroy.

These writings say that God would not utterly destroy these evil spirits as Noah asked, as their purpose or benefit would be, as God allowing them to bring trials upon and to perfect people.

God also said that these evil spirits would be "subject to satan upon the earth". Telling us that satan controls these creatures against us!

There is no record of anyone ever being attacked by evil spirits/demons prior to the flood, which would take away both the "evil spirits are from a pre-Adamic race" theory and also that "evil spirits are spirits of dead humans" theory, as evil spirits didn't show up in history, until the half-breed giants died. Would also seem to take away the interplanetary beings and inter-dimensional beings theories.

Although satan and his fallen angels are spirit and are evil, and were around prior to the flood, they were not referred to as evil spirits in these writings.

The giants roamed the earth as evil spirits after the flood and the Watcher angels who begat them, were handed their own fate—into a spiritual prison within the earth.

Now that these evil spirits are roaming around locked in and upon earth, what can we find out about their activities?

"The spirits of the giants oppress each other; they will corrupt, fall, be excited, and fall upon the earth and cause sorrow. They will eat no food nor become thirsty, nor find obstacles. And these spirits shall rise up against the children of the people and against the women, because they have proceeded forth from them." 1 Enoch 15:11-12

"They will corrupt until the day of the great conclusion, until the great age is consummated." 1 Enoch 16:1

Jubilees 7:22-24 also tells us that the nature of these beings is evil and murderous.

These verses say that these evil spirits are imprisoned here at earth and continue their oppression, corruption and attacks against people, as they had done when they were alive, doing so until the end of the age. They were, and still are, creatures of lust, hate, perversion and murder and instill this in people that they come against and inhabit.

What else do we know about evil spirits or small game that we must contend with?

Luke 4:32-35, tells us a lot about them.

"And they were astonished at His (Jesus) teaching, for His word was with authority. Now in the synagogue there was a man who had a spirit of an unclean demon. And he cried out with a loud voice, saying, "Let us alone! What have we to do with You, Jesus of Nazareth? Did You come to destroy us? I know who You are—the Holy One of God!" But Jesus rebuked him, saying, "Be quiet, and come out of him!" And when the demon had thrown him in their midst, it came out of him and did not hurt him."

This short scripture shows us seven different things about small game.

1. They can dwell in human bodies.
2. They are unclean or unholy.
3. They think, reason and speak; as it cried out.
4. It occupied a person who was at a holy place of God (synagogue).
5. The evil spirit's own words said that they can be destroyed.
6. Jesus had authority over it (Jesus gave us all authority).
7. It was <u>cast out</u> of the person.

Once it's cast out of a person, then what happens?

"When an unclean spirit goes out of a man, he goes through dry places, seeking rest; and finding none, he says, 'I will return to my house from which I came.'" Luke 11:24.

Jesus telling us, that an unclean spirit goes to "dry places seeking rest", confirms exactly what the book of Enoch says, that they are earthly evil spirits that are confined to dry earth.

"Evil spirits shall they be upon the earth, and the spirits of the wicked shall they be called. The habitation of the spirits of heaven shall be in heaven; but upon earth shall be the habitation of terrestrial spirits, who are born on earth." 1 Enoch 15:8b

Note here, that Enoch tells us where big game and small game operate from. Spirits of heaven operate in heaven (i.e. evil principalities and powers) and terrestrial (born on earth) spirits, operate on earth.

Jesus said it again in Matthew 12:43, ""When an unclean spirit goes out of a man, he goes through dry places, seeking rest, and finds none."

They have the ability to move and operate outside of a person, yet they do not like being outside of a human body.

The spirits of the half angel/half human giants, or Nephilim, are imprisoned to roam the world as spirit-beings with no bodies, looking for a resting place.

The Bible tells us, that they inhabit humans and prefer to stay in humans. When cast out, they find no rest and will go back to inhabit humans operating in the physical realm to torment us, as the Book of Enoch says they will.

"And these spirits shall rise up against the children of the people and against the women, because they have proceeded forth from them." Enoch 15:12

Perhaps it was satan's plan to corrupt the human race with these giants, so the seed (Jesus) that would defeat him (Genesis 3:15) couldn't be born. Maybe it was satan's distorted, counterfeit creation idea of a race of part human, part angel/spirit creatures.

Or maybe it was just angels that sinned on their own, having free will to make decisions, just as satan and his fallen angels did at the fall, when they were all kicked by God to earth.

We know that satan had been cast out of heaven, according to Jesus in Luke 10:18, "And He said to them, "I saw Satan fall like lightning from heaven."

Jesus witnessed this event before He became incarnate on earth.

Revelation 12:4 also indicates satan must have convinced one third of the angels (stars) to rebel with him, as this is the number that fight Michael and other holy angels in Revelation 12:7-9, "And his tail drew the third part of the stars (angels) of heaven, and did cast them to the earth."

We know from the book of Job, that Satan still had some sort of access to God and heaven after he was cast out,

"Now there was a day when the sons of God came to present themselves before the Lord, and Satan came also among them." Job 1:6

So, from all of this we see, that satan and those who rebelled with him, were cast from some or all part(s) of the heaven(s), with limited access at times, or access in certain areas of certain parts of heaven(s)—until the future war and being cast into the lake of fire (Revelation 20:10).

Many argue about when satan was cast out, as some say it was before earth's creation, others say it was between Genesis 1:1 and 1:2, when a flood covered the earth, due to satan's corrupting a pre-Adamic world.

Some say he and his crew operate in the second heaven and are banned from the third heaven or that some call the heaven of heavens…

"Behold, the heaven and the heaven of heavens is the Lord's thy God, the earth also, with all that therein is." Deuteronomy 10:14

…and 3 Enoch 17 says there are seven heavens, whose entrances are guarded.

From all the scripture and ancient writings, it would seem, that the Watcher angels acted independently from the rebellion of satan and his fallen buddies. They received a prison sentence, rather than just being cast out of heaven.

The Watchers were imprisoned and are still, for impregnating women who produced a race of giants.

The spirits from these giants are called evil spirits by God, (called small game by me) and roam the earth, rising up against people.

Some might say, that angels are spirits and thus don't have reproductive organs and/or can't mate with flesh creatures, so all of this is nonsense.

Well, I'm not an expert on the sexual functions of angelic beings, specifically a breed of angels called Watchers, but there is ample evidence to say that at least some could, and did!

We are also told in Jude 1:6, that these angels "kept not their first estate, but left their own habitation" which seems to indicate that they purposely left the spiritual realm (habitation) to become physical creatures or had the ability to operate in both realms at will.

This may be a good place to say, "Where there's a will there's a way!"

I have seen pictures of many Egyptian paintings and sculptures portraying huge men next to ordinary sized men, which may be paintings of these very watcher angels or their giant offspring.

I've visited the pyramids in Egypt, and despite the theories, science has yet to prove how those megaton rocks were made, moved and with precision, lifted and put into place by primitive people, producing these mathematical and engineering marvels.

The strength and intelligence of these angels or their giant offspring is the most probable answer.

Here's something interesting to bring up:

"For only Og king of Bashan remained of the remnant of giants; behold his bedstead was a bedstead of iron; is it not in Rabbath of the children of Ammon? nine cubits was the length thereof, and four cubits the breadth of it, after the cubit of a man." Deuteronomy 3:11

Og's bed was 18' 9" (571.5 cm) X 8'4" (254 cm) if a cubit is 25" (63.5 cm) … a big bed for a big guy! Goliath was "six cubits and a span" (1 Samuel17:4), which means he was 13' 4" (406.4 cm) tall and no doubt, he had brothers as tall!

I wonder how big their daddies, the Watcher angels, were?

Another interesting side thought… If all the giants or Nephilim were killed in Noah's flood of Genesis, where did Og and Goliath and these other giants living after the flood come from?

Did more angels leave their habitation after the flood and mate with women again?

Are there Different Kinds of Evil Spirits?

But wait you say… what about all that we've witnessed, read about and heard about, as to differences in evil spirits and what they call themselves?

Some deliverance ministers say, that demons manifest, saying they are "spirits of cancer" or "spirits of arthritis" or "spirits of pain," etc.

One minister I know says, she sees little black imp-like creatures running around and yet others have seen them in various colors.

Another minister friend of mine said they look like small insects massed together, moving inside the body.

A different deliverance minister I know claims, that outside a person's body, evil spirits are all aimless football shaped brillo-pad like things, with a little tail on top, having no power, yet when inside a human body, they become less than an inch tall and appear as humans that wear clothes! He says evil spirits come from the unsaved at their death. I've come across many evil spirits that have said they were spirits of the unsaved dead.

And yet another deliverance minister, Howard Pittman, who visited heaven, was shown the evil spiritual world and saw many kinds of creatures, including animal-creature like spirits, that wait to enter into us when we sin. Perhaps explaining the spirits of monsters from the bestiality mentioned in the Dead Sea Scrolls!

I have seen and fought what looked like various imps, ghosts and weird shaped animal and part humanoid things.

I'm sure there are many things I haven't seen, just as there are many animals I've never seen. I don't go around preaching that something doesn't exist, just because I haven't seen it! I've never seen a Tasmanian devil, but there's enough evidence to prove to me that they do exist. Because you haven't seen something or heard about something in the spiritual realm, doesn't mean they don't exist!

I've heard small game speak many times through people during deliverance. I've heard them say that they're an unsaved guy named Bob who died 60 years ago, to satan himself and everything in-between!

Remember, according to ancient writings, evil spirits have been around since the flood of Genesis and have obviously occupied, observed and been around many people during that time, obtaining much knowledge and information.

This would explain how psychics, witches "channelers", mediums, séances, etc., can relay personal information about people or departed loved ones to unsuspecting relatives, looking to contact the "dearly departed".

Are these "channeled" spirits of their dead relatives really speaking, or are they lying, deceiving evil spirits pretending to be these dead people?

Remember that Xtreme Small Game, lie, deceive and imitate by altering their shape, appearance, voice and attitude to even appear holy.

"And no marvel; for satan himself is <u>transformed</u> into an angel of light." 2 Corinthians 11:14

Many also have experiences of evil spirits in animals, physical objects, buildings and small areas of land, such as graveyards.

A "haunted house" is not unusual. One place that I was at doing spiritual warfare, the evil spirits knocked over some fruit in a bowl on the dining room table. I said to them mockingly, "That's really scary… you can knock over fruit"! They didn't like what I and some angels did to them. (Find their root or right to be there and break it… get rid of them as led by the Holy Spirit… in this case they had a right to be there, as a witch from Haiti had once lived there who had serviced an evil altar.)

Are they all just the evil spirits from the flood and perhaps the giants that the Bible tells us existed after the flood?

Is there more to it than these things that are written?

As I said in the Xtreme Big Game Sector, I studied this exact question, discussed it with others, debated it and prayed about it.

How does one hunt something, if one is unsure exactly what it is?

How do I know when I am dealing with an evil spirit, a foul spirit, an unclean spirit, a power, a fallen angel, a principality, an evil ruler, a demon, an animal creature spirit, a territorial spirit, an evil authority?

Do we <u>need</u> to know who or what they are and what the differences are between all these evil things?

God told me not to get hung up on all that. They are all the enemy. "No mercy," He said!

How Does Someone Get an Evil Spirit?

You can give evil entrance to your life through various ways. Usually it's because you've given them a legal right... your mental choices (i.e. unforgiveness, bitterness, anger and/or hatred you carry towards others, which also produces most sicknesses and diseases that evil spirits intensify. It is being said that up to 95% of all diseases and sicknesses can be traced back to a mental root.) The main mental root problem is a person's failure to accept Jesus as your personal Savior. A dead spirit and soul will manifest in the body with diseases and evil spirit intrusion. Many people have received instant freedom when they accepted Jesus as their Savior. There are times when freedom has been obtained by people from Jesus, who had no intention of accepting Jesus. Their healing and/or deliverance was a demonstration of God's power to them, to convince them to change their mind about Him!

One very successful spiritual warfare leader that I know says, that the root of all disease and sicknesses are demons. It is deeper than that, although demons are factors that must be dealt with.

Testimony: A Christian woman that was soon to die with stage 4 breast cancer found out that she needed to forgive her mother. She repented of this sin (in her mind) and to her mother face to face. She was then totally healed. The evil root was dealt with, which had produced the evil fruit (cancer).

This experience was proven by my Mom numerous times with people who had cancer, some on their death beds. When they forgave, the cancer left. Also, evil spirits leave on their own and/or can be kicked out, which produces healing, however, the person still needs to break any evil rights or they will return.

Check with the Holy Spirit after repentance and/or healing as evil spirit(s) should also be cast out once the right for them to stay has been broken. Just because the right is gone, doesn't mean they are, same as a criminal that unlawfully invades your home, who won't leave until you find him and kick him out (i.e. preferably put in prison to prevent a reoccurrence or having him go over to stay with your neighbor)!

Many evil spirits have said during deliverance, that they were in the person before they were born, while in their mother's womb. They can enter through iniquity... generational curses or the DNA sins of your parents and ancestors passed down the line. They can also enter through physical acts of transgressions and sin activity of the person. They can enter through curses you've said against yourself and/or curses said against you by others. They can enter through a trauma you've experienced (see POW's Sector). They can enter from handling physical objects where they reside (i.e. idols). They can enter through tattoos (tattoos are bloodletting/sacrifice and idol worship Leviticus 19:28- see Altars Sector). They can enter you when you are involved in occult and religious practices, which includes evil altars that you've set up and service (see Altars Sector). They can be sent against you by witches and such ilk. They can be sent against you by evil principalities and powers. They can come against you through Christian witchcraft. When a person dies, the evil spirits leave that dead body and go to a living body (which would be you if you're in the area). Just casting out evil spirits from a person can send them into another person, if they're not destroyed or sent to a spiritual prison (more on that later in Catch and Release Spiritual Warfare). They can enter through transferring from one person to the next!

Transference from one person to the next can be through touching. One spiritual warfare leader that I knew was so aware of transference, he rarely touched anyone, even during deliverance sessions, and wouldn't hug or shake hands with anyone, including while in fellowship with Christians! Most Christians love to hug each other. Besides sharing warm regards and greetings, they can also be sharing demons!

A very favorite activity that many leaders have adopted is, "laying hands" on people to "activate" someone or for healing or transfer anointing. That's not all that can be transferred!

Another non-recommended activity that we've experienced, at an internationally attended Supernatural College no less, was the main leader asks those who need healing to stand up. Then he asks everyone else (hordes) to go lay hands on them and pray. Who are these people/hordes? People do receive healing. People do also receive demons. This 'microwave healing system' doesn't address sins that people need to address; doesn't address evil spirits rights in people; nor addresses evil spirits still in people that haven't been dealt with. Spreading evil spirits around isn't a plan!

And yet one more so-called great idea someone came up with is called, "the fire tunnel"! People line up in two rows, while others shoot between these two rows, with the people in rows "laying hands" on the runners for blessing, healing, anointing… and yes you guessed it… demon transference!

Let's remember that all of these examples that I'm giving here, takes place in Christian settings by Christians, that are not addressing root problems and are passing along demons. How do I know? Because Rhoda and I have both picked up demons from others, when we participated in these activities, that we had to expel from ourselves!

In other words, we were worse off when we left, then when we walked in!

It's virtually impossible to go through life without touching others or others from touching or bumping into us. Thus, the need for daily self-deliverance. Be very careful on how you live your life to prevent demonic intrusion.

How does one cast out an evil spirit from a person, object, building or area?

Looking to the Bible, Jesus didn't get into long deliverance sessions or counseling, therapy or the use of drugs.

There was no Bible, so He couldn't tell people to go read their Bible and they would soon get well.

Did Jesus <u>pray</u> evil spirits out of people?

Never once.

He <u>commanded</u> them to go!

Did He yell, scream, bash the person with a Bible, hold them down or rub anointing oil on them?

Never once!

He didn't need to touch them.

He didn't even need to be present or see the person, such as with the centurion's servant. (Matthew 8:1-13/ Luke 7:1-10) (I've done this also many times.)

How can this happen?

It happened because Jesus operated and went in the spirit!

An example I can give is the time a lady at an assembly of Christians asked for prayer for a friend of hers who was desperately trying to conceive. She and her husband were suffering with miscarriages. I went in the spirit and saw a bull standing on its hind legs. It took its front leg and reached into this woman's womb, pulled out the baby and held it up by the legs. The word that I received was that this evil spirit was Molech (or Moloch).

I happily chopped up this bull with my spiritual sword!

The next day I searched in the Bible to look up Molech. I found out that this was a main god of Ammon and was also worshipped in Egypt. It was known as the sacred bull, where many children ended up being sacrificed/burned alive to this evil god!

About nine months after this encounter, the same lady made a testimony at this same assembly, that her friend had just given birth to a healthy baby girl!

I had never met this woman nor her husband and was nowhere near them when I conquered the enemy that was destroying their family!

Those who use alternatives to what Jesus did to exorcise evil or the enemy from a person—are they wrong?

I've done deliverance over the phone many times… should I stop doing that because Jesus didn't have a phone?

The "Glory" doctrine of Spiritual Warfare

I know some leaders who say, that they don't have to do spiritual warfare, as God's glory in the room removes demons. In other words, do nothing and let God do it. They like to say, "we don't give time to the devil. We focus on Jesus". Sounds pretty! Many people like this kind of talk. Maybe they consider Jesus spending 1/3 of His ministry on spiritual warfare, casting out evil spirits and commanding us to do spiritual warfare, is just a mistake. Such leaders (I've experienced them first hand) attack and make fun of other spiritual warfare ministers for doing spiritual warfare any other way but this "glory" way. These "types" usually also say, that we should never do high level spiritual warfare against principalities and powers, as that's the realm of God in the heavenlies, to deal with them. I guess they consider scriptures such as Ephesians 6: 12 and others brought forth in this book, and successful high level spiritual warfare testimonies by international giants (i.e. Rees Howells, Derek Prince, Peter Wagner, Cindy Jacobs, Chuck Pierce), to be lies. Their arrogance and ignorance is extremely disturbing on many levels!

One testimony from the internationally-known College teacher/speaker Mark Virkler, reports, that he refused to do deliverance or spiritual warfare for 10 years, while he had been a pastor and leader. He had cast out thousands of demons out of hundreds of people, but then stopped. He got frustrated and also "figured" (demonic suggestion) that once he was ordained, he didn't have any more sin issues. One day he asked a prayer team to "pray" for him. He got a deliverance from 20 evil spirits instead. Evil spirits that had been giving him rejection issues, anger, failure, fear and who were convincing him <u>not</u> to do spiritual warfare. He was set free and now teaches and conducts spiritual warfare again!

You gotta get rid of the root!

Again, main issues not being dealt with by "the glory zone method", "the fire tunnel method", "the hordes laying hands on you method" and others like these "quick fixes", are, that people aren't having their roots dealt with. Their soul/mental (stinking thinking) issues, their sins, their soul ties, their generational curses, their religious/idol worshipping, aren't been addressed, which continues giving them mental, emotional, spiritual and physical issues and diseases. When these roots remain, it gives evil spirits rights to stay and continue to afflict a person. IF any spirits left during these events, they still have the right to return… and they will, with 7 of their friends, making the person worse than if they had done nothing! Also, healing may manifest and does, but the danger is that it returns in the same form or another form (of evil fruit) AND WORSE… if the roots aren't dealt with!

"When an unclean spirit goes out of a man, he goes through dry places, seeking rest, and finds none. Then he says, 'I will return to my house from which I came.' And when he comes, he finds it empty, swept, and put in order. Then he goes and takes with him seven other spirits more wicked than himself, and they enter and dwell there; and the last state of that man is worse than the first. So, shall it also be with this wicked generation." Matthew 12: 43-45

EVERY Christian <u>needs</u> deliverance on an ongoing basis, ESPECIALLY leaders and ESPECIALLY when they ignore or come against spiritual warfare activities and/or refuse to get a deliverance!

One conference that Rhoda and I went to (where the main leader had made fun of spiritual warfare), the leadership team <u>commanded</u> us before every meeting, that everyone attending were <u>not</u> to do their ministry while there. One leader told Rhoda to stop, when she was "caught" praying with a woman who had asked for prayer. This conference head-lined, several internationally known leaders. Unbelievable!

Father later showed me a vision of this main leader, who publicly laughed at spiritual warfare ministry and those who did it. He was naked, being attacked by evil spirits and two principalities. The man looked to Jesus, Who was standing near him, to do something. Jesus pointed to a sword lying next to him, indicating that he should pick it up to use it. The leader looked at the sword and just curled up in a ball on the ground, as the evil entities encircled him to intensify their attacks. Jesus prohibited them from killing the leader. I was allowed to stand and watch, not help him. Please join us in prayer for any such leaders, to become aware of their demonic influence, so they may receive a deliverance to be set free.

All these are huge red flags of demonic influence!

Many of these "leaders" call themselves Dr. or Apostle and even both. When someone goes to the Dr.'s office they expect that they know what they're doing and address <u>ALL</u> of their issues. They don't expect to be clumped in a crowd and hope something happens! People don't expect to go home from a hospital and the Dr.'s did nothing. They don't expect to go home and be worse off. It didn't happen to the people who went to Jesus.

Do the job properly! Teach students/disciples how to do the job properly and fully! It's a leader's responsibility and you'll be held accountable one day!

"My brethren, let not many of you become teachers, knowing that we shall receive a stricter judgment." James 3: 1

Back to Reality Gospel

I've known physical small game to be taken with traps, snares, shotguns, rifles, handguns, bow and arrows, vehicles, ferrets and one I got was just scared stiff!

I've also done, witnessed and read about many ways that spiritual small game can be taken (destroyed, imprisoned, cast out or away).

When Jesus Christ is your Lord and Savior and you're working in His name, let the Holy Spirit be your guide.

Don't confine yourself or God to a box when doing spiritual warfare. Even Jesus did deliverance and healing in different ways.

When hunting for Xtreme Big Game, you'll encounter Xtreme Small Game, as I have while in the spirit.

Be aware that Xtreme Big Game will direct Xtreme Small Game against you, your friends, family and your life.

If you decide to <u>only</u> deal with Xtreme Small Game and not Xtreme Big Game, you may be stepping on all the ants, while ignoring the rampaging elephants that will stomp on you!

Christians who get into spiritual hunting, must not be surprised when they get attacked, <u>as evil entities will hunt you!</u>

The more you become involved in spiritual warfare and become a greater threat to the evil kingdom, the bigger the evil guns that will be turned on you to stop you! They hunt you whether you hunt them or not, so you might as well get in the game, as they say!

BAIT

One of the most effective hunting methods in the world is the use of bait. Bait brings your prey to you or to a trap. Animal hunters use bait to lure bear, deer, wolf, ducks, fish and rats. Human traffickers use bait to lure woman and children into slavery.

Evil entities use bait to lure people too!

They're using bait on you right now!

We can all think of many ways that bait is used to lure people away from salvation such as, lust for money, sex, self-importance and false religions.

Looking around at the world, we can see they're very successful at hunting people with bait. So how do evil entities hunt Christians?

It's not so hard for them to hunt Christians, as most people who think they're Christians aren't considered so by God! They're trapped in false, man-made religions, under false leaders, most living in deliberate sin, compromise and unforgiveness, thinking they're OK.

These people are caught in death traps!

Some animals are harder to bait and catch than others. The wolf is very cautious and difficult to bring in, whereas, the mouse is very easy to trick.

The Eagle Christian is difficult to bait also... but not impossible!

So how do evil entities hunt Eagle Christians?

Evil entities examine you, like any good hunter would, to find out how to bring you down. After all, <u>you</u> are big game to them!

They'll use the "G" bait on you! The three G's have been known to be very effective... Gold, Glory and Girls/Guys!

If that bait doesn't work, they'll use distraction bait to take you down a false trail, so you'll waste time squandering your destiny. They'll use your work, hobbies, family and friends to lure, delay and distract you from God's plans.

This bait can get the job done with the Eagle Christian usually not suspecting a thing!

Using emotional bait lead many down a dead-end trail. Eagles become consumed with a form of lust for political, economic, environmental or social ills and issues that they think are important.

A rarely detected form of bait is the one that lures the Eagle to a false destiny.

When an Eagle Christian makes a <u>personal decision</u> to conduct a ministry, battle, intercession, attend fellowship, etc., they have taken God's will out of the plans. This idol bait (self as god) traps many into thinking they're doing right, yet they have decided to follow their will, not God's.

"He who speaks from himself seeks his own glory; but He who seeks the glory of the One who sent Him is true, and no unrighteousness is in Him." John 7: 18

Jesus never did His will. He always did Father's will! John 5:19, 30/7:18/12:49-50/14:31, 1 Corinthians 2:13, 1 Peter 4:11

If you take the bait, you lose, others lose, and God loses and guess who wins!

Anyone who says bad things are happening to you because God doesn't want you doing spiritual warfare, remind me of Job's ignorant friends.

Stay led by God, not by people… go and do and get it done!

Leave the whiny small dogs on the porch and keep running with the big dogs, as we used to say, of those who were scared!

As the Lord leads you in the spirit, you'll see the enemy and be shown how to deal with them.

Here's a short testimony of one woman I know who had eye problems:

I (Al) could see in the spirit, a small impish looking thing floating in front of her right eye. It was smiling and poking her right eye every so often, with a long dart. Also, I could see in the past, that her left eye had been damaged by a ghost/apparition creature, that was sent against her by a curse. It put a white substance in her eye that continually changed form, from a chalky, to a snowy, to a waxy, white substance. Although both eyes had similar symptoms, after I told her what I saw, she admitted that pain came every so often in her right eye (being poked) and her left eye was more clouded at times than others (substance changing form).

I was led by the Holy Spirit to speak blindness against the impish creature, resulting in its immediately dropping its dart, putting its hands to its eyes, while screaming and jumping up and down. I also commanded it to go deaf as it was running away. It never picked up its dart again against this woman nor anyone else. Although I wanted to take on the ghost/apparition creature, God told me that the woman had to go in the spirit and do it herself.

This is just one testimony that evil spirits are not always in a person, and to wait for direction from the Holy Spirit on how to deal with problems, rather than using a "cookie-cutter" approach.

<u>And also another huge key… that the battle may not be yours!</u>

You can cast evil spirits out of anyone from a fetus, to babies to seniors.

Evil spirits in babies and children have few rights to stay in someone that hasn't sinned, transgressed or been caught up in soul ties. (Although an occultist parent may have dedicated their child to satan, thereby giving evil spirits a right. And there's generational iniquity)

Babies who constantly cry for no reason have been delivered simply with casting out the evil spirit afflicting them!

I did deliverance on a child who was in bondage due to iniquity… I had to destroy the many evil spirit attachments in this case. It took less than a minute in the spirit!

I know ministers who will never do deliverance on someone unless they are Christian. That isn't Biblical thinking!

"Then Jesus went out from there and departed to the region of Tyre and Sidon. And behold, <u>a woman of Canaan</u> (a pagan) came from that region and cried out to Him, saying, "Have mercy on me, O Lord, Son of David! My daughter is severely demon-possessed." But He answered her not a word. And His disciples came and urged Him, saying, "Send her away, for she cries out after us." But He answered and said, "I was not sent except to the lost sheep of the house of Israel." Then she came and worshiped Him, saying, "Lord, help me!"

But He answered and said, "It is not good to take the children's bread and throw it to the little dogs." And she said, "Yes, Lord, yet even the little dogs eat the crumbs which fall from their masters' table."

Then Jesus answered and said to her, "O woman, great is your faith! Let it be to you as you desire." And her daughter was healed from that very hour." Matthew 15:21-28

This woman and probably also her daughter weren't jew or Christian. Notice, that this is another occasion when Jesus did deliverance/spiritual warfare for a person He never met! Done in the spirit!

The Process Of Deliverance

You can meet with a person before deliverance, to get a list of problems or get them to reveal all that they can about their life and have them repent and renounce all activity that is abhorrent to God… this has many times proven to make a deliverance quicker and easier. (Removes rights of evil spirits to stay.)

A right to stay is like a contract that must be broken.

Usually before starting deliverance, I have the person sit in a comfortable chair or couch. This gets rid of the need for catchers if they are standing and also prevents them from being hurt if they fall.

I either sit next to them or stand in front of them.

If I don't already know, I usually start by insuring the person is a Christian and has accepted Jesus Christ as their personal Savior, although Jesus never asked a person for allegiance before He delivered them! If they don't do this, deliverance can be a struggle and even unproductive if the person carries on a sinful life afterwards.

Many times, I haven't even started to say anything, when an evil spirit manifests and starts talking to me.

I usually come against, rebuke and bind all evil spirits in the person, commanding them not to manifest except when I command them to do something (all as guided by the Holy Spirit and my discernment gift).

At this point, I know some deliverance ministers who have conversations with evil spirits to find out what they're doing, how many they are, their names, etc. I have done this myself and see no harm in this activity, as Jesus conversed with evil spirits. I'm not asking them for the winning lottery number, like some fortune teller… I'm just obtaining information to assist in getting rid of them.

Any that initiate talking to me, asking me questions, wanting to make a deal, or trying to control the process, I command them to shut up and only talk when I command them to answer my questions!

Don't let them take over!

At times, I immediately command them all to go (if led that way) into spiritual prisons and it's done. Many times, I deal with them in the spirit and say nothing… the deliverance is over without any words spoken! (Jesus did this also.) It is not always <u>necessary</u> to see or discern in the spirit in order to cast out evil spirits. I have done it and know of others who do, however, beware of other small game and their bosses if you're working spiritually blind!

If led, I command the leader evil spirit to come up that is afflicting this person in a certain area. Pre-deliverance discussions or list will advise you with what problems are probably being controlled by an evil spirit.

You will probably have to go through a separate evil spirit or set of evil spirits for each problem, sickness, pain. One evil spirit can be causing multiple problems such as a deaf and dumb spirit.

You may want to deal with the evil spirit causing cancer and the evil spirit that is causing headaches starts talking to you instead. Happens a lot.

Sometimes a stronger leader will push up a lower rank evil spirit to deal with you to protect itself.

Sometimes a "blocker" evil spirit will face you and try to block all your attempts at deliverance.

It's a process that's best learned with experience!

During deliverance, even the untrained eye can usually see evil spirits on people's faces in the distortion and/or discoloration of the face (black or red shadows.) A change in the person's attitude (i.e. sneering, smiling, anger, swearing, glaring, yawning, silence) can also be present.

There are times when the person is the same and no change appears.

Evil spirits will hide and refuse to manifest, in an effort to convince you they aren't there. (Highly unlikely some aren't there with a person who's never received deliverance!)

You will have to flush them out like a bird-dog does with a pheasant! Ask the Holy Spirit for assistance and any others in the room who may receive revelation that can assist. The person being delivered may reveal what they believe any hindrances may be.

Keep working until breakthrough comes!

Sometimes evil spirits need to be told where to come out (mouth, hands, feet) or to go out the way they came in, if they won't/can't go out a different way you're commanding them to go.

If you run across one that won't leave (does happen), ask the Holy Spirit for direction if you can't see or discern the reason why yourself or if an answer can't be found with the person. Usually its right to stay can be traced to sexual or occult activity. Find out what the right is for it to stay (sometimes the evil spirit will even tell you), then have the person repent, renounce and break the right.

While doing deliverance, don't let the occasional growling, swearing, threats, screaming, etc., concern you, as all they have to use on you is your fear.

They also try crying, begging, pleading and negotiating to let them stay, hoping you'll have mercy.

If they sense fear in you they will fight you, refuse to leave, argue with you, laugh at you, and/or refuse to talk with you.

They can also make the person drop to the floor in seeming unconsciousness or choke the person in an effort to make you stop.

They will also trick you by pretending to leave the person.

The person may know why the evil spirit is staying, but won't openly discuss their sin.

Also, many people don't want to give up certain sins and won't repent.

The well-known deliverance minister, Maxwell Whyte, ran into this situation with a woman who wanted deliverance from an evil spirit that was plaguing her, but she didn't want to give up her homosexual activity with her girlfriend. Mr. Whyte advised her that he wouldn't do deliverance on her.

If it continues to remain stubborn, remind it of its eventual judgment in front of God and that its disobedience will only make their punishment worse.

Some evil spirits will try to leave on their own before I tell it to go.

Although this sounds like a good thing, I don't agree, as they come back later when it's safe.

Let me give you a narrative to help you understand a process. Let's say there are multiple squatters living in your house. They are all evil and bad for you and perhaps at one time you enjoyed their company and invited some in, while others broke in or walked in through the open doors and windows and decided to stay on their own. They're dirtying the place up, they're breaking things, and they're hurting you. One day you decide to clean up your house and you want all these slobs out!

You tell them to go. Some laugh at you, some ignore you, some leave and then come back. Eventually you're successful in getting them all to leave (cast them out). Some stand outside your doors and windows waiting to come back in. Others go across the street and break into your neighbor's houses. What a nice neighbor you are eh!

What have you accomplished?

CATCH AND RELEASE (CAR) SPIRITUAL WARFARE

Fishing for many people in the world is necessary to stay alive, as it is their staple food and as we know, it was a full-time job for some of the disciples before they met Jesus.

Most of these people would consider sport fishing to be silly, yet this is a huge international pastime referred to as "Catch and Release".

Sport fishermen/women spend a great amount of time and money on boats, equipment and travel to exotic places to catch their prey only to toss them back in the water. Sometimes catching the same fish over and over!

Of course this activity harms no one.

When a "catch and release" spiritual warfare program is accepted by the Church, it allows death and destruction to continue, yet the Church and Christians all over the world are doing it every day!

Most Christians, including internationally-known leaders, who confront evil entities, rather than destroying them or putting them in spiritual prisons, are letting them go!

That would be like the police throwing a murderous home invader and violent thief out of a house, rather than shooting them or putting them in jail. If the police just toss them out of a house, what will this home invader and thief do next? They'll come back in or attack someone else of course! That's only logical! Same thing in the spiritual realm!

Here's another example...

Two opposing armies in war; let's call them the Black Hat and White Hat armies.

The Black Hat army is attacking, killing and destroying those in the White Hat army and the Black Hats never willingly let prisoners go.

The White Hat army's war doctrine is to ignore the Black Hat army, but when they do get involved in battle, they shoot blanks, shoo them away and catch and release any prisoners of war!

Would this make any common sense in a physical war?

It doesn't make sense in spiritual warfare either!

Just casting evil spirits out from people, out of buildings, away from land and cities or someone's life is "catch and release" spiritual warfare!

Released evil "soldiers" come back and/or attack others!

This goes for the "glory zone" way of dealing with demons also.

Such spiritual warfare accomplishes little to nothing in the full picture of warfare tactics!

Our goal is the destruction or the imprisonment of the enemy, as it is in any ongoing war!

Here's a substantiating testimony from one of my mentors. He and his wife did spiritual warfare for <u>decades</u> on thousands of people. One day, just before he was casting out an evil spirit, he asked it, "Where will you go when I cast you out"? The demon said, "I'll go to your basement"! My mentor said, "Why are you going there"? The demon said, "There's a whole bunch of us there". Demons he had cast out over the years were partying at his house! From then on, he never again did "catch and release" warfare nor ever did spiritual warfare in his house again! He of course had to get rid of them from his house.

We put an end to demonic activity when we confront them and destroy or imprison them. When their replacement troops come in, we attack them and do the same. Being able to see and go in the spirit, under God's direction, is vital to this warfare goal.

We also want to utilize angels (police/soldiers) to assist in battle to take them to a spiritual prison. Angels have assisted me numerous times by taking them to spiritual prisons.

I send evil spirits to spiritual prisons and command them to never afflict anyone ever again, and stay there bound until called by Jesus Christ for their judgment!

Spiritual warfare isn't a sport, although it is enjoyable if done right, as we're setting captives free, destroying the enemy's plans and most importantly, being obedient by doing as God has commanded us to do!

Don't do sloppy spiritual warfare. Enlighten those who have a "catch and release" (CAR) spiritual warfare ministry, to stop this terrible practice and pick up their spiritual swords and prison keys, to become more effective conquerors in this war!

There are times they are destroyed outright such as with my sword or by spiritual flames.

Do they die?

Good question!

Casting Evil Spirits out in Groups

You can also cast Xtreme Small Game out in groups, not just one at a time. Many times, leaders will cast out one evil spirit that's manifesting and then think they're done. Blame it on ignorance, poor discernment skills or they just don't care to get the job done right for the afflicted person (they'd rather move on to their personal agenda).

Frankly, casting them out one at a time is extremely tedious, so finding group leaders and <u>making</u> them take all those they're responsible for with them, is much more efficient.

You'll find that leaders can be in charge of several or I've experienced where they are in charge of dozens and hundreds!

Just group them, bind them together and cast the pile of them out! Jesus did it! (Matthew 8:31-32)

Mass Deliverance

And, you can cast multiple evil spirits out of multiple people at the same time, such as at a conference or large group. Many times, you don't have the time to deal with people on an individual basis. Mass deliverance is not a recommended option, as root issues are not dealt with.

Be led by the Holy Spirit on how to approach this, but something like… commanding all the evil spirits in the room to be bound and broken in Jesus name, cease what they are doing and come out, without manifesting, go to prison, never to return, is a simple approach. (You can have angels assist in taking them!) Discuss root issues so people can address them on their own before or later.

Be ready for lots of manifestations in the room if you forget to tell them to go quietly! I was in a room in Switzerland when a deliverance minister didn't use this simple command! Lots of coughing, choking, crying, screaming, falling on the floor going on… out of control.

Deliverance can be immediate or take many hours or sessions to complete.

In-between sessions, a person may be involved in deliberate sin; making deliverance of this person a full-time job. Again, operating in the spirit will give you knowledge of what the person is doing behind everyone's back!

Remember that you're setting a captive free with this ministry, as well as dealing with creatures that are determined to kill and destroy, unless you stop them!

To know when deliverance is complete is also discernment. The person's countenance changes; they feel relief or heaviness gone; emptiness in head feeling; pain gone; nothing else manifests; word of knowledge and/or a sense of completion, can all signal that deliverance is complete.

Ask the Holy Spirit to come and fill the void where once evil inhabited.

Remind the person to "Sin no more!"

Would God purposely send an evil spirit upon a person, even a non-sinner… meaning we can't get rid of it?

I'm hearing some people say, "God wouldn't do that!"

"But the Spirit of the LORD departed from Saul, and a distressing spirit from the LORD troubled him. And Saul's servants said to him, surely a distressing spirit from God is troubling you." 1 Samuel 16:14-15

Some say that God <u>allowed</u> this evil spirit to afflict Saul because Saul sinned, but that God didn't purposely send it.

OK… how about this one, Paul says in 2 Corinthians 12:7-9: "And lest I should be exalted above measure by the abundance of the revelations, a thorn in the flesh was given to me, a messenger of Satan to buffet me, lest I be exalted above measure. Concerning this thing I pleaded with the Lord three times that it might depart from me. And He said to me, "My grace is sufficient for you, for My strength is made perfect in weakness."

This says, that God gave apostle Paul a messenger of satan to buffet him. The original Greek wording says it was an angel of satan. Even though Paul asked God 3 times to remove it from him, God wouldn't allow it!

God told Him His strength is made perfect in Paul's weakness! In other words, "Paul you'll accomplish more for My kingdom by leaving this dark angel to harass you"!

If you're operating in the spirit, you'll know when God is purposely allowing an evil entity to stay.

SELF-DELIVERANCE

Most times Christians can never find someone to do a deliverance on them. Time then to do it yourself. Utilize the same methods I've discussed; use discernment, the Holy spirit and angels. Some go to the bathroom and point at themselves in the mirror, confronting the demon(s) commanding them to go. Self-deliverance should be done every day. We can pick up spiritual dirt, same as physical dirt that requires cleaning. Those who have never had a deliverance, with an argument like," I don't need it", is like saying all my life I've never needed a shower or a bath! Ridiculous!

Spiritual Warfare "Techniques"

"So Naaman (captain of the army of the king of Aram who had leprosy) came with his horses and his chariots and stood at the doorway of the house of Elisha. Elisha sent a messenger to him, saying, "Go and wash in the Jordan seven times, and your flesh will be restored to you and you will be clean." But Naaman was furious and went away and said, "Behold, I thought, 'He will surely come out to me and stand and call on the name of the LORD his God, and wave his hand over the place and cure the leper.' "Are not Abanah and Pharpar, the rivers of Damascus, better than all the waters of Israel? Could I not wash in them and be clean?" So, he turned and went away in a rage. Then his servants came near and spoke to him and said, "My father, had the prophet told you to do some great thing, would you not have done it? How much more then, when he says to you, 'Wash, and be clean'?" So he went down and dipped himself seven times in the Jordan, according to the word of the man of God; and his flesh was restored like the flesh of a little child and he was clean." 2 Kings 5:9-14

Notice how upset Naaman was with Elisha's cure for his leprosy. He wanted Elisha to see him in person, not send a servant, and that he would wave his hand around while calling on God, also complaining that he could just have easily washed in a Damascus river and saved himself a trip to Israel.

Naaman comes a long way to be healed of leprosy through a famous man of God, to almost leaving in anger complaining about the process. He wanted a big show to be put on by God and His servant! He thought the power of God rested in some kind of difficult technique done by some famous man. After all, Naaman considered himself important and expected special treatment from God and Elisha.

Seems kind of familiar for today doesn't it!

Did Naaman really think that Elisha pulled this technique out of a "How To" book or learned it from some conference he attended, on what technique to use on someone who has leprosy?

Yet Christians in the 21st Century want exactly that... they can't wait to hear and know the "latest technique" that someone famous is doing or teaching.

One day I talked on the phone to a long time High Level Spiritual Warfare leader, who I hadn't talked to in over a year, and he told me that he and his "church" leadership were using the latest deliverance technique they learned from an internationally known leader. This is a person who for many years has seen and gone in the spirit, attacked and destroyed evil entities in the spirit, yet now leans on a new technique for some reason!

That's like knowing how to fly a war jet in battle but then deciding one day to use your bare hands instead!

Imagine Naaman going back to Damascus to teach people the Elisha Leprosy cure technique?

Many years ago, I first learned deliverance by techniques also! I was taught that if one thing didn't work you tried the next thing and so on. I tried to remember these techniques! Imagine standing in front of a person and trying a list of packaged techniques against a demon! Now imagine doing it for a whole city and nation against a principality! Yet I've personally seen and read about Christians doing this all the time! Only God's grace and protection pulled me through such battles to where He wanted me!

Utilizing your own will and techniques are flesh doctrines that detract from God's glory, can fail (using the wrong battle plan) or backfire (evil entity counterattack against a weak, ineffective, wrong-timed, man-made plan) and can lead to being controlled by a spirit of religion, to pride and vainglory... thus to our fall!

We're not like witches or psychics who do legalistic rituals, prescribed incantations, healing formulas and magical, demonic performances for personal glory and for profit.

Techniques "can" work but why would you want to use them when God teaches you different in His Word, if one will just observe and be obedient? (BEWARE: The spirit of religion from creeping in!)

For many years I've taught people <u>not</u> to use a "cookie-cutter" approach to obtain spiritual and physical victories.

Don't confuse testimonies with techniques!

People chase after the hottest spiritual "expert's" latest book, CD or conference, to find the Holy Grail of techniques! Sadly, business-minded gurus out there, capitalize on and profit from such emotions.

Your time is better spent running closer to God and money better spent as God's perfect will directs!

Can dipping seven times in the Jordan River possibly be a scientific, medical cure for leprosy?

Of course not!

There's no healing agent in the Jordan River that works on leprosy, when dipped in it seven times! It's a one-time spiritual cure, prescribed for Naaman, performed by the power of God! So why would anyone try to repeat it over and over, because it worked once for Elisha and Naaman in approx. 850 BC?

When you hear about a famous guy like an Elisha, who cured a leper by having him dip seven times in the Jordan River, don't become a parrot squawking out the same ritual for yourself and to others! This is a testimony for the Glory of God, not a "hot" new technique or doctrine to try out on a leper colony!

What I'm saying applies to every other testimony pertaining to spiritual warfare and healing.

Now let me add, that I'm not saying this can never happen again. When we read historic testimonies in God's Word and see, hear and experience them in our own lives, God is glorified and He may repeat the circumstances through us. IF He leads us through discernment or in the spirit to do something, it will work! It may not make sense, like dipping seven times in a river, but it will work. He may advise us in a certain circumstance, to repeat a testimony we heard about in the past to bring about victory. My experience has been it's usually a new, unheard of spiritual or physical way or combination of both to be done for the victory. This is how God does a miracle, to prove it's Him, not man's works or man's plans.

Look for God's plan before going into battle. If you're going to undertake deliverance of a person, then BEFORE YOU START, find out from the Holy Spirit through discernment or seeing/going in the spirit, how the battle with these particular evil spirits afflicting this particular person are to be dealt with. The same plan if you are dealing with a group of people and especially in dealing with a city and a nation!

Picture that you're a warrior on the battlefield frontline, who must wait for directions from headquarters on when, where and how to attack the enemy and at what strength. If you're being attacked, ask God how to counterattack for the win... don't just blindly spit out some techniques... God knows where their weak spots are and how to exploit them! This goes for healing also! Healing may be a root problem, a sin problem, a demon problem or combinations of these issues. Many issues the person doesn't know, such as a generational curse. Headquarters has the big picture, as they know things that we don't know. When the plan comes, don't hesitate... ACT! Victory is the Lord's!

A specific plan for victory is obtained from God to glorify HIM, not a person nor a technique!

Where can you find Xtreme Small Game?

Probably easier to say where can you not find them!

Heavier concentrations seem to be in hospitals and places where many people have died, evil worship centers, memorial and sacrifice centers and non-Christian regions, to name a few.

Some Final Wrap-Ups

Many people receive prayer and/or "laying on of hands" and/or microwave methods such as the "glory zone method" and even deliverance sessions, but experience little or no relief from mental, emotional and physical issues and diseases. REMEMBER to look for the root, which may be generational curses; soul ties (occult and/or sexual); deliberate sin that needs repentance (unforgiveness, lying, accepting false doctrines, etc.) and other roots.

A great indicator of a root problem, is when you're trying to cast out an evil spirit and it won't leave or your struggling for hours to accomplish anything and/or it tells you it doesn't have to leave. These are big indicators of a root problem, allowing the evil spirit(s) the right to stay. A spiritual warfare teacher of mine, years ago, never addressed root issues prior to deliverance sessions. Dealing with struggling evil spirits is exhausting and unnecessary.

Also, you can speak your language (English, French, German, etc.) and evil spirits will understand, even if the people they're in don't understand what you're saying.

Look to the Holy Spirit, as it may be ALL of these roots that need to be chopped out! Just as a person in a car accident for instance, they may have multiple cuts, breaks, internal bleeding, brain trauma, etc. ALL has to be dealt with to bring about complete health.

Beyond an evil spirit issue, is that, if you have unresolved roots like unforgiveness or deliberate sin issues (believing in false/antichrist doctrines, even if you think you're Christian), you are jeopardizing your destiny; jeopardizing your health; jeopardizing a long life and jeopardizing your salvation. Resolve your root issues. Don't go to the lake of fire! Be sure!

Don't be discouraged… be encouraged… God is with you!

So, the answer to the burning question as to what all these evil Trophy and Xtreme Small Game really are… they are the enemy!

To again sum up… the giants, the Nephilim, are the children of the angelic Watchers and earthly women. They are children of fornication. God called them "bastards" in 1 Enoch 10:9. When these giants died in the flood, their spirits were confined in and upon earth by God. They have no rest and they seek human habitation and they also seek to torment us and kill us.

Not much room for other theories, when <u>God</u> tells us what happened and what evil spirits are.

I know many will not like this answer and they have their reasons. Remember that I am not your enemy, so holster your gun if you're pulling it out after reading this Sector to come against me.

Consider <u>all</u> small game the enemy and deal with them that way; and let's not argue, but work together to defeat them as <u>they must be dealt with!</u>

"Now the giants, who have been born of spirit and of flesh, shall be called upon earth evil spirits, and on earth, shall be their habitation. Evil spirits shall proceed from their flesh, because they were created from above; from the holy Watchers was their beginning and primary foundation. Evil spirits shall they be upon the earth, and the spirits of the wicked shall they be called. The habitation of the spirits of heaven shall be in heaven; but upon earth shall be the habitation of terrestrial spirits, who are born on earth." 1 Enoch 15:8

God will deal with them at some future time of judgment, but for now we must deal with them.

Now on to some of the real underbelly of spiritual hunting campaigns!

SECTOR NINETEEN

XTREME RABID GAME SNAKES, WOLVES AND OTHER CRITTERS

> **HUNTING TIP**
> Evil game are ruthless... show 'em what ruthless really means!

While hunting big game or small game, you'll come across other critters that you may want to let go by or deal with them right then. Sometimes you'll go after these just for sport or because they're pesky and a deliberate nuisance to you or someone else.

One must be careful with many of these, as they can be rabid.

Rabies is a viral disease found in warm-blooded animals that can infect others. Left untreated it will lead to death.

Many animals, although not rabid, can cause damage, injury and death with their actions. Most animals don't intend to harm people, but fact is that they do.

There was a time when a huge skunk was disturbing our moose camp every night, so I got up and put an end to him. Although it came to a very smelly conclusion, he wasn't a nuisance anymore.

Other times I have hunted ground hogs in farmer's fields, because their holes in the ground would oftentimes break the legs of cattle.

There were also fox and coyotes that raided chicken farms, and squirrels and raccoons that were a destructive nuisance to our hunt camps and buildings. (Fox, coyotes, skunks and raccoons are typical rabies carriers.)

Wolverines will kill just for the fun of it. Having crossed paths with one just once—we parted leaving each other alone!

Deer crossing over roads, have killed many people by accident… not intentional, however, still a deadly result!

Even mice, rats, and chipmunks are annoying and destructive.

Some, such as snakes or wolves, can be deadly.

Any or all of these that get into your camp or house can be a problem.

Right now, let's get into the Xtreme Rabid Game, that Xtreme Big Game and Small Game Hunters and Christians <u>will</u> come in contact with.

Rabid Game can waste your destiny, cripple you and destroy you (i.e. you can lose your salvation)!

When these get into your camp, they are "enemies in the camp" that <u>must</u> be dealt with.

Many times, they are easy to spot and get rid of… many are very difficult to see, even when standing right next to you, so great steps must be taken to uncover them or stay away from them. Even when found, trying to get rid of some can be impossible, requiring the Christian to remove themselves from the camp, where the Xtreme Rabid Game has control or access!

We'll start with the most far-removed from us, then the closer, smaller, less problematic ones and work our way up as we go along to the deadliest and dangerous game you'll probably encounter!

INTERNATIONAL RABID GAME

Some rabid varmints, are on a higher international level that we may never come in contact with, such as Islamic groups like Hamas, Hezbollah, Boko Harem, the Taliban, ISIS and al-Qaeda.

Many Christians are experiencing torture and ghastly forms of murder (i.e. buried alive, burned alive, beheaded, crucified) in various countries where these groups operate. Women are taken, bought and sold as sex slaves and made to convert to islam or be killed. Mass slaughters are taking place; with entire villages and Church structures bombed and burned, on their campaigns of genocide. They hold no mercy, even for children. They use their own children to conduct suicide attacks. They hate Christians. Truly rabid!

Nowhere is safe now from these extremely rabid creatures, as we have seen from their suicide attacks in Church buildings, restaurants, airports, sport venues, workplaces and schools in Western countries (i.e. San Bernardino, Orlando, Paris, Nice, Brussels and multiple areas in Sweden, France, Denmark, Germany, England and other EU countries). And we all remember 9/11. Criminal violence against Christians is dramatically rising in Western countries by these groups and Islamists (i.e. violent assaults and rape against the innocent). Christian assemblies need to hire armed security to protect themselves now, even in the USA. A priest in France was beheaded by Muslims while conducting a Church service. Violence against Christians by Muslims, Hindus and Buddhists all over the world, has become the norm.

They are determined and committed to kill Christians and jews, so it would be best to steer clear of areas where these Xtreme Rabid Game are known to exist, unless led there by God. Xtreme Big Game Hunting against the principalities and powers behind these groups can be undertaken. (Let God lead your battles!) Also pray for and spiritually assist the law enforcement and military forces such as FBI, INTERPOL, NATO or IDF (Israel Defense Forces) that physically confront these groups!

There are also entire countries and their governments that hate and kill Christians.

Remember in Sector Two, that in the 20th Century it was estimated that 45.5 MILLION Christians were killed just because they were Christian. This doesn't include the unknown millions of Christians in the world who are discriminated against, threatened, persecuted, imprisoned, beaten, tortured, raped, sold into slavery, have their homes burned and their human rights violated. Many governments and their police departments participate in or ignore when attacks happen against Christians.

Where does this holocaust happen?

According to International Christian Concern, headquartered in Washington D.C. (www.persecution.org); and Voice of the Martyrs, (www.persecution.com), here is the current list, as of 2017, of the countries that are guilty of such crimes:

Afghanistan
Algeria
Azerbaijan
Bahrain
Bangladesh
Belarus
Bhutan
Brunei
Central African Republic
China
Columbia
Comoros
Cuba
Djibouti
Egypt
Eritrea
Ethiopia
European Union ⟶
India
Indonesia
Iran
Iraq
Jordan
Kazakhstan
Kenya
Kuwait
Kyrgyzstan
North Korea
Laos
Lebanon

- Austria
- Belgium
- Bulgaria
- Cyprus
- Czech Republic
- Denmark
- Estonia
- Finland
- France
- Germany
- Greece
- Hungary
- Ireland
- Italy
- Latvia
- Lithuania
- Luxembourg
- Malta
- Netherlands
- Poland
- Portugal
- Romania
- Slovakia
- Slovenia
- Spain
- Sweden
- United Kingdom

Libya
Malaysia
Maldives
Mali
Mauritania
Mexico
Morocco
Myanmar
Nepal
Niger
Nigeria
North Korea
Oman
Pakistan
Palestinian Territories
Philippines
Qatar
Russia
Saudi Arabia
Somalia
Sri Lanka
Sudan
Syria
Tajikistan
Tanzania
Tibet
Tunisia
Turkey
Turkmenistan
United Arab Emirates
Uzbekistan
Vietnam
Yemen

I'm surprised that Israel wasn't on these lists, as I have heard of much discrimination there against Christians. I experienced it myself when I was in Israel. Street evangelism is banned in Israel. We can also convict the governments of Canada and the United States of open hostility and rising persecution against Christians, including from the media, the court system and various organizations (i.e. CAIR, LGBT, ACLU).

That's a total of 92, including Canada, Israel and the USA, of known countries that discriminate or restrict Christianity or are hostile against Christians on various levels! (i.e. it would be more dangerous to openly discuss Christianity or practice evangelism in Saudi Arabia, than it would be to do so in Canada.) In reality, all countries have Muslims, Hindus, Buddhists, and atheists in the population, who are hostile to Christians and can and do present a danger.

Travel bans to these high-risk countries; economic/financial sanctions; import/export restrictions; and spiritual warfare against the evil entities controlling the leaders and people are recommended hunting options. (Of course, only a Trade Minister or a President could implement sanctions, so Christians are left with few physical options ,other than refusing to travel to these countries, bringing such atrocities to their government's attention and pressing their elected leaders or the media, to make a difference, by constantly exposing the guilty people and regions to the world.) Many Christian civilians grow tired of their government's failure to act against or defeat criminal and/or terrorist groups, so have formed militias to hunt down Xtreme Rabid Game (see P.O. and R. Sector 24). It's also very practical to learn military-gauge close quarter combat (not sports martial arts), hand-to-hand and weapons methods and store weapons, for self-defense for yourself, your family and other innocents, to deal with Xtreme Rabid Game when they come to your door! Remember, you're dealing with violent predators that want to kill you and your family, only because you're Christian.

Christian residents and tourists in every country need to be on guard… more so in some places than others. If you live in these high-risk countries now, spiritual warfare is vital! Ask Father how you can turn the nation and advance His Kingdom in your country! Share the teachings from this book to help others who are exposed to danger and for them to assist in breaking nations of their evil activities and path!

"You are My battle-ax and weapons of war:
For with you I will break the nation in pieces;
With you I will destroy kingdoms." Jeremiah 51:20

David had no fear taking on nations!

"All nations surrounded me, but in the name of the LORD I will destroy them. They surrounded me, Yes, they surrounded me; But in the name of the LORD I will destroy them. They surrounded me like bees; They were quenched like a fire of thorns; For in the name of the LORD I will destroy them. You pushed me violently, that I might fall, But the LORD helped me." Psalm 118:10-13

If you think that's impossible, remember the Roman Empire was defeated by Christianity (in other words, Christians)!

Try Olafing! (See Xtreme Trophy or Big Game Sector)

Be led by God for any activity involving these countries. Pray for those Christians in these countries and assist them in intercession and spiritual warfare as led.

Many seemingly benign governments and organizations in the world are anti-Christian and may not hit these lists!

Black clouds against Christians are widening in organizations such as the Freemasons; Illuminati; Bilderberg Group; Trilateral Commission; the World Economic Forum/Davos Group and such, who are determined to form a new world government and one world religion.

This "New World Order" seeks to eliminate Christianity.

Any direct spiritual warfare against anti-Christian organizations and their spiritual roots, must also be God led.

LOCAL RABID GAME

Next, on a smaller scale, are non-Christians <u>deliberately</u> involved in witchcraft, voodoo, occultism, shamanism, sorcery, satanism, mediums, enchanters, cults, pagan religions, and new age, just to name some of the most well-known.

These people are also anti-Christian, and can be obvious to detect. Usually once they know you're a Christian, they'll avoid you!

Although many will build evil altars, do evil sacrifices, and send evil spirits against Church groups, Christian leaders, and individual Christians.

Others, in satanic groups for instance, seek also to kill and destroy any and all Christians!

People deliberately come into Church groups pretending to be Christians, to purposely bring about confusion, disruption, failure, fear, disunity, false doctrine and destruction. If anyone thinks that this just isn't possible, you need a reality check, as evil people join Christian groups with the intent to destroy them, and then they move on to the next one. People usually blame this on a "jezebel spirit."

How many Church groups have split up or failed, due to a woman or a man seducing the leader? I've lost count myself. (The leader is obviously also to blame for their sin and failure to conquer temptation.)

Many Christians are deceived into thinking, that some of these groups and occult activities are harmless, such as fortune tellers, "white" witches, shamans, or organizations that have the word "Christian" in them or that mention Jesus, leading one to believe they're OK. Some faiths consider Jesus to be just a prophet or equal to buddha, mohammed, Mary His mother or that He's just one of many ways to obtain salvation.

Stay away from occult activities of any kind and examine the belief system of any organization you become involved with, to see if they conflict with the Bible. This would also include your job.

Some of this Xtreme Rabid Game can be considered both in the international group and in the local, smaller scale group, depending on their organizational structure.

The groups and people most spiritually dangerous come from their denominations, friends, relatives, leaders and fellow Christians.

Rabid Denominations

There are many religious denominations that people assume are Christian. Their belief system must be examined, as many are antichrist or are spiritually dead, blind and deceived organizations, having no demonstration of God's power (1 Corinthians 2:4-5).

A ministry from New Zealand (www.jubilee.org.nz) writes what the clues of a spiritually dead Church (denomination) are:

Here are eight death clues:

1. Have lost their sense of mission to those who have not heard about Jesus Christ and do not pant after the Great Commission;
2. Exist primarily to provide fellowship for the "members of the club;"
3. Expect their pastors to focus primarily on ministering to the members' personal spiritual needs;
4. Design ministry to meet the needs of their members;
5. Have no idea about the needs of the "stranger outside the gates;"
6. Are focused more on the past than the future;
7. Often experience major forms of conflict;
8. And watch the bottom line of the financial statement more than the number of confessions of faith.

I would also add in a failure to spiritually equip members and a lack of evidence of spiritual gifts, healing, deliverance, miracles, signs and wonders and other demonstrations of God's power!

Here's the New Zealand's Church group's solution to a dead Church group:

"These churches are filled mostly with good Christian people, but there's no discernable spiritual power, just good Christian people-and we all know what Jesus said about being good. (Mark 10:18)

So it's obvious. Isn't it? The only solution for spiritually dead congregations is resurrection. You can't revitalize something that is dead. They must be brought to life again! And that is resurrection.

Revitalization is a waste of time. You can't breathe life into a corpse. Only God can do that, and that is resurrection.

Resurrecting a Church

My experience has taught me the resurrection of a church happens in three stages. It begins with a new pastor. Either the pastor experiences a personal resurrection or the church actually gets a new pastor. Next is the resurrection of the leaders of the church either by transformation or replacement. Finally, the church itself is resurrected and turned around through some tactical change. Then, if resurrection happens, our behavior changes:

1. The church turns outward in its focus.
2. Jesus, not the institution, will become the object of our affection.
3. The Great Commission will become our mandate, and we will measure everything we do by how many new converts we make rather than whether we have a black bottom line.
4. Membership in the Kingdom will replace membership in the church.
5. Pastors will cease being chaplains of pastoral care and will become modern-day apostles of Jesus Christ.
6. And those who try to control the church with an iron fist or intimidate the church at every turn of the road will be shown the door.

The primary reason society is shunning the institutional church is because for the most part it is spiritually dead. Spiritually alive churches, no matter what their form or where they are planted, always grow. That is the nature of the beast. That is the kind of church God honors. That is what the church was put on earth to do-spread the good news. When a church faithfully does that, it grows. Period."

End of quote from New Zealand's take on spiritually dead denominations.

Again, I'll say… ALL members operating in the spiritual realm with God's power should be evident in a spiritually alive Church group/denomination/assembly!

ALSO, VERY IMPORTANT!

Five-Fold Ministry Requirement

"And He Himself gave some to be apostles, some prophets, some evangelists, and some pastors and teachers, for the equipping of the saints for the work of ministry, for the edifying of the body of Christ, till we all come to the unity of the faith and of the knowledge of the Son of God, to a perfect man, to the measure of the stature of the fullness of Christ; that we should no longer be children, tossed to and fro and carried about with every wind of doctrine, by the trickery of men, in the cunning craftiness of deceitful plotting, but, speaking the truth in love, may grow up in all things into Him who is the head—Christ— from whom the whole body, joined and knit together by what every joint supplies, according to the effective working by which every part does its share, causes growth of the body for the edifying of itself in love." Ephesians 4:11-16

Every group should be properly "equipping of the saints for the work of ministry for the edifying of the body of Christ. "knit together"; "effective" and no longer be children, tossed to and fro and carried about with every wind of doctrine, by the trickery of men, in the cunning craftiness of deceitful plotting". Christ is the Head, not some leader and/or their spouse!

I've encountered Christians that say, apostles and prophets are no longer part of the modern Church.

"there would be mockers in the last time who would walk according to their own ungodly lusts. These are sensual persons, who cause divisions, not having the Spirit." Jude 1:18-19

Dead "churches"/denominations are the fruit of dead trees which train and sustain them… their seminaries, Bible Colleges and teaching centers! Their roots are the evil spiritual entities that keep them buried in lies and darkness. Understand that most of these seminaries, Bible Colleges, teaching centers and their fruit, have the <u>intent</u> to be right or helpful, but as many warm, cute and fuzzy animals have the same intent towards people, intent doesn't mean correct or that they aren't dangerous and can't hurt or kill you! Remember the deer vs. car can be unintentional yet have deadly results!

Spiritually dead and/or man-made religious doctrine seminaries/Bible Colleges/teaching centers produce spiritually dead and/or man-made religious leaders.

Many of these denominations also overlook or allow their leadership and members to be deliberate sinners and compromisers, (i.e. idol worship, sexual evils, mixing religions (chrislam)) without consideration of God's salvation message or repentance required in His Word!

It doesn't matter that a person thinks their leader is a really "nice guy" or "great with children" or "a great speaker" … that stuff is nice, but you need more than "nice"!

Don't get me wrong… I'm not against nice leaders who are good to people and honestly trying to be and do well.

Having a "nice" leader is great, as long as they're doing what they should be doing according to God, in addition to being nice.

If all a Christian needed to do was have a good time, no hassles and hang out with nice people who believe in Jesus, then there are lots of denominations that fit that profile already!

But, God says there's more we need to be doing!

Some people might think after reading this that I'm being too tough.

I'd rather tell God that I did my best to do as He taught us through Jesus and His Word, to do His perfect will and to teach people the same, rather than say to Him one day; "I gave them what they wanted"! I don't want people to go to the lake of fire because some twisted, false-

Christian leader or false denomination convinced them that they were saved!

Many religious groups pretend to be or sound Christian, yet are not Christian at all, such as Freemasonry (Shriners, Knights of Columbus); Mormonism (The Church of Jesus Christ of Latter-Day Saints); Jehovah's Witness; Seventh-Day Adventist; Christian Science; Universalism and the Unification church.

Some will disagree with what I just said, because "these people do good work in the community" or "they're very humble and kind", but those aren't qualifiers for salvation or teach God's truth. Jesus is the ONLY way! God's Standards are the only way! Lengthy discussions can be done on each of these groups, especially freemasonry, which has had numerous books written about this secret organization's satanic rituals and allegiances. The internet has the truth on each of these groups.

OK, don't get angry now as this next bit comes up. Read it through to make sure you're following God and not following some religion.

Main stream religions have also drifted away from the Biblical Gospel, by following their own man-made paths such as Roman Catholicism; Lutheranism; Methodist; United; Presbyterian; Anglican; Orthodox (Greek, Russian, etc.); Baptist and many that call themselves Pentecostal and non-denomination groups as well. I can't list them all here as statistics say there are 41,000 denominations, cults and groups claiming to be Christian. This is not the will of God.

Religions and denominations don't exist in heaven. Neither should they exist on earth.

"your will be done on earth as it is in heaven." Matthew 6:10

You don't need to hunt for God in some building or in some religion or in some leader.

"Do you not know that you are the temple of God and that the Spirit of God dwells in you?" 1 Corinthians 3: 16

Jude warns us not to end up with a distorted gospel, that fits into this century, instead, have our lifestyles fit into the original purposes of God. We are not relevant when we mirror the world around us.

"But I want to remind you, though you once knew this, that the Lord, having saved the people out of the land of Egypt, afterward destroyed those who did not believe." Verse 5

There are many Christians that study about and prefer to only hear about the love of God and His grace, but people will come up with their own definition of God's love and grace, to redefine what the Bible says, which is an absolute violation of scriptures. The Bible defines love, not some organization or some leader or ourselves with some "feel-good definition". Jude reminds us that there are disciplines and judgments for rebellious decisions against Christ. We can't distort a Gospel that fits a lifestyle that makes us feel good.

There are numerous denominations (unfortunately) in the body of Christ, where each has doctrines that says, depending on God's standard, "Oh no, we don't do that in our church"! This position is wrong! The Bible says: I am a believer contending for the original Gospel and I do what God is doing. Period! We are not trying to uphold a standard set by a previous generation. We are not trying to be politically or socially correct to appease the world's sensibilities. Christianity is not a country club where everybody's self-esteem gets massaged.

Every religious organization and denomination lies, compromises with, distorts, adds man-made doctrines and/or ignores parts of God's Word (which is deliberately withholding the truth or lying). A few examples: the rise of chrislam (Islam acceptance by Christians); acceptance of sexual immorality within leadership and congregants; refuses to discipline and put out of the Church body, all deliberate sinners that call themselves Christian (Matthew 18: 15-17, 1 Corinthians 5: 9-13, 2 Thessalonians 3:14); ignoring the Holy Spirit, including His direction and gifts; idolatry (i.e. praying to/revering physical objects and the dead); ignoring operating in spiritual gifts; lying to people about salvation (i.e. once saved, always saved false doctrine and/or salvation by works i.e. through good deeds or by giving money to the Church or the false doctrine of salvation through a priest or a particular religion/organization); ignoring demonstrations of God's power (miracles, signs and wonders); acceptance of merchandising (selling prayers/selling wedding, baptismal, funeral services/selling prophecies, etc.); leaders/groups who are manipulating and controlling, rather than equipping people for ministry (Ephesians 4: 11-16); replacing the true worship of God with popular songs...

"true worshipers will worship the Father in spirit and truth; for the Father is seeking such to worship Him. God is Spirit, and those who worship Him <u>must</u> worship in <u>spirit</u> and <u>truth</u>."" John 4: 23-24

It's easy to identify lies within an organization (i.e. false Church group/ministry/school), when you compare them to what they say and how they act compared to what God says is the truth.

Sheep blindly follow false denominations into thinking they're following God's will, when they are actually following man-made doctrines, worldly values and/or sinful activities that are not Christian at all.

Such places are "spiritual brothels" prostituting Christianity!

These false denominations and their teaching centers are deadly and dangerous breeding factories that pollute Christianity!

Don't get caught in one of these death traps! Locate or form a true group of Christians that are actively operating in the spiritual realm in spiritual gifts, that follows the Word of God and His perfect will for each person's life! Each person in the group should be an active participant in fellowship, teaching, equipping others, developing disciples for Christ (as Jesus taught us to do), encouraging, mentoring, giving testimonies, operating in their spiritual senses, providing spiritual gifts and fruit and so on as the Holy Spirit directs. The Holy Spirit is the Comforter, Teacher and Leader.

Spiritual Warfare against the principalities and powers manipulating these denominations need to be dealt with, the same way you would deal with them over cities, regions, etc.

Friends, relatives, fellow Church members, etc.

When you are working in the spirit, those who live in the flesh (religious and/or spiritually dead) will not understand you and usually avoid you or come against you. These are the annoying critters who don't know any better—yet they can be harmful. These can be well-meaning members and leaders of religious denomination groups, and peaceful organizations, who are deceived and living in the flesh. Although they may be kind, generous and nice people, they have been known to come against Christians, who operate in the spirit and gifts of the Spirit, with anger, hatred, discrimination, curses, bitterness, persecution, violence and un-Christian words and prayers because of their own sinful nature, fear, jealousy, pride or evil spirits manipulating them. They can and do try to control you or prevent you from doing what you are doing.

These can be from your own Church group, family, and friends.

My experience has been that they rarely listen to or accept God's truth that you would try to bring to them, so, it has been found best to do spiritual warfare for them as led and pray for them to be released from their bondage of ignorance and mental blinding by evil spiritual forces, and/or break your association with them, as God's Word directs (Romans 16:17-18)!

Deliberate sin is usually prevalent and/or accepted in a spiritually dead group of people and if so, it is Biblically recommended to end all fellowship with them. Continued fellowship with deliberate sinners, the religious and the spiritually dead will only infect you in the end. Associations with deliberate sinners that call themselves Christian, shows non-believers, that Christians are no different than anyone else and are hypocrites! This is also a slap in the face of Jesus! Listen to God.

Even those who are spiritual Christians and/or close long-time friends, can "shoot you in the back" when it serves their interests! It's happened to me many, many times!

We can quickly pick out such examples from the Bible, of those who were an "enemy in the camp".

David committed adultery with Bathsheba and then "arranged" to have her husband, Uriah, killed in battle. Uriah was one of the mighty men and a friend of David. At least Uriah's enemies had the courage to face him in battle and not behind his back. It's hard to imagine a great warrior and man of God like David would do this to a friend (2 Samuel

11). This is a perfect teaching example, that even the most unlikely person can plot your destruction!

Keep your discernment skills sharp around everyone!

Fortunately for David, he repented and reconciled with God, however, he reaped some retribution for himself and others because of his actions!

I don't need to go into the story of Samson and Delilah and how he trusted her, leading to his blindness and destruction (Judges 16). And we all remember perhaps the most infamous "enemy in the camp" in history… Judas, one of the disciples of Jesus.

The Bible is full of such stories on various levels.

Betrayal by those you trust and consider to be associates or friends strike at your heart and mind like no other enemy can reach. Keep this in mind when you spiritually hunt with others, especially strangers. People that you think can be trusted or relied upon can let you down, or in the Xtreme, turn and come against you openly to destroy you.

When such people are discerned or reveal themselves, it would be best to dispense with them, preferably not the David way, at least for the hunt you're on. Then perhaps you can talk and counsel with them, to see if they would be included on any further hunts. They may need a deliverance to clear the problem! If they do—help them—if they'll accept!

Wolf… the Xtreme enemy in the camp

The deadliest ones that I want to discuss more in depth now, are the Rabid Game <u>pretending</u> to be a Christian leader and those who really <u>think</u> they're Christian!

A favorite, most challenging hunt for some in the physical forest, is a special breed of game… the wolf! When I was a kid, the wolf had a bounty on it, because they were so destructive!

The wolf is a very worthy predator that is difficult to conquer, especially in his own back yard. If any snuck into a hunting camp, they would be quickly dealt with, unless disguised as a hunter to trick everyone. (The tail would give them away for me!)

Imagine depending on a wolf for your safety? Yet Christians are deceived into just that, all over the world!

Fortunately, the canis lupus wolves don't prey on us, as if they did, most of us would be as helpless as sheep are against them!

Wolves in Christian circles are cunning and can also be difficult to expose and conquer. Perhaps if a bounty were given to those who rip the sheep's clothing from these wolves to expose them, there would be less of them?

I'm speaking of the leaders over Christians who are indifferent; spiritually ignorant; a deliberate enemy; a non-believer; lacking the Holy Spirit; religious; idol worshipper and/or is a deliberate sinner and compromiser.

Any and all are dangerous and deadly to a person.

This Wolf is the Xtreme Enemy in the Camp!

Probably, the most destructive, dangerous physical beast that you will come across in your life! They can and do lead people to spiritual death!

God warns us many times about these enemies and warns these predators as you will see!

Jesus openly confronted these predators in His ministry:

" But when he saw many of the Pharisees and Sadducees coming to his baptism, he said to them, "Brood of vipers! Who warned you to flee from the wrath to come?" Matthew 3:7; Luke 3:7

"Brood of vipers! How can you, being evil, speak good things? For out of the abundance of the heart the mouth speaks." Matthew 12:34

"Serpents, brood of vipers! How can you escape the condemnation of hell?" Matthew 23:33

And He warned us of the wolves:

""Beware of false prophets, who come to you in sheep's clothing, but inwardly they are ravenous wolves." Matthew 7:15

""Behold, I send you out as sheep in the midst of wolves. Therefore, be wise as serpents and harmless as doves." Matthew 10:16; Luke 10:3

"For I know this, that after my departure savage wolves will come in among you, not sparing the flock." Acts 20:29

Notice that Jesus openly confronts these false leaders, rather than just ignoring them and their activities!

Good Biblical teaching for each of us!

There are the leader wolves and the regular wolves within the flock of sheep.

Some regular ones, such as witches, we've already discussed, who come in pretending to be Christian.

Besides Jesus warning us of these enemies in the camp, we can see that Jude felt it necessary to warn us also:

"Beloved, while I was very diligent to write to you concerning our common salvation, I found it necessary to write to you exhorting you to contend earnestly for the faith which was once for all delivered to the saints." Jude 3

Jude wanted to write about salvation, yet was led by God instead to urge or insist that we fight against a certain foe, for the faith which was given to us.

He next tells us who is attacking the Church.

"For certain men have crept in unnoticed, who long ago were marked out for this condemnation, ungodly men, who turn the grace of our God into lewdness and deny the only Lord God and our Lord Jesus Christ." Jude 4

They come into the Church, hiding their true intentions. They are not deceived, they are ungodly. They covertly operate to destroy and deceive… they are also called the sons and daughters of Belial by God!

There are those (wolves) who try to lead others to false gods, false religions, and false doctrines.

"Certain men, the children of Belial, are gone out from among you, and have withdrawn the inhabitants of their city, saying, Let us go and serve other gods, which ye have not known." Deuteronomy 13:13 KJV

They can be unholy "church" leaders who steal, commit adultery, purposely sin, are controlling, cruel, refuse to serve the Lord, refuse to repent, even if found out.

"Now the sons of Eli (priests) were sons of Belial; they knew not the LORD." 1 Samuel 2:12 KJV

And they can also be women.

"Count not thine handmaid for a daughter of Belial: for out of the abundance of my complaint and grief have I spoken hitherto." 1 Samuel 1:16 KJV

Quoting from Goetia, "Belial is said to be very respectful. Belial is also called the demon of lies and guilt. As a prince of hell, he commands 80 legions of demons and is specifically the prince reigning over the northern reaches of hell. It controls the elements of earth and reigns over the earth elementals (earth demons)." Many also consider Belial to be just another in a long stream of names for satan.

There is a difference between this kind, and those who are just deceived and walking in the flesh, instead of the spirit. The sons and daughters of Belial have intentionally decided to be wicked! The Bible calls them wicked, lewd, worthless, vipers, wolves, murderers, lustful, liars, deceivers, and the seed or children of the devil.

How would you like to have some of these in your hunting camp (life)?

Jude gives us some similarities to compare them with:

"Woe unto them! for they have gone in the way of Cain, and ran greedily after the error of Balaam for reward, and perished in the gainsaying of Core." Jude 11 KJV

Jude mentions Cain, Balaam and Core in this verse. Cain was a murderer, Genesis 4; Balaam was a prophet who sold out Israel, Numbers 22-25; Core or Korah, was a Levite (minister) who was a rebel, leading others to himself (Numbers 16). All of them were "enemies in the camp."

Jude warns us that these kinds are amongst us and in our gatherings, intending to destroy and deceive, "These are spots in your feasts of charity, when they feast with you, feeding themselves without fear." Jude 12a

The worst, are those who are in the role of Christian leaders (shepherds) for power, fame, and greed or some are just indifferent or although sincere, are blindly led by "head wolves" and false doctrine (dead denominations/organizations).

Many refuse such Gospel teachings as equipping the saints (Christians), as they want to keep control.

Ignorance and indifference doesn't mean they stop being dangerous… ignorance and indifference can and does take many to the lake of fire!

So how do we know one of these particular "flesh and blood" infiltrators, who are hiding in the midst of us and set on destroying us?

AND, how do we combat them?

Many are pretty obvious and easy to spot, as they are "murmurers, complainers, walking after their own lusts." Jude 16 and Jude 19, "sensual, having not the spirit."

Some are not so easy to spot.

Test them!

"Dear friends, do not believe every spirit, but test the spirits to see whether they are from God, because many false prophets have gone out into the world." 1 John 4:1

These wolves can act in various ways, yet they can be spotted by their "fruit" which is usually non-existent!

"By their fruit you will recognize them. Do people pick grapes from thorn bushes, or figs from thistles? Likewise, every good tree bears good fruit, but a bad tree bears bad fruit. A good tree cannot bear bad fruit, and a bad tree cannot bear good fruit. Every tree that does not bear good fruit is cut down and thrown into the fire. Thus, by their fruit you will recognize them." Matthew 7:16-20 NIV

When God says fruit, He means what He considers fruit, not what people consider fruit!

What does God consider bad fruit from a leader or shepherd of the flock?

In Ezekiel 34 (KJV), God commands Ezekiel to speak out against bad shepherds, with a list of 14 sins:

1. Feed themselves without feeding the flock (v. 2).
2. Eat the fat and clothe themselves with wool, but don't feed the flock (v. 3).
3. Kill them that are fed (v. 3).
4. Have not strengthened the diseased (v. 4).
5. Have not healed the sick (v. 4).
6. Have not bound up the broken (v. 4).
7. Have not brought again that which was driven away (v. 4).
8. Have not sought the lost (v. 4, 6).
9. Oppressed their subjects (v. 4).
10. Scattered the flock (v. 5).
11. Have not been true shepherds (v. 5).
12. Caused flock to be destroyed (v. 5).
13. Have not protected the flock (v. 5).
14. Ignored the true condition of the flock (v. 6).

These wolves are in religious denominations and ministries all over the world today!

Some wolves are more interested in wages/salaries; conference fees, partnership fees; selling products (merchandising); tithes and offerings and their lifestyle, than sheep. A true shepherd goes to God for their needs, not the world.

Some wolves don't equip, mentor, strengthen or heal sheep to prepare them to reproduce more sheep (evangelize). A true shepherd equips, teaches and promotes Christians to produce good fruit (i.e. reproduce or multiply themselves.)

Some wolves drive away sheep with their force, pride, cruelty, control and manipulation. Their will is supreme. They won't admit errors and expect others to overlook their errors. They demand loyalty. They won't try to protect sheep, find them, nor bring them back. A true shepherd will lovingly guide and protect his flock and hunt for any that go missing to find out why, fix what is wrong and try to bring them back (to Jesus).

Some wolves prefer to be entertainers and/or are business-minded, and therefore are not interested in correcting, rebuking, nor expelling sheep that refuse to repent, which would be lost business (income). A true shepherd teaches the flock the entire Word of God and what is expected of them, to obtain His blessings and salvation. A true shepherd will expel all those rebellious and disobedient to God from the flock, to preserve the faithful sheep.

All wolves that have left the sheep to be prey (v. 8) need to voluntarily remove themselves from the flock to save themselves from God's 8-fold judgment:

1. Woe to them (v. 2).
2. I am against them (v. 10).
3. I will require My flock of them (v. 10).
4. Their dominion will be taken away (v. 10).
5. They will not feed themselves again (v. 10).
6. I will deliver my flock from them (v. 10).
7. I will destroy them (v. 16).
8. I will feed them with judgment (v. 16).

Wolves who refuse to leave voluntarily (usually the case as wolves won't admit they're a wolf), need to be expelled by the sheep!

After teaching the Gospel to the Ephesians for 3 years, Paul left them with perhaps his most important message…

"Therefore, take heed to yourselves and to all the flock, among which the Holy Spirit has made you overseers, to shepherd the church of God which He purchased with His own blood. <u>For I know this</u>, that after my departure <u>savage wolves will come in among you, not sparing the flock.</u> Also from among yourselves men will rise up, speaking perverse things, to draw away the disciples after themselves. Therefore watch, and remember that for three years I did not cease to warn everyone night and day with tears." Acts 20:28-3

The Ephesians didn't listen to Paul's warning, as false teaching became a major problem there.

Paul later asked Timothy to help them… "As I urged you when I went into Macedonia—remain in Ephesus that you may charge some that they teach no other doctrine, nor give heed to fables and endless genealogies, which cause disputes rather than godly edification which is in faith." 1Timothy 1:3-4

Jesus warned the Ephesians through John in Revelation 2:4-5, 30 years after Paul and Timothy warned them. The Ephesians were obviously holding congregational meetings, worship services, teaching and praying in the name of Jesus, and <u>considered themselves to be Christians</u>, BUT, they were following false leaders and false doctrine as true. People trusted and believed what these false leaders said to them. The "ravenous wolves" in Ephesus were separating the one true Shepherd Jesus from His flock, with deception and false teaching, leading them to their doom!

I'm going to print all of 2 Peter 2, as Peter's warning further defines this "enemy in the camp" and God's position with them!

Destructive Doctrines

"But there were also false prophets among the people, even as there will be false teachers among you, who will secretly bring in destructive heresies (false doctrines/lies), even denying the Lord who bought them, and bring on themselves swift destruction. ² And many will follow their destructive ways, because of whom the way of truth will be blasphemed.

³ By covetousness (want of popularity and wealth to spend on their own lusts) they will exploit you with deceptive words (lies); for a long time their judgment has not been idle, and their destruction does not slumber.

Doom of False Teachers

⁴ For if God did not spare the angels who sinned, but cast them down to hell and delivered them into chains of darkness, to be reserved for judgment; ⁵ and did not spare the ancient world, but saved Noah, one of eight people, a preacher of righteousness, bringing in the flood on the world of the ungodly; ⁶ and turning the cities of Sodom and Gomorrah into ashes, condemned them to destruction, making them an example to those who afterward would live ungodly; ⁷ and delivered righteous Lot, who was oppressed by the filthy conduct of the wicked ⁸ (for that righteous man, dwelling among them, tormented his righteous soul from day to day by seeing and hearing their lawless deeds)— ⁹ then the Lord knows how to deliver the godly out of temptations and to reserve the unjust under punishment for the day of judgment, ¹⁰ and especially those who walk according to the flesh (instead of the spirit) in the lust of uncleanness (sexual immorality) and despise authority (God's will and His Word). They are presumptuous, self-willed (ignoring God's will). They are not afraid to speak evil of dignitaries (spirt-led Christians operating under God's will and God's truth), ¹¹ whereas angels, who are greater in power and might, do not bring a reviling accusation against them before the Lord.

Depravity of False Teachers

¹² But these, like natural brute beasts made to be caught and destroyed, speak evil of the things they do not understand (attack and tell lies against true spirit-led Christians that speak God's Truth), and will utterly perish in their own corruption, ¹³ and will receive the wages of unrighteousness, as those who count it pleasure to carouse in the daytime. They are spots and blemishes, carousing in their own deceptions while they feast with you, ¹⁴ having eyes full of adultery and that cannot cease from sin, enticing unstable souls. They have a heart trained in covetous practices, and are accursed children. ¹⁵ They have forsaken the right way and gone astray, following the way of Balaam the son of Beor, who loved the wages of unrighteousness; ¹⁶ but he was

rebuked for his iniquity: a dumb donkey speaking with a man's voice restrained the madness of the prophet.

[17] These (false leaders/false organizations/false "churches"/false schools) are wells without water, clouds carried by a tempest, for whom is reserved the blackness of darkness forever.

Deceptions of False Teachers

[18] For when they speak great swelling words of emptiness, they allure through the lusts of the flesh, through lewdness (lustfulness), the ones who have actually escaped from those who live in error. [19] While they promise them liberty, they themselves are slaves of corruption; for by whom a person is overcome, by him also he is brought into bondage. [20] For if, after they have escaped the pollutions of the world through the knowledge of the Lord and Savior Jesus Christ, they are again entangled in them and overcome, the latter end is worse for them than the beginning. [21] For it would have been better for them not to have known the way of righteousness, than having known it, to turn from the holy commandment delivered to them. [22] But it has happened to them according to the true proverb: "A dog returns to his own vomit," and, "a sow, having washed, to her wallowing in the mire."

In other words, these false prophets and false teachers have lost their salvation and their judgment is assured, as well as those who follow their lies (see v. 2). 2 Peter 2

Wolves are a main physical weapon used by satan to corrupt the Church!

Many wolves deceive themselves and/or are deceived into thinking that they're good shepherds, but they are still a tool of satan!

They may look good, seem sincere and sound good, but examine the fruit (what God says is fruit He expects), to see if they're wolf or shepherd!

Does their teaching hold up to scripture?

Do they fall into any of the categories listed in Ezekiel 34?

Do they live in, practice, accept or compromise with sin (sexual immorality, lying, stealing, gossip, idolatry, drunkenness, etc.)?

Are they equipping, producing, encouraging and assisting spiritually fruitful sheep, who are evangelizing and fulfilling their destiny and ministries with God?

Do they bring God's standards to the world or the world's standards to the Church!

Do the sheep they're responsible for, know God's truth?

Let's examine some "fruit" of shepherds and sheep!

A major US nationwide survey of adults' spiritual beliefs by The Barna Group in April 2009 says, that Americans who consider themselves to be Christian, have a diverse set of beliefs – but many of those beliefs are contradictory or, at least, inconsistent.

59% of Christians said they believed that satan "is not a living being but is just a symbol of evil." (Only 26% of Christians surveyed believed satan is a real entity.)

22% believe Jesus sinned on earth!

17% agreed somewhat that Jesus was a sinner. 6% had no opinion. (That's 45% of people who call themselves Christian believe Jesus was a sinner or don't know if He was.)

38% believe the Holy Spirit is just a symbol of God's power... He's not a living being. Another 20% agreed somewhat that the Holy Spirit is just a symbol. (58% haven't a clue Who the Holy Spirit is!)

Only 55% of Christians believe the Bible is accurate!

33% of Christians believe the Bible, koran and book of mormon, teach the same truths!

Of the 12 largest denominations studied, "only 41% could be classified as "born again"!"

(I believe the percentage is lower as shown in the SAFARI Sector... Barna Group's survey didn't allow for additional factors, which is why they probably said "could be classified as born-again")!

I know people who think they're Christian, because their parents were.

I know people who think they're Christian, because they went to "church" when they were a kid.

I know people who think they're Christian, because they accepted Jesus 20 years ago, but continued their sinful lifestyle.

I know people who think they're a Christian because they own a Bible and wear a cross around their neck!

I knew a woman who proclaimed she was a Christian, yet who also accepted native American beliefs and believed in reincarnation! She honestly believed "born-again" meant she would come back again after she dies, if she doesn't get to heaven this time, so she'd get another shot at life! I tried to counsel her on the correct interpretation of "being born again". She considered my teaching to be my own personal theory. I explained to her that she stood alone with her theory. This was a person who regularly read the Bible! She also told me that I should quit "playing" with evil spirits!

I said to her, "I don't play with them, I attack them".

She said, "Going after them will only make them mad"!

I said, "Mad? They hate us and they want to kill us so why would I want to leave them alone"! I pointed out the truth to her and received anger in return! (She's a "fruit" of 2 mainstream denominations… Roman Catholicism and Baptist.) She has since died. Can anyone wonder how her reincarnation doctrine worked out for her? Sad.

Try convincing someone who thinks they're a Christian that they're really lost!

That's a huge hunting campaign on its own!

"Religious" seminaries/training centers, denominational/ministry "businesses" and false leaders, who are people pleasers, accepters and compromisers of sin, teachers of false doctrines, are to blame for these abysmal statistics and testimonies and lost forever lives?

These statistics don't include all the billions of people in the world that never became nor considered themselves Christian, due to the failure of these wolves to fulfill the "Great Commission" and their sub-standard spiritual lifestyles that people aren't drawn to!

Some other teeth on the wolf include, their promoting or accepting gossip. Satan's goal here is to destroy you with your own words!

"But I say to you that for <u>every</u> idle word men may speak; they will give account of it in the Day of Judgment. For by your words you will be justified, and by your words you will be condemned." Matthew 12:36-37

How many people do the above and think they are still saved? I shudder to think!

Wolves also teach salvation is possible with other than Jesus Christ, such as through works or being a "good" person or the "once saved, always saved" false doctrine or a "priest" or religious group can absolve your sins (i.e. roman catholic indulgence)! During the many Crusades, the Roman Catholic popes proclaimed that any man that died during the Crusades would be absolved of all sins and immediately go to heaven. Wolves come up with their own salvation rules that they approve of, to satisfy their own agendas or to satisfy what others want to hear.

"Now I urge you, brethren, note those who cause divisions and offenses, contrary to the doctrine which you learned, and <u>avoid them</u>. For those who are such do not serve our Lord Jesus Christ, but their own belly, and by smooth words and flattering speech deceive the hearts of the simple." Romans 16:17-18

Some out there are proclaiming themselves to be apostles, prophets, generals and who knows what else, that shouldn't be followed through a grocery checkout aisle!

They have enough knowledge, charisma and experience to be dangerous, when <u>they</u> decide to be leaders or because some organization gave them a piece of paper! Don't bet your eternal life on anyone. Do your own research.

Beware of those who insist on being called by their title, such as pastor or apostle or prophet. I've run into a great many of those. That's a big red flag!

Paul warns of these "so-called apostles" or wolves:

"But what I do, I will also continue to do, that I may cut off the opportunity from those who desire an opportunity to be regarded just as we are in the things of which they boast. For such are <u>false apostles, deceitful workers, transforming themselves into apostles of Christ. And no wonder! For satan himself transforms himself into an angel of light. Therefore it is no great thing if his ministers also transform themselves into ministers of righteousness,</u> whose end will be according to their works." 2 Corinthians 11:12-15

Some have such a prideful, jealous and controlling spirit that they will even override the Holy Spirit's directions given to others, thinking that only they know what is best, and that only they hear from God!

Such wolves can be quite vile and ruthless. They suffer from a dysfunctional syndrome typical of dictators, the mafia, cult leaders or territorial spirits. This kind can appear loving, helpful and friendly, but when they feel any challenge to the lofty position they imagine they possess, be ready for an attack! They usually command and expect total loyalty and your surrender to their will. Many insist that they be "your covering" before you will be allowed to do anything with them or in "their" ministry or be "allowed by them" to go out on your own to conduct you own ministry! I've come across many of these wolves.

"For there is one God and one Mediator between God and men, the Man Christ Jesus." 1 Timothy 2:5

Paul teaches… "For when one says, "I am of Paul," and another, "I am of Apollos," are you not carnal?" I Corinthians 3:4

In other words, you don't belong to a person!

"For we are God's fellow workers; you are God's field, you are God's building." 1 Corinthians 3:9

In other words, God is our covering, not man! Why would anyone want a sinful person, to be between them and God? Only a wolf would want to place themselves between you and God!

For those who are led by the Spirit of God, each and every true Christian is a child of God, a saint, an heir and joint-heir with Jesus Christ to all in God's kingdom, who can personally go to Abba Father! Each of us is a living house of God; a royal priest; with Jesus as the corner-stone. (1 Peter 2)

"<u>For as many as are led by the Spirit of God, these are sons of God.</u> For you did not receive the spirit of bondage again to fear, but <u>you received the Spirit of adoption by whom we cry out, "Abba, Father."</u> The Spirit Himself bears witness with our spirit that <u>we are children of God, and if children, then heirs—heirs of God and joint heirs with Christ"</u> Romans 8:14-17

Father and Jesus paid a heavy price for this blessing for us. Anyone who presumes to take control of this blessing from us is a liar and a thief… a wolf! Don't let them get away with it for you or anyone else!

No other mediator but Jesus is needed to go directly to Father.

Young Christians need direction, guidance and nurturing… they don't need a human master… they need a humble servant… a guide!

Peter tells us in 1 Peter 5:1-4, "To the elders among you, I appeal as a fellow elder, a witness of Christ's sufferings and one who also will share in the glory to be revealed: Be shepherds of God's flock that is under your care, <u>serving as overseers</u>—not because you must, but <u>because you are willing</u>, as God wants you to be; <u>not greedy for money, but eager to serve; not lording it over those entrusted to you</u>, but being examples to the flock. And when the Chief Shepherd appears, you will receive the crown of glory that will never fade away." NIV

Wolves who command obedience and "lord" over people are not pleased with those they think are intruders or competition… they view them as a threat to their position.

Hey… we're on the same side and positioning was rebuked by Jesus! I've been attacked behind my back by very unlikely sources! Keep checking with the Holy Spirit for a "head's up" of any wolves in league against you, even if they are a distance away.

Xtreme Rabid Game in the Bible were exposed by those who operated in the spirit such as Moses, David, Elijah, Peter, Paul, Jude, and Jesus.

<u>NOTE: They were exposed, not ignored!</u>

By operating in the spirit, they knew who the wolves were! God exposes them the same way today!

If a person is not operating in the spirit, they are operating blind!

Jude tells us how to <u>prepare and defend</u> ourselves 7 ways from these "brute beasts" (Jude 10).

1. But you, beloved, building up yourselves on your most holy faith.
2. Praying in the Holy Ghost.
3. Keep yourselves in the love of God.
4. Looking for the mercy of our Lord Jesus Christ to eternal life.
5. And of some have compassion, making a difference.
6. And others save with fear, pulling them out of the fire.
7. Hating even the garment spotted by the flesh. Jude 20-23

Jude tells us that God can do two things.
Now to him that is able to keep you from falling.

1. And to present you faultless before the presence of his glory with exceeding joy. Jude 24

I know you Xtreme Big Game Hunters out there are saying, "Hey, what about offense"? How do we stop these deliberately evil people from attacking us and others, other than just preparing and defending or leaving them alone?

The children of Belial will continue to do their work, until exposed and dealt with <u>through</u> one who operates in the spirit!

David, Peter, and Paul dealt with these adversaries a certain <u>offensive</u> way. One of the secret weapons of spiritual offensive warfare that we can use against the children of Belial is… Imprecations!

Most of you are probably saying… "Impre-what?"

Not something you hear in Christian circles every day.

Actually, I've never heard it mentioned in a Church group.

David used the Imprecatory Psalms against the children of Belial! <u>God, through David, gave us an abundance of weapons</u>… "Psalm bombs" that we can drop against our <u>mutual</u> foe.

Thank You Lord!

"<u>All</u> scripture is given by inspiration of God, and is profitable for doctrine, for reproof, for correction, for instruction in righteousness: That the man of God may be perfect, <u>thoroughly</u> furnished unto all good works." 2 Timothy 3:16-17

God says that <u>all</u> of His Word is profitable to <u>thoroughly</u> equip us. No one should be cherry picking from it... leaving themselves equipment-deprived and exposed. Nor should anyone come against those using all of God's Word, as is His will!

One part of God's Word that I have never personally seen nor heard a Christian utilize, are the Imprecatory Psalms.

Many Christians may condemn the use of this segment of the Word, even though it is God's Word.

Satan and the children of Belial definitely do not want these Psalms being used against them and the evil realm...because they work!

Does for me anyway! I call them the "Psalm Bombs!"

"Seeing it is a <u>righteous</u> thing with God to recompense tribulation to them that trouble you." 2 Thessalonians 1:6

We can pray for evil people, that they will be turned from their ways, but should we allow them to continue to destroy until or if they ever turn?

Can <u>we</u> ask God to recompense tribulation?

Absolutely!

The Old Testament Levities issued curses, as set forth by God. Deuteronomy 27:14-26

Martin Luther said, "We should pray with the intent that our enemies be converted and become our friends, and if not, that their doing and designing be bound to fail and have no success and that their persons perish rather than the gospel and the Kingdom of Christ. Pray for our angry enemies, not that God protect and strengthen them in their ways, as we pray for Christians, or that He help them, but that they be converted, if they can be; or if they refuse, that God oppose them, stop them and end the game to their harm and misfortune."

Luther taught of a reformation of prayer.

When you go through these Psalms you will notice that you are asking God to act against children of Belial.

"Let their eyes be darkened, so that they do not see;
And make their loins shake continually.
[24] Pour out Your indignation upon them,
And let Your wrathful anger take hold of them.
[25] Let their dwelling place be desolate;
Let no one live in their tents.
[26] For they persecute the ones You have struck,
And talk of the grief of those You have wounded.
[27] Add iniquity to their iniquity,
And let them not come into Your righteousness.
[28] Let them be blotted out of the book of the living,
And not be written with the righteous." Psalm 69:23-28

As a child of God, you are able to request from your Father, as David did, that the physical varmints be stopped.

"And I will give you the keys of the kingdom of heaven, and whatever you bind on earth (using words) will be bound in heaven, and whatever you loose on earth (using words) will be loosed in heaven." Matthew 16:19; 18:18

When a person of authority in Christ on earth speaks certain words, especially God's Words, our heavenly Father's power is released!

"God, now step in and destroy your enemy. Use your power; <u>let your righteous wrath blaze forth</u>."

Dietrich Bonhoeffer

Bonhoeffer was executed by the Nazis—a government that refused to bow to Christ and was utterly destroyed.

Authorized agents of God (Holy Spirit-led Christians), can drop Psalm Bombs to release angels.

"Bless the Lord, you His angels, who excel in strength, who do His word, Heeding the voice of His word." Psalm 103:20

Try it… you'll like it!

My personal preference is dealing with them in the spirit, as led by God. This is by going in the spirit to confront and conquer the evil entities that are assisting and controlling Xtreme Rabid Game. You can start in prayer and worship and in bringing a situation to God that you want to deal with.

Although you may also come directly against the evil spirits manipulating Xtreme Rabid Game who are working in the spirit (satanists and witches travel in the spirit). I have done this many times, which has altered physical circumstances.

"One time I was in the spirit and could see a pentagram floating above me. I ended up in the past behind and over Jesus on the Cross. Jesus' head was hanging forward and there was blood all over Him. I grabbed the pentagram by one of its points and threw it onto the upper back of Jesus, where it stuck.

The pentagram disappeared as the blood from His head and neck dribbled down over it.

After that I was in front of this beast covered in black hair that was standing on its hind legs. It had a snout at the top of its head, nostrils up! (Never saw one of these at the zoo!) I swiped my sword through the top of it, cutting its snout off. Blood came bubbling up from the wound as he turned and ran away.

Next, I was in the midst of people in black robes who were holding candles. There were thirteen of them, and the few I could see under the hoods were women! There were also black dogs there. They didn't see me… (I like being in stealth mode!) I walked through them swinging my sword across their bodies.

I'm sure this was a surprise, although I don't know what happened to them.

The Holy Spirit told me that these people were coming directly against me.

Later I had the time to remember my moment at the Cross.

Thank you, Jesus!"

We can all do as Jude, Bonhoeffer and Luther recommends; use Psalm Bombs, receive revelation from God, and operate in the spirit.

I also speak in my spiritual language (tongue speech) which gets results!

Any who physically attack you can of course be dealt with physically to protect yourself, your family and others.

The children of Belial will continue their rebellion until the day that the son of perdition, the antichrist, comes. We can't stop this from happening, as it is Biblical prophecy. But we can work against them, to displace and disrupt the plans of the enemy and set as many POW's (prisoners of war) free!

"Let the high praises of God be in their mouth,
And a two-edged sword in their hand,
To execute vengeance on the nations,
And punishments on the peoples;
To bind their kings with chains,
And their nobles with fetters of iron;
To execute on them the written judgment—
This honor have all His saints." Psalm 149:6-9

Use your sword and accept the honor that God has given you… His saint!

"If anyone does not love the Lord… a curse be on him. Come O Lord!" 1 Corinthians 16:22 (NIV)

Imprecatory Psalms are Psalms 5, 6, 11,12, 35, 37, 40, 52, 54, 56, 58, 59, 69, 79, 109, 137, 139 and 143… given to us to pronounce against workers of iniquity.

Back to some wolf discussion… dealing with wolves can be tricky, as I've said, as usually a wolf has total power in the group and doesn't want to give it up.

When the others in the group are deceived, it will probably be impossible to get rid of the wolf on doctrine, but any evidence of sinful activity can be used to bring the wolf down. However, the effect of this procedure in a spiritually-dead, religious denomination is, that you will receive a wolf replacement!

Also, go in the spirit and destroy the evil spiritual entities manipulating this leader.

Finding a true shepherd or becoming one yourself in a group, is your best alternatives in this situation.

If you are a leader now, check yourself for your faults against what God expects of you in His Word. (No cherry-picking, compromising, altering or failing to follow the <u>entire</u> Word of God!) If you have failed the test, repent as David did and be restored to God and properly direct the flock <u>or face destruction!</u>

"But woe to you, scribes and Pharisees, hypocrites! For you shut up the kingdom of heaven against men; for you neither go in yourselves, nor do you allow those who are entering to go in." Matthew 23:13

Notice in the scripture above, false leadership and false teachings shuts off the sheep from heaven!

It is every person's responsibility to insure they are right with God! When standing at judgment in front of God one day, you <u>can</u> blame your life on the wolves, but that won't be an acceptable defense!

Many leaders start out as shepherds and because of greed, sin, pride, indifference, etc., they become a wolf!

For any Christians that are led to be leaders, be careful that you don't become a wolf of satan... "My brethren, let not many of you become teachers, knowing that <u>we shall receive a stricter judgment</u>. For we all stumble in many things." James 3:1-2

<u>This predator is a very destructive and dangerous physical enemy to your spiritual and physical life!</u>

<u>Be highly cautious and aware at all times! They are next to impossible to trap and remove from their environment!</u>

Oddly… sheep ("pretend sheep") have a greater tendency to remove a true shepherd from their midst; preferring a wolf that appeases them!

Hunting Tip: "Sheep have two speeds… graze and stampede"!

I have seen and heard of spirit-filled leaders who tried to properly lead sheep with truth, gifts of the spirit, rebuking when necessary, preaching "fire and brimstone", etc., who were fired for not "conforming" to what the sheep preferred.

I know a former leader who tried to bring in the Holy Spirit gifts to his spiritually dead denomination, only to be fired; cast out from this denomination by the "head wolves"; divorced by his wife and treated like an animal by his children and friends. This leader chose what was right in God's eyes!

These pretend sheep and head wolves will get their day in court!

Remember… the enemy isn't always out in front of you and doesn't always look like a wolf.

Always watch your back, there may be a loaded gun pointed at it!

After this study, perhaps you will be led to become a "wolf" hunter.

Replacing wolves with true shepherds would bring more sheep into the flock, producing the fruit God seeks!

CHRISTIAN WITCHCRAFT

Christian Witchcraft seems like an oxymoron (contradictory word pair) which doesn't seem possible, as how can Christians do witchcraft and still be considered Christian?

Are there any examples of Christian witchcraft in the Church today or in the Bible? The answer to both is a definite YES!

What does witchcraft mean?... "the art of sorcery; the practice of magic, especially black magic; the use of spells and the invocation of spirits."
Sorcery definition… "harness occult forces or evil spirits to produce unnatural effects in the world."

Briefly put, witchcraft is the release of evil forces that inflict evil. Evil obviously can be done innocently, deliberately and/or in ignorance.

Let's examine an instance of some Christian witchcraft from the Bible…

"A man named Simon had been a sorcerer there for many years, amazing the people of Samaria and claiming to be someone great. Everyone, from the least to the greatest, often spoke of him as "the Great One—the Power of God." They listened closely to him because for a long time he had astounded them with his magic.

But now the people believed Philip's message of Good News concerning the Kingdom of God and the name of Jesus Christ. As a result, many men and women were baptized. Then Simon himself believed and was baptized. He began following Philip wherever he went, and he was amazed by the signs and great miracles Philip performed.

When the apostles in Jerusalem heard that the people of Samaria had accepted God's message, they sent Peter and John there. As soon as they arrived, they prayed for these new believers to receive the Holy Spirit. The Holy Spirit had not yet come upon any of them, for they had only been baptized in the name of the Lord Jesus. Then Peter and John laid their hands upon these believers, and they received the Holy Spirit.

When Simon saw that the Spirit was given when the apostles laid their hands on people, he offered them money to buy this power. "Let me have this power, too," he exclaimed, "so that when I lay my hands on people, they will receive the Holy Spirit!"

But Peter replied, "May your money be destroyed with you for thinking God's gift can be bought! You can have no part in this, for your heart is not right with God. Repent of your wickedness and pray to the Lord. Perhaps he will forgive your evil thoughts, for I can see that you are full of bitter jealousy and are held captive by sin."

"Pray to the Lord for me," Simon exclaimed, "that these terrible things you've said won't happen to me!" Acts 8:9-24 NLT

Now some, perhaps most of you, are probably thinking I'm going to point to Simon as the evil example of Christian witchcraft in this example. Actually, it's Peter, the 1st disciple of Jesus, who is our case in point!

Simon was a very famous, powerful sorcerer (deliberate practiser of witchcraft) doing it for power, fame and financial gain. He became a Christian and a disciple of Philip (Jesus' 5th apostle/disciple) and was water baptised (v.13).

Peter (1st apostle) and John (4th apostle) go to Samaria to meet and pray for these new believers to receive the Holy Spirit (v. 14-17).

Three of Jesus' apostles are now here, with new Christians, a sorcerer converted, amazing signs and great miracles taking place (v.13), Holy Spirit... everything sounds great so far!

Then Simon makes a mistake. He thinks the Holy Spirit power is for sale and asks to buy it (v. 18-19). Remember that Simon is a former sorcerer, that came from a world where power was sold.

Rather than Peter taking this confused/ignorant/jealous/mistaken, new convert off to the side to correct him in how the ways of God works, to bring him to repentance, Peter curses him, his finances and his future to death!

"May your money be destroyed with you" (v. 20a) (Simon's life and finances are cursed by Peter) "You can have no part in this" (v. 21a) (Peter withholds the free gift of the Holy Spirit) "Perhaps he (God) will forgive your evil thoughts" (v. 22b) (Peter is saying perhaps God will forgive him.

What nonsense!

At this moment, standing in front of Peter, Simon is a baptised Christian, a saint, a royal priest, an heir with Jesus! God always forgives His children when they ask! And Simon did ask for help (v.24).

Obviously, Simon was terrified and asked Peter to pray for him, that these terrible curses wouldn't happen to him. There's no record that Peter, nor John, nor Philip ever helped Simon. They left Simon, this new convert, cursed!

"And if you curse someone, you are in danger of the fires of hell." Matthew 5:22c NLT

What was the result of these three apostles of God leaving this new convert cursed, without the Holy Spirit?

History of Simon taken from Wikipedia on the internet says that... Simon is "the source of all heresies... particularly St. Justin who wrote about Simon about one hundred years after his life. He is also mentioned in a great number of gnostic texts and was according to them one of the leaders of the early gnostics." (Gnosticism (briefly) is a religious combination of judaism, Christianity, Greco-Roman pagan religions, etc., teaching that knowledge brings a person to salvation.)

God doesn't bring evil upon people... satan does... "The thief's (satan's) purpose is to steal and kill and destroy. My (Jesus God, Father God) purpose is to give them a rich and satisfying life." John 10:10

So was Peter following the will of God, to give Simon a rich and satisfying life or was he commanding and authorizing the release of satan's hand into Simon's life? Fortunately, Jesus didn't treat Peter this way, during Peter's failings! Not every recorded event by the apostles, disciples, prophets and God's children in the Bible was done under God's will. Peter had power and authority over evil spirits (Luke 10:20) ... he misused this power, authority and position, to inject evil into Simon's life and ultimately to those that followed Simon's perverted teachings thereafter.

When Christians speak against others in fear, anger, jealousy, misguided prayer, self-righteousness, in spiritual pride, in revenge... they release evil, not good! This is Christian witchcraft! Many Christians and ministries have been destroyed this way!

There isn't enough space here to give testimony of all the Christians that have sent curses against me! Some thinking they were doing me a favor! Fortunately, God has given me the power and authority against evil sent against me and I break it... unfortunately, most Christians don't do spiritual warfare over their lives, therefore curses from others afflict them.

I've heard many stories of Christians being cursed by prophets, apostles, pastors, their wives and "church" members, such as when someone would dare decide to attend another "church/group" (their competition). This has happened to me and to Rhoda! Actually, it's quite common!

Sickness, financial burdens, family problems or early death, is not necessarily from sin or iniquity... it can be from curses and evil spirits sent against you... or from cursing yourself! I hear many people curse themselves!

If you have evil occurrences in your life or in the life of someone that you know and sin and iniquity isn't the answer, then speak (audibly) a rebuke and break all curses that have been sent against you (even from your own mouth) and speak (command) blessings daily over yourself and your life!

Keep this teaching in mind whenever you come across life's situations, to not act like Peter did on this occasion, but to operate under God's will, not yours or satan's, to speak "a rich and satisfying life" upon people, not destruction!

Pray for and teach those doing Christian witchcraft, to understand their mistake, for them to repent and hopefully make right the wrong (Simon could have used it) and especially not to repeat this practise! (Many will reject being corrected and curse you... so be prepared!)

Do spiritual warfare against Christian witchcraft done against leaders you know, your Church group, your ministry and for those you fellowship with!

REBUKING IN PUBLIC

The United States is well known for awarding their highest military recognition, the Medal of Honor, to those who display extreme courage and bravery... those who willingly risk their lives to save others. Ever done anything to deserve this?

Let's examine two Biblical Christians... one worthy of God's Medal of Honor... one displaying cowardice in battle!

In Galatians 2 we read of Paul's public confrontation of Peter for his hypocritical and sinful actions against the Gospel.

We learn many lessons from this confrontation and Biblical teaching.

1. Paul taught us that any Christian can rebuke false actions/teaching that is contrary to the Gospel, even if (and especially if) coming from Church leaders.

2. When false actions and false teaching are conducted in public, then the rebuke is to be conducted in public, rather than privately. (People that publicly heard or saw the wrong actions/teaching need to hear that what they saw/heard was false. The truth needs to be revealed to them).

3. Galatians informs us that Paul operated his ministry independent (no "covering") of the apostles Peter, James, John, etc. that were in Jerusalem. He only briefly met with them twice in 17 years (1:18-19, 2:2, 9). He never sought their approval, but only to work in harmony with them.

4. Peter initially acted correctly, but when jews from James came, he became a coward, which led to the corruption of the people in Antioch, including Barnabas himself (2:13)! (Peter's position in the Church, caused people to accept and follow what he was doing… even a lie!)

Peter had backslidden and became a fearful coward and a "people-pleaser". His actions were distorting the Gospel's truth, as Paul points out during his public rebuke of Peter. Peter's actions were not only leading people astray but his actions also cursed him, as we read in Galatians 1:8, "As we have said before, so now I say again, if anyone preaches any other gospel to you than what you have received, let him be accursed."

So as Christians, worthy of the Life and Blood that Jesus spent for us and the Gospel given to us that we're commanded to spread to others, we want to adopt this teaching into our lives and into the lives of those we come in contact with… through our actions and our words.

We want to at all times (especially publicly), crush anti-Gospel lies and hold the flag of courage high and in front of us like Paul did!

Every Christian is authorized and taught to publicly rebuke anti-Gospel public actions/teaching like Paul did!

So, in this Biblical teaching, how do we act like Paul (a courageous Christian) instead of like Peter (a cowardly Christian), when the opportunity or battle is in front of us?

How do we avoid being part of perverting the Gospel, thus ceasing to be a servant of Christ and how do we avoid being cursed (Galatians 1:6-10)?

How do we win God's eternal Medal of Honor?

I can pick many examples but here's a headline that we can use to assist our study… "A group of Omaha (Nebraska, USA) pastors has issued a proclamation that states homosexuality is not a sin. More than 100 ordained Christian ministers have signed the proclamation, including leaders from Lutheran, Episcopalian, United Church of Christ, United Methodist, and Presbyterian churches" (Quoted from July 23, 2011 Prophecy News Watch headlines).

These 100+ pastors and any that follow them, have ceased being servants of Christ and are cursed (Galatians 1:6-10). They are corrupting other leaders and Christians by teaching a false Gospel that many, even non-Christians, will accept as true. People in Omaha should publicly rebuke them, certainly leave their "churches" and question why all 5 of these major denominations have not fired these leaders from their positions and stripped them of their ordinations! If one was a member of one of these 5 denominations, one should sever all ties and break all verbal and written covenants/oaths/memberships/fellowship with them, in order to be set free from openings to demonic spirits, especially religious and sexual spirits. Any people that continue to accept or attend these corrupt fellowships, have by their actions (such as with Peter' actions) shown that they accept an anti-Gospel doctrine and have cursed themselves!

We must each examine our lives to distance ourselves from all leaders, denominations, people and personal actions that are anti-Gospel. We cannot be seen by others and especially by God, to be accepting of anything in our lives that is anti-Gospel/antichrist. (Old saying: Actions speak loader than words!)

Then we must boldly, gallantly and publicly step forward, when we see or hear any anti-Gospel/antichrist actions.

If someone sins in a non-public way, hidden or in private... "If your brother or sister sins, go and point out their fault, just between the two of you. If they listen to you, you have won them over. But if they will not listen, take one or two others along, so that 'every matter may be established by the testimony of two or three witnesses.' If they still refuse to listen, tell it to the church; and if they refuse to listen even to the church, treat them as you would a pagan or a tax collector." Matthew 18:15-17

If the Church leadership/body refuses to follow the Gospel (refuses to deal with unrepentant sinners), then by their actions, as with Peter's actions, they are to be publicly rebuked, as it's become a public matter.

Sin or anti-Gospel/antichrist doctrine that is done, said, and accepted or compromised with in public by leaders, must be dealt with in public, for the reasons that we just learned in Galatians 2 and this study.

Some other examples of public actions/teachings that we must publicly confront for Christ, the Gospel and to protect others are:

- Let it be known by our words and actions that we do not accept through compromise nor indifference, those who are antichrist (anti-Jesus) as the only Savior or anti-Bible (i.e. atheism, b'hai, buddhism, freemasonry, hinduism, humanism, islamism, jehovah's witness, judaism, mormonism, new age).

- We do not yoke ourselves in business, in marriage, in friendship nor in fellowship, with any who are anti-Jesus as the only Savior or any who teach a doctrine that is anti-Gospel/antichrist. This includes anti-Christian governments such as atheist, buddhist, communist, islamic or hindu-controlled countries.

- We look to Biblical Gospel in how we deal with those that sin in private and those who sin in public (Matthew 18:15-17, Galatians 2).

- We differentiate between those acceptable practices and teachings that are extra-Biblical as opposed to those that are unacceptable/unbiblical… (i.e. Sunday Schools or teaching via the internet are extra-Biblical or not mentioned in the Bible, but they're not unbiblical or contrary to what is taught in the Bible).

- That some Christians are not more acceptable/more favored by God (Romans 2:11) (Like Peter acted with Jewish-Christians vs. Gentile-Christians).

- We rebuke organizations, denominations, ministries, leaders and people proclaiming to be Christian that compromise with or accept sexual sin (homosexuality, adultery, fornication); occult practices and false religions (buddhism, islam, hindu, native cults, pseudo - Christian, etc.).

- We publicly rebuke all false, unbiblical and anti-Gospel/antichrist doctrines, actions and teachings coming through the religious church, when they present themselves (i.e. forgiveness through works/a priest; salvation through water baptism; salvation for being good or only through a specific denomination; worshipping or bowing to a communion wafer/Jesus' mother/dead saints; Holy Spirit baptism automatically received at confirmation; Jesus' mother's omniscience/immaculate conception/co-redemptrix position or her equality with the Triune God; that one person/pope holds the keys to life and death; that the communion wafer is God-incarnate; existence of purgatory; any display/reverence/devotion or worship of statues/idols/icons/"sacred objects" of the dead; "once saved, always saved" doctrine; any rejection of the Holy Spirit's gifts and demonstrations of His power; replacing the positions of Christians as saints, royal priests and rulers, with popes, cardinals, man-made priests, monks, nuns; that Church leadership can only be acceptable or come through a council/seminary/college/organization; that everyone eventually gets to heaven (universalism); that only "special" Christians are saints; that satan is chained now and/or is not a threat to Christians; that Christians can't have evil spirits in them; that there are no evil spiritual principalities/evil powers that we war against; made-up religious "holidays" that are paganist in tradition, activities and in root (lent/good friday/easter/christmas)… and any and all false, unbiblical and/or anti-Gospel/antichrist doctrines.

We are here to worship and be obedient to the Triune God... not religion; not people; not ourselves. Any acts or words contrary to this must be dealt with or why bother "playing Christian", as it will catch up to us during our judgement (Hebrews 9:27, Revelation 20: 12-13).

Be courageous for Christ!

CAN CHRISTIANS KILL?

I receive regular updates from around the world, in addition to the regular news services online, that usually ignore this news, that tell me of the Christians in many countries who are being brutalized and murdered, just because they're Christian. One of the things that always amazes me, is that I very rarely hear about Christians physically fighting back to protect themselves and their families. I understand this thinking, as I was raised in a religious "church" and we were always taught to "turn the other cheek" and "love your enemies", so we all took that doctrine to mean, that we put up with anything that's dished out to us, even if we're in the process of being murdered! But is this doctrine really what God means and wants for His children?

Should we all just sit back and do nothing, other than allow the police and military to do any "dirty work", that we can't or won't do?

Are Christian soldiers and police sinning when they must kill others to protect themselves and society?

Can a person be both a Christian and soldier or a law enforcement officer?

What is Biblical truth about this controversial issue?

The 6th commandment in Exodus 20, was mistranslated and taken out of context (satan's hand in this "mistake" is evident). The correct translation says, "You shall not murder". It refers to killing for your own personal gain; it has nothing to do with killing under lawful authority.

God says in Acts 13:22, that King David was "a man after My own heart", yet David was a man of war that the Bible says, "killed his tens of thousands" (1 Samuel 18:7). It was only when David arranged one man's murder (Uriah) in order to get his wife, did he get in trouble with God. That's one man, out of the tens of thousands he killed or had killed in war by others.

The Old Testament is full of such righteous warrior leaders of God. Moses, Joshua and Gideon are just a few of the hundreds of warriors, who found favor in God's eyes for their labors on the battlefield. God says in Proverbs 6:17, that "He hates shedders of innocent blood", but there's nothing but honor in the Bible for the soldier who kills in just combat against evil. Killing in war, under righteous (God's righteousness, not mans), lawful authority, is presented as honorable and acceptable throughout the Bible.

In the New Testament, the story is the same.

Jesus praised the Roman Centurion in Matthew 8:10 for his great faith. There's never a mention from Jesus that this man is a sinner or that he should stop being a soldier.

And in Acts 10, the 1st non-jewish Christian was designated by God, Cornelius... a Roman Centurion. Peter was shocked when God sent him to convert him, but it was because he was a non-jew. No one ever questioned that a soldier should have the honor of being the first non-jewish Christian.

Most of Acts 10 is devoted to Peter's sermon to the centurion Cornelius and his guidance as to how to be a Christian, but never once does Peter or anyone else anywhere in the Bible state, that it is incompatible to be a soldier and a Christian... the exact opposite is communicated over and over again.

Examining Luke 22:36, just minutes before His arrest and subsequent crucifixion, Jesus <u>commanded</u> his disciples..."He said to them, "But now if you have a purse, take it, and also a bag; and if you don't have a sword, sell your cloak and buy one". Jesus is saying a sword is more important to have with you than your coat! These men weren't soldiers, but Christian leaders Jesus was talking to… swords were used to protect them, their families, and each other, when physically attacked by lawless robbers and murderers.

A further proof of this command of carrying a weapon and using it when attacked, is when soldiers came to arrest Jesus, we see Peter drawing and using his sword. This proves that Peter carried a sword with Jesus' knowledge and had no hesitation in using it.

Next, we read what seems like a contradiction to Jesus' command, when he tells Peter to put the sword away saying, "He that lives by the sword shall die by the sword"(Matthew 26:52), meaning, that if the sword is your personal law (same as Exodus 20 meaning), you should die by the sword. Jesus said this, because the soldiers arresting him were operating under the law, which is different than those operating outside the law (i.e. murderers, criminals, terrorists).

God is crystal clear throughout His Word on this subject.

Law enforcement officers and soldiers are not sinning when confronted with the lethal realities of their position. Any sense of guilt, conviction or shame for doing what needs to be done, is brought to them by the evil kingdom and false doctrines, not by God.

We also learn from God's Word, that civilians are immune from sin and guilt when operating in lawful, self defense. Society's laws also allow for self defense. Not revenge, but self defense.

We can hope the police and military will prevent assaults from happening against us and the innocent, but facts are, that they can't be everywhere. Usually the police can do nothing until after the crime (assault/murder) is done and in many muslim countries, the authorities do nothing to interfere with or stop violence against Christians, most times under muslim government authority.

Besides criminal acts, there are war atrocities, terrorist acts, religious hatred, Christian hatred, mob violence, home invasions and random violence, that civilians can be suddenly confronted with, that will kill them, their family and others if they decide to do nothing.

I realize that killing can be a subject that people don't want to think about or talk about, but as I write in this book, over 45 million Christians were murdered in the 20th century just because they were Christian. That's an average of 1233 Christians a day every day for 100 years! This is an atrocity that we see is only escalating.

Prophecy News Watch November 2, 2012 Statistic: "About 200 million church members (10% of the global total) face discrimination or persecution"! (This percentage is certainly much higher now).

Don't become one of these statistics!

God doesn't ask His children to lie down under the wheels of evil that are killing them! Its satan's doctrine that wants Christians dead.

Everyone has the right to physically protect themselves, their families and other innocents when physically assaulted and attacked by others (i.e. terrorists, thieves, rapists, predators, etc.) even if you have to kill them to get them to stop. We must remember, that they are the ones that are living by the sword with their lawless actions and thus solely responsible for what comes to them, when you're defending yourself. Thus, their decision fulfills Jesus' declaration, that they "shall die by the sword".

It's time for Christians to take Jesus' advice and sell their cloak and buy a sword if they don't have one... and use it when the situation warrants it! Nowadays carrying a sword isn't practical or even lawful, but in keeping with Jesus' meaning, we are to be ready if attacked to give "the sword" or destruction to attacker(s). How you go about this wherever you are is your decision, whether you're allowed to have firearms or can only carry improvised weapons or to become self-proficient in unarmed combat.

Praying and hoping nothing happens to you or allowing violence happen to you, is not what Jesus said to do in Luke 22:36.

God's people in the Bible were many times protected from physical attack, however, they were also still expected to conduct physical battle.

As Christians, our goals are to be obedient to God; look to the Great Commission to reach others for Christ; set captives free and advance the kingdom of God... these aren't our only functions, as we must operate in a physical realm that is behind enemy lines, full of evil that uses any means available to destroy us, including evil people.

God doesn't expect us to tolerate physical attacks from people, any more than He expects us to tolerate spiritual attacks from evil spirits, unless He advises to do something different for a particular situation. There have been times when I was in the spirit when I wanted to destroy certain evil entities, yet God advised me not to or I was held back... this is His will and we obey! We may not understand, but we must obey, as He knows better than we!

"Be sober, be vigilant; because your adversary the devil walks about like a roaring lion, seeking whom he may devour" 1 Peter 5:8. He devours physically and spiritually!

"... he (satan) was a murderer from the beginning..."   John 8:44.

Evil spirits work through people, driving them to murder others! A great deception of satan is embraced and taught by many "church" doctrines, that Christians must do nothing and withstand being physically attacked and murdered, even when evil comes against women and children!

Don't allow the enemy to destroy you spiritually <u>or physically.</u>

It isn't practical, wise or Biblical!

Train hard... be prepared!

We must know how to <u>specifically</u> deal with physical evil, as well as evil spiritual game.

Hunting Xtreme Big, Small and Rabid Game is very challenging!

God will lead you, sustain you and equip you on your expeditions.

Don't ever consider hunting without Father, Jesus and the Holy Spirit!

ZONE 5

GUIDED HUNTS

SECTOR TWENTY

HUNTING 4 HEALING

> **HUNTING TIP**
>
> Hunt with the Holy Spirit… He's the best guide!

When I go into the bush hunting, I have hope that I will be successful in taking home whatever game I'm going after. There are steps that I can take to increase my odds of success. The success is up to me really, as I have to pick the right spot, at the right time, using bait, the right equipment, using camouflage and a tree stand, calling game to me, being quiet, still and patient and aim steady when the time comes. There are many facets of hunting that have to be utilized, with each one increasing the level of success.

There are also free hunting gifts, such as when the police would call me up in the middle of the night, to come and get a deer that was hit on the highway. I don't have to do anything for that!

When going out Hunting 4 Healing, the hope is certainly still there, but sadly, the odds have shown to be against the hunter at being successful. Many facets available to the hunter are not being utilized by them, nor by the hunting guides (leaders) that they're relying on for success.

Let's take a look at why Hunting 4 Healing has been at zero for most people and how to increase your success rate up to let's say… 100%!

The evil kingdom looks to steal, kill and destroy your physical, mental and spiritual health. They are very successful at this activity, as most people, including Christians, experience disease, crippled bodies, mental illnesses, pain and early death in their lives. Healing techniques and processes have been written about in hundreds of books, most of which are new age in approach or have gaping holes (the Christian ones). Almost everyone relies on the medical community for the answer to their health problems. The "church" has been sorely lacking in any kind of healing success, with very few meeting the people's needs, so people are left with little choice but to go to doctors. People try prayer, but receive frustration instead of healing and so give up on God and are back to doctors.

So, let's have some hunting guide experts show us what works and what are the long shot hit and miss approaches.

A Hunting Guide's Testimony

When my Mom, Lynn Collins, turned 50, she asked God, "Is this all there is"? She had a husband and son, a home near the lake, a stable office job and her health. She also was a volunteer officer at the lutheran church she attended. She had volunteered in one way or the other at a denominational church group, since she was a teenager. Yet her spirit knew something was missing.

God answered her question, by showing her a miracle at a prayer group one night, when a shortened leg grew out on a woman. This was something she had never seen nor heard about before (this happened in the early 1970's). She gave an enthusiastic testimony of this miracle to some women from her "church", who were just as wide-eyed at hearing about such a thing. They asked her to demonstrate how it happened. Each sat in a chair and put their feet up to see if one leg was shorter than the other. One lady had a leg that was much shorter than the other and so my Mom knelt down next to her, held up her legs, told everyone to watch, while she started praising and giving thanks to the Lord for making both legs the same length. Then the shorter leg started growing out, went past the other leg and then came back to align up together!

This was the start for her, of miracles, signs and wonders, healing, deliverance, high level spiritual warfare and raising the dead, that spanned 35 years! She had no formal, higher education (i.e. Bible College or seminary) and no "covering". She had to do "her thing" out on the street, as the "church" didn't embrace what she was doing, even though she tried for decades with them. God would bring people to her at work, in restaurants, at stores, in parking lots and on the phone. She started making regular rounds to retirement homes and hospitals where even people on their death beds were instantly healed and went home! There were times that she travelled great distances to help people.

People received healing from prayer cloths that she gave away or mailed. One baby was totally healed from a prayer cloth my Mom had mailed to his parents, who were both doctors and unable to help their own child.

"Now God worked unusual miracles by the hands of Paul, so that even handkerchiefs or aprons were brought from his body to the sick, and the diseases left them and the evil spirits went out of them." Acts 19: 11-12

Several people were raised from death. One was covered up and on his way to the morgue. Both paramedics were shocked when their declared dead patient, instantly sat up when my Mom laid her hand on his hand and commanded him to rise.

She also came directly against witches and did high level warfare (Xtreme Big Game Hunting) in forest areas where satanists and witches were operating. She came against evil spirits in physical objects and in houses. They all left. Keep in mind, this was when such things were unheard of.

She stopped and reversed the clouds and rain on command (freaked people out that were watching); snow storms bypassed just her house; had an infestation of insects in a friend's house all instantly form up in lines and leave; broken down cars suddenly start up on command… the list goes on.

Her small vial of anointing oil that she used on people for their freedom from bondage, never went empty… in 35 years!

She taught others in study groups, at speaking engagements and one-on-one.

Oh, and she did all of this without charge, without a diploma, without a title, without a "church". Her mentor and provider was God.

So, what were her secrets? How did she do all of this? How do others do the same? Was she doing what Jesus did? How can every Christian do the same as Jesus did and even greater?

"Most assuredly, I say to you, he who believes in Me, the works that I do he will do also; and greater works than these he will do, because I go to My Father." John 14: 12

What can we do?

My Mom was very compassionate and patient. She had a heart for people that were sick and in pain. She also was totally submitted and obedient to God, truly loving Him with all her heart. I never heard her murmur, complain or back-stab or slander anyone. She had a calm nature, was always joyful and loved talking about Jesus. She really had no interest in talking about anything else. She would admit to everyone that she could never heal anyone… she had faith. She never took any glory or thanks, as these belonged to God.

These attributes can certainly assist us in our path with God.

"Behold, to obey is better than sacrifice." 1 Samuel 15: 22

"But without faith it is impossible to please Him." Hebrews 11:6

"So, he (Jesus) answered and said, '"You shall love the Lord your God with all your heart, with all your soul, with all your strength, and with all your mind,' and 'your neighbor as yourself." Matthew 22:37; Mark 12:30-31; Luke 10:27

So, this position she had with God (after being a religious Christian for 50 years) had nothing to do with formal education, diplomas, titles, "church" attendance, works, mentors, "church" acceptance, or being under some leader's "covering" (or religious authorization). One pastor told her one time, that she should go to seminary to get a degree. My Mom said, "Why? I don't need it and I can accomplish much more with God without being confined under the rules of a "church" council and a governing bishop, telling me what I can and can't do".

She lectured at many different denominations in Canada and the USA, that would accept her.

So, let's see what others are doing and talk about their success or lack thereof.

MIRACLE CRUSADES

My Mom went to many Crusades, most notably run by Kathryn Kuhlman and Benny Hinn. She arranged for one Kuhlman crusade to be held in Niagara Falls, New York.

A usual Crusade can see people, mostly crippled and diseased seniors, pile up onto busses, to take the long trips to these events, wait in long lines, in hopes of being healed. People also receive gold teeth, find diamonds on the floor, hair grows on bald heads, and of course many are healed… most are not.

So why not?

Many blame it on the injured being unworthy… having a lack of faith or they're being a sinner or not being Christian or it's God's will for them to be and stay diseased.

Such absolute nonsense doctrines like this are keeping people in bondage and make them feel guilty!

"Then great multitudes came to Him (Jesus), having with them the lame, blind, mute, maimed, and many others; and they laid them down at Jesus' feet, and He healed them." Matthew 15: 30

"Beloved, I pray that you may prosper in all things and be in health, just as your soul prospers." 3 John 2

Everyone was healed at a Jesus Crusade. And none of them were Christians! So, the problem isn't with God and it isn't with diseased people. So, what's left?

AWAKENINGS/REVIVALS

There are times when miracles, signs, wonders, healing and a "move" of the Holy Spirit "breaks out" unexpectedly during meetings such as the Toronto Blessing, that can last for years. Leaders will come from all over the world to "catch" something to take it home.

Many receive healing… most again do not.

CONFERENCES

Leaders that hold healing or "glory zone" or whatever catch phrase conferences, tell some testimonies of past healing, get some spiritual insight or knowledge such as, "someone is being healed right now of leg pain". Then they ask this person to come up and tell what happened. Sometimes at conferences they'll have people line up in a pile or shoot you through a "fire tunnel" to get "something" (i.e. healing, anointing, impartation, etc.).

Again, most go home receiving nothing or can (and do) leave with picking up evil spirits that have transferred between people.

HEALING ROOMS

There are "healing rooms", following the model of John G. Lake, that have sprung up all over the world. Diseased people come in, fill out forms, sit with councilors, get prayed over and some get healed… most do not. Rhoda just talked at length to a leader in the USA from an internationally recognized, Christian healing center. The leader was disinterested in spiritual warfare and said they didn't recommend self-deliverance. This leader didn't want to look to the Holy Spirit for guidance, when asked. Instead, the counsellor went to a pre-scripted outline. They charge $99./hr., to counsel you and pray for you on Skype. Rhoda rebuked them for charging people, telling them that Jesus never charged people for healing.

The "healing room" near our location, mocked us for doing deliverance and spiritual warfare to help people.

And yet another one, insisted that we had to be under this one "pastor's covering", if we were to be part of the group. We passed.

RELIGIOUS "CHURCH"

"Is anyone among you sick? Let him call for the elders of the church, and let them pray over him, anointing him with oil in the name of the Lord. And the prayer of faith will save the sick, and the Lord will raise him up. And if he has committed sins, he will be forgiven." James 5: 14-15

Most "churches" provide no relief to the congregation when it comes to healing. The "church" I grew up in, preached that healing and other movements of God, ended with the death of the last disciple. These are called "cessationist's".

The "churches" that do hold some sort of healing process, typically have people come up to the front, while others lay hands on them. Variation of this in larger groups is, that a leader will ask people to stand that need healing and then he asks others near them, to go over and lay hands on them, while the leader speaks some kind of healing pronouncement.

One mainstream pentecostal denomination that I had an extremely brief experience with, didn't allow men to lay hands on women for healing nor women on men. Also, it had to be a group "laying on of hands" in front of the entire congregation. They wouldn't allow my Mom to lay hands on anyone by herself. They told her it was because they were protecting her from pride, when she asked, "Why". Neither of us ever saw or heard of anyone ever healed at this place. The leadership also wouldn't allow me to do spiritual warfare. They preferred that we join the choir. We both left.

The religious "church" usually experiences less than a 5% success rate in healing efforts that are tried. Most don't try.

Again, same as with conferences, most go home receiving nothing or can (and do) leave with picking up evil spirits that have transferred between people.

I left one conference with thoughts of murder and suicide plaguing me. The thoughts went back and forth. I immediately recognized that I'd picked up an evil spirit transference from someone at the conference. Which is unusual for me, as usually evil spirits want to stay away from me, because they know what I will do to them. I saw this thing in the spirit and quickly dealt with it. The thoughts immediately ended. It's in a spiritual prison somewhere now. Such an experience can explain why you read in the news of someone going on a killing rampage and then commit suicide or if they live, tell the police that these thoughts kept telling them to kill. Their friends would be interviewed and say, that they were shocked, because the person was so nice. Evil spirits change a person.

Also, many receiving a healing at these places report the symptoms/pain came back to them when they got home. Leaders tell them that they are to reject "the devils'" thoughts that you weren't healed. They tell people to "overlook" the pain and symptoms and to accept their healing.

After people do receive healing, at a crusade, conference, "healing room" or "church" they need to be counselled to repent of their sins and to stop living in disobedience (give them a list if you haven't the time), otherwise the evil roots are still there, more roots can be planted and evil fruits and evil spirits will manifest down the road. A proper job isn't done, if they continue to live in sin.

MISSIONARIES

There are missionaries all over the world. What is it that they are supposed to be doing?

"Then Jesus went about all the cities and villages, teaching in their synagogues, preaching the gospel of the kingdom, and healing every sickness and every disease among the people." Matthew 9:35

"Go therefore and make disciples of all the nations, baptizing them in the name of the Father and of the Son and of the Holy Spirit, teaching them to observe all things that I (Jesus) have commanded you" Matthew 28: 19-20. Are missionaries doing all things Jesus commanded them? This would include demonstrations of God's power, to back up preaching the Gospel.

"And my speech and my preaching were not with persuasive words of human wisdom, but in demonstration of the Spirit and of power, that your faith should not be in the wisdom of men but in the power of God." 1 Corinthians 2: 4-5

ONE-ON-ONE

Most "churches" and ministry leaders are against members of the congregation going out on their own to provide healing to another. I've attended conferences where the leadership has told the attendees <u>not</u> to practice any of their gifts from God while there! Only "accepted" leaders were allowed. This has happened in "churches" I've gone to as well. Many leaders forbid anyone from doing anything unless you're under their "covering".

"Now John answered and said, "Master, we saw someone casting out demons in Your name, and we forbade him because he does not follow with us." But Jesus said to him, "Do not forbid him, for he who is not against us is on our side." Luke 9:49-50

As we can see leaders, Jesus <u>commanded</u> us <u>not</u> to forbid people that is on Jesus' side. Forbidding the movement of God is a man-made doctrine that inhibits God. Such processes aim to protect a leader's position, power, control and/or financial flow.

There are many leaders that do go to the hospitals, nursing and retirement homes and make home visits to the sick. Unfortunately, these visits are more hand holding and verbal comforting, rather than going to specifically obtain a healing for someone that God has put them in charge of!

Fortunately, such giants in the healing arena who operated independently, like Maria Woodworth-Etter and Smith Wigglesworth… and my Mom, didn't wait for a "covering" or listen to those who came against them! They let God be in charge!

Smith Wigglesworth started working at the age of 6! He couldn't read or write until his wife taught him to read the Bible. It was the only thing he ever read in his life! He had no education, no degree, no titles, and no "church". He travelled around the world, with miracles, signs, wonders, healing, deliverance and raising the dead left behind him.

Maria Woodworth-Etter was a farm wife and mother with little education, no degrees, and no titles. She started spiritually explosive Church groups! She travelled all over the USA, setting up tents, where countless people, many on death beds were set free! She was constantly attacked by religious and medical leaders, including being taken to court many times, for healing people without a license. Religions and the world don't like those who rely on God, instead of man.

Pain

Many times, there is pain associated with disease. There are also times when people have no disease but have pain from injuries, muscle tears pulls and strains, sore joints, broken bones, cuts, sunburns, carpal tunnel syndrome, and head, tooth and ear aches, etc. Pain is very debilitating.

People spend billions on doctors and medications to relieve pain. There is loss of work productivity to the economy, when workers slow down or take time off because of pain. Chronic pain can alter a person's entire life.

My Mom used to come across people with arm slings on or moving on crutches in grocery check-out lines. She would start to talk to the person saying, "That looks painful". The person would then proceed to tell her what happened and how much pain they were in. My Mom would ask them if they'd like the pain to go away. Of course, they said, "Yes". My Mom would then look at the check-out lady and everybody in the line and say, "Would you all like to see a miracle"?

Cash register has now stopped. With all eyes riveted on her now, she would place her hand on the injured arm or leg and command the pain to go in Jesus' name and everything to go back into its proper place. The person would look stunned and say, "The pain's gone"! They'd start moving their arm or leg around, still stunned, with an equally stunned audience and say it again, "The pain's all gone"! My Mom would say, "Praise Jesus, give Him all the thanks". And then she'd pay for her groceries, leaving a stunned crowd behind her!

This happened to her weekly for decades!

What my Mom used to do was get their permission, ask what they wanted and then touch the area that was in pain with her hand. If it was a sensitive area, she would have the person put their hand on the spot and then my Mom would gently touch their hand.

She would speak directly to the pain. She would command all pain to stop in Jesus' name. She would command all muscles and cartilage and joints to go back into their proper order and place. She would ask the person how they feel. If pain was still there she'd keep going until it was gone. The person could feel heat in the area. My Mom said, that when she could feel the heat, she knew the Holy Spirit was working and it was done. She would have the person do something they couldn't do before such as touch their toes or move their formerly strained neck, to confirm to themselves it was done. My Mom would then praise and thank Jesus and tell the person that Jesus was the Healer, not her.

She was at a prayer group one time where eight ladies all had knee pain. She did the process listed here on each one. The pain left on each one!

Worked every time. At work, at restaurants, in stores, in parking lots and on the phone. She volunteered at TCT (Total Christian Television) for 13 years where over 10,000 testified to having received instant healing and loss of pain over the phone with her!

Evil spirits also cause pain. Once they are cast out, pain ceases.

Consult with the Holy Spirit for direction, as He may advise something else in a particular case.

PEOPLE LEFT DISEASED, CRIPPLED, IN PAIN AND AFFLICTED WITH EVIL SPIRITS

So why isn't everyone healed and relieved of pain at crusades, conferences, "churches", "healing rooms", revivals and by missionaries, pastors, elders and leaders?

Remember what I said earlier about how to increase your chances for success in hunting, by adding in more things to assist you? The same with Hunting 4 Healing.

A hunter may be successful within the first 5 minutes of a hunt, with doing very little preparation. It's happened to me. Then also, you can try everything and nothing comes your way. However, the hunter doesn't give up on day 1 or on day 12. The hunter adjusts, adapts, moves and keeps trying, as the hunter knows the day will come for success. It must.

Many Christian leaders never try anything at all regarding healing, beyond praying for people. Healing centers and leaders that do try, even though many are sincere, won't adjust, adapt and keep trying until they succeed with everyone. Trapped in some doctrinal rut, trying one thing that they're comfortable with or that they've been taught, achieving maybe some success for some and the rest go away lacking.

It's understandable when leaders over large crusades and conferences don't have time to personally work with each person, but they should give people a list of things that they can do, when most leave empty-handed. Wouldn't this be preferable and more productive to the suffering, than another 20-minute speech about giving offerings?

Sadly, some are wolves… more interested in entertaining and what pours into the offering baskets, as it's a job for them, moving from one conference to the next! Discussed also in the Rabid Game Sector.

What does God say to shepherds like this?

"Son of man, prophesy against the shepherds of Israel, prophesy and say to them, 'Thus says the Lord God to the shepherds: "Woe to the shepherds of Israel who feed themselves! Should not the shepherds feed the flocks?[3] You eat the fat and clothe yourselves with the wool; you slaughter the fatlings, but you do not feed the flock. [4] <u>The weak you have not strengthened, nor have you healed those who were sick</u>, nor bound up the broken, nor brought back what was driven away, nor sought what was lost; but with force and cruelty you have ruled them. [5] So they were scattered because there was no shepherd; and they became food for all the beasts of the field when they were scattered. [6] My sheep wandered through all the mountains, and on every high hill; yes, My flock was scattered over the whole face of the earth, and no one was seeking or searching for them."

[7] 'Therefore, you shepherds, hear the word of the Lord: [8] "As I live," says the Lord God, "surely because My flock became a prey, and My flock became food for every beast of the field, because there was no shepherd, nor did My shepherds search for My flock, but the shepherds fed themselves and did not feed My flock"— [9] therefore, O shepherds, hear the word of the Lord! [10] Thus says the Lord God: "Behold, I am against the shepherds, and I will require My flock at their hand; I will cause them to cease feeding the sheep, and the shepherds shall feed

themselves no more; for I will deliver My flock from their mouths, that they may no longer be food for them." Ezekiel 34:2-10

Shepherds are required to heal the sick, among many other things.

God says there are shepherds that don't feed the flock (equip them spiritually); that rule the flock with force and cruelty (control, under their "covering"); who eat and clothe themselves (obtain wealth from merchandising, tithes, offerings) from sheep and slaughter (take from) the fatlings (rich); people are deliberately driven away or left because the shepherd wasn't appropriate (cruel, immoral, money-hungry, not healing the sick); these shepherds scatter and don't recover the lost, allowing them to become food for the beasts of the field (wander the world for relief; fall prey to false religions, wander away from God and lose their salvation).

What does God do to these irresponsible shepherds?

God is against them (not a good position); He will cause them to cease being a shepherd and take away their income from the sheep.

Here's a few statistics reported by the New York Times (August 1, 2010), to back up God's promise to false shepherds:

"Members of the clergy now suffer from obesity, hypertension and depression at rates higher than most Americans. In the last decade, their use of antidepressants has risen, while their life expectancy has fallen. Many would change jobs if they could."

- 75% of leaders report severe stress causing anguish, worry, bewilderment, anger, depression, fear, and alienation.
- 80% of seminary and Bible school graduates will leave the ministry within five years.
- 1,500 pastors leave their ministries <u>each month</u>, in the USA, due to burnout, conflict, or moral failure.

I could list about 20 more just as terrible statistics.

God keeps His promises. Don't be one of these statistics. If you're a leader, operate in your spiritual senses, with the Holy Spirit leading you and be responsible for any flock that comes to you, including for healing... all of them.

My main mentor went to numerous crusades, revivals, conferences, meetings, and "churches", where leaders hurried out the door. Every time. Many have body guards to keep people away from them! My mentor wasn't a "recognized" or "authorized" event leader, but she stayed behind for hours to work with, pray for and lay hands on people in the crowd that were left empty-handed. Many received their healing. Sometimes she was there through the night and into early the next day. If there were people there in need, she stayed. If they were kicked out of the building, she worked with people in the dark parking lots.

What would Jesus do?

That was my Mom. I learned under a high standard.

STOP IT!

If you're one of the sheep that is participating in any of these spiritually lacking or dead activities (i.e. attending and financially supporting denominations, crusades, conferences, "churches", ministries) that leaves you and others hanging and in need, the question that begs is, "Why"? Why participate in dead works, and poor ministries, that don't or won't bring positive spiritual results for you and others?

Find a leader and people to walk with, that do what God expects of them.

HUNTING 4 HEALING LIST

Before I head out moose hunting up north in Canada, I get out my list I made up years ago, to make sure that I take everything that's on it. Leaving something behind can contribute to a lack of success, especially if it's ammo!

So, in this case, you're Hunting 4 Healing. Perhaps you've been to crusades, conferences and revivals and had leaders and umpteen people lay hands on you and are praying for you and nothing has happened.

What should be on your Hunting 4 Healing List? Frankly, a list that every leader should cover with people, that come to them to receive freedom from torment.

Look to the Holy Spirit foremost for your healing. He knows what ails you and what needs to be done to obtain relief. There may be a combination of many things that require treatment, same as someone who requires multiple remedies from a car accident.

If or when the Holy Spirit is silent, the following will definitely set you free in many areas, some you may not be aware of.

Disease from God?

Many Christians have disease and pain, believing it is from God and/or it is a "cross that they must bear". Meanwhile, they're going to the doctor for medications. That's hypocrisy! If they truly believe their disease is from God and they must bear it, why go to a doctor?

My Mom was at a meeting one day when a retired pastor announced to everyone that he'd had many diseases all his life, which he considered a blessing, as he was better able to counsel others who had diseases. My Mom looked at him and Biblically corrected him, that his position was false and that he had needlessly suffered all his life.

Is greater glory given to God when His children walk in health, or when they walk in disease?

Was Jesus ever sick? No.

Did He teach us to accept disease and sickness? No.

Why would Jesus bother healing and delivering people if it was Father's will that people be diseased and demonized?

Does anyone believe that there's sickness, disease, or pain in heaven? Jesus said in Matthew 6, "Your (Father's) will be done on earth as it is in heaven."

God's will is for people to be disease, pain and demon free! Disease and pain and demons come from the evil kingdom, that is allowed to afflict you, when God must remove His protection (to a degree), because a person has provided rights for the devil to afflict them. Take away these rights and God's blessings and protection is allowed to return.

Another testimony from my Mom had a woman that was in a wheelchair. My Mom was about to have the woman stand up and walk. My Mom said to her something like, "Now when you don't need that wheelchair anymore, you'll have to contact the government to stop your disability payments, you'll have to get a job and get a car, as you won't have people catering to you anymore". The woman looked at my Mom for a while and then said, "I prefer to stay in the chair"! She did.

God will not override a person's will, so if they insist on staying crippled or diseased, then suffer on!

SALVATION

Many want to be healed, but don't want the Father, Jesus or the Holy Spirit. Healing can and does come to the unsaved to encourage them to come to the One Who has healed them.

However, those walking without Jesus as their Savior, are really the walking dead, on their way to eternal spiritual death when they physically die. Don't let anyone fool you, there is no reincarnation; there is no purgatory or prayer for the dead that will change a dead person's position with God.

"And as it is appointed for men to die once, but after this the judgment." Hebrews 9:27

God will certainly bless His obedient and faithful children, as He says He will.

BODY ABUSE

"Or do you not know that your body is the temple of the Holy Spirit who is in you, whom you have from God, and you are not your own? For you were bought at a price; therefore, glorify God in your body and in your spirit, which are God's." 1 Corinthians 6:19-20

There are many, including Christians, that abuse their bodies with smoking, drinking, drugs, poor eating habits, and/or lack of sleep. This also includes improper mental (stinkin' thinkin') and religious spiritual practices that leads to disease and early death. You are expected to maintain your physical body with healthy practices.

Attacking Christians

When people verbally or physically attack God's children, there is retribution from God. Look at all the times other nations attacked Israel (when they were obedient, not disobedient) in the Bible and what happened to them. These nations received plagues to their land, diseases, war and death.

Christians are today's Israel… God's children. What do we see today with nations that attack Christians? We see the same results… war, famine, disease, drought, economic failure and death.

On a smaller scale, what can an individual expect from God, when they attack Christians? The same result in their life… failures, divorce, disease, financial loss, early death.

What can an individual (or denomination), that says they're a Christian, expect from God, when they attack true Christians that are walking in obedience to God by doing His will and operating in supernatural powers and gifts?

ROBBING GOD

Are you robbing God?

"Will a man rob God? Yet you have robbed Me! But you say, 'In what way have we robbed You?' In tithes and offerings. You are cursed with a curse, for you have robbed Me, Even this whole nation. Bring all the tithes into the storehouse, that there may be food in My house, And try Me now in this," Says the Lord of hosts, "If I will not open for you the windows of heaven And pour out for you such blessing That there will not be room enough to receive it. "And I will rebuke the devourer for your sakes, so that he will not destroy the fruit of your ground, Nor shall the vine fail to bear fruit for you in the field," Says the Lord of hosts." Malachi 3:8-11

When people, including Christians, fail to give tithes and offerings to God, "you are cursed with a curse!"

When a person does give tithes and offerings, great blessings are poured out upon them.

God promises on both points.

Many Christians, say they don't need to tithe anymore because that's changed; that's Old Testament thinking. Really? Or they just toss in a few bucks into the offering plate when it comes by.

What does God say before He talks about tithes and offerings?

"For I am the Lord, I do not change." Malachi 3:6

Tithes and offerings are still expected by God. Tithes in His Word are 10% of what you give back to God, as He gives you 100%. Offerings are extra. Almsgiving is extra.

Also, distribute your tithes, offerings and alms according to the direction of the Holy Spirit. Pray and ask Him where it should be sent, each time.

OUR TIME IS DONE

There comes a time for all of us that our physical bodies must die. Some fall asleep in their 80's and 90's and don't wake up. Yet, no one should be suffering at any age.

My Mom worked for many years with palliative care or hospice, that focuses on the palliation of a chronically ill, terminally ill or seriously ill patient's pain and symptoms, and attending to their emotional and spiritual needs. As well as working with their families.

Many were raised from their death bed. Some were not, as it was their time.

All, including the families, were counselled on getting themselves right with God. This time of life for a person is a time to reflect on life and make sure that salvation is in hand.

Work with the Holy Spirit's guidance on healing for everyone, including those in advanced years. This may be a last opportunity for some to get themselves right with God and others before they pass. As a Christian, you can greatly assist with this process with them and their families.

Evil Roots

Generational Curses

A good place to start that most people have never heard of is generational curses. I cover this in other Sectors, but it needs to be covered here as well.

Each person has picked up iniquity through their past generations. The spiritual and physical DNA of your forefathers has been passed down to you. Inherited cancers, heart disease, anger, lust for drinking, etc. Many leaders will say that this doesn't exist, as according to their religious doctrine, Jesus' Blood erases all this. Global experience and testimonies from the field, has proven them wrong.

"The Lord is slow to anger and abounding in steadfast love, forgiving iniquity and transgression, but he will by no means clear the guilty, visiting the iniquity of the fathers on the children, to the third and the fourth generation.'" Numbers 14: 18

(See also Exodus 20:5-6; Deuteronomy 5:9).

Speak something simple like, you break, in Jesus' name, all iniquity and evil roots that you have inherited or has been passed down to you from your parents. Cover specifics if you know them.

Immediate healing has been experienced by people.

Also, your DNA code will alter and become normal, ending this past genetic defect from moving beyond you. Although, any sins you are involved with moving forward (don't repent of) can alter your DNA again.

Curses Put Against You

Witches, satanists, and others, send curses against people all the time. Many Christians speak curses against others (which includes false prayers). Your boss, parents, relatives, friends and the next-door neighbor can all send curses against you… daily! These can affect you spiritually, mentally and physically.

Break all curses set against you, in Jesus' name, and cast them away from you, never to return.

CURSES AGAINST YOURSELF

People curse themselves all the time (i.e. I can't ever do anything right; that makes me sick, etc.).

Break all curses you've said against yourself, in Jesus' name, and cast them away from you, never to return. And stop doing it! Love yourself!

SOUL TIES

Soul ties I cover in the S.I.T. NO MORE Sector in depth. Soul ties involves all your sexual partners; all your false allegiances to organizations, religions and people (idol worship); and occultism you've been involved with in your life.

Break all sexual soul ties with each partner; break all wrong associations (i.e. freemasonry); break all occult activities you've ever been involved with (i.e. palm reading, prayer wheels, ouija boards, sorcerers, false religions, witchcraft, new age, etc.) in Jesus' name, and cast them away from you, never to return.

Just in breaking curses and soul ties, have been proven to easily eradicate evil spirits, which has brought on spiritual, mental, emotional and physical healing.

UNFORGIVENESS AND BITTERNESS

It's been determined that most (ranging from 80-95%) physical ailments are the fruit of an evil root. This includes cancers, heart disease, diabetes, arthritis… a long list. Your physical body reacts (i.e. chemical enhancements or immune shutdowns) to certain spiritual and mental factors (wrong thinking or stinkin' thinkin' as my Mom used to say) that alters your physical body and your mind (brain). Results can be positive or negative.

Another evil root is unforgiveness and bitterness towards others. You aren't overlooking their sin, just forgiving them. Keep in mind that people that attack you in some way, are many times driven by evil spirits. They are in bondage and in need of deliverance!

My Mom many times counselled people that needed to forgive others that had hurt them. When the person forgave, cancers instantly left. People with dozens of diseases have reported being healed from all of them, when they forgave others that they were mad at.

Many wrong emotions like anger, resentment, revenge, jealousy, hatred and thoughts of murder also disappeared when forgiveness towards others was done. Not to mention allowing peace now to be received.

When we refuse to forgive others, it doesn't hurt them. People are just drinking their own poison, many going to the grave early with their evil roots of unforgiveness and bitterness. Love others, hate the sin.

Unforgiveness affects us spiritually also. The following should make everyone forgive others, if you intend on God forgiving you.

"For if you forgive men their trespasses, your heavenly Father will also forgive you. But if you do not forgive men their trespasses, neither will your Father forgive your trespasses." Matthew 6: 14-15

CORUPTS

CORUPTS is discussed in depth in the POW's Sector. It's a study on those who are spiritual POW's or prisoners of war. Soul fragmentation or cracks in the soul can be caused by curses, occult activity, rejection, unforgiveness, physical objects, trauma and sin.

The Holy Spirit gave me the acronym CORUPTS to easily remember the attacks that <u>corrupts</u> the soul, which stands for: C-curses, O-occult activities, R-rejection, U-unforgiveness, P-physical objects, T-trauma, S-sin (includes iniquity and transgressions).

People experience fruits of rejection, lack of love, hatred, fear, anguish, stress, depression, isolation.

All of these can cause mental illness, physical diseases and evil spirit intrusion can and do intensify the damage.

Look to the POW's Sector for tips on how to be set free.

Sin

Let's talk a bit more about the "s" word. Sin covers a wide area; which God covers extensively in His Book. Some man-made denominations teach that people are no longer to be concerned about sin, because Christians are covered by grace. People think they can do (sin) whatever they want, because they're saved.

"For sin shall not have dominion over you, for you are not under law but under grace. What then? Shall we sin because we are not under law but under grace? Certainly not!" Romans 6:14-15

Grace covers those who accept Jesus and repent of their sins.

"Do you not know that to whom you present yourselves slaves to obey, you are that one's slaves whom you obey, whether of sin leading to death, or of obedience leading to righteousness?" Romans 6:16

Who are you a servant to? Sin with no repentance, leads to curses, disease, early physical death and spiritual death. Repentance and obedience to God leads to righteousness… which leads to healing and life.

God judges you on your heart towards sin. David, while a man of God, was a murderer and an adulterer, yet he repented and was forgiven. King Saul, while a man of God, did not repent of sin and was afflicted by an evil spirit until his suicide.

When we sin, we start the process of the fruit of disease growing. Continuing to sin makes it grow, like adding water and fertilizer to seed.

We need to repent and get sanctified (walk in God's truth).

Temptation is not sin. Jesus was tempted but never sinned. God will not remove temptation and trials from you. He wants you resist it and defeat it.

"If we confess our sins, He is faithful and just to forgive us our sins and to cleanse us from all unrighteousness." 1 John 1:9

If you've tried everything, but you can't shake away or stay away from some sin, look to deliverance, as it is evil spirit(s) driving you.

Repent and be healed!

Sin unto Death

"If anyone sees his brother sinning a sin which does not lead to death, he will ask, and He will give him life for those who commit sin not leading to death. There is sin leading to death. I do not say that he should pray about that." 1 John 5:16

Some interpret that the "sin leading to death" is willful, continuous, unrepentant sin. They point to Ananias and Sapphira in Acts 5:1-10, who both lied and were immediately struck dead. However, we don't know if this sin was a habit for them. According to Peter, this sin leading to their death was lying to the Holy Spirit.

God at times purifies His Church, by removing those who deliberately disobey Him. This can be a person trying to corrupt others against Jesus as the only way to salvation or perhaps a leader that permits, ignores and/or doesn't correct others about sin. Such sin is life-threatening to others, as such false doctrines leads those who listen and follow it or are ignorant of it, onto the path towards physical disease, early death and to the lake of fire.

"Sin leading to death" is obviously very serious. Don't be a part of any kind of sin nor associate with those who you know are deliberately sinning. God commands it.

"But now I have written to you not to keep company with anyone named a brother (Christian), who is sexually immoral, or covetous, or an idolater, or a reviler, or a drunkard, or an extortioner—not even to eat with such a person." 1 Corinthians 5:11

"Now I urge you, brethren, note those who cause divisions and offenses, contrary to the doctrine which you learned, and avoid them." Romans 16:17

"Now we command you, brethren, in the name of our Lord Jesus Christ, that you keep away from every brother who leads an unruly life and not according to the tradition which you received from us." 2 Thessalonians 3:6

OCCULTISM

"You cannot drink the cup of the Lord and the cup of demons; you cannot partake of the Lord's table and of the table of demons. Or do we provoke the Lord to jealousy? Are we stronger than He?" 1 Corinthians 10:21-22

Many Christians are involved in the occult. They go to palm readers, witch doctors, sorcerers, read horoscopes, use ouija boards, are freemasons, use tarot cards, new age practices. You've given evil spirits rights to come into your life and stay when you are involved in the occult.

Repent and stop this activity to free yourself from mental and physical diseases. Evil spirits will have to be cast out.

IDOL WORSHIP

People have many gods. Chasing careers, wealth, sex, power. People worship other people (priests, movie stars, sports stars). People worship Mary, dead people, icons, relics, religions. People usually worship themselves and rely on themselves.

Put God first in your life. Repent of all idol worship.

VICTIMIZATION

If you are a victim of sexual, mental, emotional, physical and/or verbal abuse (includes from Christians and Christian leaders), you don't have to resolve any issues with the assaulter for God to heal you.

Give those who have wronged you to God. Don't harbor unforgiveness or hatred or feelings of revenge.

These traumas are covered more in depth in the POW's Sector. If you've obtained fear from trauma, look also to the fear segment of this Sector.

Disobedience to God

"'"But it shall come about, if you do not obey the LORD your God, to observe to do all His commandments and His statutes with which I charge you today, that all these curses will come upon you and overtake you:" Deuteronomy 28: 15 (Read all of Deuteronomy 28 to see the blessings an obedient person receives and all the diseases that come upon a disobedient person)

"Let no one deceive you with empty words, for because of these things the wrath of God comes upon the sons of disobedience." Ephesians 5:6

"Do you not know that the unrighteous will not inherit the kingdom of God? Do not be deceived. Neither fornicators, nor idolaters, nor adulterers, nor homosexuals, nor sodomites, nor thieves, nor covetous, nor drunkards, nor revilers, nor extortioners will inherit the kingdom of God." 1 Corinthians 6:9-10

"Now the works of the flesh are evident, which are: adultery, fornication, uncleanness, lewdness, idolatry, sorcery, hatred, contentions, jealousies, outbursts of wrath, selfish ambitions, dissensions, heresies, envy, murders, drunkenness, revelries, and the like; of which I tell you beforehand, just as I also told you in time past, that those who practice such things will not inherit the kingdom of God." Galatians 5:19-21

"And even as they did not like to retain God in their knowledge, God gave them over to a debased mind, to do those things which are not fitting; being filled with all unrighteousness, sexual immorality, wickedness, covetousness, maliciousness; full of envy, murder, strife, deceit, evil-mindedness; they are whisperers, backbiters, haters of God, violent, proud, boasters, inventors of evil things, disobedient to parents, undiscerning, untrustworthy, unloving, unforgiving, unmerciful; who, knowing the righteous judgment of God, that those who practice such things are deserving of death, not only do the same but also approve of those who practice them." Romans 1:28-32

Disobedience to God can take many forms. Notice in the above scriptures that God considers such things as selfish ambitions, dissentions, backbiters, and the prideful on the same level as murder!

In Deuteronomy 28 many plagues come against the disobedient beyond many forms of diseases (God says disease is a curse), such as job loss, property loss, losing your spouse, etc.

This includes denominations and groups that are deliberately disobedient (i.e. have irresponsible leaders; follow false doctrines). If you attend such groups, you're agreeing with their activities. If they are operating in rebellion to God, so are you!

People that perform any of these activities, Christian or not, are disobedient to God and He says that there are consequences.

This is why many non-Christians experience better health than many Christians. These non-Christian are more righteous in their hearts than Christians who are not. Consequences come to all, for sin and disobedience. Actually, more is expected from Christians, as they should be aware of what God expects…

"My people are destroyed for lack of knowledge. Because you have rejected knowledge, I also will reject you from being priest for Me; Because you have forgotten the law of your God, I also will forget your children." Hosea 4:6

People experience cancers, miscarriages, psoriasis, stress, high blood pressure, anxiety, phobias and mental illnesses (insanity, dementia, Alzheimer's) when they are disobedient to God and His Word.

Look through the expectation lists that God has put in His Word and repent of all that you've disobeyed. Walk forward in obedience. Love God and His Word.

Repair and develop your relationship with Him. This brings His blessings.

Fear and Evil Spirits

"For God has not given us a spirit of fear, but of power and of love and of a sound mind." 2 Timothy 1:7

The Bible says fear is an evil spirit. Evil spirits can give thoughts, that people think are their own (anxiety, fear of heights, fear of people, fear of deliverance, etc.); can drive people with lusts (drugs, sex, gambling, drinking); they can bring guilt and despair (depression, suicide); they can make you accident prone; many say they are disease (spirit of cancer, spirit of infirmity); they do cause epilepsy, deafness and muteness; they cause heart attacks and strokes; they also can lead people into false doctrines so they'll lose their health, lose their destiny with God and lose their salvation.

I've encountered much opposition from leaders and Christians in general to spiritual warfare regarding evil spirits. You may (probably) will get the same from leaders, relatives and friends that say, spiritual warfare is nonsense, if you approach them for this aspect for healing. Many say it's impossible for a Christian to be afflicted by evil spirits. That's a religious doctrine, not a Biblical truth. Even international leaders that run supernatural Colleges avoid, ignore and/or ridicule spiritual warfare. I've experienced it!

People will eagerly accept prayer and laying on of hands for healing, but mention casting out demons and the excuses come… "no thanks", "I don't need that", "Jesus defeated satan at the Cross so we don't have to do spiritual warfare any more", "we don't dwell on satan". Walking away and running away by the demonized, are also typical responses to any talk of evil spirits. In Jesus' day, the religious leaders accused Him of working with satan, when He cast out evil spirits (Matthew 12: 22-30 see also Mark 3:22-27).

Leaders and others today would do well to heed what Jesus said to these religious Pharisees that attacked Him for casting out demons…

"He who is not with Me is against Me, and he who does not gather with Me scatters abroad." Matthew 12:30

Pray that such people you encounter, will receive deliverance one day to be set free.

The early Church leaders brought someone to salvation in Jesus; cast out their evil spirits; did a water baptism, then a Holy Spirit baptism.

The religious "church" today has dropped a couple of these necessary processes.

Go to the Xtreme Small Game Sector on how to get rid of evil spirits, including daily self-deliverance (especially when you or others notice a disturbing, negative change in your attitude). Deliverance is necessary to clean ourselves of unwanted filth picked up, same as we would take a shower daily to physically clean ourselves.

Many evil spirits don't make themselves known, so fear indicators are not always a requirement to obtain deliverance. Dirt can hide anywhere. One evil spirit I encountered during a session was residing in the person's big toe!

Once evil spirits are gone, diseases depart as well. One Christian I know had 27 diseases, which included hepatitis and lyme disease. After several deliverance sessions, he was cured of all of them (his doctor was stunned)!

Another person in his 40's had degenerative discs in his back and neck (had two operations to insert metal rods), and also had a disintegrating hip. He was in constant pain that medication couldn't relieve. The doctor told him he'd be in a wheelchair permanently within a year. After a 6-hour deliverance session, he was totally healed and pain free! As well as evil spirit free, that had also been affecting his mind! Many evil spirits took over his mind during the deliverance session, speaking through him. He didn't remember anything that happened during this session, when it was over.

One woman I know was in a mental institution (insane asylum). A leader visited her and told her she needed to repent. When she said, "I repent", all the evil spirits left her. She was soon released. She had been a Christian that got hooked up with a warlock and into occultism before she went insane. She went back to the asylum with this leader to help her friends there. Half the patients ended up leaving, after being set free from mental illness, before the staff refused them further entry. They were told, "We're losing business because of you two"!

Rarely do people know that they have evil spirits in them, until they are confronted and commanded to leave.

Remember, don't just cast evil spirits out without imprisoning them. I call this "Catch and Release Spiritual Warfare" (refer to Xtreme Small Game Sector). Otherwise, they just go out and over to someone else or they'll come back with seven of their friends and the person becomes worse off than if you'd done nothing!

"When an unclean spirit goes out of a man, he goes through dry places, seeking rest, and finds none. Then he says, 'I will return to my house from which I came.' And when he comes, he finds it empty, swept, and put in order. Then he goes and takes with him seven other spirits more wicked than himself, and they enter and dwell there; and the last state of that man is worse than the first." Matthew 12:43-45

I've received testimonies from leaders who studied and applied this book, about people who are healed of cancer, paralysis, insanity and AIDS, when they receive deliverance from evil spirits.

SELF-HATRED

There are mental and spiritual roots of self-hatred, self-bitterness and guilt. This can be brought on by many factors (generational iniquity, sin, curses, trauma, fear, evil spirits). The fruits of this root can manifest in the form of such diseases as diabetes, lupus, allergies, bone disease and arthritis, mental illness and early death.

"A merry heart does good, like medicine, but a broken spirit dries the bones." Proverbs 17:22

The immune system (in the bones) breaks down from your fear and self-hatred and now can't defeat biological enemies in your body. Disease starts and grows.

Get away from wrong people and fearful situations. Find love and trust with God. See the Fear area of this Sector.

EXPOSURE TO CHEMICALS AND THE ENVIRONMENT

Some people blame their allergies and diseases on chemical or environmental exposure. They can be allergic to foods, clothing, people, have asthma, panic attacks, fibromyalgia, angina, arterial disease, high blood pressure, strokes, ulcers, bone loss and numerous other diseases. Stress and depression from hormone disruption is typical.

"men's hearts failing them from fear and the expectation of those things which are coming on the earth, for the powers of the heavens will be shaken." Luke 21:26

When humanity is exposed to the same contaminants in the air, water, land and food supply, with only a few getting disease, you should look to an evil root as the cause, with the symptoms being its fruit.

The main evil root to look to is fear, brought about by abuse from another. Can be mental, emotional, physical, sexual abuse, especially from a parent. Legalism, sinful doctrines and cruel, forceful, controlling leaders are also abusive. Causes mistrust, insecurity and self-rejection.

A fear root in this situation can also come from exposure to war, dangerous occupations (police), and abusive spouses. Perceived or actual hatred from someone or some enemy.

Such diseases blamed on the environment or chemicals, can be traced to an anxiety disorder that is compromising the immune system, causing allergies and so on.

Your body starts to attack you physically (disruption in biological chemicals, hormones), because you live in fear, stress, and self-hatred. Brings on guilt too.

The person needs to feel safe. The person needs to be removed from the fear environment or person(s). To know that they are safe with God, and don't have to fear anyone, including themselves. Learn to trust God, yourself and others. The immune system will react positively to the mental changes of being safe (instead of fear) and symptoms will disappear quickly.

"A merry heart does good, like medicine, but a broken spirit dries the bones." Proverbs 17:22

"There is no fear in love; but perfect love casts out fear, because fear involves torment. But he who fears has not been made perfect in love." 1 John 4:18

Some with multiple diseases have reported total healing in days.

Remember that fear is an evil spirit (unloving or unclean) so must be cast out. Look to my teaching in the Xtreme Small Game Sector for assistance.

GET RIGHT WITH GOD

Another hindrance to healing is a lack of relationship with God.

"But without faith it is impossible to please Him, for he who comes to God must believe that He is, and that He is a rewarder of those who diligently seek Him." Hebrews 11:6

"Draw near to God and He will draw near to you. Cleanse your hands, you sinners; and purify your hearts, you double-minded." James 4:8

"But seek first the kingdom of God and His righteousness, and all these things shall be added to you." Matthew 6:33

This is a personal relationship with your heart, not going through any religious motions.

"He answered and said to them, Well did Isaiah prophesy of you hypocrites, as it is written: This people honors Me with their lips, but their heart is far from Me. And in vain they worship Me, Teaching as doctrines the commandments of men." Mark 7:6-7

UNBELIEF

A recipient's faith is not a requirement for healing but faith can certainly help.

"Now a woman, having a flow of blood for twelve years, who had spent all her livelihood on physicians and could not be healed by any, came from behind and touched the border of His garment. And immediately her flow of blood stopped. And Jesus said, "Who touched Me?" When all denied it, Peter and those with him said, "Master, the multitudes throng and press You, and You say, 'Who touched Me?'" But Jesus said, "Somebody touched Me, for I perceived power going out from Me." Now when the woman saw that she was not hidden, she came trembling; and falling down before Him, she declared to Him in the presence of all the people the reason she had touched Him and how she was healed immediately. And He said to her, "Daughter, be of good cheer; your faith has made you well. Go in peace." Luke 8:43-48

Jesus said in Matthew 17:20 you only need mustard seed size faith to move a mountain.

Prayer

Many people pray in error. They have a grocery list of selfish desires (money, house, job) or they use vain, repetitive, religious prayers or they're contacting the wrong guy!

The wrong guy? Most people pray to Jesus. Jesus never did that nor advised us to do that.

"And in that day, you will ask Me (Jesus) nothing. Most assuredly, I say to you, whatever you ask the Father in My name He will give you. Until now you have asked nothing in My name. Ask, and you will receive, that your joy may be full." John 16:23-24

"And when you pray, you shall not be like the hypocrites. For they love to pray standing in the synagogues and on the corners of the streets, that they may be seen by men. Assuredly, I (Jesus) say to you, they have their reward. But you, when you pray, go into your room, and when you have shut your door, pray to your Father who is in the secret place; and your Father who sees in secret will reward you openly. And when you pray, do not use vain repetitions as the heathen do. For they think that they will be heard for their many words.

"Therefore, do not be like them. For your Father knows the things you have need of before you ask Him. In this manner, therefore, pray: Our Father in heaven, Hallowed be Your name… " Matthew 6:5-9

"Every good gift and every perfect gift is from above, and comes down from the Father of lights, with whom there is no variation or shadow of turning." James 1:17

<u>Every</u> perfect gift comes from the Father. We go the Father, in the name of Jesus (our only mediator), and then the Holy Spirit performs it.

Many people also pray to Mary and dead people, and worship icons and relics, and think a religion or priest is their mediator to God… trying to obtain salvation, forgiveness, healings and blessings.

All of this activity is idol worship… disobedience… rebellion… a sin.

"For there is one God and one Mediator between God and men, the Man Christ Jesus." 1 Timothy 2:5

"Confess your trespasses to one another, and pray for one another, that you may be healed. The effective, fervent prayer of a righteous man avails much." James 5:16

Also, power in numbers together.

"For where two or three are gathered together in My name, I am there in the midst of them." Matthew 18:20

Repent if you've been wandering down the wrong path. Get on the right path with your prayer life, pray in numbers together if you can, thank Father for forgiving you and healing you, and then watch success come!

Misguided Prayer

When you ask people to pray for you or perhaps a loved one in the hospital, make sure everyone's on the same page. You may be praying for complete healing, another may be praying that the Lord takes them home soon, another that God's will be done, another that the doctor's find a cure.

"Again, I say to you that if two of you agree on earth concerning anything that they ask, it will be done for them by My Father in heaven." Matthew 18:19

Tell everyone what you want them to specifically pray about.

Laying on of Hands

One of the most important processes that should be done constantly within the Church and for and by every Christian, is the "laying on of hands".

This very important aspect of Christianity is mostly ignored throughout every denomination and group, even among those operating with the Holy Spirit. Very few Christians follow the practice of "laying on of hands", which is to be utilized for many reasons.

In this scripture, Jesus lays His hands on the children to bless them.

"After laying His hands on them, He departed from there." Matthew 19:15

Jesus commands and promises, that Christians will lay hands on the sick and they will recover.

"And these signs will follow those who believe: In My name they will cast out demons; they will speak with new tongues; they will take up serpents; and if they drink anything deadly, it will by no means hurt them; they will lay hands on the sick, and they will recover." Mark 16:17-18

Jesus lays hands on the sick and they were healed.

"While the sun was setting, all those who had any who were sick with various diseases brought them to Him; and laying His hands on each one of them, He was healing them." Luke 4:40

Jesus lays hands on an infirm (crippled) woman and she is made correct.

"And He laid His hands on her; and immediately she was made erect again and began glorifying God." Luke 13:13

Men were brought before the apostles to be ordained. Note: no diplomas or titles were issued. One of these men, Stephen the first martyr, then was performing "great wonders and miracles among the people." Acts 6:8

"And these they brought before the apostles; and after praying, they laid their hands on them." Acts 6:6

Hands laid on people to receive the Holy Spirit (baptism).

"Then they began laying their hands on them, and they were receiving the Holy Spirit." Acts 8:17

Paul and Barnabas were set apart for a special purpose and ordained for the work of the Holy Spirit and the Church.

"Then, when they had fasted and prayed and laid their hands on them, they sent them away." Acts 13:3

Paul laid hands on a man and he was healed.

"And it happened that the father of Publius was lying in bed afflicted with recurrent fever and dysentery; and Paul went in to see him and after he had prayed, he laid his hands on him and healed him." Acts 28:8 Lay hands on people to obtain the gifts of the Holy Spirit.

"Do not neglect the spiritual gift within you, which was bestowed on you through prophetic utterance with the laying on of hands by the presbytery." 1 Timothy 4:14

Lay hands on people to stir up and refresh the Holy Spirit gifts.

"For this reason, I remind you to kindle afresh the gift of God which is in you through the laying on of my hands." 2 Timothy 1:6

In God's Word, we are taught that we are to utilize "laying on of our hands" to bless; heal; baptize with the Holy Spirit; activate and refresh the Holy Spirit's power and gifts; set apart people for special purposes (i.e. missionary) and to ordain (into ministry).

I was ordained and set apart several times, receiving not only hands laid on me but also anointed with oil. Once it was with an entire bottle of oil poured over me!

Laying on of hands was the most go-to way my Mom used, when face-to-face with a person.

A hand shake and/or a hug, which is typical Christian practice, is not what is expected of us.

Ask a Holy Spirit-filled Christian to pray about you, as the Holy Spirit will most likely give this person a message (Word of Knowledge or Wisdom) for you. Then ask them to lay hands on you to bless you; baptize you with the Holy Spirit (if it hasn't been done) or refresh and stir up your Holy Spirit gifts; obtain a healing if you need it; and be ordained and set apart by God for your special purpose/your destiny with God.

When this is done, return the process to this person and then go out and do for others!

Every leader should definitely be doing this often with every person in the flock that God has been entrusted to them and with others they come into contact with (i.e. for healing), as the Holy Spirit leads.

SANCTIFICATION

"But seek first the kingdom of God and His righteousness, and all these things shall be added to you." Matthew 6:33

"Draw near to God and He will draw near to you. Cleanse your hands, you sinners; and purify your hearts, you double-minded. Lament and mourn and weep! Let your laughter be turned to mourning and your joy to gloom. Humble yourselves in the sight of the Lord, and He will lift you up." James 4:8-10

"If you love Me, keep My commandments." John 14:15

You must submit to God in holiness, otherwise little can be expected in healing and deliverance.

People can receive instant healing at a crusade, conference, "healing room" or "church" but they need to be counselled to repent of their sins and to stop living in disobedience, otherwise the evil root is still there, more roots can be planted and evil fruits will manifest down the road.

God wants to totally and long lastingly heal, to deliver, to bless. However, He can only act IF we do our end.

"Therefore, having these promises, beloved, let us cleanse ourselves from all filthiness of the flesh and spirit, perfecting holiness in the fear of God." 2 Corinthians 7:1

Paul is advising Christians to cleans yourself and perfect holiness.

Word of God

Most Christians have never read, don't read or even know the Word of God. They know perhaps a few scriptures that they like and the rest is some false or distorted doctrines that they believe is in God's Word or taught to them at some religious "church".

When people follow their own ways or some religion's ways or some leader's ways that are compromising or in conflict with God's Word, they are exposing themselves to many evil spirits (religious spirits are brutal). They can steal their salvation and are known to bring mental illness, as they are separating themselves from God's will.

Get into God's Word to discover what He expects of you. You will trust Him and He will draw near to you.

Miracles

When someone needs a limb grown or leg lengthened or eyes when there are none, this is a miracle rather than a healing. The gift of miracles is one of the Gifts of the Holy Spirt (1 Corinthians 12:10), besides the Gift of Healing (1 Corinthians 12:9).

Speak a creative miracle to that area of your mind or body that needs it, in the name of Jesus.

Divine Intervention

"I will have mercy on whomever I will have mercy, and I will have compassion on whomever I will have compassion." Romans 9:15

God intervenes to heal many instantly, even those who aren't Christian or who have no faith or belief in God. This is God's demonstration of His power to change the hearts and minds towards Him in these cases. He knows what He's doing and we rejoice and give Him the glory for the unexpected!

Going in the Spirit

Healing and deliverance can be accomplished by going in the spirit. I cover this concept in my Going in the Spirit Sector.

Angels

I discuss angels at length in the Weapons and Hunting Gear Sector. In regards to healing, we're not talking about some new age process. Angels are created beings that have many responsibilities, such as protecting people, delivering messages and fighting evil principalities.

Angels involved in healing processes have been seen by many people and you can look for their testimonies online.

Many testimonies are told of how angels assist doctors doing operations, or are guarding people in hospitals or at their homes from evil spirit attack. I've seen this many times in the spirit.

You can set angels to protect yourself and others.

Coma and Raising the Dead

When someone is in a coma, they can't go through any of the steps in this Sector. They must depend on you to set them free. A coma can be from an accident, stroke, a hemorrhage, brain damage, a concussion, tumors, epilepsy, diabetes, perhaps from drugs or alcohol. It may also be an evil spirit.

And, early death can come for many reasons, which are shown can be reversed, called resurrection.

Ask the Holy Spirit what He wants you to do and then wait to see what He says. You may have to command the body to be repaired or healed in Jesus' name or command the person to wake up or cast out evil spirits.

Doctors and Medication

I guess we have to cover doctors in a healing list. Doctors can bring relief to many patients, such as with antibiotics for bacterial infections and surgeries. For most diseases and pain, they can only provide management with drugs. They don't address the evil roots. You don't want to be managed, you want to be healed.

Medication can be a quick relief but shouldn't be our crutch. We need to find the evil root(s) that are afflicting us and address them to get rid of the fruit. This saves time, saves money, saves on suffering and it puts your reliance on God, not on man.

Relying on the world or doctors for your healing means you don't rely on God for it. Go to God first.

Here's a testimony about my aunt. She was in a bad car accident one time at night, when she was far away from home. She was brought to the hospital with many broken bones. The doctors took x-rays and were going to do surgery on her in the morning. She told them, "That won't be necessary, because God's going to heal me"! They probably thought that they should do a scan on her head after that! The next morning, she told them she felt fine and wanted to go. They ran more x-rays only to find no broken bones or any other problems. Hard for those doctors and nurses to dispute God is real after that! Demonstration of God's power is the best evangelism tool!

DISEASE PREVENTION

"And the Lord will take away from you all sickness, and will afflict you with none of the terrible diseases of Egypt which you have known, but will lay them on all those who hate you." Deuteronomy 7:15

The best place to be, is walking in perfect health. Keeping disease away from us. Follow the Hunting 4 Healing concepts that God provides us and He promises that He will take away ALL sickness!

STILL HEALING DOESN'T COME... NOW WHAT?

So, you've tried everything on the Hunting 4 Healing list and still healing hasn't come. Now what?

Continue to work at these processes. Read God's Word. Renew your mind with changed thoughts. Get away from wrong people if you can. Friends should be loving, encouraging and supporting and hold up their end of the relationship. Same goes for relatives. Dump the bad ones from your life. Your mental, physical and spiritual health is at stake. Don't believe negative thoughts about divine healing from people or from evil spirit thoughts.

Establish God's kingdom in your life. Tear down and eliminate satan's kingdom from your mind and your life. You can't serve two masters.

"No one can serve two masters; for either he will hate the one and love the other, or else he will be loyal to the one and despise the other. You cannot serve God and mammon." Matthew 6:24

Stop walking after the flesh (your job, money, your lusts) and the world.

Stop walking after legalistic, controlling, religious, spiritually dead or irresponsible leaders and denominations.

"There is therefore now no condemnation to those who are in Christ Jesus, who do not walk according to the flesh, but according to the Spirit." Romans 8:1

"Therefore, having these promises, beloved, let us cleanse ourselves from all filthiness of the flesh and spirit, perfecting holiness in the fear of God." 2 Corinthians 7:1

I pray that you are successful in your Hunt 4 Healing, whether it be for yourself or a member of your family or for a friend or perhaps for those that God has entrusted to you to shepherd. Or maybe for someone that bumped into you somewhere, like happened to my Mom for 35 years. Be a Good Samaritan and stop to give them their healing from God.

May you walk in health all your days, in Jesus' name!

All glory, victory and thanksgiving to God!

FINAL WORD FROM GOD

"See, I have set before you today life and good, death and evil, in that I command you today to love the Lord your God, to walk in His ways, and to keep His commandments, His statutes, and His judgments, that you may live and multiply; and the Lord your God will bless you… But if your heart turns away so that you do not hear, and are drawn away, and worship other gods and serve them, I announce to you today that you shall surely perish; you shall not prolong your days… I call heaven and earth as witnesses today against you, that I have set before you life and death, blessing and cursing; therefore choose life, that both you and your descendants may live; that you may love the Lord your God, that you may obey His voice, and that you may cling to Him, for He is your life and the length of your days…" Deuteronomy 30: 15-20

SECTOR TWENTY-ONE

RAISING THE DEAD

> **HUNTING TIP**
>
> "Only Believe" Smith Wigglesworth

The Bible records that Elijah, Elisha, Peter, and Paul raised the dead, as well as Jesus Christ.

Should we raise the dead?

Jesus told His disciples to raise the dead.

"Heal the sick, cleanse the lepers, raise the dead, cast out demons. Freely you have received, freely give." Matthew 10:8

Many people will argue that this command was for the disciples only. Yet, Jesus told His disciples they were to teach others to do everything He had commanded them -- even to the end of the age.

"And Jesus came and spoke to them, saying, "All authority has been given to Me in heaven and on earth. Go therefore and make disciples of all the nations, baptizing them in the name of the Father and of the Son and of the Holy Spirit, teaching them to observe all things that I have commanded you; and lo, I am with you always, even to the end of the age. Amen." Matthew 18:18-20

Jesus said believers would also do the works that He did.

"Most assuredly, I say to you, he who believes in Me, the works that I do he will do also; and greater works than these he will do, because I go to My Father." John 14:12

But, obviously, raising the dead cannot be put in exactly the same category as healing the sick.

Scripture mentions only three people that Jesus raised from death, while multitudes were healed by Him.

Healing is God's will for <u>everyone</u> who will receive it, but coming back to earth after dying, is <u>not</u> the will of God for everyone. Notice that almost all the people raised from death in Scripture were young.

Death is an enemy (1 Corinthians 15:26), and at the Name of Jesus every knee must bow (Philippians 2:9-10).

Let's look at some biblical examples of people rising from death…

We see Elijah laying on a boy three times and praying to God to "let this child's soul come into him again. And the LORD heard the voice of Elijah; and the soul of the child came into him again, and he revived."1 Kings 17:17-24

"Then he (Elisha) returned, and walked in the house to and fro; and went up, and stretched himself upon him: and the child sneezed seven times, and the child opened his eyes." 2 Kings 4:35

"So, it was, as they were burying a man, that suddenly they spied a band of raiders; and they put the man in the tomb of Elisha; and when the man was let down and touched the bones of Elisha, he revived and stood on his feet." 2 Kings 13:21

"Then He came and touched the open coffin, and those who carried him stood still. And He said, "Young man, I say to you, arise." So, he who was dead sat up and began to speak." Luke 7:14

Jesus took a girl by the hand and she arose (Matthew 9:25); Jesus commanded Lazarus to "Come forth" (John 11:43-44): Jesus just touched the man from Nain's coffin and commanded him to rise (Luke 7:11-15).

"Jesus answered and said to them, Go and tell John the things which you hear and see: The blind see and the lame walk; the lepers are cleansed and the deaf hear; the dead are raised up and the poor have the gospel preached to them. And blessed is he who is not offended because of Me." Matthew 11:4-6

"But Peter put them all out, and knelt down and prayed. And turning to the body he said, "Tabitha, arise." And she opened her eyes, and when she saw Peter she sat up." Acts 9:40

"And in a window sat a certain young man named Eutychus, who was sinking into a deep sleep. He was overcome by sleep; and as Paul continued speaking, he fell down from the third story and was taken up dead. But Paul went down, fell on him, and embracing him said, "Do not trouble yourselves, for his life is in him." Now when he had come up, had broken bread and eaten, and talked a long while, even till daybreak, he departed. And they brought the young man in alive, and they were not a little comforted." Acts 20:9-12

Paul was also stoned to death, rose and continued his ministry.

"Then Jews from Antioch and Iconium came there; and having persuaded the multitudes, they stoned Paul and dragged him out of the city, supposing him to be dead. However, when the disciples gathered around him, he rose up and went into the city. And the next day he departed with Barnabas to Derbe." Acts 14:19-20

Perhaps one of the most well-known example of raising multiple dead at the same time was the moment Jesus died on the Cross.

"Then, behold, the veil of the temple was torn in two from top to bottom; and the earth quaked, and the rocks were split, and the graves were opened; and many bodies of the saints who had fallen asleep were raised; and coming out of the graves after His resurrection, they went into the holy city and appeared to many." Matthew 27:51-53

Some more testimonies…

Missionary in Uganda

"On September 25, 1999, after preaching in a village near the town of Bostime, Uganda, he was preparing to leave the meeting when a Muslim man approached him. The man had met a weeping mother walking along the road on her way to bury her dead child. He had told her that there was a man in town preaching about Jesus' power to raise the dead. The Muslim man brought the woman with the dead infant to Rev. Idrifua wanting him to pray for the dead child. Rev. Idrifua asked the mother if she was a believer. She said she was. The Spirit of God came on him. He told the woman, 'Remove your breast and prepare to nurse the baby' (a common practice in Africa). She did so and he laid hands on the baby and strongly rebuked the spirit of death, then commanded life to return. Immediately the baby came to life crying and began to swing its arms and legs, then quieted down and began to nurse! The Muslim man got so excited he went to a friend's house whose baby also had died several hours before the first baby. This dead baby was the child of a Muslim cleric (or pastor), a Haji. He brought this dead child and its mother to Rev. Idrifua. God raised the second baby to life too!

Five Muslims gave their hearts to Jesus that day -- including the Haji!"

This story again proves you don't need faith of non-believing bystanders to raise the dead.

Another one from Africa

One of Heidi Baker's key leaders is Pastor Rego. In 1998, the wife of the district secretary contracted AIDS and died. Pastor Rego takes God at His word, he tells the following story of praying for a co-worker's dead wife in <u>Always Enough</u>. When asked how he can do something so radical, he says, "I open the Bible and do what it says."

Pastor Rego went with the district secretary to his house. When they got to the house, they found everyone crying. Here's his description:

"His wife's head was covered already. Suddenly, I felt something touch me. I thought, 'Oh, God, I need to pray now for you to give me power to do a miracle.' So, I got up. I started to feel strength and great power coming into me.

I told everyone to be quiet and not cry anymore, because this mother who died is a Christian. Nobody wanted to be quiet. I asked again, 'Please be quiet now. Calm down.' They wanted to keep crying and feel sad, but eventually they were quiet.

We sang and worshiped the Lord. Then my friend Francisco, one of our counselors, also started to feel the power of God.

I got next to this dead mother. I took the cover off her head and began to pray. I prayed for over an hour. She was very cold. The second hour I started to feel warmth coming into her. I could feel her body warming up. I prayed all the way down her body. When I got down to her legs, the bottom of her legs were still cold.

I picked her up, and then her eyes were open. She began to vomit and vomit. I can't even explain it.

I told a woman, 'Sit here and hold her,' because she could see everybody now. 'Let's keep praying,' I said. Her legs were beginning to get warm. We prayed some more. The third hour her whole body had movement. She was alive!'" by Seth Barnes of Radical Living October 16, 2006

This testimony shows that it may not happen instantly.

Mexico and Central America

This is the testimony of David Hogan, a missionary who has lived in Mexico and the jungles of Guatemala for the past 35 or so years, preaching and planting Church groups (600+) among the villagers under the most dangerous and primitive conditions.

He has also seen over 400 people raised from the dead!

He has been shot, stoned and beaten, losing 11 of his native pastors to martyrdom.

But not everyone for whom Hogan has prayed is raised from the dead. He estimates that only a fifth have been, and says adamantly: "I want that to be really clear. We're not 100 per cent. Only Jesus is 100 per cent. We just pray for everybody."

According to Hogan, there is a price to pay for the kind of faith that will trust God to raise the dead. "In order to help people through the power of God, my wife and I were seriously aggressive in our own lives against barriers and offenses to God through prayer and fasting and meditation in the Word of God for about four years before we saw the first person raised from the dead."

Now, says Hogan, they are on a continual fast. "We fast every other day -- meaning no food. Sometimes we go on extended fasts for three or more day's just drinking water or juice depending on how we feel led by the Holy Ghost."

He believes that prayer and fasting, and the Word of God are tools believers can use to keep their flesh submitted to the Holy Spirit, allowing Him to use them however He desires.

Hogan's testimony is electrifying. He has seen thousands of miracles and healings.

USA

(MIAMI, FL)—The audience of 120 doctors from 50 countries sat in stunned silence, as a renowned heart doctor produced evidence of how, after he had prayed for a patient who had died and was being prepared for the morgue, was brought back to life after prayer.

Dr. Chauncey W. Crandall IV, who serves at the Palm Beach Cardiovascular Clinic in Palm Beach Gardens, Florida, made his dramatic presentation on Friday, July 13th, 2007 at the 4th Annual World Christian Doctors Network Conference in Miami, Florida.

He produced dramatic evidence that was shown on the screen and then, afterwards, agreed to tell the story to *Assist News Service* in an interview with Dan Wooding.

"The following is the interview as conducted by Dan:

Dr. Crandall began by saying that the dramatic incident took place in West Palm Beach, Florida. "We had a fifty-three-year-old man who came to the emergency room with a massive heart attack and actually his heart had stopped," he said. "The medical people had worked on him for over forty minutes in the emergency room and then declared him dead.

"They called me in to evaluate the patient towards the end of his treatment where they had unsuccessfully tried to revive him. The nurse was preparing his body to be taken down to the morgue when the Holy Spirit told me to 'turn around and pray for that man.' When the Holy Spirit talks to you, you have to respond. It's sometimes a quiet voice and this was a quiet voice and to honor the Lord I did turn around and I went to the side of that stretcher where his body was being prepared.

"There was no life in the man. His face and feet and arms were completely black with death and I sat next to his body and I prayed, 'Lord, Father; how am I going to pray for this man? He's dead. What can I do?' All of a sudden, these words came out of my mouth, 'Father, God, I cry out for the soul of this man if he does not know You as his Lord and Savior, please raise him from the dead right now in Jesus name.

"It was amazing as a couple minutes later, we were looking at the monitor and all of a sudden a heart beat showed up. It was a perfect beat; a normal beat; and then after a couple more minutes, he started moving and then his fingers were moving and then his toes began moving and then he started mumbling words.

"There was a nurse in the room—she wasn't a Believer—and she screamed out and said 'Doctor Crandall, what have you done to this patient?' And I said, 'All I've done is cry out for his soul in Jesus name.'

"We quickly rushed the gentleman down to the intensive care unit, and the hospital was by now buzzing about the fact that a dead man had been brought back to life. After a couple of days he woke up. He had an amazing story to tell after I had asked him, 'Where have you been and where were you on that day that you had that massive heart attack? You were gone and we prayed you back to life in Jesus name.'

"He said, 'Doctor Crandall, it's the most amazing thing. I was in a dark room and there was no light. It was complete darkness and I felt I was in a casket and I kept repeating that I was so disappointed.' He said the disappointment came from the fact that none of his family, friends or colleagues, had come to visit him. Then he told me, 'All of a sudden, these men came in and they wrapped me up and they threw me in the trash.'

"Dan, he was in hell that day and as he told me that story, I cried out, 'Lord, this gentleman needs to accept You as Lord and Savior.' I then explained the salvation message to this man as he sat in that bed and I held his hand and I cried out, 'Father God, in the name of Jesus, I pray that this man accepts you as his Lord and Savior right here in the intensive care unit.' He held out his hand and accepted Christ as his Savior with tears rolling down from his eyes and now he's a child of God.

"I told him, 'You never have to be thrown in the trash into total darkness now. The life of Christ is in you and the light of the kingdom of Heaven is on you now.'"

I asked Dr. Crandall if there had been any brain damage to the patient.

"No there was no brain damage at all; his brain was completely normal," he said. "I was most concerned about his hands because his fingers were completely black and he had some numbness in his fingers and his feet, but now that is totally resolved."

I asked Dr. Crandall if he could give the name of the man and he said he couldn't as the patient had requested that it would not be revealed.

"All I can say is that he was fifty-three years old and he was a car mechanic," he said. "He had a family who were Believers, but he left them twenty years ago, because he didn't believe in the Lord. His family continued to pray for twenty years for his salvation, and his ex-wife was on her hands and knees praying for the salvation of her ex-husband, who came to know the Lord that day."

I then asked the doctor if he had seen other similar miracles in his practice.

"I've been witness to three cases of people being raised from the dead," he said. "One other case was when another patient came to the hospital with a massive heart attack. It was on the very day that I received the Baptism of the Holy Spirit and I'd been praying for weeks that I would receive this mighty baptism that the Lord can give us. We were working on this patient that came in again with a massive heart attack and who didn't survive in the operating room.

"All of a sudden, that Baptism of the Holy Spirit hit me and I started speaking in a spiritual language and crying over this patient who, in the operating room theater, had passed away. And then, within five or ten minutes, the heartbeat came back and life came back to this patient. Once again, the nurses who are not Believers looked at me as if to say, 'There goes Doctor Crandall on another case.'"

I concluded the interview by asking Dr. Crandall what he would like to say to doctors who do not believe in supernatural healing.

"I would just like to say to my colleagues and physicians out there, that the Lord is real. We've seen many miracles and we pray for our patients daily. There is not one week that goes by that we don't see a mighty miracle in our office. The people need this; they need the power of Christ in their life and they need the power of Christ for healing.

"I would just encourage my fellow doctors to get involved in a church, meet with a minister, and attend a healing service run by people that believe in the power of Jesus Christ. We love our colleagues in medicine—we pray for them."

One researched testimony tells of a leader in Africa that told all of the people attending a meeting, to go and bring back their dead. Numerous dead were dug up from their graves and brought to the meeting rolled up in carpets. They were resurrected and restored!

Here's a testimony from someone who applied this book to raise a child the Centurion way!

"Hi Al,

A happy new year to you and Rhoda too.

Thanks for the update on the text book. Fantastic job.

We are fine here at Lae. We are doing another month of fasting to complete our 70 weeks. While praying in tongues on Saturday, I saw waring angels as big and tall as skyscrapers descend into the church area. They were here to ensure the 70 weeks was completed on schedule.

November last year, Gabi and Joel went to Kimbe for a meeting. The meeting was organized by the university students from Madang. My elder sister lives at Kimbe and attended the meeting. One of the lady students prayed with her for healing of cervical cancer and she was instantly healed. She is now well and putting back her weight.

On new year Monday, she called me and related to me that since that meeting at Kimbe after Joel and Gabi prayed with her for spiritual activation, the spiritual gifts in her seemed to have doubled in operation. Just last week she was at her house sitting under a tree. She felt the Holy

Spirit urged her to turn and look across to her neighbor's house opposite a soccer field. There a child had just died and his parents were mourning. The Holy Spirit urged her to pray in tongues. She continued to pray until the child rose from the dead. The parents and all those around were very surprised but did not know what or how it happened. All the while my sister never approached them or even gone near them.

God is still in the miracle business.

Many blessings,
 Martin R., Papua New Guinea", January 4, 2017.

Who raises the Dead?

"For as the Father raises the dead and gives life to them, even so the Son gives life to whom He will." John 5:21

"Why should it be thought incredible by you that God raises the dead?" Acts 26:8

Romans 8:11 says, "If the Spirit of him who raised Jesus from the dead dwells in you, he who raised Christ Jesus from the dead will also give life to your mortal bodies through his Spirit who dwells in you."

Permission

You should obtain permission from the dead person's family, hospital and/or funeral home before proceeding. There are times when people have made it known to family, that they don't want to be resuscitated if they die, so any attempts later, would be against their will.

Continued Handicap/Injury

Keep in mind that you may resurrect someone who was in perhaps a bad car accident and now will have to recover and perhaps be cared for (if they aren't instantly healed).

What's the Process to Raise the Dead?

Sometimes the dead were touched or even laid upon, sometimes not. Some were commanded to rise. Some are just prayed for and not touched. Once the person was surrounded by many disciples. As we can see, there is really no method. Certainly, no evil roots to cover with the dead or evil spirits to cast out.

My Mom raised a person from the dead by touching his hand. The paramedics, who had confirmed he was dead, were shocked when he rose up from under the sheet! Another was by her appealing to God to rise a person up, like Elijah did.

Some people have been dead for a long time and were commanded to come back into their bodies and rise.

One leader told me that they commanded a person to come back to their body. Jesus then appeared with the dead person to tell the leader, that it was this person's time, so they wouldn't be coming back to their body.

Some were brought back to life immediately and others took days.

In some testimonies that were researched, people can be either young or old. Some people have fulfilled their destiny for God at a young age and so won't be returned from heaven and some that are seniors are brought back to life, as God has more for them to fulfill.

One of the main processes is, to command the person's spirit to come back to their body.

We know that Jesus must have come across many who had died, but did not raise everyone from death. So, as Jesus did, we should raise someone from death, when we are sure it is the will of God. In this, we must be led by God's Spirit. When we are certain of God's will, we should command with authority and not give up.

SECTOR TWENTY-TWO

POW's

HUNTING TIP

When evil game has you surrounded... take no prisoners!

As mentioned in other Sectors, Xtreme Big Game, Xtreme Small Game and Xtreme Rabid Game Hunting have as a goal, freeing those who are being blinded from the gospel and/or being tormented.

To most, this seems like an easy process of just doing spiritual warfare, the bad guys go away, people open up to Jesus, problems go away and all is right with the world.

Sounds nice, but it isn't that easy, unless one would consider Xtreme Big, Small Game and Xtreme Rabid Game Hunting easy!

In the physical world, there are those who are imprisoned because of criminal activity, political activity, religious activity, and military activity.

There are minimum, medium, and maximum-security prisons.

There are federal, state, county, and city prisons, and jails.

These are just some of the physical prisons.

Then we have emotional and mental prisons.

We have doctors, psychologists, psychiatrists, and various counselors, dispensing advice and/or drugs to try to free people from these kinds of prisons.

There are different kinds of prisons and prisoners in the spiritual realm also.

Such as prisons for fallen angels.

"For if God did not spare the angels who sinned, but cast them down to hell and delivered them into chains of darkness, to be reserved for judgment." 2 Peter 2:4

"And the angels who did not keep their proper domain, but left their own abode, He has reserved in everlasting chains under darkness for the judgment of the great day." Jude 6

"This place is the prison house of angels; they are detained here forever." 1 Enoch 21:10.

We're all aware of being under the curse of death or the prison of death, if one hasn't accepted and held onto salvation through Jesus Christ.

We've also discussed freeing the cloudiness of people's minds and casting out evil spirits, to free people from imprisonment.

What else is there?

In the military, when going into enemy territory, in addition to destroying enemy troops, structures, and securing the area for your forces, you can come across prisoners of war, or POW's.

POW's can be <u>known</u> to be where military troops are going, and at times, when they find some, it is <u>a surprise</u>.

Sometimes commandos will go into enemy territory on a raid with the <u>only purpose</u> being to release prisoners.

The same can happen in the spiritual realm.

During one hunt, I came across what some would say are unusual POW's, as you'll read in one testimony in the Sector on "XBGH Stories and Testimonies".

Other Xtreme Big Game Hunters have also released these same kinds of spiritual POW's.

Let's examine some other prisons and POW's and see how a POW can escape or be released.

Are you a POW?

If you are going to be a spiritual warrior, it's best not to be working from behind a prison wall or perhaps several prison walls!

The devil rules by holding people captive in various ways.

For instance, the soul is a spiritual substance and satan can capture pieces of it. He wants as many pieces or areas of your soul as possible. He especially wants the piece that will give allegiance to him, not God. If he can't have this piece, because you are a Christian, he works through the pieces of a Christian that he does hold captive to damage them with sickness and tragedies, etc.

He uses various means to do this, through the occult, iniquity, our sin, our fears, trauma, and other means; and puts holes, snares, and traps out to take a piece when we aren't careful.

Any trauma that you experience in life can crack or fragment your soul, putting a portion of it into captivity.

This has nothing to do with spiritual salvation; I'm talking about your soul.

This part of your imprisoned soul stays imprisoned until released, as with any physical prison restricting a person.

When you see Christians that have depression, desperation, anxiety, anguish, and fear who cannot obtain a solution—part of their soul is probably in captivity.

Let's examine a spiritual meaning behind this in Isaiah 7.

"Let us (evil forces) go up against Judah (people) and trouble it (cause trauma), and let us make a gap in its wall for ourselves (crack/fragment), and set a king over them (demon leader), the son of Tabel (Hebrew meaning good for nothing)." Isaiah 7:6

With trauma and fear, satan makes you useless and destroys you.

Isaiah 24 speaks of a prison where captives are kept:

"They will be gathered together, as prisoners are gathered in the pit, and will be shut up in the prison;
After many days they will be punished." Isaiah 24:22

This is speaking of satan in the end times being gathered, yet note that they will be as prisoners are gathered in the pit and shall be shut up in the prison. This is speaking of something other than a physical prison.

"You have laid me in the lowest pit, in darkness, in the depths." Psalm 88:6

Holes and traps to capture enemies have been used by military forces and hunters throughout history and spiritual wars use the same devices, as David tells us in Psalm 35:7 and Psalm 9:15-16.

"For without cause they have hidden their net for me in a pit, which they have dug without cause for my life." Psalm 35:7

"The nations have sunk down in the pit which they made; In the net which they hid, their own foot is caught. The Lord is known by the judgment He executes; The wicked is snared in the work of his own hands." Psalm 9:15-16

We see here that the wicked are captured in a net or snared, and sink into a pit by their own hands.

"Lord, how long wilt thou look on? Rescue my soul from their destructions, my darling from the lions."Psalm 35:17 KJV

David's soul needed rescue from destructions.

"I am shut up, and I cannot get out." Psalm 88:8

This speaks of a person who tries, but can't worship God.

"Bring my soul out of prison, that I may praise Your name; The righteous shall surround me, for You shall deal bountifully with me." Psalm 142:7

David wants to be brought out of prison so he can worship God.

"O Lord, You brought my soul up from the grave; You have kept me alive, that I should not go down to the pit." Psalm 30:3

David speaks of his soul being brought up from the pit or freed:

"He also brought me up out of a horrible pit, out of the miry clay, and set my feet upon a rock, and established my steps." Psalm 40:2

Your soul is trapped in whatever you put your trust in, besides God.

"Give glory to the Lord your God before He causes darkness, and before your feet stumble on the dark mountains, and while you are looking for light, He turns it into the shadow of death and makes it dense darkness." Jeremiah 13:16

Don't lead a life that does not give all glory to God, to prevent your stumbling and going into the darkness of prison.

"As for you also, because of the blood of your covenant, I will set your prisoners free from the waterless pit." Zechariah 9:11

"by whom also He (Jesus) went and preached to the spirits in prison." 1 Peter 3:19

Isaiah 49:8-9 says that <u>God makes a covenant with those who are deliverers, that he will cause us to inherit the desolate… in other words… if we will go to set prisoners free, they will be freed!</u>

"Thus, says the Lord: "In an acceptable time I have heard You, and in the day of salvation I have helped You; I will preserve You and give You as a covenant to the people, To restore the earth, to cause them to inherit the desolate heritages; That You may say to the prisoners, 'Go forth,' To those who are in darkness, 'Show yourselves.' "They shall feed along the roads, and their pastures shall be on all desolate heights." Isaiah 49:8-9

Say to the prisoners "go forth."

"I, the Lord, have called You in righteousness, and will hold Your hand; I will keep You and give You as a covenant to the people, as <u>a light to the Gentiles</u>, to open blind eyes, to bring out prisoners from the prison, those who sit in darkness from the prison house." Isaiah 42:6-7

God says He will be with those who are rescuing the imprisoned.

"Thus says the Lord to His anointed, to Cyrus, whose right hand I have held—To subdue nations before him and loose the armor of kings, to open before him the double doors, so that the gates will not be shut:

'I will go before you and make the crooked places straight; I will break in pieces the gates of bronze and cut the bars of iron." Isaiah 45:1-2

God says He will go before you and break in pieces the brass gates of prisons and cut asunder the iron bars (Isaiah 45:1-2) that hold all pieces of a soul captive.

Let God lead the way and <u>command</u> that souls be set free, to be ministered to and restored by the Lord.

In the spirit, with the Lord's guiding, with speaking His Word, using your authority, and also with angels, you can open a person's prison cell and set them free… even your own!

You can go to people, areas, and nations that are held captive and you will find gates of hell, especially where idols are worshipped and sacrifices made.

You can command these gates to be opened and set the captives free.

Many are delivered from evil spirits, but never set free from prison!

Ever hear of a prison break by prisoners?

The Bible says we can!

"<u>Deliver yourself</u> like a gazelle from the hand of the hunter, and like a bird from the hand of the fowler." Proverbs 6:5

When there isn't anyone available to help, people can escape from prison and set fragments of their own soul free from captivity!

When a person is physically sent to prison, certain factors will determine the kind of prison it will be, which may be minimum, medium or maximum-security.

When I visited Alcatraz (that's visited, not stayed), I would say that this is an example of an Xtreme security prison.

Yet, comparing Alcatraz next to what I saw at Mamertine prison in Rome, where Paul waited for his execution, I'd take Alcatraz!

Various factors can also determine how deeply a soul is imprisoned; however, the Lord can free those who are willing to follow His escape plans to freedom!

Let's examine more on the soul and soul imprisonment that the Bible speaks of, for God's escape, extraction and evasion plans to set ourselves and others free.

SOUL IMPRISONMENT

Jesus suffered from a crown of thorns on His Head, shedding His blood for the healing of our mind.

The price for our mental, emotional, and spiritual healing is paid!

We must believe it and take it!

But how do we do that?

Many times, prayer, counseling, laying on of hands, and deliverance are very successful, yet there are times when these methods don't heal the mental and emotional pain of our life.

The world's methods of drug therapies, hypnotism, psychiatric counseling or hospitalization do not effectively deal with the spiritual roots.

Even talking to friends and family is a comfort, but not a cure.

And the old saying that "time heals all wounds" is a nice saying, but some wounds fester for a lifetime and never heal.

There are a few other alternatives that God has provided that are extremely successful.

This involves the freedom and healing (of the soul that has been imprisoned) from some sort of a crack, or fragment.

Many call it inner healing.

The human spirit in the brain gives us a mind, making us a living soul.

The soul is a multi-faceted thing made up of the mind, intellect, emotions, and personality.

The soul is heavenly material.

"And the Lord God formed man of the dust of the ground, and breathed into his nostrils the breath of life; and man became a living being." Genesis 2:7

We are a spirit being living in a physical body, possessing a soul.

The soul is the center of the vitality of life, connecting us to the spiritual and physical.

We are told to love and magnify God with all our soul.

"You shall love the Lord your God with all your heart, with all your soul, and with all your strength." Deuteronomy 6:5

The soul connects us to God and with most people, this link is disrupted.

"But the natural man does not receive the things of the Spirit of God, for they are foolishness to him; nor can he know them, because they are spiritually discerned." 1 Corinthians 2:14

Only through Jesus is a soul brought back to life; and we should submit our soul only to Him.

"For you were like sheep going astray, but have now returned to the Shepherd and Overseer of your souls." 1 Peter 2:25

The devil wants souls, and he controls most of them in the world right now!

He relies on people working only within their physical senses and feelings, in order to deceive them.

Satan allows the unsaved to think they have their own will, but really, they are puppets.

Ephesians 2:2-3 says before a person is a Christian, satan controls their will, body and mind.

"in which you once walked according to the course of this world, <u>according to the prince of the power of the air</u>, the spirit who now works in the sons of disobedience, among whom also we all once conducted ourselves in the lusts of our flesh, <u>fulfilling the desires of the flesh and of the mind</u>, and were by nature children of wrath, just as the others."

Ezekiel 13:17-23 says souls can be captured.

Satan wants to capture what he can and put a ruling demon in place.

Souls can be cracked, fragmented, torn, imprisoned, displaced, and thankfully, restored.

Luke 21:19 says that <u>we</u> are responsible for our souls.

"By your patience possess your souls."

We can lose control of our minds from certain incidents in our lives that crack or fragment our souls.

How does a person get a cracked or fragmented soul?

Like a physical body that can receive wounds from a cut, a tear or an amputation, the soul can experience wounds also.

Physical wounds can come from a variety of sources and wounds of the soul can also be from many causes.

I learned a great deal about <u>soul fragmentation</u> from an old charismatic teacher, Dr. Marcus Haggard; and about <u>cracks in the soul</u>, from an anointed teacher and author, Dr. Dale M. Sides.

I use both terms—as either or both can be experienced.

Their experience, my personal experience, and the experience from other Xtreme Big Game Hunters tells us, that these are factors in spiritual warfare that must be dealt with, yet are largely unheard of!

I agree with Dr. Sides' teaching, in that most typical soul wounds come from seven sources.

Dr. Sides uses the acronym TRUCOPS to describe attacks that <u>crack</u> the soul in his fantastic book, *Mending Cracks in the Soul* (highly recommended study material).

The Holy Spirit gave me the acronym CORUPTS to easily remember the attacks that <u>corrupts</u> the soul, which stands for: C-curses,

O-occult activities, R-rejection, U-unforgiveness, P-physical objects, T-trauma, S-sin (includes iniquity and transgressions).

Use whatever method allows you to simply remember these wounds when you're in the field.

These seven areas cause cracks and fragmentations, corrupting certain emotions and feelings and opening the doors for evil intrusion.

Areas of our soul (some call gates) become imprisoned behind a stronghold, which can have jailer demon(s) posted as guards and tormentors.

Regardless of how long you've had this crack or wound, or how many wounds you have, there are ways to escape or be rescued from captivity.

Besides God going before you, leading you, assisting you, and self-escape, as we just examined, let's look at some specific plans.

First is the cracking of a soul, using the study of Dr. Sides' analogy and remedy, which I like to call;

THE DUAL STRIKE FORCE ESCAPE PLAN

One of God's escape plans is a dual strike force plan.

The Holy Spirit knows exactly where the wounds are and He can allow them to be healed.

"But the Helper, the Holy Spirit, whom the Father will send in My name, He will teach you all things, and bring to your remembrance all things that I said to you. Peace I leave with you, My peace I give to you; not as the world gives do I give to you. Let not your heart be troubled, neither let it be afraid." John 14:26-27

In this dual strike force process, the Holy Spirit does His part and the person must do their part.

Just as with a physical prison, if a crack commando team breaks into a prison and blows open a cell door, it won't do much good if the person won't leave the cell and go with them.

The Holy Spirit's part is to <u>initiate</u> the healing of a person's mind… "He has sent Me to heal the brokenhearted." Isaiah 61; Luke 4:18c

The person's part requires faith and patience. Romans 8:27 and 1 Corinthians 2:10 says, the Holy Spirit searches our hearts and our minds and is sent by God to be our Helper, to cure the areas in our heart.

He cures us by binding up or piecing together what has mentally injured us (bad memory), by showing us the true picture of what happened during any traumatic event.

Luke 4:18f says "to set at liberty them that are bruised." KJV

The original Greek word for bruised is "thrauo" meaning to "break in pieces or shatter."

Experiencing or seeing something traumatic, produces a shock to the soul or mind. The good news is that the Holy Spirit can set people free from this soul damage.

A great Biblical teaching of this dual strike plan is revealed to us in the story of the Good Samaritan in Luke 10:34 "So he (the Good Samaritan) went to him and <u>bandaged his wounds</u>, pouring on <u>oil and wine</u>; and he set him on his own animal, brought him to an inn, and took care of him."

This is a dual strike cure, as the wound was bandaged and then both the oil and the wine were poured into the wound. So, it is with the mind or soul wound. The Holy Spirit is the oil, and the Word of God is the wine or blood of Jesus.

We know that spiritual warfare's objective is to set captives free, especially ourselves. A prime example of a captive was a man at Gadara in Mark 5, that Jesus cured/delivered, by getting him back in his "right mind."

"Then they came to Jesus, and saw the one who had been demon-possessed and had the legion, sitting and clothed and <u>in his right mind</u>. And they were afraid."

This man wasn't in his right mind, which allowed demons to come in.

Evil spirits can cause accidents producing trauma and bad feelings and emotions, specifically to open doors in order to enter. This man got the dual strike cure, in that he was freed by the Holy Spirit and then received the Word from Jesus. Jesus healed the crack, expelled the demons and they could not return, as the stronghold was gone.

As a medical doctor would do, you locate the injury, find the cause and give the cure, which includes cleaning and care of the injury. Failure in any area can result in a longer healing time or non-healing.

Physical wounds can hurt when being cleaned and prepared for healing; and the same can happen with soul wounds.

Impression, repetition, and association are what affect the soul. Impressions, especially if they are violent, shock the soul (traumatize) leaving the mind or soul wounded.

The crack in the soul will cause the mind to go back to this place to repeat the event, especially under similar circumstances, causing something the medical profession calls associative dysfunction.

Emotions attached to the impression cause deep wounds and repetition of the memory causes the wound to deepen.

What the Holy Spirit does is to go into your mind, <u>when invited</u>, to retrieve the memory and heal the way that you think about it, cutting the associative attachment, or creating a new associative attachment to the memory, with the truth.

<u>You might want to read that last important aspect again.</u>

If you won't go to a doctor for a physical wound, he can't help you. Neither can the Holy Spirit help your soul, if you won't go to Him!

Once this is taken care of, demons have no further stronghold or right to be there, as fear, anger or any bad emotions and feelings have been removed.

Your spirit can be saved, but your soul and body can be attacked by the enemy.

You must keep up your defenses of the body and soul from evil intrusion.

Evil spirits come in on the trauma and emotions and take control of certain areas, while other areas they do not affect.

The seven entry points again that they take advantage of are CORUPTS… curses, occult practices, rejection, unforgiveness, physical objects, trauma and sin.

Reactions to these memories or activities differ in people, from anger, to fear, to drinking or drug abuse, etc. Each person responds generally where they are weakest.

For instance, if fear manifests during a trip back into your memory, then the Holy Spirit must remove the root of the fear factor. Any demons can then be cast out very successfully, as they will no longer have a stronghold or access through a closed door.

Memory healing is done by the Holy Spirit exposing the emotion where the stronghold was set.

<u>He does this by opening our spiritual eyes to see the truth, which exposes the lie of the event.</u> Once the truth is revealed, we are no longer traumatized by the event.

The traumatic event experienced was seen by the natural eyes and not the spiritual eyes.

The Holy Spirit takes us back to the event and opens up our spiritual eyes to see the truth. The truth will destroy the negative emotions, the evil stronghold, and the lying memory, to be replaced with God's love. The memory is not forgotten; it's just replaced with a true memory.

This may sound unusual, but I have personally seen this work with people who have had troubles for years. People who are strong Christians, who have had prayer and deliverance, used this dual strike force plan and were released in minutes!

I taught this plan to an entire audience at a conference, giving them all time to implement the first strike with the Holy Spirit. People testified to immediate freedom from decades of imprisonment, when other efforts had failed!

You must allow the Holy Spirit to move within you to bring about healing.

"He will… bring to your remembrance all things." John 14:26

Let the Holy Spirit bring forward in your mind this memory, even though it may be painful, so that He may minister and show you the truth.

"In all your ways acknowledge Him, and He shall direct your paths." Proverbs 3:6

God designed us perfectly and knowing that we would run into these problems with satan, He designed us to be spiritually fixed.

"Search me, O God, and know my heart; Try me, and know my anxieties; And see if there is any wicked way in me, and lead me in the way everlasting." Psalm 139: 23-24

Allow God to search us and lead us to healing.

He can even take us back to the womb to deal with inherited iniquities.

"For You formed my inward parts; You covered me in my mother's womb." Psalm 139:13

"It is the glory of God to conceal a matter, but the glory of kings is to search out a matter." Proverbs 25:2

In searching how God does soul healing, He shows us not once, but three times in Matthew 13:15; John 12:40 and Acts 28:27.

"For the hearts of this people have grown dull. Their ears are hard of hearing, and their eyes they have closed, lest they should see with their eyes and hear with their ears, lest they should understand with their hearts and turn, so that I should heal them." Matthew 13:15

Looking backwards in this verse, we are healed in our heart by being converted; when we understand with our heart, when we see with our spiritual eyes and hear with our spiritual ears.

God tells us that this is a reality.

The Holy Spirit "opens the eyes of our heart" or in other words, shows us the truth.

A good example of this is one of my favorite stories in the Bible in 2 Kings 6:17, where Elisha and his servant were surrounded by enemy forces at Dothan. Elisha's servant saw with his physical eyes, that destruction was about to come. When his spiritual eyes were opened, he saw God's forces. He saw the truth.

The Holy Spirit opens the eyes of our spirit.

"the eyes of your understanding being enlightened; that you may know what is the hope of His calling, what are the riches of the glory of His inheritance in the saints." Ephesians 1:18

"to open their eyes, in order to turn them from darkness to light, and from the power of Satan to God." Acts 26:18

We are born into spiritual darkness and only the Holy Spirit can open our eyes to the light.

You don't <u>need</u> a minister or healing or deliverance teams to accomplish this healing.

The Holy Spirit knows what to do and where to go. He just needs you to let Him go!

When the Holy Spirit takes you back and shows you the event in the spirit, He is giving you one of the gifts promised in 1 Corinthians 12:8… the gift of knowledge. He can give a person knowledge of the future and He can also do so for the past. Let your teacher and comforter do this for you. Just have faith that He will move and let Him do His work when He comes. You must be humble and be quiet to prepare for Him.

To enter into the spirit realm, you need to control your soul and body and remove distractions from the physical world.

If you are distracted you will lose your focus.

God gave us music to assist us in entering the spirit realm, as it can stabilize the body, especially if it is synchronized to the heart beat. Elisha used music in 2 Kings 3:15 when a minstrel played for him to be at peace and receive word from God. "But now bring me a musician." Then it happened, when the musician played, that the hand of the Lord came upon him."

A good way to prepare for this ministry is to be somewhere quiet, away from all distractions, with some calm instrumental music. (Personally, I prefer no music.) A place where you will have no interruptions when the Holy Spirit is working.

The Holy Spirit will work with you when you admit that you need Him.

BE HUMBLE.

Jesus couldn't heal or deliver people that did not seek Him or want Him.

If you do not trust the Holy Spirit, this plan cannot succeed.

Depend on Him… He will help you.

Don't be afraid and don't resist as He leads you, even though it may be an experience you don't want to remember. He will relieve the hurt by opening up your spiritual eyes to see in the spirit the truth of this event. As you relive the event, let the emotions also happen, which may be fear or anger or rejection, or a combination of emotions.

If assisting people with this ministry, you may find that they will go back to an event that happened when they were a child and have emotions of that childhood again, such as crying.

As the Holy Spirit takes you… stop and take note of your feelings and emotions, such as shame, hurt, anger, rejection, etc. These feelings can inform you of any demons that have entered and hidden behind damaged emotions and feelings from traumatic events and from the other CORUPTS door portals.

As mentioned, when your feelings and emotions are damaged, a portal or door is opened and demons come through this tear. Don't let this alarm or concern you, but use this information for your healing and the healing that others need, especially when continued attempts at deliverance are a struggle, or when demons reoccur later.

We must shut the doors of the prison after we're free and kick them out for good!

The lie of the event has been guarded by the emotion which has prevented the healing and recovery. The lie will be exposed by the Lord, when He reveals Himself to you! The Holy Spirit will show you how the evil realm took this event and made a bad situation worse. Such as a demon entering from the trauma of being rejected, beaten or raped as a child, having this demon tell you that it wouldn't have happened if you weren't a bad person. Or perhaps witnessing a murder, with a demon telling you that you could have acted to stop it.

Once they get in, they actively work at deepening the wounds.

Take an account of your feelings and ask yourself, "How do I feel right now"? These feelings will be associated with the lie that you have believed.

During your encounter with the Lord, He will speak the truth to you, which will dispel the lie.

After this… examine your feelings, and you should see that your feelings have changed and the root of the dysfunction was removed through spiritual healing.

Do not be surprised where the Holy Spirit takes you; or that you are experiencing certain feelings and emotions.

While you are there, look around and expect to see something you didn't see before. When you look around with your spiritual eyes, expect now to see or hear Jesus.

Focus on perhaps a light or a color or something that comes to your attention.

Look for Him.

While reliving this event, you may see the Lord or He may just give you a Word or maybe just a new feeling inside, as you know He is present and you now know something He wants you to know.

<u>When the Lord appears to you by sight, sound or perception this is the most significant moment of the ministry</u>!

He will reveal the truth to you with a Word that will dispel the lie. He may encourage you, comfort you or He may reprove you and ask you why you did something. Speak and talk to Him, as He leads. He may also rebuke you and ask you to confess your sin. Obey what He says.

"Trust in the Lord with all your heart, and lean not on your own understanding; In all your ways acknowledge Him, and He shall direct your paths." Proverbs 3:5-6

<u>The Word He speaks to you is the key to your prison break!</u>

It is important to remember what He says, as it will be used to do the second strike of the escape plan later.

This Word that the Lord gives you will be so impacting that it will <u>instantly</u> heal your emotions and break the lie that you have lived with!

After your experience with the Lord, examine your feelings again. Your revised feelings will be your evidence of healing.

The Holy Spirit may now take you to another event and if so, repeat the process again and again, as He leads.

One woman testified to me that the Holy Spirit took her back to three different areas and showed her the spiritual truth… all in minutes!

One man testified to me that he invited the Holy Spirit to do this and he was taken to a trauma that he hadn't thought of since he was a child. His spiritual eyes were opened and he was released from a secret prison he wasn't aware he was in!

Other fruits of this ministry are, that now you realize that you have a closer relationship with your Lord, that the Holy Spirit is in you and you know that you can rely on him, and not alternative therapies or counseling from people.

Important to note again… now that one's emotions are back in order and the truth has overcome the lie, any demons present are no longer hidden or allowed to stay, as their stronghold is gone. There <u>may</u> be a demon in you, just as there may be a burglar in your house if you left the front door open. You must look for it, as you would in every room for a burglar.

One person put this plan in operation and while spiritually searching himself, he found two unwanted evil intruders in his intestines and promptly kicked them out!

Demons have a right to be in a person if they are allowed and they are also easily cast out when the blood of Jesus is applied to that portal that is now closed.

If you had previously lost control of any area of your life, then you can call it what it is, such as "spirit of fear" or "spirit of rejection or lust" and say something like: "In the name of Jesus Christ, I have authority over you, you evil spirit of (whatever) and you have no right in or over me— and I command you in the name of Jesus Christ, to come out of me without manifesting and never return."

You speak to the evil spirit and command it.

You can have variations of this as the Holy Spirit leads and you also can and should command them to go somewhere (prison) as the Holy Spirit leads, as Jesus cast the legion into a herd of swine:

"And He said to them, "Go." So when they had come out, they went into the herd of swine. And suddenly the whole herd of swine ran violently down the steep place into the sea, and perished in the water." Matthew 8:32

Any evil spirits in you must go.

Holy angels will also assist in chasing demons out, once their right to stay is gone.

There may be a manifestation or sense of them leaving. Breathing out forcefully for instance or you may moan, or scream or there may be silence when they go.

This evil entity is not you, and not part of you, as you are a Christian who belongs to God.

When the demon(s) leaves you have control back in that area and now let Jesus sit on the throne— so if demons come, they will find Jesus over your heart, mind, body, soul, and spirit.

Declare war on the enemy and claim victory over them by the blood of Jesus.

Don't be afraid... be free!

If you happen to be helping someone through this process, sit the person down and ask the Holy Spirit to take them back into their memories to cure them of any dysfunctions. When they are reliving the event ask the Lord for help and to reveal Himself to the person and ask Him to show the person what they need to know.

When this is done have the person command the evil spirit to come out or you can assist and expel it for them.

Failure in this comes when the person will not allow the Holy Spirit to operate or the person will not adhere to their part of the strike plan.

This is a dual strike force escape plan, requiring two strikes to secure the cure.

The Holy Spirit does His strike, now the person must do a follow-up strike.

As with the oil and the wine used by the Good Samaritan, we have utilized the oil of the Holy Spirit on the wound and now we must use the wine, or the Word of God.

The Word of God will give strength and health to the wound.

Like a physical wound, there is more needed besides cleaning and closing, as the wound can still be vulnerable initially and until the cure is done, such as daily antibiotic medicine and/or treatment to a physical wound. The Holy Spirit initiates the healing and the Word of God completes it.

In the Bible, we find all sorts of two-part combinations such as bread and wine, Spirit and truth, and praise and worship. The Bible is full of two-part activities and it is no different with healing the soul.

Once you receive the Word/truth that the Lord gave you when you revisited the event, you reinforce this Word from the Lord with the Word of God being engrafted into you.

"Therefore, lay aside all filthiness and overflow of wickedness, and receive with meekness the implanted word, which is able to save your souls." James 1:21

It is your responsibility to hold onto the Word you received from the first strike, and truth that has been revealed; and take the medicine of the scripture to reinforce the cure.

Do not think that the process is done totally by God?

He expects you to do your part.

Be patient, as one must be for a total physical healing.

Find scriptures that relate to the Word given to you by the Lord.

If the Word given related to fear or rejection, find scripture verses that relate to this, such as "Lo, I am with you always, even unto the end of the age." Matthew 28:20

Through study of Dr. Dale Sides' ministry in this area of inner healing, I learned a truth regarding Jesus referring to satan as Beelzebub, the prince of demons, in Matthew 12:24, which means lord of the flies. A fly's life expectancy is forty days and this is the exact amount of time that the lord of the flies tempted Jesus in the wilderness before he stopped. This teaching has held true for this cure of the soul process also. When people confess the Word given them by the Lord and the scriptures over their mind and body for forty days, that usually within this time, total healing manifests!

If people don't do their part and take this medicine, often times their healing is lost and they can become re-imprisoned!

Another aspect of the fly is that it reproduces every six hours, meaning we can expect an attack against our wound every six hours, for forty days!

We need to combat this attack by quoting the word of God to our minds at least every six hours. Just like pills we must take at regular intervals to prevent infections and complete a physical healing; it is the same with the soul.

Dr. Sides suggests that a person find three verses in the Bible relating to the rhema that the Lord gave them during their operation with the Holy Spirit.

Use three scriptures, as this is how many times Jesus quoted scripture at the devil during his temptation.

Speak these three verses <u>out loud</u> four times a day (every six hours) for forty days.

Put a note somewhere to do this so you don't forget to take your medicine.

The Word permeates the affected area and keeps the flies off.

Don't be concerned about overdosing on <u>this</u> medicine… it can't happen!

Interesting to note that science tells us that 75-80 % of all diseases are rooted in the mind (some say its 80-95%)!

When our souls are cured our body bears the fruit!

Go get the truth with the Holy Spirit, get the Word (rhema) from the Lord and then take three gospills, (as Dr. Sides calls them) four times a day for forty days.

"Trust in the Lord with all your heart, and lean not on your own understanding; In all your ways acknowledge Him, and He shall direct your paths." Proverbs 3:5-6

Besides a cracked soul, which is like a rip, cut or tear in the flesh, the soul can also fragment or have a piece torn away, same as with flesh.

As one person can end up with multiple cuts and pieces ripped or cut away from the body, so also can one's soul.

Don't be in a hurry to deal with one or two issues and then think you're done, as some do.

Tending to just one wound and not another would be foolish.

When dealing with a POW, we must look at <u>every</u> wound!

Dr. Haggard taught that a damaged soul can be fragmented.

One way to deal with fragmented souls is what I call:

THE SAINTS AND ANGELIC PRISON BREAK PLAN

This next plan for inner healing is the prison break of fragmented souls.

This can be done in addition to the preceding method, as it relates to various other situations of what CORUPTS the soul.

There are situations that are directly and indirectly affecting us and our souls that we need to be made aware of, requiring attention and action.

We covered rejection, trauma, and sin in the dual strike escape force plan, so now let's go over some other areas of CORUPTS.

Curses can be put against us by others, and also by ourselves. Not only specific attacks can come against us from witches, satanists, and occult practitioners, but also from family, friends, and even fellow Christians! People can speak words against us in spite, anger, jealousy, fear, hatred, and also in ignorance.

People very often curse themselves!

I hear this almost on a daily basis!

Curses can <u>indirectly</u> come against us such as with food grown on cursed land or by cursed people. Which in this case, shows us the wisdom of blessing food before it is eaten and even taking communion with every meal. Certainly, taking communion often increases your spiritual and physical well-being.

Occult practices can imprison us… many are involved in the occult, willingly and in ignorance. Such activities as astrology, palm and tea readings, charms, tarot cards, prayer wheels, hypnotism, white and black magic, freemasonry, spells, incantations, etc., can all tear away at our soul. God wants us to go to Him for wisdom, knowledge, and revelation, not the devil.

During one of Dr. Haggard's teachings about retrieving fragmented souls, he spoke of a man in Guatemala brought to salvation who gave a startling testimony I'd like to share.

This man was an occultist, who, to the world, was a happy family man and a photographer, but unknown to anyone, he would go to his basement, and through witchcraft, capture portions of people's souls that lived in his town and put them in sealed jars!

He would keep these jars on a shelf and enjoy watching people in town get sicker and sicker.

Once this man became a Christian, he was told he had to put all these fragments back into people, yet he had never done that before and didn't know how.

He asked the Holy Spirit for direction and was able to put all these soul fragments back where they belonged, after which he noticed that all the people in town had recovered!

Another unusual testimony is of fragmented souls of people in a "church" congregation, kept in jars that were guarded by a pastor and his wife!

Can anyone ever imagine a congregation being controlled and in bondage by a priest or minister?

Doesn't seem out of the realm of belief, as we see and hear of that often.

What we don't see and hear is, what is happening in the spiritual realm behind this bondage.

There are many other testimonies of people's souls being fragmented and imprisoned somewhere else.

Idol worship is another activity that many people, including Christians, are involved in. People idolize and worship the dead and the living, including themselves. (i.e. Dead idols: dead Mary, dead disciples, dead priests, dead nuns… Living idols: Movie stars, sports stars, music stars.)

Physical objects are also idolized such as money, cars, houses, etc., which captures a piece of their soul.

It was found out through deliverance of a person, that a fragment of their soul was in various places such as the Vatican, the pope, and in a statue of Mary!

The Vatican means, "hill of the soothsayer" and demons who have manifested during deliverance, speak of how many souls are trapped there!

"For where your treasure is, there will your heart be also." Mathew 6:21

Unforgiveness of others is another huge door that opens within us damaging our soul, jeopardizing our salvation, and permitting demons to plague us.

All of these CORUPTS activities can crack and fragment your soul, open doors and allow demons to come in, to stay and corrupt.

"For what profit is it to a man if he gains the whole world, and loses his own soul? Or what will a man give in exchange for his soul?" Matthew 16:26

Examine yourself… do some soul searching… ask the Holy Spirit to help.

Is your memory as good as it could or should be?

Can you love as well as you should?

Are there any parts of your soul cracked or missing?

Are you reigning or are you being reined?

What have you traded your soul for?

Many people may not agree that a soul can be fragmented or cracked or imprisoned, but whatever you want to call it, the Bible warns us of what can happen and testimonies have proven God's Word is right.

Escape and inner healing is possible, if we act, or someone acts on our behalf.

"Lest he tear my soul like a lion, rending it in pieces, while there is none to deliver." Psalm 7:2 KJV

A few other situations that can damage the soul:

- Illicit sexual encounters.
- Taking care of the sick and the invalid form unhealthy 'sympathy' attachments.
- Fire worship, such as lighting candles in a religious "church" to the dead and for favors.
- Soul ties with non-Christians.

"If anyone comes to you and does not bring this doctrine, do not receive him into your house nor greet him; for he who greets him shares in his evil deeds." 2 John 10-11

Unhealthy social fellowships

We are to fellowship with the Father, Son, Holy Spirit, and other true Christians—there are over 40 classes of people mentioned in the Bible that we are <u>not</u> to fellowship with.

All sin and iniquity

"His own iniquities entrap the wicked man, And he is caught in the cords of his sin." Proverbs 5:22

All graven images of worship

"You shall burn the carved images of their gods with fire; you shall not covet the silver or gold that is on them, nor take it for yourselves, lest you be snared by it; for it is an abomination to the Lord your God. Nor shall you bring an abomination into your house, lest you be doomed to destruction like it. You shall utterly detest it and utterly abhor it, for it is an accursed thing." Deuteronomy 7:25-26

Adultery destroys the soul

"Whoever commits adultery with a woman lacks understanding; He who does so destroys his own soul." Proverbs 6:32

How do we get our pieces back and restored?

<u>Send angels</u>, with the authority that you have in Jesus Christ, to have them break the bondage on the soul, which may be also at evil altars, go get any fragments and bring them back and restore them.

"Are they not all ministering spirits sent forth to minister for those who will inherit salvation?" Hebrews 1:14

They are waiting for you to activate them for God's glory! Send them into battle! Have them raid the prisons where any fragments of a person's soul are kept and release them to be restored where they belong.

We must do more than break soul ties…we must restore the soul! This can be done by ourselves or we can do it for others, even from a distance.

Soul fragments of others may also be in you…if anyone worships you! Many Christians worship leaders, instead of God. Command any and all soul fragments of others in you to go out and go to where they belong. Have angels take them back.

Let the Holy Spirit guide you on which plan to use in a specific situation.

You might end up using all the plans on many missions with the same person.

One person I know has helped one person break free from dozens of different soul prisons over many months.

This next plan is another one the Holy Spirit may lead you to use.

THE COMMANDO PRISON BREAK PLAN

I like this one!

You can send special commandos into a prison. Call for the enemies of sickness, infirmities, and disease to come and attack these evil things and set people free.

This plan has freed those with palsy, paralysis, and from wheelchairs!

Against the mind, there may be an evil spiritual squid or octopus spirit binding the mind and draining energy. (Hey… don't look at me like that… I have come against these things!)

The Holy Spirit may show you all sorts of evil things in and on people that would require a certain plan to deal with it.

One time I could see an evil entity standing on a woman's back with its fingers in her ears causing her hearing loss… my sword ending its torment of her and her hearing returned!

The Holy Spirit may direct you to call for the natural enemies of these creatures, such as a spiritual sperm whale against a squid or octopus affecting a person's mind.

You can also send angels to assist the sperm whale in battle. Although this sounds unusual, there are natural enemies in the physical realm, such as the eagle against the snake or the lion against the hyena.

Testimonies from those who operate in the spirit have seen these creatures, including me, and results have been dramatic!

Although these plans are all spiritual plans, this next one is you going in the spirit to release a POW.

GOING IN THE SPIRIT PRISON BREAK PLAN

As a spiritual being and a born-again Christian, you may also go in the spirit to set captives free.

When I have done this, there really hasn't been a preplanning stage, I simply did as I was led during the operation.

I went in the spirit one time to the door of a prison cell. There was a huge spiritual boar that was blocking my way to the cell. Always willing to get acquainted with such evil creatures, I introduced myself by shoving the point of my sword into its right eye! From its hasty departure, I discerned that it didn't really want to stay to get to know me!

I walked up to the cell, struck my sword down upon the huge lock and opened the door.

I didn't know what was in the cell or what would come out, as it was pitch black in there.

To my surprise, a little girl in pigtails came out, took my hand, and came with me as we left the area. She had the face of an adult acquaintance of mine.

She is now free of this prison that she has been in probably since a child. I have no idea what this imprisonment was about.

During this "Going in the Spirit Escape Plan," you may also have the assistance of angels to move evil forces, extract POW's, and seal off gates of hell.

Don't be shy towards angels or about using them.

Seek the Holy Spirit for guidance and assistance in a situation.

A person I know in Europe has gone in the spirit to many soul prisons of various kinds such as caves, cages, valleys, blackness, and ice, releasing the imprisoned soul fragments with the assistance of Jesus and angels. Some prison breaks have been simple, taking only minutes, while others took hours.

When I say soul fragment, what you'll see looks like the whole body, not just a piece of a body such as an arm or leg.

Once this fragment is released, it goes back to the person.

The person usually notices that a positive change in them has happened.

I was in the spirit to help someone and could see that they were in a coffin-shaped cage. I opened the top of the spiritual cage door and told her she had to come out on her own. Jesus and I waited for her to decide, as she seemed unwilling to leave this comfort zone. She finally came out and as Jesus hugged her, He said, "I will never reject you!", releasing her from a lifetime of rejection torment.

She became a totally transformed person after that event… in minutes!

And remains so to this day!

A final note on POW's, is that our souls are always in danger of being wounded and captured.

The devil will never give up on you and will have strategies to attack you, tempt you, trick you, trap you, traumatize you, and if he can't get at you the way he would like, he will attack areas around you such as your family and finances, to wound, confuse, delay, disrupt, and destroy you.

He will talk to you in such a way to have you think he is God.

He will also leave you alone for a while to see if you will drop your defenses and then he will attack.

Keep your heart, mind, body, spirit, and soul guarded, your defenses fortified, and daily be in touch with command headquarters of God, as Jesus did, for your battle plan, and any necessary escape plans.

"Therefore, do not fear them. For there is nothing covered that will not be revealed, and hidden that will not be known." Matthew 10:26

Raid the prisons and set the captives free!

SECTOR TWENTY-THREE

ALTARS, STRUCTURES AND STRONGHOLDS

> **HUNTING TIP**
> Words make a mighty weapon… use them wisely!

As a big game hunter, you will have your favorite spots to hunt. Many hunters will travel hundreds of miles, then fly into a place only to then boat to a spot from there, and walk for miles to reach that sweet spot where they consistently experience success.

Certain sweet spots have brought me to them every year and they rarely fail me.

These places are where game love to hang out or pass through for some reason such as water, food, protection and/or migration.

Many hunters also have spots they regularly go to prior to a hunt, servicing it with bait to bring the game in where you want them. If you want to bring in a deer you can use salt licks, apples and doe scent. Want a coyote… use a rabbit call or a smelly animal carcass. Want a bear… try donuts. (I'm not kidding… this works on people too!) My father used to use dead fish to bring mink to his traps.

Try African jungle drums for spiritual dragons! These drum sounds have been ignorantly played at religious "church" events, thinking it was entertainment or somehow pleasing to God.

People also use sweet spots such as clubs, bars, dating services (even Church group events) and attractions (bait) like perfumes, clothes and make-up to bring in the big game (the opposite sex).

Make sure you're using the correct lure for the correct game. Coyotes could care less about apples and women aren't attracted to hunters that have been in the bush for a week.

Well, maybe some would think it's manly, until they got downwind of us!

What is the success rate if you don't go to a sweet spot or don't lure the game you're after?

I don't need to answer that one!

So, you're thinking, Al, what does this have to do with altars?

If you want to attract God, angels, evil entities, blessings, curses, success, failure, health, sickness, wealth, poverty, life or death, an altar, or lack of one, can help do the job. I've mixed in the good and the bad here because there are holy altars and evil altars.

Many Christians think that the need for altars ended in the Old Testament or are only at the front of a "church" to hold up a gold-plated cross. Yet, very effective, extremely successful altars are serviced by millions, probably billions of people in <u>every</u> country all over the world.

<u>Many people who call themselves Christian are servicing altars every day!</u> Unfortunately, the altars I speak of here are evil ones!

Hard to believe, isn't it?

Are you servicing any evil altars?

Are there any evil altars set up against you?

Are you servicing a holy altar daily?

Better be sure before you head out Xtreme Game Hunting!

<u>Altar:</u> Place that serves as a center of worship or ritual. (Mirriam-Webster Dictionary) An altar can be holy or evil; a physical place or a spiritual place.

At an altar, a person makes contact with the spiritual realm through prayer or sacrifice to produce a covenant and serve a covenant either with God or evil entities.

Anyone who has authority or represents one with authority, can build an altar for blessings or destruction.

Blessings or destruction upon a person, people or places (Church group, neighborhood, city, nation)

<u>Covenant</u>: a written agreement or promise usually under seal between two or more parties, especially for the performance of some action. (Mirriam-Webster Dictionary)

A holy altar connects a person with God to receive His grace, His anointing, His revelation, His intimacy, His assistance, His favor, His covering, His blessings and His judgments against enemies.

The first physical altar in the Bible is built by Noah after the flood. God was very pleased and made an everlasting covenant with Noah and the world to never destroy all living things again by water, sealing His pledge with a token, in the form of a rainbow. Genesis 8:21-22; 9:8-15

<u>A token is a sign that a covenant is in existence and operating.</u>

There are too many altars and covenants in the Bible to cover here, so I'll just mention a few.

Abraham built altars to God and God made covenants with him. One well known everlasting covenant was made for his descendants. The token or sign of this covenant was the circumcision of all males. Genesis 12:6-8; 13: 4-18; 17-2; 17:9-14

Jacob had a dream, God made a covenant with him and his descendants and Jacob built altars wherever he lived. God even commanded Jacob to build an altar. Genesis 28:10-1; 33:18-2; 35:1

God made a covenant with Moses and the children of Israel that had an "if".

"Now therefore, <u>if</u> you will indeed obey My voice <u>and</u> keep My covenant, then you shall be a special treasure to Me above all people; for all the earth is Mine." Exodus 19:5

God has many covenants with the "if" word attached to it that people ignore.

<u>Each</u> party that enters into a covenant or contract (i.e. accepting Christ as your Savior) must <u>each</u> service the terms of the contract.

God <u>must</u> and will service His terms of the covenant (i.e. salvation, healing, joy, blessings, success, protection, peace that surpasses all understanding, etc.) and a person <u>must</u> service their terms of the covenant (i.e. praise, worship, thanks, prayer, forgive others, obedience, no sin, etc.)

<u>If the terms of the covenant aren't being provided for you by God, look to yourself!</u>

God didn't institute altars and their very specific servicing because they don't work. And if they didn't work, satan and his breed wouldn't use them!

David and Daniel serviced their <u>spiritual</u> altars to God three times a day!

"Evening and morning and at noon
I (David) will pray, and cry aloud,
And He shall hear my voice." Psalm 55:17

"Now when Daniel knew that the writing was signed, he went home. And in his upper room, with his windows open toward Jerusalem, he knelt down on his knees three times that day, and prayed and gave thanks before his God, as was his custom since early days." Daniel 6:10

Jesus serviced the spiritual altar to God every day, even the day of His death.

"Now in the morning, having risen a long while before daylight, He went out and departed to a solitary place; and there He prayed." Mark 1:35

"Coming out, He went to the Mount of Olives, as He was accustomed (habit), and His disciples also followed Him. When He came to the place, He said to them, "Pray that you may not enter into temptation." Luke 22:39-40

Christians are expecting God's glory and for Him to meet His Word for them, yet they wander around ignoring <u>their</u> requirements!

"When Solomon had finished praying, fire came down from heaven and consumed the burnt offering and the sacrifices; and the glory of the Lord filled the temple. And the priests could not enter the house of the Lord, because the glory of the Lord had filled the Lord's house." 2 Chronicles 7:1-2

Ever been <u>unable</u> to enter somewhere (i.e. a religious "church" building), because the glory of the Lord was residing there?

God doesn't want the servicing of His altar to stop.

"A fire shall always be burning on the altar; it shall never go out." Leviticus 6:13.

Nowadays the main altar is located in our heart and we should be servicing it to God continually!

Blood sacrifice is what God's altars needed to take effect.

Jesus' blood became the final and only holy sacrifice that God needs. Come to God continually using the blood of Jesus as your sacrifice!

Let's see what happened in the war between the house of Israel and the Philistines in 1 Samuel 7:3-13:

"Then Samuel spoke to all the house of Israel, saying, "<u>If</u> you return to the Lord with all your hearts, <u>then</u> put away the foreign gods <u>and</u> the Ashtoreths from among you, <u>and</u> prepare your hearts for the Lord, <u>and</u> serve Him only; (Israel had to do 5 things first) and He will deliver you from the hand of the Philistines." (<u>then</u> God would move to protect them against the Philistines) ⁴ So the children of Israel put away the Baals and the Ashtoreths, and served the Lord only.

⁵ And Samuel said, "Gather all Israel to Mizpah, and I will pray to the Lord for you." ⁶ So they gathered together at Mizpah, drew water, and poured it out before the Lord. And they fasted that day, and said there, "We have sinned against the Lord." And Samuel judged the children of Israel at Mizpah.

(They put away their evil altars and gods, served the Lord only, gathered together, fasted, asked for forgiveness and were judged. Their hearts were turned and prepared.)

⁷ Now when the Philistines heard that the children of Israel had gathered together at Mizpah, the lords of the Philistines went up against Israel. And when the children of Israel heard of it, they were afraid of the Philistines. ⁸ So the children of Israel said to Samuel, "Do not cease to cry out to the Lord our God for us, that He may save us from the hand of the Philistines."

⁹ And Samuel took a suckling lamb and offered it as a whole burnt offering to the Lord. Then Samuel cried out to the Lord for Israel, and the Lord answered him.

(High Priest Samuel serviced the altar and asked the Lord to protect Israel. Israel was God's again, and He was theirs. God would fulfill His end of the old covenant.)

¹⁰ Now as Samuel was offering up the burnt offering, the Philistines drew near to battle against Israel. But the Lord thundered with a loud thunder upon the Philistines that day, and so confused them that they were overcome before Israel. ¹¹ And the men of Israel went out of Mizpah and pursued the Philistines, and drove them back as far as below Beth Car. (Israel was saved and the enemies were driven back) ¹² Then Samuel took a stone and set it up between Mizpah and Shen, and called its name Ebenezer, saying, "Thus far the Lord has helped us."

¹³ So the Philistines were subdued, and they did not come anymore into the territory of Israel. And the hand of the Lord was against the Philistines all the days of Samuel."

God's protective hand and blessings stayed in place… for a time… until Israel reneged (for the umpteenth time!) on their covenant with God.

Some will say we must go to a specific place, as did Moses to the mountain, Ezekiel at the Chebar river, Daniel at the Ulai river or Jesus in the wilderness, <u>but</u>, we know that Jesus wasn't in the same place all the time and the holy of holies was ripped asunder when Jesus died on the Cross (Mark 15:38).

We no longer have to go to a specific physical place to be with God.

We can go to physical places such as a prayer closet in order to achieve silence and be alone, but a physical place or physical altar isn't a requirement, as every true Christian is a high priest and has direct access to God from anywhere!

Not just once a year, but all the time!

If a Christian is derelict in their altar service to God, what can we suppose can happen or not happen?

On that note, let's move over to evil or satanic altars.

Evil Altars

Christians, and especially Silver Bullets of God and Xtreme Game Hunters, will come into contact or suffer attacks from satanic altars!

Christians can be feverously praying, fasting, singing songs, tithing, fellowshipping, reading the Bible, having people intercede/pray for them, hands laid on them, deliverance done, inner healing methods done and yet problems persist. They are doing everything they can think of, but bad stuff keeps happening.

The marriage, family or their Church group is inexplicably failing; they are plagued by nightmares or hearing strange voices and footsteps; irrational behavior pops up, such as violence or tantrums or uncontrollable urges (i.e. alcohol, drugs, sex, gambling, etc.); they can't seem to get ahead or succeed or get a good job; money just oddly disappears; they are constantly suspicious, fearful for no reason or sudden suicidal tendencies or a death wish. This happened to Elijah when Jezebel spoke a curse against him in 1 Kings 19.

Mysterious marks are showing up on their bodies.

They experience sickness or depression, especially when it happens on a timetable.

This happened to me every day for a while at four o'clock in the morning, when I'd wake up, having a feeling of intense dread and hopelessness. It would go away, but come back again the next morning at the same time. Warfare against evil entities didn't work. Warfare against the evil altar against me took care of it.

Ongoing accidents or maybe family members are killed!

Maybe early death comes for them!

"The thief does not come except to steal, and to kill, and to destroy. I have come that they may have life, and that they may have it more abundantly." John 10:10

Where's God, they cry?

<u>These people are perhaps servicing evil altars (in ignorance) AND/OR evil altars are set up against them.</u>

The devil counterfeited and perverted altar use to produce curses and destruction against God's people and creation.

Satanists and witches build evil altars and regularly offer sacrifices upon it to send out evil entities.

Christians also service evil altars (deliberately and in ignorance), keeping evil covenants in place, that keep evil entities in place.

Whether deliberate or in ignorance, building and servicing evil altars produce and maintain evil results!

Evil altars connect with the evil spiritual realm invoking evil entities to afflict people or areas.

An evil altar is serviced by a person(s) by giving sacrifices to evil entities.

As Christians depend on the spiritual realm for Father God, Jesus, the Holy Spirit and angels to assist us, evil people depend on the spiritual realm for evil spirits and territorial spirits to assist them.

These evil spirits are sent out to afflict a person and monitor them.

Evil altars can help these people know a person's strengths and weaknesses, to determine their attacks.

They also use human agents/spies to assist them in reporting on a person, which can be religious "church" members. Animal spies are also used, such as birds that evil spirits will use to keep an eye on you and report back to the evil altar keepers.

Altars will be used to destroy and hold a person back in various areas of life, especially any spiritual areas.

Let's examine some Biblical examples of evil altars.

In Ezekiel 8, Ezekiel was taken in the spirit to see what was going on at night in Jerusalem. Seventy elders and Jaazaniah were worshipping idols <u>in the temple</u>; a woman was worshipping the god Tammuz, and he was shown twenty-five sun worshippers.

Quite a lot going on when others were sleeping, eh!

This resulted in filling the land with violence and turning God away in jealousy, anger and pronouncing judgments. These people were bringing the nation to destruction.

More than forty men in Acts 23:12-14 made and serviced an evil altar to produce Paul's death, which was approved by Jewish leaders.

"And when it was day, some of the Jews banded together and bound themselves under an oath (curse), saying that they would neither eat nor drink till they had killed Paul. Now there were more than forty who had formed this conspiracy (evil covenant). They came to the chief priests and elders, and said, "We have bound ourselves under a great oath (curse covenant) that we will eat nothing until we have killed Paul."

Such things still go on today all over the world.

Many areas, towns, cities, regions and nations were built by leaders who did not dedicate them to the one true God, but made covenants with evil entities, giving these evil entities spiritual authority over these areas.

These covenants and evil entities stay, unless spiritual warfare is done to bring repentance and have covenants revoked in Jesus' name.

These evil covenants and evil entities are serviced by people every year by their culture, traditions, festivals and holidays.

Culture's root word is cult.

Looking at some culture, people for centuries have been getting tattoos, incisions and piercings of their bodies for various reasons.

"You shall not make any cuttings in your flesh for the dead, nor tattoo any marks on you: I am the Lord." Leviticus 19:28

Tattoos are a bloodletting practice of idol worship, allowing demons to enter and bring bondage. Many tribal/cult tattoos and incisions can bring specific problems which are only upon them when they are in certain areas.

A person can notice that they are not struggling with perhaps depression, anger, addictions, thoughts of suicide, etc. when they leave the area, only to have the problems return, when they go back home.

The power of the territorial rulers against them ends until they return.

Fortunately, there is a remedy… read on!

People regularly celebrate special occasions, festivals, holidays and traditions throughout the year such as honoring shrines, monuments, idols, statues, the dead, halloween, etc., which keep evil covenants serviced and satan happy.

These activities keep evil entities and their power over areas and people in place.

Evil spiritual rulers are receiving support and worship to continue; and the curse over the people and land thus continues.

"They served their idols, which became a snare to them." Psalm 106:36

"Thus, they were defiled by their own works, and played the harlot by their own deeds. Therefore, the wrath of the Lord was kindled against His people, so that He abhorred His own inheritance. And He gave them into the hand of the Gentiles, and those who hated them ruled over them. Their enemies also oppressed them, and they were brought into subjection under their hand.Psalm 106:39-42

"Therefore, my beloved, flee from idolatry." 1 Corinthians 10:14

People, including those who say they are Christian, are involved in horoscopes; palm, psychic, tarot card and star readings; witchcraft; sorcery; ouija boards; crystal balls; good luck charms; prayer wheels; false religions and personal doctrines; new age stuff; and spirit channeling, to name a few.

"You are wearied in the multitude of your counsels; Let now the astrologers, the stargazers, and the monthly prognosticators stand up and save you from what shall come upon you. Behold, they shall be as stubble, the fire shall burn them; They shall not deliver themselves From the power of the flame; It shall not be a coal to be warmed by, nor a fire to sit before!" Isaiah 47:13-14

Generation after generation of unsuspecting people, are cursing themselves, their children, their grandchildren and the land.

These are some of the things people are doing to themselves.

What about people who are doing it to you?

There are evil people who have evil altars that they service against Church groups, leaders, Christians in general and specific people.

One case I'm aware of, is of evil words, incantations, spells and ceremonies being recording on tape and then placed on the property of a Church! These words would be in place, continually affecting the spiritual atmosphere.

There are many cases of former witches testifying, that their job was to go to Church services to destroy the assembly. Fortunately, some received salvation and became warriors for God!

Another case that I'm aware of, was of a woman that went to a Church group and stayed there until it was destroyed, through seduction of the pastor or one of the Church leaders and then she moved on to the next Church group.

There are countless stories of these things going on… pastors and Christian leaders becoming controlling, committing adultery, stealing Church funds, becoming disillusioned, and quitting.

Evil altars are set up and being serviced against them.

Evil people can do this in a variety of ways.

They can make an image of the person, put it on an altar or in a shrine and then pronounce/invoke evil words against the person, conjuring/sending out evil entities to fulfill the affliction against that person.

This image can be a 3D image or a picture.

They also will strike the image or poke it with sharp objects to inflict pain and disease upon the person they're after (voodoo).

They can do this just with a person's name that is pronounced over their altar and what they want done to them.

They will also use hair, nail clippings, the person's clothing and even menstrual pads of an individual to attack that person.

They will suspend people's names and images in trees to suspend their life from success.

They will do the same, by putting people's names and pictures in bodies of water, or in the ground to suspend a person's life to never advance.

Those experienced in astrology, can attack the zodiac or star sign of an individual to also produce curses.

A Christian can do spiritual warfare to destroy these altars, remove these images and names, reverse the rituals, break the curses and turn it all into blessings.

IMPORTANT… Break the curses and evil covenants set up against you/a person first and THEN destroy the altar.

This is important because a person is spiritually attached or connected to the altar and if you destroy the altar first, the effects will affect the person.

Pronounce that your name/person's name/image/picture is removed from this altar in Jesus' name, and sever all ties with this altar and those working them.

Evil people that are setting up and servicing these altars, and how to deal with them, are discussed in more detail in the Sector on Xtreme Rabid Game.

> Briefly we use the Imprecatory Psalms or "Psalm Bombs." Imprecatory Psalms 5, 6, 11, 12, 35, 37, 40, 52, 54, 56, 58, 59, 69, 79, 109, 137, 139 and 143, were given to us to pronounce against workers of iniquity.

Although bringing them to Christ would be our aim, we must also stop their works.

Prophesy over them that they will receive Jesus as their Savior. We can't just turn a blind eye to evil, as we are to <u>resist</u> (fight/oppose/defy) the devil.

"Resist the devil, and he will flee from you." James 4:7

To deal with evil altars we must realize that they exist and what they do. This knowledge can keep a person from setting up and servicing evil altars in the future, but more is needed to combat them.

Ask God to show or reveal to you any altars that are against you and how to destroy them.

He can do this in a dream, a vision, revelation, and taking you in the spirit, as He did with Ezekiel.

If there is evil activity in your life, this must be dealt with, as evil spirits will keep a rightful hold and/or be difficult or impossible to conquer, until you place yourself into obedience with God.

If there is an attack against others, your family, Church group, or marriage, as a royal priest of God, you can stand in the gap, and intercede, asking God to forgive the sins of the evil altars, sacrifices and tokens given.

When God has reveals certain evil altars to you, you can speak prophetically against them, as a child of God. The Word of God against them is an excellent weapon. Ezekiel can teach you on speaking prophetically against evil altars.

Once you have detached yourself from these altars and they are destroyed, now command that all has been stolen from you/person/place be restored in Jesus' name.

Once delivered, possess what is yours.

"But on Mount Zion there shall be deliverance, and there shall be holiness; The house of Jacob shall possess their possessions." Obadiah 17

Don't forget to praise, worship, rejoice and thank God after all of this.

IMPORTANT… Keep up this warfare especially at night, when evil altars are usually serviced, until you receive results and blessings are flowing.

Key times are midnight and three in the morning.

Also, specific dates such as April 30, halloween, solstices, and equinoxes, are a few of the high holidays with heavy evil altar activity.

Check in your area, city and nation what dates are celebrated with festivals such as Mardi Gras in New Orleans or the festival of the dead in Mexico, to assist with your warfare plans. As an Xtreme Game Hunter, you don't have to wait until evil altars are set up against you.

Hunt them down with God's help, destroy them for others and restore people and areas that have been under a curse.

This can be done in the spirit, as I did one time, destroying an evil entity that was blocking a huge Christian festival that was cursed, from taking place. I was physically hundreds of miles away when this was done.

The next day, funds started flowing into this event, Church groups started joining in instead of coming against it and volunteers showed up. Before the warfare it was heading towards being a lackluster event or cancellation.

There are many areas in the Bible that can be studied about altars.

Here's some that stand out of what God thinks of evil altars and their gods and that He wants His people to destroy them:

"But thus, you shall deal with them: you shall destroy their altars, and break down their sacred pillars, and cut down their wooden images, and burn their carved images with fire." Deuteronomy 7:5

"You shall utterly destroy all the places where the nations which you shall dispossess served their gods, on the high mountains and on the hills and under every green tree. And you shall destroy their altars, break their sacred pillars, and burn their wooden images with fire; you shall cut down the carved images of their gods and destroy their names from that place." Deuteronomy 12:2-3

"Son of man, set your face against Pharaoh king of Egypt (evil spiritual principality/ruler), and prophesy against him, and against all Egypt (evil dominion). Speak, and say, 'Thus says the Lord God:

"Behold, I am against you, O Pharaoh king of Egypt, O great monster who lies in the midst of his rivers, who has said, 'My River is my own; I have made it for myself.'

But I will put hooks in your jaws, and cause the fish of your rivers to stick to your scales; I will bring you up out of the midst of your rivers, and all the fish in your rivers will stick to your scales.

I will leave you in the wilderness, you and all the fish of your rivers; You shall fall on the open field; You shall not be picked up or gathered. I have given you as food to the beasts of the field and to the birds of the heavens." Ezekiel 29:2-5

"And it came to pass in the twelfth year, in the twelfth month, on the first day of the month, that the word of the Lord came to me, saying, "Son of man, take up a lamentation for Pharaoh king of Egypt, and say to him: 'You are like a young lion among the nations, and you are like a monster in the seas, bursting forth in your rivers, troubling the waters with your feet, and fouling their rivers. 'Thus says the Lord God: "I will therefore spread My net over you with a company of many people, and they will draw you up in My net. Then I will leave you on the land; I will cast you out on the open fields, and cause to settle on you all the birds of the heavens. And with you I will fill the beasts of the whole earth. I will lay your flesh on the mountains, and fill the valleys with your carcass. "I will also water the land with the flow of your blood, even to the mountains; and the riverbeds will be full of you. When I put out your light, I will cover the heavens, and make its stars dark; I will cover the sun with a cloud. And the moon shall not give her light. All the bright lights of the heavens I will make dark over you, and bring darkness upon your land," Says the Lord God." Ezekiel 32:1-8

Let's do it!

<u>Structures and Strongholds</u>

In a nut shell they are, foundations or the beginning of an area or of a city's life, as with a person, reflecting what it becomes later in life.

Rip off the veil of darkness over the area in the spirit and see what is over the area.

"And He will destroy on this mountain the surface of the covering cast over all people, and the veil that is spread over all nations." Isaiah 25:7

In the physical world, there are governmental structures and strongholds of nations that are controlled from the cities.

In ancient times, cities were fortified with walls and protected by armies.

An invading army can take all the forests, fields and deserts, but they must eventually take the cities or fortress of an area to overthrow the government.

Many times, a kingdom or government will fall when you destroy the evil king or leadership and replace it with a new leader and government.

Although sometimes defeating the king of an area or people was not enough for God.

He wanted all of their influence destroyed.

"So, the people (Joshua and the Israelites) shouted when the priests blew the trumpets. And it happened when the people heard the sound of the trumpet, and the people shouted with a great shout, that the wall (of Jericho) fell down flat. Then the people went up into the city, every man straight before him, and they took the city." Joshua 6:20

"But they burned the city and all that was in it with fire."
Joshua 6:24

When I visited Jericho years ago, I saw the wall that they had excavated. The ancient wall was still there standing under the ground.

When the Bible says "the wall fell down flat," did it mean the walls dropped flat down into the ground, rather than over?

In hunting jargon, I just went off on a rabbit trail, so let's get back on target.

Under God's plans, Joshua defeated 33 kings in a war that lasted 5 years. Many cities, towns and villages were taken. These evil strongholds and structures had to be methodically taken down under the direction of God.

Had Joshua and the guys went in and attacked them all at the same time or in the wrong order or at the wrong time or with the wrong strategy, they would have failed.

Remember that as an Xtreme Game Hunter!

Actually, they initially failed to take Ai, because one of them with Joshua failed to follow God's orders (Joshua 7). He was an enemy in the camp.

Notice that God gave the Israelites the land, but they had to war to take possession!

The earth belongs to God's people, but we have to war to take possession!

"For though we walk in the flesh, we do not war according to the flesh. For the weapons of our warfare are not carnal but mighty in God for pulling down strongholds." 2 Corinthians 10:3-4

God says here that we don't war in the natural and that strongholds exist that must be pulled down.

Some will say that this scripture pertains to mind strongholds, not spiritual structures. Mind strongholds exist. Yet, we know that there are spiritual structures as Jesus speaks of mansions in heaven (John 14:2) and a city of God, the new Jerusalem in Revelation 3:12; 21:2,10.

We know who is setting up evil spiritual strongholds against us.

"whose minds the god of this age (satan) has blinded, who do not believe, lest the light of the gospel of the glory of Christ, who is the image of God, should shine on them." 2 Corinthians 4:4

So how best can satan blind the minds of people from the gospel of Christ?

How best can satan control the most number of spiritual beings possible?

He controls them with a spiritual government!

A collection of individuals (souls) make up a city and are controlled by the government of that city, region, state and nation.

The birth of a city of individuals, patterns the birth of an individual. An individual's formative years are instrumental (usually) in the way they govern themselves when they are older. If a baby is mistreated and wounded in some way, it most likely will grow up dysfunctional, sick and cursed. If a city or area of people is birthed and is wounded by war, murder and violence (bloodshed), evil religion; then it will grow up to be dysfunctional, sick and cursed.

"Woe to him who builds a town with bloodshed,
Who establishes a city by iniquity!" Habakkuk 2:12

<u>Look to the past of a city.</u>

"For inquire, please, of the former age, and consider the things discovered by their fathers; For we were born yesterday, and know nothing, because our days on earth are a shadow." Job 8:8-9

Add more violence, bloodshed and sin into a person's life and they will become more violent, sicker and more cursed. Same with a city, a region and a world.

To rid a person of their dysfunctions, sin, iniquity and evil, they need the government of the one true God.

To rid cities/regions of their dysfunctions, sin and iniquity and evil they need the government of the one true God.

Remove the evil government and replace it with a holy government.

How do we do that with people, a city or a region?

Daniel spiritually came in intercession for Israel to God repenting and asking forgiveness for them to be set free. (Daniel 9:5-19)

Rees Howells spiritually came against Hitler, Mussolini and Stalin and those evil governments fell… and he never left Wales (see Why Do Xtreme Big Game Hunting Sector).

To have an effect on a physical government, the spiritual government over it must be dealt with.

People perpetuate evil structures over their lives, families, homes, neighborhoods, cities, regions, nations and the world with their activities!

I know we'd like to blame everything on satan and his followers, but if you'll recall, it was Eve and then Adam that decided to go against God.

People have that same decision today and if they compromise with and/or turn on God, they should expect much the same as those in the Bible received in this life and the lake of fire in the next!

The book of Revelation shows us the root or foundation of all structures.

We can't tear down this root foundation, as Revelation says it will be firmly in place at the eve of Christ's return.

"So, he (angel) carried me (John) away in the Spirit into the wilderness. And I saw a woman sitting on a scarlet beast which was full of names of blasphemy, having seven heads and ten horns. [4] The woman was arrayed in purple and scarlet, and adorned with gold and precious stones and pearls, having in her hand a golden cup full of abominations and the filthiness of her fornication. [5] And on her forehead a name was written:

MYSTERY, BABYLON THE GREAT,
THE MOTHER OF HARLOTS
AND OF THE ABOMINATIONS
OF THE EARTH.

⁶ I saw the woman, drunk with the blood of the saints and with the blood of the martyrs of Jesus. And when I saw her, I marveled with great amazement.

⁷ But the angel said to me, "Why did you marvel? I will tell you the mystery of the woman and of the beast that carries her, which has the seven heads and the ten horns. ⁸ The beast that you saw was, and is not, and will ascend out of the bottomless pit and go to perdition.

And those who dwell on the earth will marvel, whose names are not written in the Book of Life from the foundation of the world, when they see the beast that was, and is not, and yet is." Revelation 17:3-8

What John saw is not an actual woman, but representative of a structure.

This structure or stronghold is a religious system that satan started.

As there is a holy Church, or system, there is an unholy church or system.

The Church or bride of God is made up of Christians.

The false-church or bride of satan is made up of his followers or anti-Christians.

Where and what is this stronghold or false-church of followers of satan?

The evil system is called "Babylon the Great" in Revelation.

John was told that this beast "was, and is not, and yet is."

What does that mean?

The Babylonian empire (stronghold/religion) was, and is not, and yet comes back and exists today. The city no longer exists, but the stronghold or system does.

There is a religion that currently exists and it was said in 1987 to have 875 million followers in the world. (Commission Update Report March 1988 on December 31, 1987. World Healing Day by John Randolph Price, head of the powerful Planetary Commission.)

That's almost 1 BILLION people!

AND that was over 30 years ago… imagine how many there are today!

This religion is the largest and fastest growing religion today. (No, it's not Islam, although Islam does have a major role in end-time prophecy.)

This religion is a revival of ancient Babylon, wallowing in its lustful desires; sexual promiscuity; drug abuse; drunkenness; and especially, a hatred of Christianity.

Acceptance and practice of witchcraft; reincarnation; nature worship; infanticide (abortion); euthanasia (assisted suicide); idolatry; astral travel; spiritism; astrology; magic; psychic powers; goddess worship; occultism; evolution; globalism; divination; necromancy (communication with the dead); false Bibles; and promotion of the merging of a world religion, government and science (a new world order).

It preaches that humanity is evolving into God or self as Christ.

This "mother of harlots and abominations" wants it all… one world government; one world currency and one world antichrist religion.

This whore returns in its new form and new name, seducing people's minds, sexual energies, passions and lusts. This religion infects our systems of education, government, entertainment, medicine, economics, science, media, internet, television, radio, religions, families and the Church.

It's fancy, it's desirable, it's seductive, and it's popular!

Its apostles and prophets are numerous sports figures, actors, liberal media and music personalities that draw in millions of "fans" (converts).

<u>The god of this religion is satan!</u>

This false religion even infects the most elite of Christianity today!

Babylonian Queen Ishtar (pronounced Easter) declared herself queen of heaven to be worshipped, as she said she was immaculately conceived and birthed from a moon egg. She commanded a specific day of the year be called "Easter Sunday" after her and that it be celebrated with 40 days of mourning (lent) in advance, with rabbits, eggs, people "T" crossing their hearts and a cooked ham to remember her son-god Tammuz.

Christians all over the world do exactly that every year!

Babylon also celebrated a holiday called the feast of the son of Isis on December 25 with gift giving and singing door to door (caroling). The Roman Catholic pope Julius 1 decided in 350 A.D., that all catholics would celebrate Jesus' birthday (a special mass held for Christ… Christmas) this same day, with much the same traditions, not counting Santa Claus!

These pagan religious holidays/dates were being celebrated long before Jesus was born on earth!

If you're celebrating these Babylonian holidays do you still think you don't service evil altars or don't compromise with God!

This is the liberal, new age, world religion… the revised Babylon!

The Holy Spirit is a Christian's guide. The "higher self" (demon) is the new age person's guide.

Satan's main target is much the same as it was in the Garden of Eden, in that he goes after the woman/women first, as he did with Eve, who will capture their husbands and children.

There is much more that can be discussed on this topic, which is not the goal of this book.

This new Babylon or new age religion is a mighty stronghold and structure that can only be approached as led by the Holy Spirit, as only God will ultimately bring down this entire religion and its god.

Be led by the Holy Spirit to find the strategy to warfare against a false religion or for a city/region/nation.

Don't fear to take on such a beast.

Daniel was by himself; and Rees Howells had only a small team of people with him.

The Holy Spirit may have you do spiritual mapping, intercession and/or battle evil principalities, powers and rulers, perhaps with angels.

Ask the Holy Spirit how to take down <u>specific</u> spiritual structures and strongholds of a <u>particular</u> area and you will receive the strategy, as did Joshua for every campaign of the five-year war in Canaan (see the SAFARI Sector on different phases of the war).

Go with God!

SECTOR TWENTY-FOUR

P.O.A.R IT ON PURSUE, OVERTAKE AND RECOVER

> **HUNTING TIP**
>
> When they attack your home, your family, your life…
>
> hunt them down and end it!

The fox, the coyote, and the wolf are wild game that are known to sneak in, while others are asleep or away, to rob and kill.

When I was a kid, I used to go out after hunting and trapping with my father, to some chicken farms where pheasants were raised for both the government's Ministry of Conservation and the Canadian Sportsman's Club program. The mature pheasants would be released to repopulate the area.

Many times, there wouldn't be anything left in the pheasant cages but a few feathers in the snow. The marauders had successfully figured out a way past the defenses and taken their spoil.

There are four things that could have been done:

1. We could have done nothing and said "Oh well, that's life." If you knew my father, that wasn't a considered option.
2. We could beef up the defenses, such as strengthening the cages or putting some farm dogs outside, which are a good idea; however, defense without offense eventually fails.
3. Offensively thinking we could set traps (we did), which were successful.

4. Hunt them down and dispatch them. "Dispatch" is a kinder, gentler word that one uses when talking to the sensitive… it means kill.

The fox, the coyote, and the wolf are not inherently evil; they are just doing what comes naturally for them to survive. Unfortunately, when their world collides with the farmer's, the farmer must win in order to survive.

One farmer that I know, lost his entire sheep herd in one night—not once but twice—from packs of coyotes! Those coyotes killed all the sheep, beyond what they needed to eat. They enjoyed killing.

The wolverine is another animal known to kill just for fun. Wild cats (tigers, lions) and bears have been known to develop a taste and liking towards "dispatching" people.

Here's something I pulled off the National Geographic website on man-eating tigers: "The Sunderbans in India are one of the last enclaves where tigers hunt, kill and eat humans. Fishing or gathering firewood in the gnarled mangrove forests can prove fatal in this region. Here, up to 80 people every year are killed and eaten by tigers. The villages here are filled with orphans, widows, and people who have harrowing tales of survival. In the Sunderbans, people understand that humans are not the most dominant animal. If a tiger decides to kill, it can… and will…"

Imagine waking up every morning, wondering if you'll be breakfast that day! Of course, again, the options are obvious as to how to stop these man-eaters.

There were also robbers, killers, and destroyers (RKD's) in the Bible.

One example that we'll examine is in 1 Samuel 30. Let's read it all and go through it on the other side:

"Now it happened, when David and his men came to Ziklag, on the third day, that the Amalekites had invaded the South and Ziklag, attacked Ziklag and burned it with fire, ² and had taken captive the women and those who were there, from small to great; they did not kill anyone, but carried them away and went their way. ³ So David and his men came to the city, and there it was, burned with fire; and their wives, their sons, and their daughters had been taken captive. ⁴ Then David and the people who were with him lifted up their voices and wept, until they had no more power to weep. ⁵ And David's two wives, Ahinoam the Jezreelitess, and Abigail the widow of Nabal the Carmelite, had been taken captive. ⁶ Now David was greatly distressed, for the people spoke of stoning him, because the soul of all the people was grieved, every man for his sons and his daughters. But David strengthened himself in the Lord his God.

⁷ Then David said to Abiathar the priest, Ahimelech's son, "Please bring the ephod here to me." And Abiathar brought the ephod to David. ⁸ So David inquired of the Lord, saying, "Shall I pursue this troop? Shall I overtake them?"

And He answered him, "Pursue, for you shall surely overtake them and without fail recover all."

⁹ So David went, he and the six hundred men who were with him, and came to the Brook Besor, where those stayed who were left behind. ¹⁰ But David pursued, he and four hundred men; for two hundred stayed behind, who were so weary that they could not cross the Brook Besor.

¹¹ Then they found an Egyptian in the field, and brought him to David; and they gave him bread and he ate, and they let him drink water. ¹² And they gave him a piece of a cake of figs and two clusters of raisins. So, when he had eaten, his strength came back to him; for he had eaten no bread nor drunk water for three days and three nights. ¹³ Then David said to him, "To whom do you belong, and where are you from?"

And he said, "I am a young man from Egypt, servant of an Amalekite; and my master left me behind, because three days ago I fell sick. ¹⁴ We made an invasion of the southern area of the Cherethites, in the territory which belongs to Judah, and of the southern area of Caleb; and we burned Ziklag with fire."

¹⁵ And David said to him, "Can you take me down to this troop?"

So, he said, "Swear to me by God that you will neither kill me nor deliver me into the hands of my master, and I will take you down to this troop."

16 And when he had brought him down, there they were, spread out over all the land, eating and drinking and dancing, because of all the great spoil which they had taken from the land of the Philistines and from the land of Judah. 17 Then David attacked them from twilight until the evening of the next day. Not a man of them escaped, except four hundred young men who rode on camels and fled. 18 So David recovered all that the Amalekites had carried away, and David rescued his two wives. 19 And nothing of theirs was lacking, either small or great, sons or daughters, spoil or anything which they had taken from them; David recovered all. 20 Then David took all the flocks and herds they had driven before those other livestock, and said, "This is David's spoil."

21 Now David came to the two hundred men who had been so weary that they could not follow David, whom they also had made to stay at the Brook Besor. So, they went out to meet David and to meet the people who were with him. And when David came near the people, he greeted them. 22 Then all the wicked and worthless men of those who went with David answered and said, "Because they did not go with us, we will not give them any of the spoil that we have recovered, except for every man's wife and children, that they may lead them away and depart."

23 But David said, "My brethren, you shall not do so with what the Lord has given us, who has preserved us and delivered into our hand the troop that came against us. 24 For who will heed you in this matter? But as his part is who goes down to the battle, so shall his part be who stays by the supplies; they shall share alike." 25 So it was, from that day forward; he made it a statute and an ordinance for Israel to this day.

26 Now when David came to Ziklag, he sent some of the spoil to the elders of Judah, to his friends, saying, "Here is a present for you from the spoil of the enemies of the Lord"— 27 to those who were in Bethel, those who were in Ramoth of the South, those who were in Jattir, 28 those who were in Aroer, those who were in Siphmoth, those who were in Eshtemoa, 29 those who were in Rachal, those who were in the cities of the Jerahmeelites, those who were in the cities of the Kenites, 30 those who were in Hormah, those who were in Chorashan,

those who were in Athach, ³¹ those who were in Hebron, and to all the places where David himself and his men were accustomed to rove."

David and his men were living in Ziklag. While they were away, the Amalekites came and destroyed Ziklag, departing with the women, children, and other spoils. David and his men returned to absolutely nothing! <u>All</u> of their treasures were stolen or destroyed. We read how these brave conquerors reacted. They wept until they could weep no more, and were so angry they wanted to stone David, their leader! Obviously, the defenses of Ziklag were insufficient.

Further examination of 1 Samuel 27 shows, that David and his men were living in Ziklag, which was in Philistine territory, to escape the wrath of King Saul. As we know, the Philistines were the enemies of Israel and while David was there, he deceived King Achish into thinking he was killing and destroying people and towns within Israeli territory. David lied to Achish about what he was doing. David was ruthless, in that he was killing even women and children in their raids, so the truth would never be heard by Achish. 1 Samuel 27:8-12

So, David was lying, deceiving, murdering, and plundering the countryside around Ziklag like a pirate, for over a year.

Some might say that David opened the door for the retribution of Ziklag. A lesson to any who would think the end justifies the means!

Meanwhile, back with the sobbing and angry Ziklagonians, (or is it Ziklaganites?) we have David on the verge of being stoned. David goes to God and says," Shall I pursue after this troop? Shall I overtake them"? and God says, "Pursue: for thou shalt surely overtake them, and without fail recover all."

God sanctions this action… pursue, you <u>will</u> overtake them and <u>without fail</u> you <u>will</u> recover everything!

David knew the result long before it actually happened.

Now… after reading this Silver Bullet of God, Xtreme Big Game Hunting book up to this point, do you think that such a thing is possible in the spirit realm?

Evil spiritual game wait for your defenses to come down or they look for weaknesses that they can exploit. They wait for you to be spiritually asleep or spiritually dead to come to rob, kill, and destroy. When a person is spiritually incapable of stopping spiritual beasts, what are spiritual robbers, killers, and destroyers (RKD's) capable of doing?

The answer is self-evident.

We've discussed options earlier when other RKD's have come and gone. We can shrug our shoulders and say, "That's life." We can plead and pray to God for Him to do something, although we see with the Ziklag situation and other examples in the Bible, that God didn't strike the enemy dead, and send the captives back.

<u>We're</u> expected to take action.

We can and should boost our defenses to stop further invasions—although in Ziklag's case there was nothing left to defend!

Just curbing sin, pleading the blood of Jesus over ourselves and our life, surrounding ourselves with protecting angels, etc., is a good defense and will close doors to evil, but what about going to God in the spirit, get His approval and assistance regarding the RKD's that have been attacking us, our family, our life, the lives of others… to hunt them down, overtake them, destroy them, and recover <u>all</u> they took!

Hmmm… let's see… which option would a conqueror choose?

In August 2007, a lady in Vermont contacted me to ask if there was anything that I could do in the spirit about a multiple-day Christian event that wasn't coming together. They couldn't get any local interest from Church groups or volunteers, nor were the needed funds coming in.

Vermont is about an eight-hour drive for me so going in the spirit there was much handier (and cheaper) than a personal trip.

Once in the spirit, I was in a huge open area that had a forest in the distance. A rampaging rhinoceros with a golden horn ran up to me. With my sword, I cut the golden horn off of its face and then slipped to the side to cut his head off. He slumped down onto his belly. I then knew I was to climb over his carcass, rather than go around it.

Another rhino then came running up. Yet this one was all white. This one was the Holy Spirit! (Don't ask me to explain how or why the Holy Spirit came in the form of a Rhino!)

I turned and could see this lady who had contacted me, with a group of others, looking at this rhino carcass wondering what to do. I told her to lead the group in climbing over the carcass as I had done. I told her and the group to follow the white rhino to the forest.

The forest was too thick to walk through, so the white rhino (Holy Spirit) started pushing over trees to clear a pathway through the forest. I told the people to follow the Holy Spirit, stay on the path and not to go off the path into the woods.

I could see evil spirits waiting in the trees for any who would step into their area. The people looked back for me to lead them, but I told this lady that she was to lead them to where the Holy Spirit was going, as my job was done.

I watched as they went in single file through the forest and came out on the other side into a seemingly endless field of ripe, almost white, wheat. The people started gathering up wheat under their arms. There was more wheat than they could possibly gather.

"Then He (Jesus) said to His disciples, "The harvest truly is plentiful, but the laborers are few. Therefore, pray the Lord of the harvest to send out laborers into His harvest." Matthew 9:37-38

All of this took just a matter of minutes. I found out later that this huge event was a spectacular success! Local Church groups and volunteers "suddenly" wanted to be involved. Money and resources "suddenly" started pouring in. The harvest was taken for God and the glory is His!

The evil game that was guarding the golden horn (funds and resources) had been pursued in the spirit, overtaken, and destroyed… with all that it had taken (made captive) recovered!

Are you, your family, your friends, people in your Church group, Christian lives, health, blessings, and resources being robbed, killed, and destroyed?

Have you come home one day and <u>your</u> Ziklag was destroyed and looted?

Perhaps you're sitting now in the ruins of your Ziklag, wondering what to do. Perhaps like many others, you blame God, as David's men blamed him. Whining about it, worrying about it or shrugging your shoulders about it, won't solve the problem.

When evil spiritual game are doing this to you, get up off your pew and do something about it! Go to God as David did. See if the problem is a Ziklag problem that can be overcome with a Ziklag solution!

If so, and God sanctions your attack, then POAR it on (<u>P</u>ursue, <u>O</u>vertake <u>A</u>nd <u>R</u>ecover)

"for you shalt surely overtake them, and without fail recover all."

Let me tell you something else… something really exciting!

When I started to POAR it onto evil game, guess what happened?

Instead of fighting from just a defensive standpoint, i.e., casting out evil spirits already present, I moved into a new arena—hunting them down, overtaking them, and destroying them!

Guess how the RKD's approach toward me changed?

How many evil spiritual game do you think want to move against me now? They know that if they do, I will come after them and they will pay.

I was at this home one time and could see numerous evil spirits outside the property looking in at me.

I said to them, "Why don't you come on in"? (Notice I was enticing them to attack me.)

They said, "We don't want to".

I said, "Why not"?

They said, "Because you can destroy us"!

I just smiled and thought, "Nice to be appreciated"!

Another time I went hunting in the spirit to pursue those who were attacking my wife. Assorted evil game had me surrounded in an enclosed circle. They were about forty feet away from me in all directions. I moved around the center area looking into all of their eyes, pointing my sword at all of them and said, "Any of you want some of me come and get it"!

They just stood there, saying nothing, not allowing me to get close enough to them to destroy them. I motioned with my sword for some of them to move aside and we walked through and past them. They left her alone after that!

Another time I went hunting in the spirit to an area over earth and quickly came upon a small herd of dragons. (Do dragons move in herds or flocks?) Should I have been politically correct and called them serpents, leviathans or behemoths instead or perhaps principalities? Anyway, I destroyed one of them… the others ran away. Bunch of sissies!

There are many more testimonies in the Hunting Expeditions Sectors.

When hunting in the physical, a hunter knows how to increase his success rate by baiting and/or calling in game. Bears like donuts… really! You should hear my moose call!

Christians, leaders and deliverance ministers are struggling against attacks from RKD's that enjoy their work—and know that retaliation against them is usually non-existent or a joke.

I saw one principality laughing at a huge prayer rally of Christians, that were praying against the fruit of what it (the principality) was doing! (Hunting reminder: You shoot the root, not the fruit!)

I say bait 'em, snare 'em, trap 'em, entice 'em, call 'em in, hunt 'em down, bring 'em down… show no mercy!

Remember Ziklag, the next time you look over the ruins of your life!

If this next sentence sounds like a broken record, then it's for good reason.

<u>Start and continue operating and going in the spirit!</u>

Go to Father God in confidence, as you are an heir to the throne. (Romans 8:17)

Plead with Him if you must (I did) that you need this ability. He <u>wants</u> you to operate in the spirit. It might start out with glimpses here and there or maybe happen fast. I know people who've had various experiences and timetables of progression. Get this ability… have no fear… be an Eagle!

If your Christian leader won't equip you; or help you develop your ministry; or allow you to exercise your spiritual gifts; or allow you to leave this leader's private religious nest… go to the edge of that nest, fling yourself out and soar!

Go on God's hunting expeditions!

Take angels with you.

Send me pictures of your spiritual trophies! (If you can do that, teach me how, as I haven't figured out that one yet!)

Your life <u>will</u> change!

ZONE 6

HUNTING EXPEDITIONS

SECTOR TWENTY-FIVE

XTREME BIG GAME HUNTING STORIES AND TESTIMONIES

> **HUNTING TIP**
> When evil game hit you… smile… then hit 'em back harder!

After a hunt, hunters sit around and recount the stories of what happened. Usually they are vivid, exciting and pleasant memories they'll remember for the rest of their lives.

Reliving these moments seems as good as the hunt sometimes, as you get to relive it as many times as you want.

Also, having a mouthwatering meal as a bonus of your success, blends in nicely with these stories.

What makes an Xtreme Big Game Hunt even more satisfying is that your memories are there, as well as the thoughts of how many people you have helped, which you will never know the extent of until you get to heaven. Most important is that you have been a hunter for God and did it for his Glory, to advance His kingdom and to set people free and have been building up your treasures in heaven… sticking it to the evil realm is also a plus!

I have never had a meal of this game and from what I've seen, that would be a good thing!

All in all, an Xtreme Big Game Hunt is tough to beat!

I know there are hunters from Safari Club International and many sportsmen's clubs that have some thrilling moments to impart. Many TV programs have given us a close-up of some of these adventures.

I've got some pretty good big game hunting stories myself.

None of them come close to the thrill of taking down Xtreme Spiritual Big Game!

I've also never heard a natural big game story that matched an Xtreme Spiritual Big Game hunting story!

In addition to the obvious unmatched experience of the hunt, we mustn't forget the outcome of these hunts.

I've mentioned previously, and it's worth repeating, huge areas suddenly open up to evangelism and to the gospel, that had been barren for years, decades and centuries! Results have even included a renewed spiritual revival among Christians in these areas.

<u>This kind of hunt or spiritual warfare can affect hundreds of thousands and millions of people at a time!</u>

Dramatic changes have been witnessed and documented and can be expected in cities, regions, areas and countries, in politics, finance, religion, education, economies, in Church groups, and with people. Heathen festivals, evil worship, celebrations of idols, witchcraft, crime, drugs, and sexual immorality are disrupted, and fail in areas, as people will lose interest in evil things. Corruption in governments and finance crumbles.

People will start to seek out their Lord and Savior Jesus Christ!

Although there are lots to choose from, let's get into some of these stories.

Sit closer to the campfire and let me share some good ones with you! The Bible is full of spiritual hunting stories with one of my favorite testimonies being the Xtreme Big Game Hunter, Elisha. 2 Kings 6 tells of this <u>one man with the Lord's forces</u>, defeating an entire army and ending a war!

Through spiritual means, (the Holy Spirit, by angels or by going in the spirit), Elisha knew the plans of the Syrian king and army and frustrated their war campaign (and satan's) against Israel 3 times! (V.8-10)

I'd like to think he went in the spirit and stood invisibly in the room with the Syrian king as he plotted war against Israel!

Elisha was considered so dangerous to Syria that the king sent a great host to capture him!

<u>Imagine an army sent to capture one man, that's how dangerous they knew Elisha was!</u>

Let's each be that dangerous to the evil spiritual realm!

The Syrians moved at night to surround Elisha at Dothan. Elisha's servant was so startled and afraid he said, "Alas, my master! What shall we do?" Elisha said, "Do not fear, for those who are with us are more than those who are with them." 2 Kings 6: 15-16

We could doubtless sense Elisha's servant thinking, "Two of us against a great military host?"

Many today think like this servant, through ignorance of spiritual warfare… generating true pity from those who know better.

Probably to reassure his servant, Elisha prays for his servant's spiritual eyes to be opened and he saw "the mountain was full of horses and chariots of fire all around Elisha."

When the Syrian army moved in to capture Elisha, he prayed that they would all be made blind. (Imprecation!)

Then Elisha tells this <u>blind army</u> that he will bring them to "the man whom you seek," which in truth really was the king of Israel they were warring against; and so, leads them to Samaria, which is about <u>14 miles</u> from Dothan!

Picture a blind army being trotted along the countryside for 14 miles, with hopes of capturing the very man who is leading them!

<u>Instead of an army capturing one man, one man captured an army!</u>

Elisha led them to the king of Israel, and incredibly had them treated like honored guests and released… ending this war!!! (2 Kings 6: 19-23)

First off, I must say, that I enjoy God's sense of humor in having Elisha do all of this!

Elisha always knew the war plans of Syria and it is most likely he knew they were secretly coming to capture him.

Instead of leaving Dothan, he stays and waits for this army to surround him and instead of slipping away when they are all blinded he leads them all into captivity.

Despite satan's attempt to destroy Elisha and Israel, and of course many Syrian troops; despite satan's power and potency; despite all that satan must have brought to bear for this victory and destruction, he was defeated through one man!

Now that's funny!

It shows how really pitiful satan and his war plans are against one man and an omnipotent God.

This stands to reconfirm that we deal with the <u>only</u> Being in the universe Who has <u>never</u> made a mistake, Who has <u>never</u> been caught at a disadvantage, Who has <u>never</u> been surprised by a superior force or strategy.

"The Lord is high above all nations, His glory above the heavens. Who is like the Lord our God, Who dwells on high." Psalm 113:4-5

Satan may do his very best with the forces he has under his control, but he is impotent outside of the will of God and can only accomplish what is permitted.

Elisha taught each one of us what one person, a Silver Bullet of God, <u>can</u> accomplish with God's spiritual direction and forces, <u>anytime</u>... <u>any place</u> and certainly, when it appears that we're up against "seemingly" overwhelming evil forces.

<u>They</u> are no match against <u>Us</u>!

One of my favorite modern-day testimonies from an Xtreme Big Game Hunter, is from Dr. Dale M. Sides, *Closing Gates of Hell*, 2005.

He tells of a hunt he was on in January 2005, in Southern India, in the city of Madurai, also called the temple city:

"When the time came, "the Holy Spirit delivered a revelation utterance through me (Dale Sides). The message was a curse against the temples and gods of this area. A command came from the Lord for angels to close this gate of hell."

(There was an immediate clap of thunder over the top of the temple area and rain began to fall. Rain had not been here for two months.)

"Warfare erupted in heaven and evil spirit strongholds that were in place for millennia came under siege."

(The gate of hell here was shut!)

"Thousands and potentially millions of people can be freed from the tyranny of evil spirits. I rejoice that the names of people who were headed through these gates into the region of Death will not go there because they are now written in the Lamb's Book of Life and are headed to Paradise instead. I rejoice, not just that a gate of hell was closed, but that people who were under the control of the demons and principalities are freed from the curse of hell.

Within two weeks after these gates were closed, the government bulldozed over 200 surrounding temples and shrines. Then, temples throughout the state of Tamilnadu were closed and bulldozed. To date, over 500 temples and shrines have been removed since the day that gate was closed."

Now that's Xtreme Big Game Hunting!

God has blessed me, by allowing me to experience many beautiful, international cities in my life, but this small and also very beautiful city, offered me a hunt that I really enjoyed.

I was physically in Savannah Georgia USA in 2006, where I found the oldest Masonic temple in the Western Hemisphere.

While there, I went in the spirit.

God laid this city out before me, revealing many gates of hell in the ground that looked like large round holes.

I was led to do warfare to seal off all but one of these gates or portals of hell, with a mixture of the blood of Jesus and oil from heaven.

They were sealed with what looked like a membrane over these portals and then angels came and stood guard around them.

I left the last gate closest to me open and then commanded angels in Jesus' name to start binding <u>all</u> the evil powers and principalities over the city and <u>all</u> the evil entities in every building on every block and take them all down through that portal.

Many angels started doing this.

Then I saw soul captives (POW's) in prison-like cells beneath this gate, so I commanded other angels to go down and bring up all the captives, leading them and carrying them if necessary.

I commanded all these cells beneath the city to open in Jesus' name and as they did, angels went down through the portal and started bringing them up, as the other angels were taking evil entities down.

The angels were passing each other through this portal.

I directed the angels getting the captives to take them to where they belonged.

The angels were to continue this process until it was done and then this last gate of hell was to be sealed like the others were.

Savannah has a very well-known college and students attend from all 50 States in the United States and from over 85 countries.

I was led to make sure that the light of God, Jesus and the Holy Spirit and God's kingdom, filled this place when this last portal was sealed. Also, that all the students that came to this place now and every year hereafter, would have their blindness lifted from them (2 Corinthians 4:4) and would be <u>able</u> to accept the Gospel and take the Word, the truth, and their own ministry back to where they came from and like a seed… grow and spread out across their lands.

Every few hours I would check in the spirit and could see the angels still doing their work passing each other through the portal.

Many hours later, when I checked again, I could see the work had been completed.

I commanded the last gate to be sealed with this heavenly membrane and I could see angels were now standing guard around them all!

A year later, I did an online crime statistics search for Savannah.

This was a quote from one of this city's news sources:

"A recent FBI report claims crime rates are rising nationwide, but what's going on in Savannah? According to latest statistics released by the FBI, last year violent crimes and murders increased nearly two percent across the country and robberies increased just over seven percent. But not on our streets. City police say in 2006, they saw a 15 percent drop in property and violent crimes. "It's a combination of the community and the police working hand in hand which contributes in large part to the reduction," says assistant police chief."

Another report said crime went down further in 2007!

Statistics are difficult or impossible to obtain in many areas, however, positive results like this are also expected in this city in its schools, Church groups, government, and financial institutions, in occult circles, in homes and in businesses.

Realize that God put this hunt instantly in front of me... there was no spiritual mapping done, no intercessors, <u>no other warriors involved</u>... indicating that these extras are <u>NOT</u> a requirement!

God's Glory was achieved with the smallest number... only one... such as with Elisha at Dothan... such as with Dale Sides at Madurai! No numerous works or numbers of people can be said to have accomplished this.

In Buffalo, New York, where I lived for one year, the startling crime statistics was a headline in the paper... overall crime was <u>down 20%</u> that year and <u>down 17%</u> in Niagara Falls, New York, the city next door!

Remember the testimony in the SAFARI Sector about the crime rates when Daniel Nash and Finney were done in Rochester, New York... "<u>Even the courts and the prisons bore witness to its blessed effects. There was a wonderful falling off of crime. The courts had little to do, and the jail was nearly empty for years afterward.</u>"

When God puts a hunt in front of you and wants you to go, there is no need for all the formality and procedures and rituals to go through first.

If God has us do lengthy mapping and procedures with many people and physical prophetic acts after spiritual warfare has been done, then that is what should be done, but it isn't a requirement.

He also told me that books, conferences, and leaders teach on <u>limiting</u> Him in many ways… He told me not to do that… He's not in a box.

Amen to that!

Some of the testimonies in the next Sectors from different parts of the world that I went to, may stun you. You may think I'm delusional or a liar or perhaps a superhero!

I'm just an ordinary guy, who God uses as a Silver Bullet.

If some of it is too much for your mind to handle right now, then have the Holy Spirit bring you into teaching and going in the spirit at your comfort level and be at peace during the process.

<u>All</u> Glory to you Heavenly Father, Jesus and Holy Spirit!

SECTOR TWENTY-SIX

AUSTRIAN/HUNGARIAN NETHERLANDS HUNTING EXPEDITION

> **HUNTING TIP**
> No distractions... stay on target!

Spiritual hunting expeditions into Europe are never a disappointment. I only wish there was as many moose and deer around when hunting season opens here in Canada!

For those of you who have never eaten moose, I can only repeat some words my Dad used to say on that topic, "You've never lived, you've only existed!"

On December 19, 2008, I went on a mission into Austria, Hungary, and the Netherlands. Although most times I go in the spirit to different locations on earth, the heavens or the underworld, this time it was a personal vacation...with hunting as a bonus.

As I never leave home without God and am always eager to hunt, the hunting grounds in these three countries was full of "trophy-class" game that didn't disappoint me.

"Then He said to His disciples, "The harvest truly is plentiful, but the laborers are few. Therefore, pray the Lord of the harvest to send out laborers into His harvest." Matthew 9:37-38/Luke 10:2

As my plane was approaching the ancient city of Budapest Hungary, I could see a target at a bridge over the Danube River... a colossal black dragon! (Call it a serpent, python, leviathan, behemoth or principality, if you don't like the word, dragon.)

It also knew I was coming!

Budapest is considered an important political, economic, commercial, industrial, transportation hub of Central Europe.

The beast not only knew I was coming, it was eager for me to come fight it right away!

It was taunting me to come to the bridge.

This bridge, known as Freedom Bridge, <u>was</u> infamous for its attraction to those committing suicide… sacrifices to this beast!

I was also eager to face this beast; however, we must move in God's timing, not ours. It was not time.

The next Monday, Rhoda and I left Budapest for Vienna and Salzburg Austria.

Austria is a strategic, economic, influential location not only for Europe but also for the world.

Vienna and Salzburg are beautiful cities, having a mixture of old world charm, mountains, many lakes, and of course the smell of money everywhere.

One Inn that we passed outside of Salzburg charged 4700€ a night!

I can only expect that the Queen of England served you tea, in order to justify such an amount!

Over Vienna were two dragons.

I immediately went in the spirit after one of them.

I ripped open its green belly and as its insides fell out, it crumpled down out of the sky.

I turned to face the other one, but it had left the area during the fight. (I do prefer to destroy them, but I'll settle for displaced!)

I wasn't called to any further warfare in Austria, although while I was there, the beast in Budapest continued to taunt me to come face it.

I said to it, "Don't worry, I'll be coming for you!"

When I said this, I sensed its boldness crack a little, when it realized it wasn't scaring me.

After returning to Hungary from Austria, I awoke one morning and said to Rhoda, "Today we go to the bridge!"

I do have to appreciate the courage of the beast for not running away scared.

It allowed me to come to its lair, rather than making me hunt it down.

Of course, if it ran away, it would have only died tired! (I love hunting humor.)

As we approached the Freedom Bridge by foot, this beast towered high above the top of the bridge and said to me, "You can't destroy me; I've been here over 1000 years… I've been here over 2000 years!"

I just chuckled at it and said, "So what!"

Now I know you'd like to hear what happened next, but first I have to tell you about a new sword that Jesus gave me the previous month.

On Nov. 23, 2008 I popped in at a Church assembly in St. Catharines, Ontario, Canada.

I could see Jesus standing behind the leader, as he was teaching about getting to really know the living Jesus, not just someone in a book that lived 2000 years ago.

Interesting topic, considering that Jesus was standing in the room!

I could also see a golden, jewelled, crown on the leader's head.

Jesus went up to the leader; hugged him, blessed him, and then came down to hug and bless everyone in the Church group!

When Jesus came to me, I said, "Do everyone else first Lord and me last."

During fellowship afterwards, the leader's eyes became very wide, when I told him what had happened during his teaching.

I didn't sense that I was to tell him what happened next.

When Jesus was done blessing everyone, He then came up to me.

I was instantly in the spirit in armor kneeling down on one knee in front of Jesus.

Whitey, my horse, was standing next to me when Jesus said, "Give Me your sword."

I pulled it out from the scabbard on my left side (still kneeling) and handed it to Him.

Another sword came down from above.

It was more iridescent than the ones I had in the past, with an unusual hilt.

Jesus handed the sword to me; I put it in the scabbard; arose and got on Whitey.

Jesus said, that I would be going to more places and doing more now.

I could see a door open up behind Jesus in the heavens… Whitey and I rode through the doorway.

On the other side of the door it was very sunny, with rolling hills, trees, grass, and a river.

I rode up next to a huge tree by the river and got off of Whitey.

It was all very tranquil.

As far as I could see in the distance, there wasn't anyone else or any buildings.

Not what I'm accustomed to when I'm in the spirit!

I took out my new sword and thought, "I wonder what this can do?"

The earth shook like an earthquake, when I touched the sword's point to the ground.

Whitey was startled and looked at me as if to say, "What was that?"

Then, I put the blade in the water and stirred it a little.

Huge waves sprang up and roared down the river.

Next, I put the sword up over my head and waved it a bit in the air. Huge winds like a tornado appeared and went out from where I was standing.

My thought was, "This will be interesting to see how the Lord will have me use this sword!"

Then I said Lord, "Where is Rhoda?"

As I turned, I saw her in the distance coming over a hill riding Isaiah (her white spiritual horse). She was wearing armor, which included her sword. She rode up to me; got off her horse… I showed her the river and my new sword.

It was very serene; her and I, watching the river and the beautiful scenery; our two horses grazing.

As I was thinking that this place is so peaceful, I said, "Lord can we take our armor off here?"

He said, "You never take off your armor."

Meanwhile, back at the Freedom Bridge, I pointed this sword at the dragon's head!

The best that I can describe what happened is, a sonic wave or boom emanating from the sword's tip, caused the dragon's head to explode! Pieces sprinkled away like confetti; its body slid into the Danube.

I directed the angels that came, to pick up its body and take it to a prison.

Its body was miles long.

As they were doing this I could see five smaller dragons at five other bridges.

I stuck the blade of the sword into the river and started spinning it.

Water was twirling in a circle, sucking these five dragons into a huge water tornado.

I raised my sword high; released the water and dragons into the air where waiting angels caught them in bags.

These sword upgrades are pretty cool!

Then I saw many eagles flying into the city attacking black birds. When I told Rhoda what was happening, she said that these birds in Hungary are mythical creatures called "turuls", considered messengers of God. (Yeah right!)

When the last of the turuls were attacked, killed, and chased away, all was still.

Then they came!

White doves… they landed on the bridge, the buildings… everywhere!

I told Rhoda that they bring love and contentment.

Later, I saw four warrior angels on either end of the bridge had turned away someone who had come to commit suicide.

Six dragons… six in the hunting bags… a plethora of turuls smacked… ahhhh, a good day of hunting eh!

THE NETHERLANDS

As my plane was heading into Amsterdam, in the Netherlands, it wasn't a pleasant sight that greeted me. There were black snakes over the entire city, with many gates in the ground to the underworld.

Angels of light were battling dark angels in the heavens.

I was standing there with my sword looking up.

Then the rain came.

This was no ordinary rain… it was a rain of fire coming down, like napalm or fire bombs would rain down from aircraft, in a battle on earth.

God's napalm was coming down and burning into the snakes.

They were squirming in agony, trying to escape; trying to escape down their gates, yet the fire was dropping in after them.

I struck the ground with my sword; the earth trembled and the gateways started filling in.

The angels in the heavens were watching, but they had little time to help or applaud, as they were in heavy battle themselves.

The battle was continuing when I had to leave.

Message to all Conquerors for Amsterdam and the Netherlands… carry on the fight… I will come if God sends me and stand by your sides.

Give them both barrels for me!

(Giving something "both barrels" is a hunting idiom, meaning blasting away with all you have (two shots) from an old double-barrel shotgun.)

SECTOR TWENTY-SEVEN

CANADIAN HUNTING EXPEDITION

> **HUNTING TIP**
>
> Just keep pulling the trigger... let God keep score!

I've been to many countries in the world, but home for me is Canada! The second largest country in the world... of only 37 million friendly people! Mountains, forests, abundant wildlife, fresh air, 3 oceans and over 31,000 major lakes including the largest group of freshwater lakes on earth... the 5 Great Lakes, that holds 21% of all the surface-fresh water in the world!

Hunting of moose, deer, elk, caribou, bear, duck, goose, pheasant, partridge, rabbit, cougar, mountain goat, coyote, fox, and more, is popular.

I've spent many pleasurable times hunting in Canada... including... Xtreme Big Game Hunting!

My favorite sport in my favorite country!

It would be impossible to recount all of the spiritual game that I've brought down here, so I'll just hit on some of the highlights.

In the summer of 2007, I headed an Xtreme Spiritual Warfare Conference in Niagara Falls, Ontario.

With the other teachers, brought in from Europe, we not only had classroom teaching on Xtreme Big Game Hunting, but we took the students out for some actual gang hunting in the field. We were equipping the saints as God commands.

We were led to hunt what is considered the most haunted cemetery in all of Canada!

Ahhhh… fresh air, good hunters, perfect weapons, angels, working in the spirit, God with us… equals conquered game!

Every hunter took a shot… there was breaking of war, death, and murder curses… there was the closing of a huge gate of hell that evil spirits were using as a portal… assistance of angels taking away terrified evil spirits… there was shofar blowing… there was healing of the land with oil, salt, and wine… we were Conquerors!

Another hunting expedition to this cemetery was needed later to eliminate a gigantic spiritual octopus that was contaminating the area.

Each tentacle had a name on it such as crime, prostitution, drugs, and gambling, that reached far out of the cemetery, wrapping itself around various parts of the city.

I instructed angels to take it away, but as they tried, they couldn't remove it from the ground, nor its tentacles from around the buildings and structures throughout the city… they kept struggling and looking to me to help.

Stepping in front of the creature, I thrust my sword into it and twisted. He went limp. The angels were now able to release its tentacles, wrap them around its body, pick it up, and take it away.

As we were leaving the cemetery there were hundreds of angels on either side of the walkway, standing, watching, and clapping to congratulate us for our successful hunt!

I said to the angels, "Don't clap for us, as we are nothing without God!"

This didn't stop them, as the clapping continued, until we walked passed them and left the area!

Once on a hunt in the spirit, I could only see a huge smoke cloud over the area. As I moved through the smoke to get to its source, I came directly in front of a creature with enormous eyes, that was spewing smoke from its mouth. Instinctively and quickly I attacked its eyes, which stopped the smoke and turned it away running!

Although I prefer to destroy these guys, rather than wounding them, it did stop the smoke, which God told me was clouding the minds of the people.

"In whom the god of this world hath blinded the minds of them which believe not, lest the light of the glorious gospel of Christ, who is the image of God, should shine unto them." 2 Corinthians 4:4 KJV

Right after it, I turned to see a huge, black, crow that was about 50 times bigger than me.

Now that's a lotta bird!

Again, another wounding as I attacked its heart. It turned to fly away with a countless number of smaller crows following it.

"And as he sowed, some seed fell by the wayside; and the birds came and devoured them." Matthew 13:4.

I'll catch up with these guys again someday, to enjoy finishing them off!

Another time in the spirit, I was hunting a great number of spiritual lions, as so-called Christians were standing around watching.

I yelled at these "Christians" to join in.

They only shrugged their shoulders, saying they had no weapons.

I've set angels in motion patrolling the area over Lake Erie (one of the 5 Great Lakes bordering Canada and the U.S.).

Another time I was shooting water-spirits with arrows, while angels with me were using crossbows. The angels took their skewered bodies away to parts unknown.

As they were doing this, a huge leviathan beast came up out of the water on the American side of the lake. Perhaps it wanted to stop what we were doing. I did one of those Clint Eastwood stares on him, which prompted its quick retreat back down into the water!

Must have been one of those chicken leviathans!

I've been in the spirit on hunts in Canada assisted by white eagles eating snakes; with huge angels on chariots; fire balls being launched into the area, that were snuffed out into the waters by angels; chased an evil entity out of an underworld tunnel; and one of my favorites… there were eel-like spirits that filled the Niagara River and the famed Niagara Falls, that were coming out of a massive gate of hell.

The evil aura and history about this spiritual gate was so strong, it was called the Devil's Hole for hundreds of years by the locals.

Niagara Falls… the most famous address in the world was being used by the evil realm to infect the world!

These eels all had a word branded on them such as lust, hate, theft, murder, incest, and idolatry.

One eel would wrap itself around the neck of every tourist that came to visit Niagara Falls!

More than 12 million people a year from every country in the world were taking home a special souvenir from satan!

These eels scattered down the Devil's Hole before it was closed.

If you ever feel like doing some great hunting… come to Canada!

There always seems to be some kind of game around you can hunt!

Messages From Father And Jesus

Rhoda and I go to our special spot by the lake many times to walk with God. This is a spot that my Mom went to for many years to commune with God. A portal. I share some of Father's and Jesus' messages here for your edification.

In December 2015, Father said, "Come to Me often as I am here waiting for you. Stay in My presence. Walk in My presence. Carry My Light in front of you. Put your life in My Hands. Pursue holiness. Pursue righteousness for your lives. Open yourself to Me like never before. Reach deep into My Heart and hold onto the love that is there. Bring all of yourself to Me. Lay your troubles and concerns at My Feet. The time is near. Bring sheep who are lost into the pasture past the gate before it closes. There are so many to be brought in.

Your opportunities with Me are endless. Keep asking for My blessings, as I love to give to you. Seek My Face in all things. Praise Me and glorify Me. Enjoy all that I have given you. Find strength in Me to complete your tasks. I will take care of everything in your life. Time is fleeting. I am eternal. You are eternal. Finish the race strong."

Jesus took me in the spirit and showed me the earth, the valleys and mountains and said to me (and all Christians), "You have dominion over all this. Take your place. You are a king among men. Rule with the power and authority I have given you. Speak in My name. Overlook, overtake, conquer. Use angels to help you. Move back the blackness. Trust in Me, as I am with you always."

SOME MORE HEAVEN

Rhoda and I have been having a blast in the spiritual realm over the last month in November 2105. We've been getting long messages and gifts from Father and Jesus. Many evil entities have been defeated.

I (Al) saw an army of angels in the heavens, many with swords, some on chariots. I saw dark angels in the distance being held back by holy angels. Jesus said, "A great war is coming. It is close". I saw angels about to blow long horns. Angels lining up in ranks getting ready. I also see the enemy getting ready. Each army is on mountains overlooking a fighting ground between them. Jesus is walking around the angels talking to them saying, "Prepare; the time has come. This will end the struggles. The enemy will lose but this war must be fought. The enemy will suffer a mortal wound that they can't recover from. They will be judged from the book and punished".

Jesus then spoke to me, "More people must occupy more before this time comes. The time is short. Don't delay what is needed. Strengthen your armor. The armor of God upon you and in you. Meet the enemy with the power that is in you both Rhoda and Al. You are both strong and ready. Be faithful and determined. Climb on your horses and ride. Destroy the enemy. Save the weak. Protect them from the enemy's ways. Stand bravely against all attacks which will be a loss for the enemy. Dig them out of their secret hiding places, expose them and imprison them. Strike them down wherever they are. Attack them without mercy. Don't fall for any of their tricks. Take angels with you to assist. You will see and hear what you need to do and how to do it. Your hands are My hands. The power is yours. Take and occupy for the kingdom. Move forward in strength and determination, as We are with you at all times. Cast all your burdens and cares on the fire and leave it."

THE COURT OF HEAVEN

In September 2015, I was in the court of God in heaven acting as intercessor for those who contacted us as well as for myself. Jesus and the Holy Spirit were there, as were some of my relatives. The accuser was also there. Cases were presented, heard, argued (by the accuser) and justice was served. When court was adjourned, I hugged all my relatives and then walked out the doors into the gardens of heaven, that was full of beautiful grass, trees, bright flowers, people walking, birds flying. I walked and listened to Jesus about plans and different things that are to come for me. I was given much encouragement, counsel and blessings.

Some main advice given to me was, "Put away the things of man. Pick up the things of God."

Soon enough, each of us will be standing in front of God to give an account of our life.

Let's look forward to that accounting!

SECTOR TWENTY-EIGHT
THE CARIBBEAN

> **HUNTING TIP**
> Wait until they're right on top of you and then... show 'em the power of God!

COZUMEL MEXICO

Principality that Destroys Civilizations Was Destroyed!

In May 2015, Rhoda and I went to the Cayman Islands, as well as to Cozumel Mexico. A Mayan city called Tulum in Mexico, had a Mayan temple where they had once sacrificed people. The Mayan civilization once had 2 million people and was considered very advanced in astronomy, mathematics and in the development of a complex calendar system. Also, advanced in evil entity worship!

Before we got there, I could see in the spirit that there was a snake/dragon creature in this ancient Mayan temple. Before we arrived, I chained it in the spirit to a post in the middle of the temple so it would stay put. I don't know why I couldn't have dealt with it before we got there, but with this warfare, I apparently had to be physically on site. There were 2 angels with swords that were stationed in the temple with it. It struggled to get away, but the chains only tightened on it.

When we finally got to Mexico, I could see in the spirit it struggling more, as it knew I was coming. When we got physically on site, I watched as fire from heaven came down and burned it. Its body split open and many smaller beasts that looked like big lizards came out and tried to get out of the temple. The 2 angels were stabbing them with their swords, getting all of them. This beast was over a portal to hell which I knew was now closed by the righteousness of Christ. Interesting to note that this land was full of big lizards running around everywhere (iguanas).

I then saw in the spirit, a huge beast come out of the water right next to the temple. This was much bigger than the one in the temple. It was associated with the one in the temple. I was on Whitey now and flew up to its head and drove my sword down the top of it and as it split open many smaller lizard type beasts came out and started to swim away.

Angels on chariots came with bows and arrows. There were 2 baskets on either side of each chariot. The angels started shooting the smaller beasts in the water, pulling them up with ropes attached to the arrows, putting them in the baskets. When they were all shot, the angels rode off to a mountain. They rode through an opening in the mountain. I understood them to be taking these things to prison.

I was told that this large beast was a destroyer of civilizations. The smaller ones out of it would have gone to many countries to try to destroy their civilizations.

This Mayan civilization disappeared for unknown reasons around 900 AD. Unknown reasons until now!

All glory to God for this victory. I thank You Lord for allowing me to be a part of this battle to advance Your kingdom and thank You as You guide me to what to do for You next!

"And they have conquered him by the blood of the Lamb and by the word of their testimony, for they loved not their lives even unto death." Revelation 12:11

John says we conquer by the word of our testimony.

"Only let your manner of life be worthy of the gospel of Christ, so that whether I come and see you or am absent, I may hear of you that you are standing firm in one spirit, with one mind striving side by side for the faith of the gospel, and not frightened in anything by your opponents. This is a clear sign to them of their destruction, but of your salvation, and that from God. For it has been granted to you that for the sake of Christ you should not only believe in him but also suffer for his sake, engaged in the same conflict that you saw I had and now hear that I still have." Philippians 1:27: 30

BARBADOS

Rhoda and I were on the island of Barbados in the Caribbean for a conference in May 2106.

At the start of the conference I saw 2 spiritual lions from Jesus' throne room come and walk through the crowd. They were hunting for evil spirits!

I saw the lions jump on two people in the room and devour evil spirits. They then walked around some more and then both laid down at the platform. I then saw a staircase come down from the heavens with angels lining the sides of the stairs. I was told they were elite angels. I had never seen angels that looked like this with glimmering helmets. I saw Jesus and Father sitting on thrones at the top of the stairs!

Jesus stood up and came down the stairs. The elite angels dropped to one knee and bowed their heads. The King of Kings was coming to our conference!

Jesus proceeded to walk around the room and personally minister to, and lay Hands on everyone there!

Awesome!

JAMAICA

A leader who teaches Xtreme Big Game Hunting at his College in Uganda and Kenya, was in Jamaica for two months June-August 2016, training people in Xtreme Big Game Hunting.

I went in the spirit to see what God had for him on this hunting SAFARI.

I told him, "Yes, for angels to surround you more for protection. I see them coming in now some on chariots. These angels are very battle-hardened I see. Very muscular. Many weapons. Fire surrounds them.

As I am writing this I was shown 2 Kings 6. These angels were also with Elisha!

"So, he answered, "Do not fear, for those who are with us are more than those who are with them." And Elisha prayed, and said, "Lord, I pray, open his eyes that he may see." Then the Lord opened the eyes of the young man, and he saw. And behold, the mountain was full of horses and chariots of fire all around Elisha." 2 Kings 6: 16-17

You've got some very serious troops with you. I see them surround you. Fire moving in circles and around. I see that you are to run boldly with these troops into the enemy's camp and destroy them! They flee before you. They leave behind their spoils, which are people in chains, in caves, blinded from The Light, the Light of Jesus. They are covered in sicknesses and sores and dirty with sin. I see you and others strike the chains off their hands and feet and necks. They are being cleansed by the blood and the spirit of the Holy Spirit. They will become clean as they walk through the fire of the Holy Ghost. When they came out, they were issued a sword by an angel to join the fight against evil.

Some are staring at the sword not knowing what to do. I see warriors teaching them, equipping them. I see Jesus giving them bread and drink from Himself. I see Him anointing them into The Family of God. I see Him washing their feet and teaching them to 'Follow Me". I see Him giving each a robe. I am told they are now royal priests and rulers. I see each getting a different kind of ring. Some with a red stone, some have a blue stone, one a green stone. One with a diamond stone. I see a new crown being given to you and the others by Jesus, for those who fought this battle with you. I see Lights shining out from the shores for people to see. I see this in the spirit high above Jamaica. Lights, especially on the west side and north-west corner. I am shown that these special angels will work there for a while, then they will leave. Others will stay. I hear the words, "Jamaica's time has come".

There's more than just sun, palm trees, turquoise waters and good food in the Caribbean! Excellent hunting too!

SECTOR TWENTY-NINE

GERMAN HUNTING EXPEDITION

> **HUNTING TIP**
>
> Be a fire spitter... not a pew sitter!

On Monday June 19, 2006, I went in the spirit to Germany from the USA, for a hunt with angels against astral projecting satanists and witches!

This was about three months prior to my leaving for Germany on September 8, 2006, to spend three weeks there for some Xtreme Big Game Hunting.

Angels are really great hunting partners... no worries of an enemy in the camp with them!

It was night and I was in the spirit at the base of this mountain in Germany, as an angel rode in on a golden chariot.

The entire chariot was gold, including the wheels, and was being pulled by a white horse. (In other hunts, I have seen huge chariots pulled by six horses!)

The angel had a quiver on his back full of golden swords and as he pulled a sword out, he stuck it into a satanist or witch (astral projecting), leaving the sword sticking in.

(A few hunter associates in Germany, later told me in September when I was physically there, that satanists and witches offer sacrifices and worship on this mountain, as these bad guys go there often physically and spiritually.)

These Xtreme Rabid Game were here this night spiritually!

This angel then pulled out another sword and did the same to another and then another.

Then, a different angel pulled up on a chariot further down along the base of the mountain and he had a bow and arrows.

He was shooting arrows into another satanist who was on the mountain.

Many arrows went into this particular satanist.

Another angel pulled up on a chariot further down and started throwing spears into another Xtreme Rabid Game creature (astral projecting).

The angels always remained on their chariots.

I had divine knowledge that these were satanists and witches in their spiritual bodies that we were attacking.

I didn't see that they were being killed, just severely wounded and in pain.

I sensed that this would happen to all satanists and witches, that would be on the mountain.

Moving in the spirit higher up, I could see that many angels on chariots were stationed all around the base of the mountain.

I didn't get any knowledge that they were attacking any Xtreme Big or Xtreme Small Game, just the Xtreme Rabid Game made up of satanists and witches.

I had directed all this action to be done without speaking... the direction was all done with directing them with my thoughts.

A teaching that angels can be directed by spirit-filled Christians.

After I arrived in Germany in September 2006, I went to this mountain again physically and also in the spirit.

While physically there, I could see spiritually, that the entire top of the mountain was the head of a serpent and its mouth was open wide, with a gate of hell in the center (where its throat was) going down into the mountain.

Obviously a very big serpent!

One of the German hunters did some research on the internet that night and found out that long-ago, people worshipped a snake god there.

A modern-day cult was reactivating this worship and was looking for members to join them there for serpent worship!

A gate of hell is an entry point, gate or portal to the underworld, considered a front-line battle position.

One day while there, I was in the spirit, standing on the stairway of the Thingstätte, which are the ruins of a Nazi worship center that was built on top of this mountain, oddly called the holy mountain… where Druids, Romans, serpent worshippers, satanists and witches for thousands of years had also stood and worshipped at this gate of hell.

A spiritual lion was walking away from me to my right, unaware of my presence.

This was an evil guardian spirit over the gate of hell at this place and the hunt was about to begin!

I stood looking down towards hell's gate and out of the corner of my eye watched the lion as he patrolled looking for intruders.

When I called out to the lion, he spun his head around, quite startled that I was there.

He turned, came running toward me and jumped high in the air to pounce down on me.

I stood still, facing forward.

Then my right arm drew across my waist and pulled my spiritual sword of light out from my left side, that Jesus had given me.

I turned right, crouching down and sliced the sword across the lion's chest as he was about to come down on me!

He fell down onto the steps of the ruins.

I walked over to him and thrust the sword's point into his head.

The Big Game guardian of this place was slain.

Several of us went there physically again the next day to do warfare and we could see a spiritual lion resting up where I had conquered the lion the day before, while in the spirit.

This was very odd, as I knew that I had destroyed him.

He lounged there until dusk, eventually getting up and walking into his spiritual cave into the side of the mountain.

I sensed that he was the day time guardian and that he would be replaced by night time guardians.

I was really at a loss as to why this lion was back, until the Holy Spirit told me, "There was more than one lion!"

WOW... now it made sense, as this lion was on the opposite side of where I had destroyed the other one and he stayed to the one side.

Ever see a crest of a city with a lion guarding either side of the city's shield?

A few days later I was standing behind some cars and the Holy Spirit directed my attention to the license plate on one of them, which had the crest of this city on it.

It was a symbol with <u>three</u> lions!

I felt like walking over and putting an "X" through one of them on that plate!

I also wondered where the third lion was!

Another site that I hunted, was at Buchenwald in Eastern Germany... a death camp built by the Nazis in WW II, operated by Hitler's elite SS troops, who brutalized, tortured and slaughtered jews, Poles, Russians, Gypsies, jehovah witnesses, and others.

This place is a horrific memorial to how brutal humanity, under the influence of evil spirits, can be. I can't remember an uglier feeling.

It was a nauseous sensation, all the while I was there.

After walking over the grounds, God agreed that I could sprinkle earth from Herrnhut, Germany in each oven in the former crematorium, as a prophetic act of peace over this area.

This "special" earth, as God called it, (that was prayed over for more than 100 years by the Moravians of Herrnhut), joined the earth filled with the innocent blood of Buchenwald's victims.

I had been drawn to go to Herrnhut for years, not only by the Holy Spirit, but also due to the great sacrifices Moravians had given of themselves for Jesus, even to the point of selling themselves and their families into slavery.

They sacrificed in order to be put on ships to bring the Gospel to new lands.

Now that's commitment to evangelism!

While in the tower that the Moravians built, that overlooks vast stretches of Eastern Germany and the Czech Republic, God told me to gather earth from there.

I was to sprinkle a small amount when and where He told me to on an area and it would bring the area peace.

During prayer and worship in Germany, I again was in the spirit and Jesus walked towards me smiling.

He was wearing robes of two colors and sandals and was very happy, as He came upon the German hunters.

He hugged them saying, "My brothers, come… walk with Me, talk with Me, listen to Me!"

They walked towards a bright light and as I looked, I saw that they were walking on water!

Jesus… King, Savior, Healer, Deliverer, and Brother!

Walk on water with your Brother Jesus… talk with Him, listen to Him!

All in all, very successful hunting in Germany I would say!

SECTOR THIRTY

MEXICAN/AMERICAN HUNTING EXPEDITION

> **HUNTING TIP**
> We're always behind enemy lines... that's unfortunate for them!

As I look out my window, I see new yellow buds on the small bush outside. A season of renewal and birth.
Not what is considered hunting season conditions in Canada.

In God's kingdom, renewal and birth is always in season and so is hunting, as it was in early 2006 at the El Paso, Texas USA/ Juárez, Chihuahua Mexican border!

During my time there, one day at spiritual hunting camp, I could see a fallen angel watching us, who I knew was sent to destroy us.

The Holy Spirit gave me a hunting strategy to end its evil plan. I had to find the person in the group, who the Holy Spirit had chosen, to deal with this situation. When He pointed this person out to me, it was then their job to listen to the Holy Spirit and get directions on how to deal with this fallen angel's plans. He told her to anoint and pray over each one of us separately for protection.

Once this was done, he disappeared!

Listen, go, do, done!

Also during this time at camp, the Holy Spirit revealed to me that this intercessory group was not doing what they were supposed to do, as they were casually talking about different things.

They were supposed to be interceding for certain hunters who were out on a hunt.

The Holy Spirit gave me an urgent message to immediately pray in tongues in my head for these hunters, as they were in danger.

I did this, as the group continued talking.

I continued praying until the Holy Spirit told me they were safe.

The Holy Spirit had me point out later to the others what He said and what happened and that they must be ready <u>before</u> hunting starts, not during.

After this, I went in the spirit.

I saw the heavens open up like a womb and fire started pouring down in a column, which continually poured down upon the hunters.

The fire surrounded them and was bouncing up from the ground, licking up in front and behind, as they moved along.

It was like God's consuming fire for the Israelites against the children of Anak in Deuteronomy 9:1-3,

"Hear, O Israel: You are to cross over the Jordan today, and go in to dispossess nations greater and mightier than yourself, cities great and fortified up to heaven, a people great and tall, the descendants of the Anakim, whom you know, and of whom you heard it said, 'Who can stand before the descendants of Anak?' Therefore, understand today that the Lord your God is He who goes over before you as a consuming fire. He will destroy them and bring them down before you; so, you shall drive them out and destroy them quickly, as the Lord has said to you."

"For our God is a consuming fire." Hebrews 12:29

Later that night in my hotel room, God the Father said to me, "You want to see something cool?"

I had never imagined Him talking that way, but that's what He said!

He showed me the same column of fire that I had seen previously, showering down over the hunters. I could see the column getting thicker and getting thinner, back and forth.

I asked God the Father, "What does this mean?"

He said," Whenever the intercessors were doing their job and praying, the fire intensified and the protection was greater. Whenever they were distracted and stopped praying, the fire and protection started to die down."

Teaching that it is very important, that any intercessors who have been brought into the hunt, must be focused, even though the hunt may be an all-day process, or sometimes over many days, as this hunt had been.

While I was there on this hunt, I saw, heard, and even smelled many things in the spirit, which the Holy Spirit blessed me with during that time.

We hunted in a cemetery and saw remnants of bird sacrifices, done by witches or those in voodoo or Santeria.

We hunted in a national park where native Americans had worshipped. Paintings of spirit creatures were on the cave walls.

We hunted at the Rio Grande, in many heathen worship centers and also at the Texas/Mexico border and into Mexico.

As prophetic acts were done, where much bloodshed had been spilled in this area between these two countries, the wind of the Holy Spirit came through in a mighty way.

It was a wonderful experience of Him blowing in a new season.

Many strongholds of evil powers and principalities were brought down!

"For though we walk in the flesh, we do not war according to the flesh. For the weapons of our warfare are not carnal but mighty in God for pulling down strongholds." 2 Corinthians 10:3-4

As my plane was rising above the clouds, ending my 12-day hunting expedition in Texas, I could see this city in the spirit.

I saw the mountain overlooking all the neighborhoods, where there were many, shining lights on the ground.

They were everywhere... all over every block.

It looked like lights of a city at night, except this was the daytime.

God told me I was looking at all the souls of this city, like diamonds waiting to be "mined" or picked up, and since the hunt was over, they were ready for Jesus!

That's a population of about <u>750,000 people</u>!

Now that's a lot of diamonds!

Once the warfare is completed and the strongholds are down, the souls who were freed need salvation.

The Xtreme hunt was just the means to accomplish Mark 16:15, "And He said to them, "Go into all the world and preach the gospel to every creature."

The Lord blessed me again before I left that place, allowing me to "mine" a few of His precious "diamonds" from the captives (minds) who had been set free during that hunting period.

While I was waiting in the hotel lobby for my airport shuttle, the Lord had me open my suitcase and take out two of the three Gideon Bibles that I had and put them in my pocket.

I didn't know what He had in mind, as I would soon be leaving.

And why just two of the three Bibles?

I didn't have to wonder for very long.

He brought exactly two people to me before I walked away from the shuttle into the airport and they gladly accepted the Bibles!

In my younger days, I used to work at a mine, but there is no mining like mining for our Lord Jesus!

SECTOR THIRTY-ONE

NORTH CAROLINA USA HUNTING EXPEDITION

> **HUNTING TIP**
>
> Ephesians 6: 12 says that we war against principalities! Go get some!

There are many States in the USA that I've hunted, from New York to California, from Florida to Hawaii and many in-between, that offered Xtreme Game, which varied in each State, with something different happening during each hunt.

But the teaching I wanted to share with you now, was one that took place in one State… North Carolina. For those not familiar with the positioning of this State, it is about mid-point on the East coast of the USA.

The hunt in North Carolina was a long awaited one, as I was waiting for the Lord to release me and give me directions on how to do the hunt here <u>for almost three years</u>!

All in God's timing, not ours.

During this waiting time, I was at a Christian home meeting one night and as I was sitting there, a cup materialized in front of me.

I looked at this cup, that was just a bit higher than eye level and about two feet in front of me.

I looked around at the others in the meeting, who obviously weren't seeing what I was seeing.

I sensed that I was supposed to grab this cup, so my right arm reached out in the spirit.

As my hand went around the cup, a blade of light shot out from the bowl of the cup!

This blade was a few feet long with no discernable edges.

I was amazed as I sat there looking around in the physical, while at the same time looking at my spiritual arm out in front of me, holding onto this cup, which now was a sword!

I asked the Lord "What is this?"

Jesus said, "This is the cup that I used at the last supper and this is my sword which I give to you!"

I think I gulped a few times.

Jesus didn't say anything else so I just sat there holding this for a while.

Eventually, I let go of the sword and brought my spiritual arm back to my physical body.

As I did this the sword disappeared.

I have used this sword on many hunting expeditions.

Finally, the wait to start the hunt in North Carolina was over on the eve of June 6, 2006 (666), when the Holy Spirit told me that it was finally time.

The anniversary of the longest day at Normandy in World War II and also a numeric symbol of evil! (Revelation 13: 15-18)

Two of us (my Mom Lynn and I) were led to fast, praise and worship and hunt over a 24-Hour Period. The creative Holy Spirit had special plans for this area, as He knew what was needed!

"Thus, saith the Lord God to the mountains, and to the hills, to the rivers, and to the valleys; Behold, I even I, will bring a sword upon you, and I will destroy your high places." Ezekiel 6:3 KJV

We were to go out many times over the entire day to various locations… mountains, forests, valleys, rivers and "high places" or evil worship centers and conquer them for the Lord!

"For they also built for themselves high places, sacred pillars, and wooden images on every high hill and under every green tree." 1 Kings 14:23

We were led to go out… at start and then every three hours… hitting three categories… four places in each category…nine hunting missions… twelve locations… over 24 hours!

We ended up going to four different mountains, four different rivers and four different heathen worship centers!

Every three hours the Holy Spirit told me where to go next and what to do there.

One stop was a 1,000-year-old ancient native American mound at the center of town… said by the Cherokees, to hold the ever-burning sacred fire.

They believe it is the dwelling place of the immortal spirit-beings, the nunne'hi, who were seen in historic Indian wars in the past, coming out of the side of the mound, as through an open doorway to defeat the local tribe's enemies!

This battle was at three in the morning, and although one would think all would be quiet at that time, a huge black helicopter came into the area, just as I got to the top of the mound to start.

Rather than just flying by, it kept circling around over me!

As it was pitch dark, I just laid down on my back and waited, expecting the search light to come on and police cars to come streaking out of nowhere, wondering what I was doing on this historic landmark!

The helicopter eventually left and I finished that segment of the hunt.

At each place, I blew the shofar.

"The sons of Aaron, the priests, shall blow the trumpets; and these shall be to you as an ordinance forever throughout your generations. "When you go to war in your land against the enemy who oppresses you, then you shall sound an alarm with the trumpets, and you will be remembered before the Lord your God, and you will be saved from your enemies." Numbers 10:8-9

As directed, at each place, I put in place a twelve-stone altar to God, made up of rounded, uncut river stones.

At some places, I planted a Bible and poured salt and holy oil on the land or in the waters and said the words the Holy Spirit wanted me to say.

On this hunt, I didn't see anything in the spirit.

I was guided by Him and faith alone on <u>when</u> to go, <u>where</u> to go next and <u>what</u> to do and <u>say</u>.

A lot of activity was accomplished in a very short period of time, all for His Glory and His kingdom!

If this is the way you are led, to work in the physical, doing prophetic acts as directed by the Holy Spirit, then you must go and do.

However, if you decide to go around a neighborhood or city and just proclaim it for the Lord and other such activity (because you want to), this can be extremely dangerous.

You would not be working spiritually, but in the flesh.

I'm not saying it can't work, as I've known cases when it did, just that it is not wise to do so under these conditions.

If it were that easy, we could just claim that the entire planet is the Lord's and we'd be done!

A three-year wait, for a 24-hour hunting expedition!

All Glory to You Father for Your kingdom being advanced in this place!

For those of you who say you're too old for warfare… my Mom was 83 years old when this took place!

You <u>can</u> do it!

SECTOR THIRTY-TWO
PAPUA NEW GUINEA HUNTING EXPEDITION

> **HUNTING TIP**
> You don't need a degree. Just get serious and work with God!

I have asked two leaders in Papua New Guinea, to share their experiences, since downloading this book online, in order to encourage others, of what can be accomplished when what is in this book is applied.

Martin R.'s Testimony

"In the year 2013, I was searching on the internet for e-books on healing, deliverance and spiritual warfare. It was then that I stumbled into the *Xtreme Big Game Hunting* spiritual warfare text book, by Al Collins. I was astounded by what I read in there. Excited, I shared the book with two of my spiritual brothers, Gabi and Joel. Gabi took the book back to Madang and began a season of periodic fasting throughout 2013 and 2014, using *Xtreme Big Game Hunting* as his study material.

In 2014, while fasting with a group of people, the Lord activated supernatural experiences of going in the spirit. In February 2015, Gabi and his team from Madang visited us in Lae and testified of how God was working among them. Gabi prayed with the church and for an impartation and activation of the supernatural move of God This is the story of how *Xtreme Big Game Hunting* text book impacted our church and the coming of the Seed of Holiness. It is a summary of the major events that marked our spiritual journey from the year 2015 to 2016-current. 2015.

THE SEED, THE PLANT AND THE TREE OF HOLINESS

The church then declared a corporate 21-day fasting in March. The children experienced going into the spirit. They relate stories of their spiritual experiences. The main message they always bring back from heaven is; HOLINESS, RIGHTEOUSNESS AND TRUTH. The Lord always reminded the children to tell his people to live in these aspects. One of the many things God did for us at Lae, was giving us a seed of holiness in the spirit. During the 21-day fasting, the devil tried to destroy this seed before it was planted. However, the children would go into the spirit and battle these demonic forces with the guidance of Ps. Joel and I, to ensure the seed was not destroyed. We would discuss and confirm the status of what was happening in the spiritual realm around us and take note of what was required of us to do next.

Our task was yet far from over. Towards the end of the fasting, we noted that the seed had been planted and had become a small plant. At the end of the 21-day fasting, the general church congregation went home, but a few of us and the children remained with Ps. Joel, to continue for another 120 days of partial fasting. The Lord also showed to the children a conduit being built in the spirit realm, connecting heaven and our church and 12 rings of brick walls circling one another outwards and a mighty white eagle that wanted to land and rest in the church. The Lord had instructed us to look after this plant, to ensure that it became a tree, for the conduit and 12-ringed brick walls to be built completely before the White eagle can land and the Tree to be transplanted into the spiritual location of the church on earth.

Around the month of July, during a prayer session, the children saw that the plant had become a tree and the conduit pipeline and the 12-ringed wall were nearly complete. Now the Lord instructed us to press on into prayer, especially in praying in tongues, praise and worship and declaring his word. We organized ourselves and at weekends, we would pray all night. There were many spiritual experiences we experienced during those times. In August 1st, at exactly 12 am midnight, the pipeline and 12 ringed brick wall were completed. There were 7 children and I and we were praying and worshipping from 7:00 pm till 12:00 am. When the walls and the pipeline were completed, a mighty white eagle flew into the church building. The eagle flapped its wings and a very strong presence of God filled us. The presence of God knocked us off our feet. The children were caught up into the spirit and the Lord instructed them that not many days from now, the Tree of Holiness will be transplanted from the heavenly realm to the spiritual location of the church on earth and we must all be ready.

I remember distinctly when that happened. It was at the end of the month of August. We gathered with Ps. Joel at 7pm one Saturday and it happened. I saw in the spirit the tree uproot itself from the heavenly realm and it walked into the church area! None of us could withstand the presence of God at that time. Every one fell to the ground. The tree is now planted within the church!

After this, the children broke up camp and went home, but they continue to come for prayers and keep in touch with me and the pastor. In September, the Lord revealed that the church would go into period of 70 weeks of dealing process. The Lord gave a scripture in Daniel 9:24. The Lord revealed that He had chosen this church congregation for a special task, but He had not yet anointed it. After the 70 weeks, the Lord will anoint the church for the task. Since then, we had gone through a lot of problems and difficulties. However, in all these the Lord had proven His faithfulness to keep us. His grace is sufficient."

HOW TO GO IN THE SPIRIT WHILE HAVING DINNER

"I am in debt to Al Collins for his teaching on the subject. His testimony has been a guide I used to help others going in the spirit. For an in-depth study of the subject, please refer to the *Xtreme Big Game Hunting* text book. Although it is not necessary, as I have gone in the spirit while at a variety of places, even sitting down for dinner in a restaurant! (Al Collins - *Xtreme Big Game Hunting-Going in the Spirit*)

"For I indeed, as absent in body but present in spirit, have already judged (as though I were present) him who has so done this deed. In the name of our Lord Jesus Christ, when you are gathered together, along with my spirit, with the power of our Lord Jesus Christ" 1 Corinthians 5:3-4

"And the spirits of the prophets are subject to the prophets." 1 Corinthians 14:32

"Supernatural eyesight is a FUNDAMENTAL BYPRODUCT of the born-again, Spirit-led life. But just as in the natural, it must be trained, honed and perfected through practice." Dr. Morris Cerullo

"The mind is the bottle neck of the spirit." Clark Taylor

Testimony: "Thank you Man of God. We had supernatural experiences that started yesterday. One of our youth was transported in the Spirit to Melbourne and prayed for a lady by the name of Jane Ferguson, who had cervical cancer. And later, he went to Sydney to minister to a millionaire and later, one of our boys went in the Spirit and prayed for a lady with breast cancer at the Washington public hospital. Lastly, a girl went in the Spirit to Egypt and saw Christians hiding under an old temple worshiping God. She and Jesus went to Cairns (Australia) and appeared to a millionaire, who for 15 years prayed for which country or direction would the last revival come. When he saw Jesus, he fainted to the floor of his house. Jesus lifted him up and he asked the young girl to stay with his family, but Jesus said to him, she cannot stay, as we come in the Spirit to visit you only and I'll take the girl back, leave her and I'll go back to My Father.

Thank you, Man of God, for the many spiritual blessings that we encounter through your ministry… and lastly JESUS said to us that the last Revival is the Revival of HOLINESS, RIGHTEOUSNESS AND TRUTH…God bless, Gabi M., January, 2015."

Testimony: "Thank you for the teachings on spiritual warfare. I shared your book, *Xtreme Big Game Hunting*, with a pastor friend and he and a group of children have fasted and prayed using the teachings of your book. There are about 60 people in the group. Majority are children and teens with a few adults, some who are parents of the children. They are now experiencing spiritual encounters such as visiting heaven and hell, travelling to England, USA and Australia praying for sick people. Just last month a group of children travelled with Angels of God down to the Bermuda Triangle and closed the gate of hell there. Initially, only 4 children ages between 8 and 13 got caught up in the spirit during a fasting and prayer meeting. Now the number has increased from 4 to 12 which include some teens. The impact of your teachings is astounding.

We have never seen spiritual warfare of such nature. The children related instances of how they went into the spirit realm and followed the Archangel Michael into battle against the strongman of the town. Spiritual experiences are still taking place at this time but are too many to capture in writing. The outstanding of all these is, God the Father's command for holiness, righteousness and truth in the lives of His people. This is the last revival before Christ returns.

Please remember us in your prayers. God bless you.

Martin R., February, 2015."

Testimony: "The Kamkumu area where our church is located is a notorious place. All sorts of illegal things happen there. People throw stones and bottles of beer at the church building while we are at prayer or church services. Along the main road, are a lot of black market stalls illegally set up. These are points where alcohol and marijuana are sold, hidden from the eyes of the law. During the 21 days fasting, drunkards would be seen at almost any time of the day or night swearing at the church congregations, smashing bottles at the church gate. The children at various times would go in the spirit and battle the evil spirits that influenced the surrounding community. One week right after the 21 days fasting, the police raided and burnt down all the black-market stalls! Even the streets along the church are now quiet all the time. No more drunken brawls, smashing bottles and swearing directed at the church to this day at the time of this writing. Martin R, March, 2015."

Testimony: "My name is Emmanuel. I live in Lae, Kamkumu. I work as a static guard with a local security firm. However, on my off days I used to rob people of their money, mobile phones, watches, shoes or bags and any other valuables I could get my hands on to resell for money just to sustain my drinking habit. One evening on March 2015, after a heavy drinking spree, I stumbled home, had a quick dinner and tried to sleep. The moment I closed my eyes I felt like someone was looking at me. His eyes were piercing into my soul and I felt the guilt of all my sin coming over me. I got up and said a short prayer asking God to forgive me and show me what to do. In an instant, I saw a picture of

Ps. Joel's church come into my mind and knew I must go there to seek help. It was 2 am in the morning when I knocked at the gate of the church. The church congregation were all camping there and I called out to an elderly man who was out walking and praying in the church yard. He came over to me and let me into the church. The kind gentleman counselled me and led me to the Lord. I made Jesus the Lord of my life that fateful morning. Today I am married to a beautiful woman and we are both committed members of Ps. Joel's church. By spending time in fasting, prayer and being trained, the Lord has activated both our spiritual senses and He is using us to minister to others in our community. To Jesus be all the glory. Amen Emmanuel M., 2015 March, 2015."

Testimony: "One of the kids tells me of the battles he fights with you (Al) around the world. He said once after a battle in India, both of you sat down in the clouds and chatted for a while. Regards, Martin R., October, 2015."

Testimony: "Here are some of the events that Kupa, my four-year-old son experienced.

One evening at dinner, he told me to ask Papa Jesus, as he calls Him, to bring his sword and his Angel to him. Kupa was sitting on my lap and eating a bowl of rice when he made this request in his simple childlike way, so I said ok, I will pray and ask Papa Jesus. I made a simple prayer and then asked Kupa if Jesus was coming to him. He stopped eating and looked up to the ceiling and said Jesus is coming, bringing his sword and his Angel, but they are not here yet, so he continued to eat his food.

After a few minutes had passed, I asked again if the Lord had arrived. He looked up to the ceiling and shook his head, saying the Lord was not here yet. A few more minutes passed and then Kupa just pushed his bowl of food away from him and laid down on my lap quietly.

I asked him again if the Lord is here now and he nodded his head and went off to sleep. I asked him in the next morning if he went to do battle and he just nodded his head and ran off to play!

Another time in the night, I carried him on my shoulder while walking and praying. He looked up to the moon and said Papa Jesus and the angels are up there fighting. I stopped praying to ask him what else he was seeing. He said 'koko-man', referring to the devil, was fighting against the Lord and His angels. Kupa was trying to relate from his 4-year-old mind how he was also involved in the fight up in the heavens! He was showing me how he was stabbing and cutting with his sword at the enemy! He said Jesus gave him something to cover his chest. I could only make it out that he was referring to a breastplate. I asked him if he saw the Blood of Jesus and he gestured with his hand that the Blood covered him from head to toe!

Then he said that Papa Jesus took him to His house and gave him fruit to eat and water to drink.

I had stopped asking him questions and seeing that he was now yawing, I took to bed and laid him to sleep.

Almost every day Kupa talks about going to Papa Jesus' house and eating fruits, drinking water or bathing in rivers. His favorite fruits are apples, strawberries and watermelon. He describes the strawberries, as big as a coconut, as very juicy. I am many times surprised by spiritual things he mentions which I did not teach him. Like he says, that we must worship Papa Jesus alone! Will write to you again soon.

God bless! Martin R., November, 2015."

Testimony: "Smith is in grade 8. In June one afternoon after school, he went home had a snack and decided to take a nap. When he lay down in bed and closed his eyes, instantly he was in the spirit. His angel beckoned him to follow him. Smith went with his angel to Bugandi Secondary School. This school is known for student violence, drug and alcohol abuse and cult activities. The angel took Smith to specific spots around the school yard where cult members had buried human bones grounded to powder. Smith was instructed to remove these bones, collect them into very large containers and angels came and took them away. The demonic spirits that ruled over the school sensed what was happening and they came to attack Smith. Smith called on the waring angels and they came and fought off these demons. Smith was taken away by his angel back home. In August, the student's Christian fellowship hosted a crusade in the school. Many of the cult groups came forward and surrendered their craft, confessing and renouncing their activities publicly. The school board is now contemplating on doing away with boarding students in order to stop completely the cult activities which are considered to be the main factor behind students' violence and lawlessness. Coincidence? I don't think so. Somebody did spiritual hunting in that school earlier on, secretly. Martin R., June, 2016."

Testimony: "Stanley is a sales and ticketing officer at an airlines company. He also leads worship at the church, however Stanley does more than that. He is one of the young people we trained to do spiritual game hunting and he is a good one too. One-day Stanley came to me told me of a dream he had about his elder brother. In the dream, his brother was dressed up for work however he was stabbed with a dagger by a man with a traditional mask on. Stanley comes to his brother's aid at the road side and tried to help him. He could see that he will definitely lose his brother. But the dream ends suddenly and Stanley woke up very troubled. We interpreted the dream to be related to his brother's struggle for many years to find a job. I tell Stanley that a dream is like going into the spirit realm only that it occurs when you are asleep. What he could do now is enter the spirit to when the dream occurred and change the end of the dream to be a good one. While I was still explaining this to Stanley, he turns around, and looks at me and tells me that it is done. Approximately a week after the discussion, Stanley's brother was hired by the postal company. This is a miraculous breakthrough for him because he had been struggling for many years trying to secure a good job. I asked Stanley what he did. This is what he related to me. While I was talking to Stanley about the relation between dreams and spiritual encounters, he went into the spirit and changed the dream. He went to the last place in the dream where his brother was wounded and he took him to a hospital. There the angels treated his wounds and nursed him back to health. The result manifested in the natural with a break through. Martin R., 2016."

Testimony: "August 2016 I found my 5-year-old son Kupa playing with his friend Ziba, our neighbor one day. Ziba is 6 and his family attend fellowship with us. I called them over to wash and have lunch together. While we were eating, I asked Ziba if had ever seen angels. He said no but he had once seen Jesus in a dream and Jesus had told him that one day he will become a pastor. I asked Ziba if he would like to see angels and he nodded yes. I then instructed Ziba to imagine himself at the gate of their house where his mother was selling fire wood. Ziba said he could see himself there and he gave me the number and the names of the people who were there. I quickly ran over there and confirmed that it was correct. Now I asked Ziba to see where the angels were and he said the angels were flying in circle over where we were sitting. Kupa and I could also see them. We finished lunch and both boys were off to their playing. Gabi M."

Testimony: "October 2016 I sat down with Ps. George at 11:00pm sipping cola and discussing about the spirit realm and how to see into the spirit realm. He had seen at the Madang crusade how I had coached a young person to go into the spirit while we were having dinner one evening and desired the same. Ps. George moves in the gifts of the Holy Spirit like the word of knowledge, but this "going in the spirit" was something different. Since he was keen to know how, I helped the young person in Madang, I suggested we do a little exercise on how to go in the spirit. I instructed him to see himself outside the house. Once he could see himself I then asked if his "other self" could see, hear, speak and move. When he could do all those, it was not hard for him see angels and demons. He was now very aware of the spirit realm around him.

In an instant, we were at Ela beach, Port Moresby. We were standing at the beach shores. I told George there was a demon like a fish with human body and it was coming out of the sea. I asked if he could see the demon and he affirmed it. The demon was roaring, when out and from behind us, a black puma came sprinting to attack us. George spun around and cut off the head of the puma with a sword that suddenly appeared in his hand. The puma disintegrated with a puff of smoke as the demon fish-man sank back into the sea and disappeared. Gabi M."

"The above experiences contain the basic steps to go in the spirit whilst you are engaged in any natural activity. Here is the outline; however, the Lord may show you a better way.

HOW TO PRACTICE GOING IN THE SPIRIT

1. Find a quiet spot, sit down and worship, pray or read the scriptures, which ever feels appropriate to you.

2. Then in a relaxed state, imagine or see yourself at another place that is familiar to you. Maybe back at your church.

3. Now try to see if your "other self" can see, hear, speak, move or feel at the other location right now; in this case in your church. It will be like watching yourself in a TV screen.

4. Now see the angels of God in the church and around you. If you can do that, the Holy Spirit will lead you to do exploit in the spirit realm.

Some thoughts to remember…

- You must understand that you are a spirit being capable of moving in the spirit realm.

- You must know that the mind is a window into the spirit realm.

- You must understand that you can control your spirit with your mind at will (1 Corinthians 14:32).

- You must remember that practice sharpens your spiritual skills.

- ALWAYS remember that the HOLY SPIRIT is your guide and teacher.

- Holiness is not an option.

In your initial experience, your spiritual sight may not be too clear. Things may be blurry but continue to practice. It would be better to practice with someone who knows how to go in the spirit or who can see in the spirit. They will be able to coach and guide you through the experience. But once you can maneuver in the spirit, everything will become easy. You can lose your connection in the spirit if your mind becomes distracted. Be focused and concentrate.

I have assisted mostly young people and children become activated in their spiritual gifting. All of them could almost operate at will. Those who are students tell me how this had helped them to go in the spirit when the Holy Spirit moved on them while they were doing their school work.

Embrace the Lord Jesus Christ with all your heart; live and walk in the Holiness, Righteousness and Truth. I pray the Lord Jesus bless and enhance your faith and use you for his glory with this article. Be blessed. Martin Raurela LAE, and Gabi Mandari MADANG, Papua New Guinea"

Al commenting now. Such wonderful testimonies and teachings from everyone in Papua New Guinea, especially from the children and youth!

These young supernatural saints testify, that God uses them in powerful ways, so they shouldn't be kept to the side until they're adults, as they can accomplish great miracles in God's Kingdom now!

These men of God, Martin and Gabriel and others in these groups, have stepped out boldly with God to do His will on earth and to accomplish their destiny with Him. Not only to fulfill their own destiny, but to equip children, youth, adults and other leaders to do the same. And to change the demonic affects taking place in their neighborhoods and schools. Even going into other nations!

These bold ones in Christ are fulfilling the Great Commission, in demonstrations of God's power and equipping the saints.

And Jesus said, "Well done, good and faithful servant; you have been faithful over a few things, I will make you ruler over many things. Enter into the joy of your lord." Matthew 25: 21, 23

SECTOR THIRTY-THREE
SWISS HUNTING EXPEDITION

> **HUNTING TIP**
> Donuts build great hunters... not really... but Canadian hunters always hope!

Hunting in Switzerland was a wonderful experience, as I was able to be part of a large hunting gang and really bring it to the Xtreme Big Game that was there!

Little do people realize, that the peaceful, neutral nation of Switzerland... is in reality... full of marauding Xtreme Big Game that pull strings on an international basis!

Switzerland is a focal point of world finance and banking and satan doesn't overlook such power!

These evil forces do not recognize neutrality... they are always working to destroy us... everywhere!

Christian spiritual conquerors from Europe, North America, Asia and Africa mobilized in a gang hunt or combined forces operation, to destroy some of these evil forces in late September/early October 2005.

This Xtreme Big Game Hunting Gang, was made up of almost 175 of God's spiritual conquerors! We went to various locations, hunting Xtreme Big Game that were in, under and over that region. They were clouding the minds of countless numbers of Swiss, French, Italians and Germans, as Switzerland is at the crossroads of these three countries.

One of the main evil spiritual rulers over the region we were in, was the Baselisk.

The city of Basel was named after this creature and its head, claws, wings, tail and body, cover the shield and crest of the city.

Interesting, was that before the hunt, while in the spirit, it was revealed to one of the conquerors that one of the angels commissioned to assist us in this expedition, was the same one seen by John in Revelation 20: 1-3, as the angel that will one day in the future, bind satan and throw him in the bottomless pit for 1000 years!

Nice guy to have on a hunt!

During the hunt in the spirit, a huge spider with its web was seen in the underworld guarding bags of gold and money. It was destroyed by our shouting several times at it, "The sword of the Lord destroys you!"

Next there was a huge frog sitting on a giant egg, that was full of small asps, which was another spiritual foundation of the area and region. The frog was bound and taken away by angels; the egg was destroyed and the asps were stomped under the feet of the hunters!

These spiritual creatures are the historic foundation of the Basel region!

The basilisk was seen next. The heavenly angels that were commissioned to assist us appeared and chained the basilisk, after it had been spiritually attacked, blinded and crippled.

The basilisk was just one of the five principality/ruler Xtreme Big Game brought down in this region.

Due to the numbers of people and nations affected and connected to finance in Switzerland and around the world, such pivotal influential areas are considered major hunts or turning points.

The victory was the Lord of Lord's!

While I was in Switzerland, on Wednesday September 28, 2005, I had an experience with one of the Xtreme Big Game there.

I was in the spirit and saw a town or city far away, like I was on a hill. I was looking out at it from a distance. There was a river in front of the city, flowing from right to left… perhaps the Rhine. I looked up and could see a womb in the sky over the city, bleeding all over the city. Blood moved out, covering all the houses and buildings, poured into the river and started filling the river, as it flowing to the left.

Moving further away in the spirit, this city became much smaller. I could see a huge naked female creature standing over the city with her legs spread out. The houses were only reaching to the tops of her ankles!

She was standing on either side of the city, bent forward towards me with her head down and hair hanging down.

She looked like a young woman with long blonde hair, who was resting her hands on her upper thighs, watching her blood come out of her, as it poured out onto the city. Her long hair flew back, as she lifted her head up.

Our eyes met and she could see me!

She was smiling in sheer pleasure at what she was doing to this place.

The Word I received when I first saw the womb pouring out blood, was miscarriage and then destruction.

With this particular creature, I was just an observer, as the Lord didn't have me do any hunting. The experience was over when she lifted her head and I saw her smiling.

I found out later, that this region has three female deities associated with lakes and waters that are worshipped. Loreley, is the entity they say, is the goddess of the Rhine River, a seductress who sexually lures men.

I also learned later, the worshipping of the womb is very strong in this city and region, including freemasonry temples built in the shape of a womb!

Not a usual hunting story that one hears around the campfire is it, but one that I'll enjoy telling in the future around heaven's campfires!

SECTOR THIRTY-FOUR

DRAGON SLAYING

> **HUNTING TIP**
>
> Hunt until the death of the last dragon… then you can relax!

The first time that I killed a dragon I was 6 years old! It was in Mrs. Baker's Grade 1 class where she insisted that I be Prince Charming in the play that we were doing in front of all our parents.

I was somewhat reluctant, as I had to kiss a girl (a.k.a. Sleeping Beauty)!

This play was to be a prophetic act of my future!

Despite the number of times I've been out hunting in the woods, I never have come across a dragon. Don't imagine my 30.06 semi-automatic rifle (a.k.a. Barkin' Bertha) would have done the trick if I had!

What is a dragon?

Wikipedia says: The dragon (from Ancient Greek δράκων - drakōn, meaning a serpent of huge size, a python, a dragon) is a mythical creature typically depicted as a gigantic and powerful serpent or other reptile with magical or spiritual qualities.

Leave out "mythical" and that pretty much is correct.

Dragons are depicted in civilizations in Asia, Europe, Africa, and the Americas, as well as in the hindu, buddhist, and Christian histories. The Bible depicts Leviathan and Behemoth, as dragon-like creatures, with dragon and dragons mentioned 35 times in the Bible (KJV)! And Satan is also called a dragon.

St. George killing the dragon, is the most notable dragon-slayer, who is celebrated in many countries yet today. Although others, including women, are depicted in Medieval and Renaissance artworks as dragon-slayers.

Could all these many civilizations and religions just make up a dragon?

Did these separate civilizations get their beliefs and similar depictions of dragons from the physical or the spiritual realm?

As I've never seen a dragon in the woods nor on any of the National Geographic specials, I'll have to go with they are a spiritual beast!

Anyway, that's the only kind that I've ever seen!

Are dragon's principalities?

Are they fallen angels?

Are they Nephilim?

Are they pythons, leviathans, behemoths or perhaps dinosaurs?

Do you need to know, other than they're the enemy?

I call them a dragon, as that's what they look like to me!

On November 5, 2006, about a week before I went to Omaha, Nebraska USA to speak at the "Advancing God's Kingdom" conference, I was at home alone. As I was walking through a room, (I wasn't praying), I could see in the spirit a huge python/dragon shoved down inside a tall, transparent, standing upright, rectangular box. Its tail was at the bottom of the box and his head was at the top. It totally filled every part of the box with its body... no empty spaces.

Looking at this thing I went into hunting mode.

Nothing like hunting in your own living room eh!

I commanded that the box be filled with the blood of Jesus and watched as the blood poured down over its head, eyes, and body. The blood seemed to have very little effect against it. It just kept blinking its eyes as the blood dripped into them. It was spitting blood away from around its mouth, as the blood poured over the edges of his mouth. Other than that, it didn't seem to mind the blood of Jesus!

An important lesson, that even though people all over the world plead the blood of Jesus against and on everything, believing that nothing more is required... evil activity can still continue.

So, I pulled out the sword Jesus gave me (it is always there when I want it) slicing the sword down through the top to the bottom of the box... cutting it up in many pieces, slicing back, and forth, and across. It was bleeding all over in the box.

I noticed that the sword had no effect on the box. I cut off its head and shoved the sword's point into both of its eyes.

Then two angels showed up with a huge white bag, that was, I would say, five times bigger than the angels. I told them to put all the very huge pieces of this creature in the bag, which they did. Then the angels started wrapping up the top of the bag with a golden cord and left with this huge bound bag between them, having all the pieces of this thing in it.

I looked back to the box which was now empty... none of the blood of Jesus or any of the creature's blood was left in it now. It was just a transparent, empty box.

I discerned that I couldn't leave it like this so I asked God to come fill this box with His presence. A small light started to shine in about the middle of the box. The light started getting brighter and brighter as I asked God to fill the box. The entire box became full of this light, starting from the center until the box was full of just light.

That was the end of my spiritual experience.

I shared this with a leader, who said that he had come across a python doing deliverance on two people on two different occasions. Both times the python spoke to him, saying he couldn't hurt it because it was in a box. Both times the people had been deeply involved in witchcraft!

Of course, he did get to both of them and dealt with them, despite their claims of invincibility.

Interesting, as he had never told me this before!

He also said the Holy Spirit was telling him, that what I had just defeated was a principality over an area where I was going. The light was the area being replaced with the kingdom of God!

At the conference, I told this to the crowd in Omaha, who were very happy to hear this, although I told them that I was in Cincinnati, Ohio, Iowa and Atlanta, Georgia (besides Omaha) during this trip and I couldn't say with certainty that this Xtreme Big Game was over Omaha.

I told them if it was in Omaha, things should start to noticeably change, especially in the witchcraft and occult areas of the city.

The python is associated with witchcraft, as we learn from Paul when he was confronted with a spirit of divination, which in Greek is a spirit of python, or Apollo.

"Now it happened, as we went to prayer, that a certain slave girl possessed with a spirit of divination (python) met us, who brought her masters much profit by fortune-telling (witchcraft)." Acts 16:16

"And this she did for many days. But Paul, greatly annoyed, turned and said to the spirit, "I command you in the name of Jesus Christ to come out of her." And he came out that very hour." Acts 16:18

This experience that I had again teaches, that you don't have to be physically at a place to do Xtreme Big Game Hunting and that it can be done alone, without a lot of preparation work or physical acts!

Just be ready to go hunting… even in your own living room!

Another time, I was in the spirit when I went into a stable to get my white horse (Whitey). I jumped on him and rode out of the stable down a long road towards a huge dragon that I could see in the distance. This dragon was standing on its hind legs… becoming larger as I got closer. It was standing in a forest of dead black trees, leaving no way around him.

I said to God that I didn't know how I was going to destroy this thing, as its head was too far up for me to strike with my sword. Just then Whitey spread out wings and we flew up over top of the dragon. The dragon was looking up at me with eyes that were hypnotic. The

Holy Spirit told me to point my sword at its eyes and speak spiritual words against it. As I did that, I saw a flash come out of the tip of my sword, striking its eyes and blinding it! Whitey then flew down, allowing me to slice my sword across its neck… finishing him off. We flew past the dragon to a castle where I had to chop through the door with my sword to get in. The castle and its interior were all grey, as I made my way to a room where a woman was imprisoned. (I know… sounds like a Grade 1 play!) I took her back to Whitey and we flew away from the castle, passing the dead dragon below us. I left this lady at a Church building, as I returned to the stable.

Mrs. Baker would be proud!

There was the time that one of the biggest dragons I ever saw came against me. I didn't know how I was going to defeat this one and then I grew in size, becoming much bigger than him! I took him up in my hands and gave him a bad day! (Ophiuchus Constellation and "they will <u>take up</u> serpents (principalities)" Mark 16:18a

One time I found myself in almost total darkness at the edge of a large body of water. I could barely see the black body of a serpent-like creature moving up from the water, rising above and in front of me. He must have thought he had me, as it was too dark to make him out. As I looked up, I could see two huge white eyes staring down at me. Attached to eyes is head and below that is neck… right? I made a slash across below the eyes and heard the blade go through it, followed by some black blood pouring into the water. White lights out!

Late summer of 2007, I saw in the spirit, a huge black dragon that filled almost the entire sky. This was the biggest dragon I've come across! It hung over the area like a large constantly moving cloud. I couldn't see any spaces in-between its body and only occasionally its head poked out below its body… always in a different spot. Its head was black with gold streaks on either side of its face. I wanted this thing destroyed! I went in the spirit streaking up through and back down through the tight spaces between its body. I was having fun doing this until God said to me, "It's not a toy!" Getting serious, I took my sword and sliced every time I streaked up and back through the tight coils of its body. The cuts were bleeding black blood down upon the area and I sensed that this was not wise. I needed to get to its head. He never did show his head again, ending this phase of hunt. He wasn't so fortunate the next time we met!

It was about four months later; I was in the spirit in a huge valley that had mountains in the distance. I was putting on a new suit of armor that was much brighter than what I was used to. My sword was sticking in the ground in front of me as I was putting on the final pieces of armor... my gauntlets. As I looked up, my old nemesis was looking down at me. The gold streaks clearly visible on its black face. Digging my feet into the ground I grabbed my sword and pulled it out of the ground as the dragon came down at me. I readied and struck up through the bottom of its mouth, which dropped him to the ground. I could see and hear his entire body fall out of the sky into the valley which was many miles long. I walked over and cut off its massive head. Make a nice trophy over the fireplace in my heavenly mansion! God told me to take off the gold streaks that were on its face. They were a metal-like substance that I put into a canvas bag at my side. Next, I commanded angels to come and take this dragon away.

It took a number of angels to lift it all up. They flew to the far end of the valley through a tear in the sky that opened. Another one bites the dust!

As I was standing there, I looked to my sides and behind me, to see angels in the valley and in the mountains around me on golden chariots! Tall flames were coming from these chariots, as they were moving closer to me. I still get chills when I remember this experience! Just then, Whitey came from behind me and with his head, went between my legs, scooped me up and onto his back without missing a stride! We were riding down the valley with the angels on chariots following to the sides and behind me. A crown came down from the sky towards me, which I waved away saying to God, that I didn't want any glory, as all the glory is His! Just ahead I could see someone standing facing us.

It was Jesus!

I stopped Whitey, jumped down, and prostrated myself at Jesus' feet. Jesus pulled me up to Him, hugged and kissed me two times on my right cheek and said, "Thank you My brother! Turning, I got back on

Whitey and headed back down the valley with the army of angels on chariots moving with me. That night I felt that I had been to this valley before, but couldn't put my finger on it. Then the Holy Spirit enlightened me! I went to the internet in the morning to find pictures, of exactly where I had been years before and now to slay this dragon. It was the Jezreel valley or valley of Megiddo in Israel... the place of Armageddon! The same area where Elisha had come against the Syrian army with angels on chariots of fire!

"And Elisha prayed, and said, "Lord, I pray, open his eyes that he may see." Then the Lord opened the eyes of the young man, and he saw. And behold, the mountain was full of horses and chariots of fire all around Elisha." 2 Kings 6: 17

The story gets better!

Over the next several days I wondered about the gold pieces that God wanted me to remove from the dragon. I asked God what He wanted me to do with these things. The next time that I was in the spirit, I was pulling the pieces out of the bag, forming them into a golden bow with a thin gold string and golden arrows! Anticipation was deep, as I waited for what would be done with this new weapon! The first time I used this golden bow was against a creature that I could see miles away standing next to a roman catholic monastery! God told me to shoot an arrow at it, which brought it down from that distance! God had me go to this place, finish this creature off and retrieve the arrow. As I pulled the arrow out of it, I looked up to see a huge stingray-type creature in the sky about the size of several city blocks! Perhaps wondering what happened to its friend. I thought, "Hey, why not!" As I started putting the arrow in the bow, the stingray quickly turned, snapped its tail and was gone. Guess he didn't want me to reach out and touch him with my new weapon!

Another time I was in the spirit at night, below a basilisk, that was sitting on top of a war monument. I could see what looked like beams of light coming from its eyes, as it looked around. I loaded the arrow, brought him to the ground and finished him off with my sword!

There are various colors of dragons such as black, green, red and yellow as well as coming in a variety of sizes. One dragon that my spiritual horse Whitey stomped on, was about as big as a squirrel or rabbit and yet others have been many miles long!

I've destroyed many dragon-looking creatures in the spirit, over areas such as the Arizona Grand Canyon and Mexican Yucatan peninsula and high in the heavenlies over earth.

Most people would say that dragons don't exist.

Perhaps all these ancient civilizations and the Bible are wrong.

Follow the guidelines in this book and God will show you one-day what's what!

Are You Game?

SECTOR THIRTY-FIVE

THE SPIRIT OF DEATH

> **HUNTING TIP**
> Spit in death's eye... he doesn't like it!

In mid-July 2006, I was in North Carolina when I found out that a friend of mine in Niagara Falls, Canada had just suffered a severe heart attack.

She had actually died before being resuscitated, although she remained unconscious and in a coma since the attack.

As I prayed for her, I ended up going in the spirit to her hospital room.

I could see a huge, black, eagle-like, bird standing on her chest, with the talons of one foot embedded into her chest, wrapped around her heart. I walked up to her bed and with my right-hand, karate chopped across the bird's leg.

The leg snapped off and the bird disappeared.

The leg was still there and I sensed that I couldn't just rip off the leg, as it would tear the heart. So, with my spiritual hands, I snapped off each talon from the leg, until they were all removed from the heart. I then tossed the bird's leg and talons off to the side.

Next, with my hands, I went into her chest, cupping her heart for a while until it started to glow.

From there I moved my hands up to her head and around her brain for a time. I discerned something was being done, but I didn't know what.

Finally, I sensed that my work was done, so I turned to leave.

As I got away from her bed, I turned around to look at her again and could see this all black shape standing at the foot of her bed.

I knew it was the spirit of death!

I called for an angel who came with his sword and forced the spirit of death back through the wall of the hospital room, which was transparent.

The angel kept his sword up in front of death keeping it back, just to the other side of the wall.

I could see the both of them facing each other, with the angel's sword in-between.

I then placed other angels around her bed.

As I turned to leave, I could see the glow still emanating from her heart.

I was told, that she very briefly regained consciousness the next day.

I pray that she made peace with her heavenly Father through Jesus, before she passed away.

Although I had desired a total healing for her with my hunt, we cannot question why things do not happen the way we desire.

We must go when the Lord sends us, do as we are led… leaving the rest up to the Lord and His plans.

All praise and all glory to you Father, as only You have all the answers.

Thank you for giving us the peace in areas that we may not understand.

ZONE 7

HUNT'S END

SECTOR THIRTY-SIX

THE SILVER BULLET OF GOD

> **HUNTING TIP**
>
> The Bible is full of God's Lone Rangers... be one!

Back in the 1950's, when I was a kid, I watched a TV show called, The Lone Ranger.

The main character was a masked Texas Ranger in the Old West, who galloped about on his trusted white horse, Silver; righting injustices with his two six-gun silver revolvers, shooting only silver bullets.

The usual opening announcement was: "A fiery horse with the speed of light, a cloud of dust, and a hearty 'Hi-yo Silver!' The Lone Ranger!"

His horse would rise up on hind legs, as he was in pursuit of the bad guys.

Episodes usually ended with one of the characters lamenting the fact, that they never found out the hero's name asking, "Who was that masked man?" Only to be told, "Why, that was the Lone Ranger!" as he rode away, leaving one of his silver bullets behind, as a reminder that good triumphs over evil and that he was always around.

My favorite memory of The Lone Ranger, is when he galloped past me one night at a local county fair and yelled his famous line," Hi-yo Silver!"

I watched in awe as Silver's front legs came up and kicked!

It doesn't get much better than that at that age!

THE SILVER BULLET OF GOD

The metaphor of "the Silver Bullet", applies to any straightforward solution perceived to have extreme effectiveness. Something that acts as a weapon; especially one that instantly solves a long-standing problem.

The term traditionally originates from ancient days; said to be the only kind of bullet that is effective against monsters.

In military strategy, it would be the ultimate weapon or tactic that ends the battle or war… the Xtreme example that comes to mind was the dropping of "the silver bullets" (atomic bombs) that ended World War II.

In the Bible, a good example would be, Israel's "Silver Bullet of God", against the Philistine's monster at Shochoh's valley of Elah.

Goliath, the man of satan, never had a chance against David, the man of God!

I sit here looking at my Dad's commando fighting knife that he used in WW II and his many medals from Britain, Canada, and France for combat actions at Spitsbergen, Dieppe, Normandy, and Cain.

Actions where he had been wounded several times; carrying a bullet in his shoulder and shrapnel in his leg for the rest of his life.

Actions that resulted in his family in Canada being told that he had died in battle… two different times!

Hitler considered the commandos so dangerous and so effective, that he commanded his troops to never take one as prisoner.

They were all to be shot immediately if taken alive!

My Dad laughed when he told me this story, as he said, "Hitler was so stupid that he didn't realize that his order just made us fight fiercer and to the death, as we would never give up!"

Most of the time he couldn't speak of what he saw and went through, as it was too much for him to bring to mind… and he was perhaps the toughest man I ever knew!

I can't imagine what he went through in his fight against evil forces that were holding people and areas captive… to help set them free.

After the war, he continued his fight for justice as a police officer, justice of the peace and judge.

He was a true Silver Bullet against evil!

There's was a small vial of anointing oil in my Mom's purse that she used for 35 years. God told her, that she should use it only for healing others and it would never run out… it never did.

It still hasn't!

She never put more oil in the bottle and she used it on an unimaginable number of people who were instantly healed by God!

People in stores, in parking lots, at Church groups, at meetings, in restaurants, and so on.

There were over 10,000 people that she kept track of that received healing on the telephone… she never saw them nor touched them. They received healing as the Centurion's servant received in Matthew 8:5-13.

She led numerous Bible study and prayer groups, and lectured in many Church groups and Christian meetings.

Doing all of this into her mid-eighties!

She was a true Silver Bullet of God!

So, what is a Silver Bullet of God, when it comes to Xtreme Big Game Hunting, Xtreme Small Game Hunting and Xtreme Rabid Game Hunting?

You need to have a fire in your gut for righting injustices, fighting unrighteousness and evil and not care what anyone says or does who try to stop you… even if you must do it alone, as did Moses, Samson, David, Elijah, Elisha, Daniel, Ezekiel, and many, many more, including Jesus.

Most of those who wrote the books making up the Bible were God's "Lone Rangers" and commandos!

It would be preferable that the entire Church of God worked together in unity, but in reality, that isn't the case. Depending on your circumstances, if you can't find others that are willing to step up to their destiny with God, don't let that stop you, if where you live, you stand alone with God's Standards! You can always search, find and fellowship with like-minded individuals on the internet. You all can support each other in encouragement, fellowship, prayer, intercession, spiritual warfare, etc. You can also start a group to teach others how to develop their destiny with God as His Silver Bullet, if they're willing. He's looking for Silver Bullets.

The Bible has numerous references indicating how powerful we are—with God.

"Though an army may encamp against me, my heart shall not fear; Though war may rise against me, in this I will be confident." Psalm 27:3

"Jesus answered, "You could have no power at all against Me unless it had been given you from above." John. 19:11

Jesus said that to Pilate… same goes for us in the physical and spiritual realms.

When you've got the power of God and are led by God, there isn't a force in existence that can withstand you!

This is the Silver Bullet of God!

YOU!

YOU are God's Silver Bullet!

Shoot Straight…

Shoot True…

Stay on Target…

Never Give Up…

Be the Silver Bullet of God wherever He sends you.

You'll receive your medals for your actions in heaven!

SECTOR THIRTY-SEVEN
GLORY TO GOD

HUNTING TIP

Keep the trophy… give the glory!

At the end of a hunt it is typical to see many pats on the back all around; high fives and words of praise to those very successful hunters… and most often a party to celebrate.

Hunting alone doesn't produce such revelry, other than self satisfaction.

In Xtreme Big Game Hunting, you can enjoy what you are doing to free people and areas and bringing down evil strongholds for God… however, take no glory for yourself, as all of it is God's.

If you start taking God's glory, your hunting days will be over.

"Give unto the Lord the glory due to His name; Worship the Lord in the beauty of holiness." Psalm 29:2

"Declare His glory among the nations, His wonders among all peoples. For the Lord is great and greatly to be praised;
He is to be feared above all gods. For all the gods of the peoples are idols, but the Lord made the heavens.
Honor and majesty are before Him; Strength and beauty are in His sanctuary. Give to the Lord, O families of the peoples, give to the Lord glory and strength.
Give to the Lord the glory due His name; Bring an offering, and come into His courts." Psalm 96:3-8

"For Yours is the kingdom and the power and the glory forever. Amen." Matthew 6:13b

"Glory to God in the highest." Luke 2:14a

"He who speaks from himself seeks his own glory; but He who seeks the glory of the One who sent Him is true, and no unrighteousness is in Him." John 7:18

Jesus here said never take glory for yourself, especially glory when God sent you, as this is unrighteous.

"And I do not seek My own glory; there is One who seeks and judges." John 8:50

Even here we see, that Jesus never took glory for himself nor glory that was the Father's alone.

Paul wrote, "For of Him and through Him and to Him are all things, to whom beglory forever. Amen." Romans 11:36

Paul also wrote, "Therefore, whether you eat or drink, or whatever you do, do all to the glory of God." 1 Corinthians 10:31

Peter wrote, "To Him be the glory and the dominion forever and ever. Amen." 1 Peter 5:11

Take the advice of David, Matthew, Luke, John, Paul, Peter, and Jesus… give <u>ALL</u> the glory for <u>ALL</u> things, <u>ALL</u> the time, to our Father in heaven.

Get down on your knees after a hunt; thank Him for guiding you to success and allowing you to be His Xtreme Big Game Hunter!

Hallelujah… thank You Lord!

THE LAST SHOT

> **HUNTING TIP**
>
> Once you become an Xtreme Big Game Hunter...
> become even deadlier... teach others to hunt... then... teach others to teach!

One time I was at the feet of Father God in His throne room. Every Christian is welcome here.

I was gripping a glowing, transparent substance that was alive.

It was His Robe!

"Bless the Lord, O my soul! O Lord my God, You are very great: You are clothed with honor and majesty, Who cover Yourself with light as with a garment, Who stretch out the heavens like a curtain." Psalm 104:1-2

This substance started to slowly melt down over my hands and arms.

As I stood up, this substance formed around my shoulders and hung on me like a robe.

God said, "This is My Mantle that I give you."

"I will greatly rejoice in the Lord, my soul shall be joyful in my God; For He has clothed me with the garments of salvation, He has covered me with the robe of righteousness, as a bridegroom decks himself with ornaments, and as a bride adorns herself with her jewels." Isaiah 61:10

What can I say about such a gift from Father?

It's the best hunting coat that I've ever owned!

How about this... His Mantle is available for you too!

Well... here we are... at the end of this Silver Bullet of God, Xtreme Big Game Hunting book, full of war hunting campaigns! Heaven vs. hell. Holy vs. evil.

When you think of it, military war campaigns in the world, are just another form of hunting, are they not?

This nation hunts that nation; our army hunts their army.

Except their hunts are only operating in a limited, physical dimension.

This is when everyone would probably like to hear, those last inspiring words motivating them into hunting mode.

Whenever a hunter only has one round left, it has to count when fired.

So, here's my Last Shot!

One day, Father God told me that I was a predator!

I was puzzled at first with this Word, as most might consider this to be a bad thing.

It is a bad thing... for Xtreme Big Game and their buddies, Xtreme Small and Xtreme Rabid Game!

"Look, a people rises like a lioness, and lifts itself up like a lion; It shall not lie down until it devours the prey, and drinks the blood of the slain." Numbers 23:24

"Can you hunt the prey for the lion." Job 38:39a

(Are You Game?)

"I will send him against an ungodly nation, and against the people of My wrath I will give him charge, to seize the spoil, to take the prey." Isaiah 10:6

"'Therefore, all those who devour you shall be devoured; And all your adversaries, every one of them, shall go into captivity; Those who plunder you shall become plunder, and all who prey upon you I will make a prey." Jeremiah 30:16

"I have set the point of the sword against all their gates,
That the heart may melt and many may stumble.
Ah! It is made bright; It is grasped for slaughter." Ezekiel 21:15

"Our pursuers were swifter than the eagles of the heavens. They pursued us on the mountains and lay in wait for us in the wilderness." Lamentations 4:19

As a Christian, we can and should conduct many hunts… hunt to set people and areas free in Christ; hunt for more of God in our lives, and hunt for evil game (Big, Small and Rabid)!

Any international big game hunter will tell you, that the most satisfying hunting expedition is against the most dangerous game… the predator… the lion, the tiger, the panther… the man eaters!

For the Xtreme Big Game Hunter, the most satisfying hunting SAFARI expedition is <u>to hunt and bring down the most dangerous predators known to exist (Big, Small and Rabid Game), to capture for God the most precious beings known to exist (which is people)</u>!

I have been, am currently, and will continue to operate as a Silver Bullet for God! I've hunted all kinds of wild game in many countries and in the heavenlies. I've gone in the spirit to the past, to see Jesus on the Cross; walked with Him in heavens gardens and ridden with Him in the future to Armageddon, into the war of all wars. I've witnessed people dropping into the lake of fire and stood face-to-face with satan. Father has had me in His throne room many times; I've attended His courtroom; visited the Garden of Eden, the New Jerusalem and my magnificent mansions and met many of the great ones from the Bible. I've been in the spirit to multiple places at the same time.

Great ones of God all over the world, have stepped up to their positions and responsibilities, as saints, royal priests, heirs with Christ and rulers, to train themselves to do the same… and more!

This book has gone into over 190 countries and is being taught from in Universities, Colleges, Church assemblies, Sunday Schools and by an unknown number of groups! I've received a vast amount of emails over the years from all over the world, testifying of people's freedom, healing, deliverance, miracles, wonders, destiny direction and success.

Witchdoctors and witches have abandoned satan and become leaders for Jesus, thanks to the spiritual warfare done by students of this book. Such an honor and blessing, to be associated with so many of God's great superheroes around the world, aged 4 to 85, who engage in these incredible adventures of God. Individuals, families, neighborhoods, regions, areas and nations have been so positively affected, by people acting upon their God given power and authority.

And all of us keep going in Him and for Him.

As for me, as long as Father wants me to hunt… I'll keep hunting to the far ends of the heavens and to hell and back!

What about you?

I have a very immense trophy room in one of my heavenly homes!

When we're there full-time, I pray that you'll stop by my chateau with the waterfalls and mountain lake, so I can share my Silver Bullet hunting stories with you. Even more so, I look forward to coming to your trophy room in your mansion… to sit in a wonderfully comfortable chair, beneath one of the trophy heads that you took while on earth, as I want to hear all about it!

Perhaps under a dragon's head!

This gives me a such big smile just thinking about it!

I would also love to see there, all of the people whose lives you helped change and save, so we can all hear about your hunt together!

Save me a good seat… near Jesus if you can!

Till then… hope to see you out there in the field one day!

Good Hunting!

BIBLIOGRAPHY

Angels in the Army, Dr. Dale M. Sides, Liberating Publications, Inc. VA 2004

Apocrypha, The Fourteen Books, edited by Manuel Komroff,
Tudor Publishing NY 1936

Art of War, Sun Tzu, Ralph D. Sawyer, Barnes and Noble 1994

Closing Gates of Hell, Dr. Dale M. Sides, Liberating Publications, Inc. VA 2005

Dake's Annotated Reference Bible, King James Version Text,
Commentary-Finis Jennings Dake
Dake Bible Sales Inc. 1991

Daniel Nash, Prevailing Prince of Prayer, J. Paul Reno, Revival Literature, NC 1989

Dead Sea Scrolls, A New Translation, translated and commentary by Michael Wise, Martin Abegg Jr. and Edward Cook, Harper San Francisco Publishers 2005

Josephus, The Complete Works, translated by William Whiston,
Thomas Nelson Publishers Nashville 1998

Like A Mighty Wind, Mel Tari, Creation House 1971

Mending Cracks in The Soul, Dr. Dale Sides-Liberating Publications Inc. VA 2002

New Age Lies to Women, Wanda Marrs, Living Truth Publishers TX 1989

Paradise of the Holy Fathers, Volume 1 & 2, Wallis Budge
Chatto & Windus London 1907

Pseudepigrapha, Volume 1, edited by James H. Charlesworth

Doubleday & Company NY 1983

Pseudepigrapha, Volume 2, edited by James H. Charlesworth

Doubleday & Company NY 1985

Scroll of the War of the Sons of Light against the Sons of Darkness, Yigael Yadin, Oxford University Press Great Britain 1962

The Sanctified Body, Patricia Treece, Doubleday 1989

War in Heaven, Derek Prince, Chosen Books MI 2003

War Psalms of the Prince of Peace, Lessons from the Imprecatory Psalms, James E. Adams,

Presbyterian and Reformed Publishing Company New Jersey 1991

WayOfTheEagle.org

www.ingramcontent.com/pod-product-compliance
Lightning Source LLC
Chambersburg PA
CBHW071132300426
44113CB00009B/954